CALIFORNIA STATE UNIVERSITY, SACRAMENTO

the last date stamped below.

on the date due will result in assessment

M/

Policing American Society

Nelson-Hall Series in Law, Crime, and Justice

Consulting Editor: Howard Abadinsky
Saint Xavier University, Chicago

Policing American Society

Randy L. LaGrange

*University of North Carolina
at Wilmington*

Nelson-Hall Publishers/Chicago

Project Editor: Rachel Schick
Cover Painting: "Nightlight" by Mary Selfridge
Photo Researcher: Randall Nicholas
Illustrator: Corasue Nicholas

Library of Congress Cataloging-in-Publication Data

LaGrange, Randy L., 1956–
     Policing American society / by Randy L. LaGrange.
          p.   cm.
     Includes bibliographical references and index.
     ISBN 0-8304-1267-0
     1. Police—United States. 2. Police administration—United
States. I. Title.
     HV8138.L26   1993
     363.2′0973—dc20   92-28103
                                                                    CIP

Manufactured in the United States of America

10 9 8 7 6 5 4 3 2 1

TM The paper used in this book meets the minimum requirements of American National Standard for Information Sciences—Permanence of Paper for Printed Library Materials, ANSI Z39.48-1984.

CONTENTS

PREFACE

This is an important time to be studying the role of police in American society. Recent research has produced an explosion of new knowledge taking us to a higher level of understanding about the police. Virtually every aspect of modern police work has been closely examined, and many established police practices have been openly challenged. Thus, as we move toward the twenty-first century, we find it increasingly necessary to search for renewed purpose and direction in American policing.

Policing American Society is intended to be a comprehensive introductory textbook for undergraduate students in either two-year or four-year programs. The book is largely descriptive and is written from an eclectic perspective with no single theoretical orientation or methodological strategy promoted over another. Instructors may wish to use *Policing American Society* alone or supplement it with additional readings. A test bank is available, with multiple choice, true/false, and fill-in-the-blank questions. Although the book draws most heavily from the discipline of sociology, important insights from other disciplines are incorporated into this work as well.

Most important, this book is written with the student in mind. The emphasis is on engaging discussions of important topics and issues in policing, not erudite discourse. Internal citations are kept to a minimum to enhance readability, and numerous inserts are embedded in the text to stimulate student thinking. Throughout I have tried to reach a satisfying middle ground between responsible, thorough coverage and lively prose.

Policing American Society is organized into five parts and fourteen chapters. Each chapter builds to some extent on the previous one. Part I, **Introduction and Background** examines the origin of the police from a broad historical and cross-cultural perspective. Three chapters trace the evolution of policing from its earliest forms and demonstrate how it has become the instrument of social control and social service that we recognize today. Part II, **Police and Society,** sharpens the focus of analysis. This section begins with an examination of the role of the police in modern society and ends with a discussion of what it is really like to "work the streets." Part III, **Legal Parameters of Policing,** and Part IV, **Police Administration,** discuss contemporary issues that pose substantial challenges to police officers and administrators. Students interested in criminal justice as a career will find these sections of particular interest. The book's last section is entitled **Contemporary Concerns and Future Challenges.** Chapter 13 probes a number of critical issues confronting American policing today such as deadly force, AIDS and affirmative action. Finally, chapter 14 draws our study to an end with a synthesis and conclusion.

The general thrust of *Policing American Society* is on issues, ideas, theory, and research. The techniques of policing, such as how to handcuff, frisk, use a nightstick, or lift fingerprints receive little attention. The book attempts to present a realistic look into the work of policing—not overly glamorous or romantic or dangerous as portrayed in some popular police shows, nor overly critical as periodically portrayed by police writers who, like myself, have never worn a badge. My aim is to have students glean a deeper understanding of the role of police in modern society, and to challenge those who currently hold strong opinions one way or the other about the police to reexamine their views. It is imperative that students grasp early on a fundamental lesson woven throughout the book: who the police are, what they do, and how they do it is not carved into stone. *Policing could be different and it could be better.*

Randy L. LaGrange
Wilmington, N.C.

PART I

Introduction and Background

This first section of our study establishes the necessary foundation for understanding American police. Chapter 1 begins with an examination of crime in the United States and what the police as formal agents of social control *can* and *cannot* do about the problem. Chapter 1 also suggests several reasons why the study of police in American society is worthy of serious academic attention. Chapter 2 takes us back through time in order to show how earlier societies grappled with the problems of crime and disorder. We shall see how the police evolved slowly over time in response to emerging societal needs, and why police systems today are so strongly influenced by the past. Chapter 3 completes our basic foundation with a descriptive analysis of police systems in contemporary American society. Here we examine the size and cost of police protection in the United States, and how police systems differ at the local, state, and federal levels.

CHAPTER ONE

CRIME AND CRIME CONTROL

There are three things and only three things that a guy can count on in life: death, taxes and being ripped off.

—*Man on the street*

Policing American society is a complicated and multifaceted role. As the major enforcement arm of the government, the police are responsible for upholding the law and protecting the public. This important role finds the police investigating crimes, arresting criminals, issuing traffic tickets, and so on. Without doubt crime control is an important role of the police and a central justification for their very existence. Yet the police are responsible for other duties as well. The police spend much of their time maintaining social order and rendering services to the public. In other words, the police often assist in problem situations which are not of a "law enforcement" nature, such as providing directions to a lost tourist or giving aid to an injured child. Indeed, policing American society is no simple task.

In this chapter we establish the basic parameters of our study. We begin with a sober discussion of crime in the United States and an assessment of what the police can and cannot do to control the problem. Once this groundwork is set, our attention then turns to what "law" and "justice" actually mean in the daily operation of the criminal justice system in general, and for the police in particular. Finally, we note why the study of the police is an important topic worthy of our very serious consideration. By the chapter's end you should have a better understanding of the larger issues involved in policing American society.

CRIME IN THE UNITED STATES

It is difficult to put into meaningful perspective the severity of the crime problem in the U.S. Almost everyone knows there is a great deal of crime in our society; the newspapers and TV news programs overwhelm us with daily reports of murders, rapes, and robberies. Almost everyone is concerned about crime and wishes that more could be done to fight crime, such as hiring additional police or building more prisons. And almost everyone has experienced fear of crime in their daily lives—when walking alone on the city streets, when riding public buses and subways, when approached by a stranger in a parking lot, or when someone knocks on the door late at night. Despite our heightened sensitivity to crime, few people fully grasp the magnitude of the problem. Crime directly affects so many people so permanently in such profound ways. Crime also affects everyone indirectly in immeasurable ways. *No one escapes crime.*

Crime: The Problem

Researchers are not able to pinpoint precisely how much crime occurs each year. The United States covers a huge expanse of land populated by millions of people who commit thousands of crimes everyday. No reporting system, regardless of how thorough and accurate, could identify all the crimes that are committed. (Just think of how many crimes you have seen or heard about or committed in your lifetime that were never discovered by the authorities.) Nonetheless, we can get a fairly good approximation of the crime problem from two different information sources: the **Uniform Crime Report** (UCR) and the **National Crime Survey** (NCS).

Since the 1930s when Congress first authorized the fledgling Federal Bureau of Investigation to be the official keeper of crime statistics, the Uniform Crime Reports have been the major barometer of the nation's crime problem. The FBI collects and tabulates crime data sent in by police agencies from across the country and publishes the results in its yearly report. The central feature of the UCR is the eight major felony offenses that comprise the Part I **index offenses.** The index offenses include four crimes against persons (murder, rape, robbery, and aggravated assault) and four crimes against property (burglary, larceny-theft, motor vehicle theft, and arson).

The most dramatic feature of the UCR is the *crime clock*. The crime clock depicts the frightening frequency with which serious crimes are committed. As shown in figure 1.1 for the year 1990, an index offense was committed, on average, one every two seconds of every minute of every hour of every day, 365 days a year; a violent crime every seventeen seconds and a property crime every two seconds. Even murder, the most serious of the index offenses, albeit the least frequently committed of the group, still occurs nearly three times an hour. In absolute numbers, these crime-by-time tallies amounted to over 14 million index offenses committed in 1990. Of this number, criminal homicide ended the lives of over 23,000 people.

As shocking as these crime statistics may seem, they do not come close to profiling the true extent of crime. For one thing, the UCR index offenses are based on the crimes *known to the police*. The problem is that the police never find out about many crimes, mainly because citizens fail to report when they have witnessed a crime or have been a crime victim. People do not report crimes to the police for a variety of reasons: they do not want to get involved, they feel there is nothing the police can do, or they may fear personal retaliation if they report the offender to the authorities. Criminologists refer to these unrecorded crimes as **hidden crime,** or the "dark figure" of crime.

Among the eight index offenses, some crimes are more hidden than others. For instance, almost all murders and the great majority of motor vehicle thefts are reported to the police (murders are hard to conceal and most people report when their cars are stolen for insurance refunds). However, approximately 50 percent of burglaries and forcible rapes are reported to the police, and less than 30 percent of larceny-thefts are reported.[1]

Another drawback to the index offense section as an exclusive barometer of the nation's crime problem is that it is based on only eight crimes. Yet there are hundreds of criminal offenses on the statute books. It may well be that the American public is especially concerned about the eight "street crimes" represented in the offense index. After all, murders, robberies, and rapes are serious crimes that cause immeasurable damage to our society. But these are not the only crimes deeply troubling the American public, and they are not the only laws the police are required to enforce.

To partly compensate for the limited focus of the Part I index offenses, the Part II section of the UCR provides arrest data on many additional crimes such as forgery, fraud, vandalism, embezzlement, gambling, and disorderly

FIGURE 1.1
Crime Clock, 1990

The crime clock should be viewed with care. Being the most aggregate representation of UCR data, it is designed to convey the annual reported crime experience by showing the relative frequency of occurrence of the Index Offenses. This mode of display should not be taken to imply a regularity in the commission of the Part I Offenses; rather, it represents the annual ratio of crime to fixed time intervals.

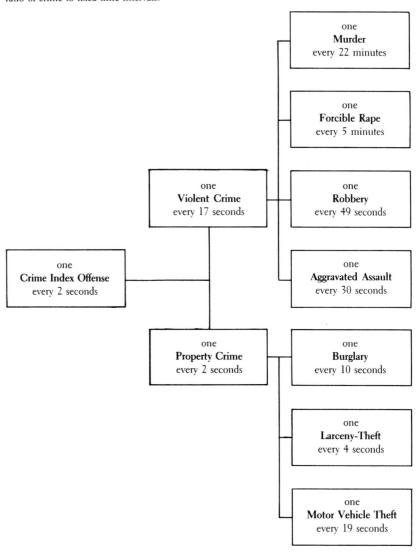

Source: U.S. Department of Justice, *Uniform Crime Reports, 1990* (Washington, DC: U.S. Government Printing Office, 1991), p. 7.

conduct (Part II offenses exclude traffic-related crimes). According to FBI figures, there were over 11 million arrests made in 1990 for Part II offenses.[2]

An alternative barometer of the nation's crime problem comes from the National Crime Survey sponsored by the U.S. Bureau of Justice. Since its inception in 1972, the NCS has collected information on the extent of criminal victimization in the United States by using a national probability sample of approximately fifty thousand households and one hundred thousand individuals.[3] The UCR and the NCS data are quite different; the UCR is based upon the crimes known by the police while the NCS reflect responses to a scientific survey asking about the interviewee's past victimization experiences. The NCS collects information on victimization rates for all index offenses except homicide and arson.

There are several distinct advantages of the NCS over the UCRs for research purposes; however, the most important advantage for our concern is the fact that the "hidden crime" problem is greatly minimized.

The National Crime Survey determined there were an estimated 34.4 million crimes committed against individuals and households in 1990. Over 60 percent of these crimes were never reported to the police. Thus, the crime clock depicted in the UCRs ticks much faster than figure 1.1 would lead us to believe.

If we only look at the yearly estimates of the amount of crime in the United States, even the NCS data may lull the typical American into a false sense of security. For example, the victimization rate for robbery in 1990 was just 5.7 out of every one thousand persons aged twelve or older, and the victimization rate for aggravated assault was only 7.9 per one thousand persons.[4] Given such seemingly low probabilities of criminal victimization for serious crime, it is not surprising that many people believe "it is not going to happen to me." The deception of yearly rates of victimization is they do not provide a realistic estimate of one's chances of being victimized over a period of time greater than one year. One criminologist views the deception this way: "If the Earth revolved around the sun in 180 days, all of our annual crime rates would be halved, but we would not be safer."[5] So then, just what is the likelihood that a person will become a victim of a crime during his or her lifetime?

Statisticians at the Bureau of Justice Statistics, the research arm of the U.S. Department of Justice, have calculated the lifetime likelihood of criminal victimization for various offenses based upon the NCS data.[6] Their findings are absolutely startling. According to statistical projections, 83 percent of the population aged twelve or older will be victimized by a violent crime (rape, robbery, or assault) during their lifetime. Ninety-nine percent of the population will be victimized by a property crime (purse snatched, pocket picked, bicycle stolen, umbrella taken, etc.) sometime in their life. Generally speaking, white females are least likely to be victimized by violent crime while black males are most likely to be victimized by violent crime. But for the crime of rape, which according to the 1990 NCS data occurs at an *annual* rate of "only" 1.0 per one thousand females age twelve or older, the odds are that one out of every twelve females (8 percent) will be forcibly raped sometime during her life.

The most startling lifetime statistics are the Justice Department's estimates of the probability of being murdered. On average, one out of every 133 Americans will be a murder victim. The situation is more bleak for males than females: statistical projections estimate one out of every eighty-four males will be murdered and one of every twenty-one black males will be murdered. The murder rate among young black urban males is so high that it has become their leading cause of death.

On a global perspective, the U.S. is regarded as having one of the highest crime rates in the world. This is true for most types of property crime and is especially true for serious violent crime. The rate of violent crime is from four to nine times higher in the United States than in European countries. The rate of property crime runs about twice as high.[7] Crime statistics compiled by the International Police Organization (INTERPOL) places the U.S. first among selected countries for rates of completed homicide, forcible rape, and robbery.[8] Judging by the best available evidence, the message is painfully clear: crime is rooted in the American way of life.

Crime: Its Causes

If crime is rooted in the very foundation of American society, what are these "roots" and where do they grow? These are difficult questions to answer. Individuals have differing points of view about the causes of crime. Many God-fearing people believe the cause of crime, particularly violent crime, is simply Satan at play. Others believe that humans are basically self-serving,

---

THE RISK OF BEING MURDERED

Coroner and medical examiner reports compiled by the National Center for Health Statistics show that during the years 1978–82 the prevalence of homicide reached its highest level in 1980: in that year one of every ten thousand Americans was murdered. Although a one in ten thousand chance of being murdered may seem remote to most people, it would be wrong to conclude from the statistic for a single year that the chances of *ever* becoming a homicide victim is equally remote. When the annual homicide reports are analyzed to determine the lifetime probability of being murdered, the likelihood jumps to one in 133. Black males, who have the highest probabil-ity of all, have a one in twenty-one lifetime chance of becoming a homicide victim. The results of this lifetime probability analysis are summarized here:

Lifetime Risk of Being Homicide Victim

	1 out of:
U.S. Total	133
Female	282
White	369
Black	104
Male	84
White	131
Black	21

Source: From U.S. Department of Justice, Bureau of Justice Statistics, *The Risk of Violent Crime* (Washington, DC: U.S. Government Printing Office, 1985), p. 2.

pleasure-seeking excitement chasers and, if given the chance, will break the law for their own benefit. Among criminologists—the modern day scientific experts on crime—there is also vigorous debate regarding the fundamental causes of crime. Some criminologists look to biological factors to explain crime, others focus on psychological causes, and still others search for the roots of crime in the social environment (e.g., urban decay, poverty, social disorganization, unequal distribution of social rewards, family breakdown, peer pressure). Thus, with such a proliferation of "root" causes of crime in the United States, one gets the feeling that there must be either a tangled mess of roots in the American soil, or that many of these roots do not hold much water.

What can the police do to eradicate the root causes of crime? The regrettable answer is they can do very little. Even if we could agree on what the root causes are, the police operate only on the surface of society, which is to say the police are not well suited for attacking the roots of crime. For example, we can request the police to aggressively patrol drug infested inner-city ghetto areas in order to suppress the trafficking of illegal substances, but the police are unable to do much about the causes of drug abuse (i.e., poverty, unemployment, high density slum housing, personal despair, minimal ties with mainstream society). Likewise, we could expand the enforcement powers of the police by limiting the constitutional rights of citizens, or we could increase the efficiency of the police by the use of sophisticated computers and tracking devices. But this would only make the police better *crime fighters*, not better *crime eradicators*. The roots of crime would still flourish.

As students of the police, it is necessary to have a realistic understanding of the contribution the police can make to the control of crime. *At best, the police cannot cure the crime problem—they can only help to control it*. In the absence of fundamental social and economic changes in the American system, there is little anyone can do to eliminate the root causes of crime. Yet the effective control of crime by the police is attainable provided there is sufficient public support and political leadership.

Crime: Its Consequences

Crime is never a single, solitary event; crime transcends the direct and immediate harm done to the victim just as ripples transcend a pebble's entry into water. "H.S. CHEERLEADER RAPED: SUSPECT STILL LOOSE," reads the headline of a small-town newspaper. Word spreads like wildfire. The townspeople are frightened; doors are bolted, windows are locked, strangers are feared. Friends and family are shocked, the local media voices its outrage, and the police intensify their efforts to capture the rapist. And the young girl, the target of the crime, the one who was raped, deals with an emotional trauma of almost unbearable intensity. She has been savagely violated and will forever feel vulnerable. The actual act of rape may have consumed less than fifteen minutes, yet the young girl will likely experience the emotional and behavioral consequences of the rape for the rest of her life.

As unpleasant as these types of victimizations are on the individual level, it must be understood that every society has to tolerate at least some crime. Crime is an inescapable fact of social life. Emile Durkheim, a famous early sociologist, made the classic observation over a century ago that crime is a *normal* part of every society:

> Crime is present not only in the majority of societies of one particular species but in all societies of all types. There is no society that is not confronted with the problem of criminality. Its form changes; the acts thus characterized are not the same everywhere, but, everywhere and always, there have been men who have behaved in such a way as to draw upon themselves penal repression.[9]

There are times when crime may provide secondary benefits to a society. Nothing brings townspeople closer together than when they share a common fate, such as the collective exhilaration of being the World Series champions or the collective outrage of a local political scandal. Crime often enhances social bonds among community members as the people react to promote and protect their common interests.

While crime may be a normal part of every society, no society can tolerate for long serious crime on a wide scale. If unchecked, crime breaks down social order by destroying the delicate threads of trust woven throughout the social fabric. People begin to restrict their behaviors and constrain their social relationships. The middle classes flee the high-crime central cities for the security of suburban life. Urban folks become less inclined to mingle freely on city streets. Strangers are avoided, eyes do not meet, "hellos" are not exchanged. Inevitably the quality of community life diminishes. So what is the American public doing to control crime?

Crime Control: Public

When we speak of "public crime control," we are referring to the entire criminal justice system (i.e., police, courts, and corrections) as well as the subcomponents of the justice system (probation, parole, alcohol and drug abuse centers, mental health centers, diversionary programs, etc.). We are also referring to the criminal laws passed by legislative bodies regulating human behavior.

In the past quarter century, public sector crime control has grown dramatically. In fiscal year 1991, American taxpayers were billed for approximately 75 billion dollars worth of justice system expenditures.[10] This was an increase of over 50 percent since 1985. In addition, state and federal lawmakers have gotten tougher with criminals. Tired of rising crime and lenient punishments, legislatures across the country have increased the length of sentences, enacted mandatory minimum sentences for serious crimes, and passed habitual offender laws ("three time loser laws") for repeat offenders. One noticeable result of our increased efforts at public sector crime control is the serious overcrowding of our nation's prisons and jails.

By all indications, public sector crime control will only intensify in the near future. The **war on crime** is here to stay, at least until the current crime crisis subsides or a major new national crisis emerges.

While on trial, subway vigilante Bernard Goetz had supporters and detractors outside the courtroom as well as inside.

In communities across the United States people are fed up with crime and are beginning to fight back. The "get-tough attitude" is transforming into "get-tough behavior" as law-abiding citizens try desperately to reclaim the streets. Crime prevention programs that rely on the *passive vigilance* of citizens in cooperation with the police (such as neighborhood watch programs, placing the faces of missing children on milk cartons, or engraving serial numbers on home valuables), are increasingly giving way to more *active vigilance* on the part of citizens. Much of the country cheered for Bernard Goetz, New York's "subway vigilante," after he shot four youths in December of 1985—two of them in the back—who apparently planned to rob him.[11] The Guardian Angels have attracted national attention as a self-appointed citizen crime squad that patrols the alleys, streets, and subways of several large American cities. And in some communities angered residents have torched crack houses operating in their neighborhoods. In one Detroit incident, a jury refused to convict two residents who admitted to burning down a local crack house.

Recently the entertainment industry discovered that thief catching can be profitable, so they too have become vigilant. Following the successful lead of *Crime Stoppers*, a program emulated nationwide (crimes are reenacted on television in thirty to sixty second slots with a phone number to call if you have information about the crime), television writers have created several weekly shows. These programs are not only exciting to watch but also encourage the national television audience to help solve the crime.

The consequences of crime are evident in other areas of private sector crime control. The private security industry has grown at a much faster rate than public policing. Currently it employs nearly twice the personnel and costs nearly twice as much as our public police system.[12] While the average person cannot afford to hire someone for protection, they can usually afford to buy extra security at the hardware store (burglar alarms, dead bolt locks, guns) or at the pet store (watchdogs, vicious cats).

Despite our efforts to control crime in the public and private sectors, the extent of crime in the United States remains seriously high. The unsettling conclusion is that the American public is not well protected from crime.

POLICE AND THE JUSTICE SYSTEM

A fundamental duty of the police in every society is to bring to **justice** those who violate the law. On first reading this duty sounds reasonable and straightforward; criminal suspects are arrested, then taken to court for prosecution and punishment. But when we more carefully consider what "justice" means in the daily operation of the criminal justice system, this simple duty of the police loses some of its clarity. This should become apparent in the following paragraphs.

What is justice? *Webster* defines justice as "the maintenance or administration of what is just especially by the impartial adjustment of conflicting claims or the assignment of merited rewards or punishments."[13] This definition may be technically accurate but it lacks intuitive appeal. A more useful

CRIME-TIME TELEVISION

By the 1980s, there was a resurgence of public interest in crime dramas. Responding to viewers' demands, networks revamped their programming schedules. But, the television shows took on a new look—a new direction.

Dramatized, factual recreations or "reality programming" now appear on the screen. Viewers are asked to help identify or locate criminals. Crime-time television has taken a premier position in modern-day programming.

Two of the most popular shows, *America's Most Wanted* (AMW) and *Unsolved Mysteries* (UM) have become potent law enforcement tools. They are basically a more visual and more interesting extension of the "Top Ten" Program that has captured America's attention since the 1950s. While AMW centers on factual fugitive recreations, UM's format is more varied, covering not only fugitives but also unsolved criminal cases and unexplained mysteries. Both shows factor in entertainment, and that, combined with the public's desire to help, accounts for the audience draw.

AMW, hosted by John Walsh, whose son Adam was brutally murdered, premiered on February 7, 1988, on select Fox TV affiliates.

John Walsh describes *America's Most Wanted* as a "weekly nationwide criminal manhunt." The show attempts to accurately reenact crimes at the actual scene whenever possible. However, only serious crimes which merit nationwide exposure and which can be solved with the public's help are reenacted. In May of 1992, AMW celebrated its two-hundredth capture.

Unsolved Mysteries, created by NBC's entertainment division, is hosted by Robert Stack.

Although crime-time television is common in such European countries as England, West Germany, and The Netherlands, the genre is still fairly new to the United States. Yet, the FBI has cooperated with certain crime-time television shows from the very beginning, recognizing the programs as unique opportunities to catch fugitives and solve cases through public/private involvement.

CROOKS CATCH A CROOK

Mark Austin Goodman, booked under the alias of James R. Eide, was serving a seventy-five-day sentence for a burglary charge at a minimum security stockade. On Sunday, May 15, 1988, inmates of the stockade were watching *America's Most Wanted* on the Fox television network. Goodman was portrayed on the program as one of the U.S. Marshal's Top Ten Fugitives. These same inmates recognized Goodman as being James R. Eide, a fellow inmate.

The inmates learned from the segment that Goodman was wanted for ten bank robberies in Oklahoma, six escapes, (one from a federal prison) and numerous other charges in four states. The inmates then reported Goodman to prison officials, who called the hotline. This tip was one of 274 from people from across the country who thought they knew Goodman.

The corrections officers, in order to guard against his escape, decided to transfer Goodman to a more secure jail. He never made it. Goodman escaped from his captors by scaling a fence around the stockade. The U.S. Marshal's office in West Palm Beach then initiated a search. Goodman was arrested by Jupiter, FL, authorities on May 16, 1988, and turned over to U.S. Marshals.

Source: Scott A. Nelson, *FBI Law Enforcement Bulletin* (U.S. Department of Justice, Washington, DC: U.S. Government Printing Office, August 1989), pp. 2–9.

definition of justice is "the process by which everyone gets what he or she deserves," better known as the **just deserts** principle. Criminals get punishment, victims get compensation, and society gets protection, retribution, and peace of mind. In earlier times when a crime was committed, the responsibility for seeking justice was almost fully the burden of the victim or the victim's family. This usually meant some form of physical retaliation. In modern times the responsibility for seeking justice has shifted from private hands to the state.

Justice does not really exist!—at least not as things exist, such as a chair, a desk, or a person. The concept of justice is a mental invention; it is never constant nor ever fixed. Justice varies over time as the collective sentiments of right and wrong change (the heretics of yesterday are often the heroes of today). Justice also varies by geography. On this latter point, Islamic countries like Iran are known for their "harsh" punishments for violators of the *Koran*, the Islamic holy bible:

> Theft, in accordance with Islamic law, is punished by amputation, as are other offenses. The first conviction for theft results in amputation of the four fingers of the right hand. The second conviction leads to the dismemberment of the left foot. In 1984 Iranian officials introduced an electric guillotine which is able to sever a hand in less than a tenth of a second. During 1985 and the first half of 1986, eleven amputations were reportedly carried out.
>
> The death penalty is prescribed for offenses ranging from adultery to repeated lesbianism and wine drinking, and thousands have been executed. Between July and December of 1981 alone, 2,444 individuals were killed, and there were a reported 470 executions in 1985.[14]

By comparison, thieves in the United States receive fines, probation, and sometimes jail; adulterers and lesbians receive community consternation. But whose justice is more just? And how can you know for sure?

Justice is a highly elusive concept. Because there are so many differing views of what is just and what is unjust, society will never achieve universal agreement. An act that is perfectly warranted in one situation (the mercy killing of your terminally ill pet) is perfectly wrong in another (the mercy killing of your terminally ill uncle); what is legally right in some states may be considered by many to be morally wrong (abortion, capital punishment); what is against the law for some is not against the law for others (underage drinking, unmarried sexual activities, delivering babies without a medical license, etc.). The elusiveness of the concept of justice is the major reason there is continual debate over the proper mix of law and punishment.

Equal Justice Under Law

The principle of **equal justice under law** is the cornerstone of our system of justice. We eagerly teach this to our children and proudly preach it to other nations. The ideal is so fervently held by Americans that the words "Equal Justice Under Law" are impressively engraved in marble over the entrance to the U.S. Supreme Court Building in Washington, D.C.

As admirable as this principle may be, we usually fall far short of achieving equal justice in reality. Indeed, *we do not have equal justice under law, we will never have equal justice, and we would not even want it if we could have it!* This statement may appear excessively cynical, but it is not.

Consider for a moment one of the most deadly and destructive type of law violator on the streets of America today—the traffic offender. On any given day there are millions of traffic violations committed by the driving public. Cars zig and zag and zoom and roar up and down the streets of America breaking every conceivable traffic law. Accidents occur with astounding regularity. People are injured, crippled, and killed by the thousands. As luck has it, a few violators are caught, but most are not. In fact the same could be said of most criminals—a few are caught, but most are not.

It is axiomatic that when two persons commit essentially the same criminal act, yet one is caught and punished while the other is not, we have not achieved "equal justice." It is also axiomatic that we will never have equal justice under law because it is impossible to equally enforce all of the laws all of the time. This would require, at minimum, one police officer for every man, woman and child who would follow their assigned citizen twenty-four hours a day. And if this impossible feat could somehow be managed, we would have to program all police officers to think and react exactly alike so no two officers would enforce the law differently. Of course all of this is rather absurd.

More importantly, society would be unwilling to tolerate complete and equal enforcement of the law even if it were possible. Returning to our traffic violator, it is fairly easy to think of numerous situations where the unbending enforcement of the rules of the road would not serve the ends of justice. Imagine yourself driving home after a long evening of studying for a criminal

Traffic accidents occur with astounding regularity, and police must arrive on the scene to assist victims and gather evidence.

justice exam at a friend's house. It is now 3:00 A.M. The streets are dark and deserted. You carefully approach a stop sign. Noting there are no cars or pedestrians in sight, you slowly "roll" through the intersection. A police officer spots your illegal movement and pulls you over. Do you deserve a ticket? If you think you deserve one, do you want one? Will you be disappointed if the officer does not give you one? Would you try to talk the officer out of the ticket? Have you ever tried to talk yourself out of a ticket?

There are two conclusions to be gained from this discussion on the police and the justice system. First, we can still have justice under law even if it is not equal justice. Second, the police can often contribute more to maintaining an orderly society by the underenforcement of the law than by its full enforcement. These ideas are so critically important to our study of the police that we will be returning to them in later chapters.

WHY STUDY POLICE IN SOCIETY?

Is there something special about police in society that make them inherently more important to study as an occupational group than, shall we say, carpenters in the community or nurses in the neighborhood? As a general observation, the public seems to be fascinated with crime and crime fighters, more so than with nursing and nurses, and far more so than with carpentry and carpenters. Consider all the successful detective novels, gang buster movies, and television police shows that have entertained us over the years. Something about policing captivates us. Perhaps it is the danger and suspense that thrills us or the sex and sleaze that excites us. Whatever the attraction, this tells us only that the police are *interesting* to study (which is not to say that nurses and carpenters are boring). But why is the study of police *important*?

First, if you can understand how the police operate in a given society—their powers, their authority, and their relationship with the people—you can also learn a great deal about that society. For example, to know about the police in South Africa is to know something about South African society. Similarly, to learn more about how and why the police operate as they do in the United States is to learn more about the United States. In this sense, the police are a reflection of the society in which they serve.

Second, the police are the most visible representatives of governmental authority. While the average citizen seldom has contact or conversation with elected representatives of government, such as governors, congressmen, or senators, the police are everywhere. We see them on the streets, on school campuses, at athletic events, and in the malls. We may not speak to them, but we see them. Their presence is constantly felt by the public. In this sense, the police serve as a daily reminder of the power of the state to regulate the lives of its citizens.

A third and critically important reason to study the police is because their capacity to act goes far beyond the capacity of the general public to act. The police can do things that ordinary citizens cannot. For instance, the police have the ability to (1) investigate crimes (i.e., gather documents, search property, seize evidence); (2) withhold personal liberty (from brief stops on the street for simple questioning to full-fledged arrests); (3) use physical force in non self-defense situations (i.e., subdue a suspect, shoot a sniper); and (4) violate the law in the performance of their duty (buy and sell illegal drugs, solicit prostitutes, etc.). What we are referring to here is **police authority.** Police authority may be defined as the *legitimate right* of the police to act on behalf of the health, welfare, and safety of society.[15] In all societies that have a police, the immediate source of their authority comes directly from the state.

The counterpart to police authority is **police power.** Although often used interchangeably, the two terms are not synonymous. One group of writers have suggested the following distinction:

> *Authority* is the right to direct and command. *Power* is the force by means of which others can be obliged to obey. Power without authority is tyrannical; authority without [power] is meaningless.[16]

Max Weber, a highly regarded early German sociologist, defined power as "the possibility of imposing one's will upon the behavior of other persons."[17] Another way of expressing the same point is that power is the ability to make

A transit police officer checks the platform of a New York City subway station. His very presence is a reminder to citizens of the government's control of their lives.

an individual or an entire group do something even if they do not want to do it.

We may define police power as the force used by police when acting on behalf of the health, welfare, and safety of society.[18] Consider the following: one officer questions a burglary suspect at the police station after properly reading the suspect his rights; a second officer questions a different burglary suspect at the police station without reading the suspect his rights. Both officers are using police power—that is, they are using "force" (persuasion, influence, leverage) to solve a crime. The difference is that the first officer is well within his legal authority while the second officer is not.

To summarize our point, whereas police authority by definition implies the legitimate right of the police to act, police power does not. Police power may or may not be legitimate, and power is easily abused. For this reason alone the police in every society ought to be carefully scrutinized and closely controlled. The police in our society wield an awesome amount of power; fortunately, they use it with proper authority most of the time.

On a broader historical perspective, one should be mindful that our Western cultural heritage has long been distrustful of excessive state power. Two of history's most important documents reflect this distrust: England's **Magna Carta** and the Constitution of the United States. An important purpose of each of these documents was to restrict the capricious power of the state. Although at the time the U.S. Constitution was being drafted there were no public police patrolling the streets—public policing had not yet been established—the framers of the Constitution were all too familiar with the abuses of military power to maintain domestic control over the people.

Our founding fathers were clever enough to not only separate the powers of government but also to devise a system of checks and balances. This arrangement was to ensure that no one person, group, or governmental entity garnered excessive power at the expense of individual freedom. To simplify it greatly, Article I of the Constitution established the legislative branch of government with the authority to make laws. Article II established the executive branch with the authority to veto bills and with the responsibility to enforce the law. And Article III created the judicial branch, holding it responsible for interpreting the law and rendering decisions. In theory, therefore, the enforcement responsibilities of the police make them a part of the executive branch of government.

As testimony to the genius of our founding founders, our system of government has lasted over two hundred years, thus making the United States one of the oldest governments in the world. What is more, we have found it necessary to amend the original Constitution fewer than thirty times. Today few citizens worry that our police forces pose a serious risk to our personal freedoms. But there are no guarantees in life, and nothing lasts forever.

CONCLUSION

The United States is host to what may well be the most crime plagued society in the world. Among all the public servants and agencies that share the burden of doing something about the crime problem (mayors, governors, judges, city councils, etc.), it is the police that shoulder the majority of the burden. But is this realistic? Do we expect too much from the police? The police are not able to attack the root causes of crime. They cannot make greedy people less greedy, and they cannot change the social, cultural, and historical conditions that shape people's lives. The police can only help to control the crime problem. Alone, they can do little to eliminate it.

Should the police enforce *bad* laws? While seat belts are credited with saving thousands of lives, some say mandatory seat belt laws are "bad" because they encroach excessively on freedom of personal choice. Should *unjust* laws be obeyed? For example, the "separate but equal" laws of the past seem, at least in retrospect, incredibly unjust. What about laws that serve a useful purpose but may at times get in the way of achieving a greater good? Should these good laws be conveniently circumvented? For instance, is it OK for the FBI to infringe on the civil rights of known political subversives through illegal wiretaps and eavesdropping devices? Should the police be allowed to illegally search and seize incriminating evidence from known drug dealers and other despicable folks?

It is commonly agreed that *ours is a society of laws, not of men.* A society of men is little more than a society of whim, for who decides what is in the best interest of our country—a police official, a military leader, an Adolf Hitler?

We have only begun to scratch the surface of some of the more important issues relating to criminal law. We shall return to these and many other critical issues in American policing in the chapters to follow.

KEY TERMS

Uniform Crime Report (UCR)
National Crime Survey (NCS)
index offenses
hidden crime
war on crime

justice
just deserts
equal justice under law
police authority
police power

DISCUSSION QUESTIONS

1. Why do you think it is called the "criminal" justice system and not the "victim" justice system? Do you believe most crime victims receive less justice than they deserve?
2. In what ways can the police contribute to the maintenance of an orderly society by the underenforcement of the law? What are some of the problems with underenforcing the law? What are some of the problems with full enforcement of the law?
3. It is commonly pointed out that the criminal justice system focuses more attention on controlling the crimes of the powerless than the crimes of the powerful. Why do you think this is so? Do you think it should be different?
4. What are your thoughts on the root causes of crime? What would you recommend we should do to control crime?

CHAPTER TWO

DEVELOPMENT OF PUBLIC POLICING

The basic mission for which the police exist is to prevent crime and disorder as an alternative to the repression of crime and disorder by military force and severity of legal punishment.

—Sir Robert Peel

The creation of a paid, full-time, uniformed public police for the purpose of protecting and serving the general citizenry is a fairly recent social invention. Public policing as we know it has been around for less than two hundred years! The English were the first to develop the professional model of public policing in the early 1800s. Early British police officers were sworn to protect all citizens in the crime-infested city of London. The idea of public policing spread quickly throughout the rest of England, and the idea inevitably made its way across the Atlantic Ocean. By the mid-1800s, many of the larger cities in the United States were adopting the British style of policing. At the turn of the twentieth century, almost every small town and big city in the United States had its own public police system.

This chapter traces the history of the police from ancient times to the present. We pay particular attention to the major events that have shaped the development of the police and the leading people who have made significant contributions to the field of policing.

TRACING THE HISTORY OF THE POLICE

The following discussion examines the historical development of the police through four time periods: Ancient History (from prehistory to 500 A.D.); Middle Ages (500 to 1500); Early Industrial Europe (1500 to 1829); and Modern Public Police (1829 to present). Because we are covering thousands of years of human history in only a few pages, our discussion is limited to the major developments relating to the police.

Ancient History (Prehistory to 500 A.D.)

Piecing together an accurate picture of early forms of policing is difficult to do because there is limited documentable evidence of much of our past. Historians note that representatives of the human race have roamed the earth for a million years, yet we are able to trace the course of human events less than one percent of that time.[1] It was just six thousand years ago that humans began to record their achievements (i.e., the beginning of written history), thereby passing their society and culture down through time.

The absence of a documentable history on the life and times of early humans prohibits us from being very confident in our statements about prehistoric policing. Storytelling of this sort rests on the subjective interpretation of archeological findings combined with imaginative recreations of what life in prehistoric times must have been like. As one group of police scholars has written, "the beginnings of formal law enforcement activities are clouded within a historical mist."[2] Nonetheless, we are still able to make some general observations.

In ancient times there were, of course, no police. There was neither the need for a formal institution in prehistoric society to police clan members (informal mechanisms of social control worked sufficiently well), nor was prehistoric society organizationally advanced enough to support a police. Initially, small groups of families banded together for mutual protection from wild beasts and from the hostile environment. Crimes were normally vindicated by the person who was injured or by the victim's family. We can call this early type of crime control **kin policing** because the family or clan was responsible for seeking justice.[3]

As these clans grew in size they appointed a chief as their leader. The tribal chief and his warriors were responsible for protecting the interests of the entire clan, which included clan property (tools, weapons, caves, animal skins, etc.) and clan members. Certainly there were times when the clan needed protection from the disruptive behavior of fellow clan members—persons we would now classify as deviants or criminals; yet the most important protection provided by the tribal chief and his warriors was from outside invasion of an enemy clan. The dual protective duties of the clan leader was an early combination of military and domestic police functions.[4]

Egypt and Mesopotamia

Two of the earliest known civilizations sprang up at about the same time (circa 5000 B.C.) in the great river valleys of the Middle East.[5] The ancient Egyptians, best known as the people who built the pyramids, developed their civilization in the fertile valley of the Nile River in North Africa. Mesopotamia was the other early civilization nestled in the rich valley region between the Tigris and Euphrates rivers (present-day Iraq). Compared to other population centers during this period in history, these two great civilizations were highly advanced. This was especially true of ancient Egypt. The Egyptians devised a twenty-four letter alphabet three thousand years before the birth of Christ; learned how to make paper and to write with pen and ink; discovered copper (thus entering the Age of Metals); invented indoor plumbing; and developed the Egyptian calendar based on 365 days in a year.[6] Historian Joseph Reither notes that the early Egyptians developed the necessary ingredients for recording history: "an accurate time measurement and a system of writing."[7] The earliest recorded date in human history is the date assigned at the beginning of the Egyptian calendar—4241 B.C.[8]

But the greatness of ancient Egypt and Mesopotamia was also the source of a growing problem—namely, crime. As centers of early trade and culture, these regions attracted many people of varying backgrounds and personal interests. Of particular concern at the time was the large number of drunks and deviants who roamed the streets pestering the public. Drawn to these population centers because of the huge concentration of riches and the anonymity of urban life, thieves, pickpockets, and swindlers preyed on innocent people with relative impunity. Perhaps for the first time in history we find that the established methods of private retribution (kin police) and informal social control (townsfolk watching townsfolk) were insufficient to control crime. It was about this time in history that the achievement of justice was becoming the public and formal responsibility of royalty.

The beginning of formal written law dates back to this period. Two thousand years before Christ, Hammurabi came to power as King of Babylonia (formerly Mesopotamia). King Hammurabi desired to unite the entire region by creating a strong centralized government. He ordered his governors to collect taxes, enforce the laws, and protect the country from attack with the aid of a standing army.[9] But to Hammurabi's disappointment, his governors encountered tremendous confusion enforcing established laws because the laws were not the same everywhere. Determined to centralize his authority, Hammurabi ordered his men to *record* and *standardize* all existing laws, thus making his code the law of the land.

The **Code of Hammurabi** was based on the age-old principle of *lex talionis* ("an eye for an eye, a tooth for a tooth"). For example, if a house collapsed due to faulty craftsmanship and killed the homeowner's son, the homeowner would have the right to take the life of the son of the builder. Although the punishment for criminal acts was generally harsh, it is criminologically significant that the code assigned a penalty to each crime in a fashion similar to criminal statutes today. The Code of Hammurabi was literally carved into stone and buried in the temple of Marduk in Babylon. Archaeologists unearthed the code decades ago and placed it on display at the Louvre in France. The Code of Hammurabi survives today as the oldest preserved written law from ancient times.[10]

The **Mosaic Code** of the Israelites (1200 B.C.) was another famous early law that embodied the formal rules of the ancient Jews. The Mosaic Code is best known for its *Ten Commandments*, which forbid such acts as lying, stealing, killing, and adultery. For three thousand years the Mosaic Code has been an important source of law and moral thought for European and American legal systems.[11]

Greece and Rome

The ancient Greek civilization made important contributions to the early development of police (the word "police" comes from the Greek word "poli," meaning city).[12] There is evidence that the kin police system developed into a rudimentary form of community policing in early Greece. Draco, an early Greek lawgiver, introduced a severely harsh code in 621 B.C. that granted the government sweeping powers to intervene in the lives of citizens. This is the origin of the word *draconic*, meaning extremely harsh. Under Pisistratus (605 to 527 B.C.), ancient ruler of Athens, a guard system was established to protect the tower, the highways, and the men of the crown. And in Sparta,

---

THE MOSAIC CODE: THE TEN COMMANDMENTS

1. I am the Lord thy God.
2. Thou shalt have no other gods before me.
3. Thou shalt not take the name of thy God in vain.
4. Thou shalt observe the sabbath day, to keep it holy.
5. Thou shalt honor thy father and thy mother.
6. Thou shalt not kill.
7. Thou shalt not commit adultery.
8. Thou shalt not steal.
9. Thou shalt not bear false witness against thy neighbor.
10. Thou shalt not covet thy neighbor's wife, nor any of thy neighbor's possessions.

Source: Holy Bible, American Standard Version.

One of the first police forces was the Roman Praetorian Guard, an elite military corps assigned to protect the emperor's palace and ensure his personal safety.

another great city-state of ancient Greece known for its strong centralized government, a ruler-appointed police system was developed to spy on citizens. Sparta's police system was the first "secret police" in history.[13]

Ancient Rome had considerable influence on modern day policing as well. The Roman empire was continually expanding and eventually conquered much of the Mediterranean world. The rein of Augustus, grandnephew of Julius Caesar and first emperor of Rome (27 B.C.), introduced many advances to law enforcement. Under Augustus the *Praetorian Guard* was created. These men were an elite military corps assigned to protect the palace and ensure the personal safety of Caesar.[14] The *urban cohorts* were comprised of five hundred to six hundred military men who were responsible for keeping the peace in the city. Finally, the *vigiles of Rome* were civilian peacekeepers (i.e., nonmilitary) who patrolled city streets and performed the combined duties of law enforcement and fire fighting.[15] The Roman vigiles predate by two thousand years the integrated police and fire department that still can be found in a few U.S. cities.

Middle Ages (500 to 1500)

Historians of Western civilization refer to the thousand year interval between 500 A.D. to 1500 A.D. as the "Middle Ages" (also the "Dark Ages" or "Medieval" times). The Middle Ages signify a time when intellectual, literary, and artistic achievements stagnated. The Middle Ages also signify a time when the church dominated nearly every aspect of daily life.

The collapse of the Roman empire in the first few centuries A.D. brought years of conflict in Western Europe. Fierce nomadic tribes swept through the countryside pillaging and plundering the land. One highly feared Germanic tribe known as the *Vandals* overran much of Europe around 455 A.D., sacking Rome and terrorizing people everywhere. It is from these savage marauders that we get the term "vandalism" to describe malicious, destructive behavior.

Policing seems to have lost its historical pattern following the fall of the Roman empire. It was not until the **feudal system** of government started in England and France around 700 A.D. that a stable system of policing re-emerged.[16] Just prior to this time, or from about 450 to 650, successive waves of Anglo-Saxons of Dutch and German descent invaded the Romano-Celtic inhabitants of England.[17] The new Anglo-Saxon inhabitants settled throughout much of England. They worked the land and developed the feudal system of local government. This Anglo-Saxon feudal system helped establish a degree of social order and stability that had not existed for some time. Several centuries later, in 1066, England was again invaded. This time it was from the south by the Duke of Normandy, William the Conqueror. King William set out to revamp the established feudal order by creating a much stronger, centralized government. The new social order allowed William to effectively control his kingdom and collect taxes. The infamous Domesday Book, kept by King William and his proficient revenue men, was an extensive listing of every landowner and their property in the kingdom. The Domesday Book allowed King William to collect all the taxes due to him.

The reign of the Norman kings brought a number of advances to policing. King William himself instituted the practice of curfews to keep people off the streets and out of trouble after sunset. King Henry I, the son of William, formalized the concept of *disturbance of the peace:* ". . . there will be certain offenses *against the king's peace*, arson, robbery, murder, false coinage, and crimes of violence."[18] Henry I also made the distinction between *felonies* (the word "felon" at the time identified a person of low character) and *misdemeanors*.[19] A few years later Henry II initiated the jury trial, and Richard I appointed knights to the job of *peace wardens* to enforce the law. The practice of recording the decisions of the courts, the beginning of the *English Common Law*, also dates back to this period.

Norman rulers were known for their flagrant abuses of power. Traditionally thought to be the birthright of the common people, basic rights and political liberties were denied. Criminal defendants were charged, tried, and convicted with minimal due process protection. By the early thirteenth century, during the reign of the worst ruler in English history, mean King John (1199 to 1216), resentment toward the crown rose to a critical level. It was not just the common people who were unwilling to tolerate the abuses of power any longer; the resentment was widespread and included many nobles, landowners, and the clergy. As one of history's earliest civil rights movements, the voice of the people struggled to be heard. The confrontation culminated in King John's forced signing of the **Magna Carta** in the year 1215, thereby limiting—but certainly not eliminating—the capricious and ruthless power of the crown. Initially the document served mainly to protect the rights and privileges of nobility. Only with the passage of time and the increased democratization of the British system of government did the Magna Carta fully serve the interests of the common man and woman.

Policing in the Middle Ages

Let us take a closer look at the type of policing that existed in feudal England. It is known as the **tithing system** (also the frankpledge system). In the many small towns and villages that dotted the landscape, the responsibility for maintaining social order was that of all able-bodied men. Every male over the age of twelve—females were excused from duty—had to form an alliance with nine of his neighbors called a *tithing*. Tithingmen were obliged to apprehend anyone caught committing a crime in their jurisdiction and deliver that person to court (an early form of citizen's arrest). If a crime was committed or a fire detected, the first tithingman to become aware of the problem would raise the **hue and cry.** The remaining tithingmen had to drop whatever they were doing and respond to the emergency.

One of the keys to the success of this way of policing was to hold the entire tithing responsible for each of its members; if one tithingman committed a crime and escaped justice, the nine remaining members could be fined, punished, or forced to make restitution. The practice of punishing the entire tithing for the actions of one of its members made it a wise strategy to form a tithing alliance with nine trustworthy males—which was not always easy to do—and then to keep a watchful eye on them all. It was common to find tithings trying to conceal the criminal behavior of a fellow tithingman so as to avoid being punished.[20]

A group of ten adjacent tithings formed a *hundred* (i.e., one hundred families). The hundred was a recognized judicial jurisdiction that held court, settled disputes, and exacted punishment. The *reeve* was the head man of the hundred. The reeve had some limited enforcement authority. Larger areas, called *shires*, were comprised of several hundreds. The head of the shire was the *earl*. The earl's duties combined a few law enforcement responsibilities with numerous administrative chores.

Yet far more important and powerful than the earl was the king-appointed **shire-reeve.** As official representative of the crown, the shire-reeve was the primary law enforcement officer in the jurisdiction. The position was arguably the first *general* police officer in English history, since the shire-reeve was responsible for protecting not just his immediate kin and neighbors but everyone in the jurisdiction. The shire-reeve enforced the law while also attending to other duties of the crown (such as collecting taxes). The office of shire-reeve in feudal England is the direct historical ancestor of the modern-day office of sheriff.

The tithing system was originally a highly localized type of citizen policing during the Anglo-Saxon period in feudal England (around 700 to 900 A.D.). Local lords and nobles tended to the administration of justice without interference from the crown. However, the invasion of the Normans in 1066 greatly increased the crown's authority in such matters.[21] First, the king's sheriff took over the job of supervising the tithings from the local lords and nobles. Second, errant tithing members were taken to the king's central court instead of the local manorial courts. Third, the money collected from tithing fines went directly into the crown's coffers.[22] In fact, the frequent imposition of stiff fines by the king's courts on all ten tithing members when they failed to perform·their required duties was an effective way to keep the tithing in check. As criminologist Carl Klockars contends, the fines are what made the tithing system a form of **obligatory avocational policing;** "obligatory" meaning mandatory, "avocational" meaning part-time, unpaid, amateur status.[23]

As a form of citizen policing, the tithing system worked reasonably well in the stable social setting of early feudal England. As English society became more urban and the population more geographically mobile, the tithings were increasingly unable to police the growing numbers of transients, vagrants, beggars, and peddlers who were not bound by a tithing alliance. Moreover, since the tithings were unpaid for their crime control services they had little incentive (other than to avoid punishment) to aggressively control crime.

The Statute of Winchester (1285) sought to replace the growingly ineffectual tithing system of policing with the **parish constable** system. In actuality, the statute simply replaced one ineffective type of mandatory citizen policing with another. The statute ordered that one man from each parish serve an entire year, unpaid, as constable. Parish constables were general police officers and, as such, had to protect the entire community. For additional protection of the cities at night, constables were expected to band together a group of citizen watchmen (also unpaid) to guard the town's gates from dusk to dawn. Similar to the tithing system, if the parish constable became aware that a criminal was loose in the area, he was authorized to issue the traditional hue and cry. As in the past, this required all able-bodied men in the immediate area to cease whatever they were doing and go to the constable's aid. The new law even required every man to own a weapon so they could help catch crooks and protect personal property. Thus, while the Statute of Winchester shifted the formal responsibility of policing directly to the parish constable, every man continued to be responsible for policing as well.

It is not hard to understand why few men wanted to be constable. The job was time consuming and financially unrewarding; yet if selected, a man had no choice but to serve (or be sent to the pillory), usually while continuing to work his regular job. The parish constable system was another form of obligatory avocational policing thrust on the people to replace the older tithing system.[24] Partly because of the personal hardship it created, the misfortune of serving as parish constable was passed to someone new each year.

In 1362 England passed the Justice of the Peace Act. **Justices of the peace** were established in the cities to work in concert with parish constables to maintain order and control crime. During the early years of this new office, justices of the peace were highly respected townspeople of considerable wealth. They accepted the unpaid position because it was viewed as an honorable way to serve the community. Eventually, justices of the peace became the superiors of the undistinguished parish constables because of their loftier social status.[25]

Parish constables and justices of the peace were the dominant forms of policing over the next several centuries. Yet as we shall soon discover, they were far from satisfactory solutions to the serious crime problem that existed in early industrial England.

Early Industrial England (1500 to 1829)

As Western civilization emerged out of the Middle Ages, England experienced sweeping social change. On the one hand, it was a time of great excitement and optimism; the New World had been discovered, commercial activity was increasing, and great riches could be made. On the other hand, not everyone was sharing in the dream or the profit; events of the day foreshadowed a new era when poverty, despair, and crime would reach unprecedented levels.

The worst to suffer were the small farmers. By the late 1500s, the large landowners discovered they could make more profit by raising sheep for wool than crops for food. They began to convert large portions of their farms to grassland pasture.[26] The result was mass migration of landless farmers from the small hamlets and villages to urban centers. Having lost their livelihood, these homeless and dispossessed people were eager to accept any type of employment regardless of the working conditions. Men, women, and even children worked up to sixteen hours a day, six days a week at starvation wages just to make enough to survive. And these were the lucky people because they had employment.

Crime soared as people needed to steal to survive. Places like London and Liverpool grew almost overnight from small sleepy towns to dens of deviance and decadence. The streets were unsafe; citizens were terrified. A desperate plea for help to the Mayor of London in the early 1700s captures this gripping fear:

> The Whole City, My Lord, is alarm'd and uneasy; Wickedness has got such a Head, and the Robbers and Insolence of the Night are such, that the Citizens are no longer secure within their own Walls, or safe even in passing their Streets, but are robbed, insulted and abused, even at their own Doors. . . . The Citizens . . . are oppressed by Rapin and Violence; Hell seems to have let loose Troops of human D– – –ls upon them; and such Mischiefs are done within the Bounds of your Government as never were practised here before (at least not to such a degree) and which, if suffered to go on, will call for Armies, not Magistrates, to suppress.[27]

The problem of crime intensified throughout the 1700s. In larger cities around the turn of the nineteenth century, the people saw themselves threatened by a growing mass of vicious criminals produced by the burgeoning unattached and unemployed population—referred to as the **dangerous classes** in the writings of the time.[28] Crime and disorder prevailed.

Looking back it is obvious that the system of obligatory avocational policing was not sufficient for such large scale criminal activity. Part-time citizen police (parish constables, justices of the peace, magistrates, and night watchmen) had neither the know-how nor desire to fight crime on a large scale. As Carl Klockars sees it:

The deterioration and demise of the parish constable system illustrates the central flaw in all systems of obligatory avocational police. As the work becomes more difficult, demanding, or time-consuming, obligatory avocational policing takes on the characteristics of forced labor. Unpaid, it has to compete with earning a living. Motivated only by the threat of punishment, it becomes unwilling and resistant. Offering no one any reason to learn or cultivate the skills necessary to do it well, it becomes undependable, uneconomic, and of poor quality. *In short, the more we expect a police to do, the less we can expect obligatory avocational police to do it. For all of these very good reasons, obligatory avocational systems cannot serve as a basis for a satisfactory modern police.*[29]

The twin problems of rising crime and ineffective citizen police do not mean that early industrial society was in complete disorder. First of all, while many criminals escaped the arms of the law, a sizable number of criminals were caught and faced stiff fines or harsh physical punishment. By the latter part of the eighteenth century there were over 160 offenses in England—some as minor as stealing a loaf of bread—that could send a criminal to his grave.[30] In reality, however, the death penalty was seldom inflicted for most minor crimes.

Second, existing alongside the dominant obligatory system of citizen police was a patchwork of other police forms. For example, paying private guards for added protection became popular for those who could afford it, like the business people who hired their own *merchant police* to protect their property. Also, vigilantes and lynch mobs, though more a tradition of early America, periodically became active as dissatisfaction with the regular citizen police peaked. Klockars refers to the vigilante method of getting police work done as **voluntary avocational policing,** which was debatably effective and often brutal.[31] Finally when all else seemed to fail, England began offering handsome rewards for the capture of criminals. The passage of the High-waymen Act of 1692 was a desperate attempt to entice the average, everyday greedy citizen into the crime control business, or what Klockars calls **entrepreneurial avocational policing.**[32] As luck would have it, there were plenty of entrepreneurially spirited citizens willing to chase after criminals. The problem is that these so called **thief takers** were easily corrupted by all the money that could be made. They resorted to lying, blackmail, and extortion to earn a living. It is ironic that many of the thief takers were more despicable than the criminals they sought.

This entire constellation of police forms available in the seventeenth and eighteenth centuries created only a semi-workable system of social control, a system that was soon to wither away as the dominant form of policing society. Citizen policing was on the way out as a new form of paid, full-time "professional" police was soon to be developed. It was about this time that we entered into the modern era of public policing.

Modern Public Police (1829 to present)

Tuesday, September 29, 1829, was a historical day in the annals of police.[33] As darkness blanketed the cool, crisp autumn evening, swarms of uniformed officers marched from their Scotland Yard headquarters to assigned posts throughout the city of London. Charged with the duty of preserving the peace and preventing crime, they commenced policing. The importance of this day in Britain is nearly impossible to overstate—modern public policing had been born.

Sir Robert Peel, the "Father of Police," is given credit for establishing the first modern police. As British Home Secretary at the time, a high-level cabinet position, Peel introduced a controversial piece of legislation to the British Parliament entitled "An Act for Improving the Police In and Near the Metropolis." The bill was to replace the disjointed system of citizen police with a select body of well-trained and highly disciplined public police officers. Better known as the Metropolitan Police Act, Peel's plan finally passed Parliamentary vote in 1829. To this day British police officers are called bobbies, so named after Sir Robert (Bob) Peel.

The idea of an organized public police force was not applauded by all. Peel had his hands full convincing parliamentary colleagues that such a system was in England's best interest. Peel's plan prevailed in the end because the creation of a public police was simply the lesser of two "evils" confronting the British people. The first and greater evil was the absence of a viable police system in the face of steadily rising crime and pervasive fear of victimization. By the early 1800s it was obvious that something had to be done, though exactly

---

JONATHAN WILD (1682–1725): THIEF TAKER GENERAL

Jonathan Wild was a famous English robber, fence, thief taker, and crime boss of London's underworld. While serving four years in debtors' prison, Wild met a whore named Mary Milliner who later introduced him to leading robbers in the city. Wild soon organized a gang of thieves who were responsible for countless robberies over a ten-year period. Wild was known as the "Prince of Robbers." With branch offices and warehouses throughout the city of London and a fast-sailing sloop for smuggling stolen goods, Wild became the key player of a major crime ring. He divided the city into districts and assigned gangs to work each area. Anyone refusing his rule would be hunted down, framed for a crime and eventually executed. Wild was so audacious he even had one man hanged in order to sleep with his widow.

Meanwhile, Wild set himself up as a private *thief taker.* He opened an office where victims of robberies could hire him to catch thieves and return the loot for a reward. He advertised his services under the self-appointed title of "Thief Taker General of Great Britain and Ireland." As an added show of authority, Wild carried a baton with a crown on it. Wild is credited with sending up to one hundred criminals to the gallows as thief taker while simultaneously operating one of the largest criminal organizations in London.

An angry highwayman named Blueskin, whom Wild helped to frame, slit Wild's throat in court. Blueskin was hanged. Wild survived the wound but soon found himself on trial for receiving stolen goods. Wild was convicted and sentenced to die. The night before his execution, Wild tried unsuccessfully to commit suicide with a powerful opiate drug. On the ride to his execution site the next day, the crowd pelted him with stones and mud. Wild was hanged on May 24, 1725.

Sources: George C. Kohn, *Dictionary of Culprits and Criminals* (Metuchen, NJ: The Scarecrow Press, Inc., 1986), p. 384; Sir Harold Scott, ed., *The Concise Encyclopedia of Crime and Criminals* (New York: Hawthorne Books, Inc., 1961), p. 337.

what was not clear. The second evil eventually proved to be surmountable, but it too was a serious problem: what is to stop a benevolent *policed society* from becoming a malevolent *police state?*[34] The thought of plainclothes police agents living secretly among the people and spying on citizens was repulsive. In France, England's southern neighbor and historical nemesis, soldiers, spies, and paid informants had been used to control the masses since the Middle Ages.[35] The French *Gendarmerie Nationale*, a highly trained military unit used by Napoleon for domestic control, was a form of policing that the English did not wish to emulate.[36]

Crime Prevention

Among the many important features of the new police system, none was more basic to its mission than **crime prevention**. In the words of Police Commissioner Charles Rowan as he addressed the first group of police officers in 1829:

> It should be understood, at the outset, that the principal object to be obtained is the prevention of crime. To this great end, every effort of the police is to be directed. The security of person and property, the preservation of the public tranquility and all other objects of a police establishment would thus be better effected than by the detention and punishment of the offender after he has succeeded in committing the crime.[37]

The concept of crime prevention had been taking shape for more than half a century before the first police officers set foot on the streets of London.

SIR ROBERT PEEL (1788–1850)

Robert Peel was born on February 5, 1788 in Lancashire, England. As the eldest son of a wealthy businessman, Peel was fortunate to receive an excellent education. He studied at Harrow School and Christ Church, Oxford, where he earned degrees in the classics and mathematics.

Peel was a tall, handsome, and ruggedly-built man with red hair and blue eyes. He was fond of sports and was an excellent marksman. Peel was highly intelligent and had an immense capacity to work, although he often appeared shy and uneasy in public. In 1820 Peel married Julia Floyd, the beautiful daughter of General Sir John Floyd, and the two shared a very happy life together.

Sir Robert Peel's political career was truly brilliant. Early in his career Peel became a member of the House of Commons where he began developing an impressive reputation. He later served as Chief Secretary for Ireland, Parliamentary member for Oxford University, Home Secretary, and two terms as Prime Minister of Britain.

As Home Secretary of Britain, Peel introduced a bill into Parliament called "An Act for Improving the Police in and Near the Metropolis," better known as the Metropolitan Police Act of 1829. The bill was an attempt to stem the problem of rising crime in the city of London. The British police are called "bobbies" after Robert Peel's nickname.

After a brief illness, Sir Robert Peel—the founder of the modern police—died at the age of sixty-two in 1850.

Source: Edward Eldefonso, Alan Coffey, and Richard C. Grace, *Principles of Law Enforcement*, 2nd ed. (New York: John Wiley and Sons), pp. 68–70.

The "Father of Police," Robert Peel.

Leading criminological thinkers of the time such as Jeremy Bentham, Cesare Beccaria, and Patrick Colquhoun were debating its virtues. In the mid-1700s, novelist Henry Fielding and his blind brother John put the concept of crime prevention to the test by organizing a group of six plainclothes detectives to investigate crimes and to run known criminals out of the Bow Street section of London.[38] The measurable success of the **Bow Street Runners** in countering the crime problem encouraged those promoting the concept of prevention. Peel was so impressed with its practical application that he insisted crime prevention be the cornerstone of his police.

Gaining Legitimacy

The passage of the Metropolitan Police Act of 1829 gave formal approval to organize the police, but the enabling legislation did not ensure the public would immediately accept the police. And in fact there were a great many skeptics of the first British police. For instance, the industrial labor movement during this time in England posed what appeared to be a substantial risk to the social order. Critics were concerned the new police were really intended as a political instrument to control this labor movement. Therefore it was up to Peel and his appointees to develop the new police in such a way that the police could effectively control crime while at the same time win the respect, support, and confidence of the people. This is where the organizational skill and creative genius of Sir Robert Peel was unmistakable.

The first order of business was to hire over three thousand men of sound mind, body, and character as officers of the law. This was no small task. The entrance requirements established by Peel and his first two police commissioners, Colonel Charles Rowan and Irish barrister Richard Mayne, were as follows: recruits had to be at least 5'11" in height, no more than thirty-five years old, capable of reading, writing, and taking orders, and not a criminal.[39] The pay was modest, but this assured that the men who sought the job "would not adopt a superior air toward the public and that they would speak the same social language as most of the people with whom they would have to deal."[40] Incredible as it seems, in the first ten years of the new police force nearly five thousand police officers were fired and another six thousand officers resigned (many of these officers were given the choice to resign or be fired).[41] This is more than just an amazing turnover of police personnel—it was a test of Peel's commitment to recruit the best available men as police officers.

PEEL'S PRINCIPLES OF LAW ENFORCEMENT

1. The basic mission for which the police exist is to prevent crime and disorder as an alternative to the repression of crime and disorder by military force and severity of legal punishment.

2. The ability of the police to perform their duties is dependent upon public approval of police existence, actions, behavior, and the ability of the police to secure and maintain public respect.

3. The police must secure the willing cooperation of the public in voluntary observance of the law to be able to secure and maintain public respect.

4. The degree of cooperation of the public that can be secured diminishes, proportionately, the necessity for the use of physical force and compulsion in achieving police objectives.

5. The police seek and preserve public favor, not by catering to public opinion, but by constantly demonstrating absolutely impartial service to the law, in complete independence of policy, and without regard to the justice or injustice of the substance of individual laws; by ready offering of individual service and friendship to all members of the society without regard to their race or social standing; by ready exercise of courtesy and friendly good

humor; and by ready offering of individual sacrifice in protecting and preserving life.

6. The police should use physical force to the extent necessary to secure observance of the law or to restore order only when the exercise of persuasion, advice, and warning is found to be insufficient to achieve police objectives; and police should use only the minimum degree of physical force which is necessary on any particular occasion for achieving a police objective.

7. The police at all times should maintain a relationship with the public that gives reality to the historic tradition that the police are the public and that the public are the police; the police are the only members of the public who are paid to give full-time attention to duties which are incumbent on every citizen in the interest of the community welfare.

8. The police should always direct their actions toward their functions and never appear to usurp the powers of the judiciary by avenging individuals or the state, or authoritatively judging guilt or punishing the guilty.

9. The test of police efficiency is the absence of crime and disorder, not the visible evidence of police action in dealing with them.

Source: W. L. Melville Lee, *A History of Police in England* (London: Methuen, 1901).

Peel was convinced that the police must be highly visible to the public. As long as the police were easily recognizable, citizens would have little reason to fear they were being watched by secret spies carrying out the espionage functions of the government. (This is the main reason why there were no plainclothes detectives in the early years of the British police force. The detective division appeared only after the police gained the confidence of the public.) Citizens also would know who to turn to if there was trouble that required the officer's attention. This meant that officers had to wear an identifiable uniform so citizens would know who they were, where they were, and what they were doing. Furthermore, since the police force was a civilian organization separate from the military, Peel wanted to be sure his police officers in no way resembled the British soldiers.

Peel settled on a conservative-looking dark blue uniform to distinguish it from the bright red of the military. This marked the early beginning of such colorful phrases as "man in blue" or "the blue curtain" to describe the police. The uniform included a top hat, a blue tail coat, a truncheon hidden in one of the coat tails, and a badge clearly pinned to the uniform which identified the precinct and patrol number of each officer. Citizens were encouraged to report officers who were discourteous or who acted without proper authority. Allowing the public to monitor the police in this fashion had the dual benefits of (1) holding individual officers accountable for their misdeeds, thereby keeping the entire police force in check; and (2) accentuating citizens' feeling of control over the police.

The police earned the confidence of the English people in only a few short years. Part of their success was due to Peel's dogged determination to fill the police ranks with quality officers. Another factor was the nonthreatening, "underdog" image of the police that Peel was able to create. As one observer of British policing sees it, "the real art of policing a free society or a democracy is to win by appearing to lose, or at least to win by appearing not to win."[42] Lastly, but of no less importance, the new police force proved to be fairly good at fighting crime and maintaining public order. The tense confrontation in Cold Bath Fields on May 13, 1833 between the unarmed police and an armed angry mob dramatically helped turn public opinion in favor of the police.[43] Frightened, outnumbered, and armed only with wooden truncheons, the small disciplined group of public police lead by Colonel Rowan himself successfully dispersed the crowd with only a minimal amount of force. The only person to be killed in the incident was a police officer—he was stabbed to death in what was later ruled to be "justifiable homicide."[44]

To summarize, from their earliest days the British police have been relatively effective in controlling crime and maintaining public order. Thus we see the formal transition from citizen policing as the dominant method of crime control to public policing.

DEVELOPMENTS IN THE UNITED STATES

The development of the police in America shares a great deal in common with the experiences of England.[45] This is hardly surprising since the English comprised the first large waves of settlers to inhabit the Eastern seaboard of the New World. As recently as 1800, an estimated 90 percent of the people in the United States were of English descent.[46] There were sizable pockets of New World settlers from other countries who established their own brand of justice (e.g., the Louisiana French). Yet it is the English influence that is indelibly printed on the pages of U.S. policing.

The English settlers of the New World brought with them the style of law enforcement to which they had grown accustomed. For instance, the early inhabitants of New England found it convenient to settle close together in small towns for mutual protection and emotional support. It was only natural for them to rely on the English urban police model of town constables and night watchmen. The sparsely settled farmers of the South found the English-styled office of sheriff more suited to its county form of government. And the adventuresome settlers of the West blended these two forms of policing depending on their changing needs and local conditions; town constables and marshals were usually found policing the small communities while county sheriffs policed the vast open lands of the west.[47]

The early settlers did not completely adopt the ways of the English. The colonists had to adapt the English style of policing to the unique character and needs of this country. There are a number of critics who suggest that the early colonists retained only those aspects of English policing that were not

The early British bobbies were also referred to as "Peelers."

effective. The following statement by criminologist Robert Pursley conveys this sentiment:

> If the history of law enforcement in England up to the nineteenth century can be considered shameful, the American experience must be considered a disgrace. America seems to be uniquely adept at ignoring the lessons of history. During the 200 years of our existence, we have overlooked the repeated lesson that laws are meaningless in the absence of the authority to secure the *observance* of those laws.[48]

Criticisms like these notwithstanding, there are still numerous milestones in the development of U.S. police. The first organized citizen night watch was established in Boston in 1636.[49] New York established its famous **rattle watch** in 1658, so named because the night watchmen were armed with rattles that allowed them to communicate with other watchmen.[50] Philadelphia developed a citizen night watch in 1700, Cincinnati in 1803, and New Orleans in 1804. Because crime was not limited to the dark hours of the night, the first *daytime watch* was created in Philadelphia in 1833—almost two hundred years after the first night watch. Day watches spread quickly to the small towns and big cities across the United States as the problem of crime intensified.

Unfortunately, Americans had to learn the same hard lesson as the British—that is, the exclusive use of amateur citizen police to combat a serious and growing crime problem was not sufficient. A wave of riots and disorder swept over many cities in the 1830s and 1840s.[51] The year 1834 in New York was declared the "Year of the Riots,"[52] and in 1838 Abraham Lincoln warned citizens of the United States of the "increasing disregard for law which pervades the country."[53] Indeed, just as in England, the growing unwillingness among citizens—especially the merchants and other men of "position"—to serve as watchmen when it was their turn adversely affected the calibre of men on watch. This lead to the practice of paying anyone willing to volunteer as watchmen to take their place.[54] The courts even sentenced minor offenders to night watch duty,[55] partly as punishment and partly to at least have someone watching the city.

In 1845, just sixteen years after the Metropolitan Police Act formed the British police, New York City became the first city in the United States to make the formal transition from citizen police to public police. However, this development was to be expected; police service was just one of many types of services that urban centers began providing about this time in history. Fire protection, healthcare, and sanitation were other governmental services that grew rapidly in the late nineteenth century.[56] In short, modern public policing in the U.S. was underway. Within a few short decades, the "Peelian plan" had been adopted in most cities and towns across the nation.

The list of early accomplishments in U.S. policing is quite lengthy. Space limitation precludes discussing them thoroughly here. However, the general pattern outlined in the development of police in England applies to the United States as well. As society modernizes, the people become less bound to the traditional way of life. The growing population becomes more diverse, mobile, and anonymous. Wealth accumulates, material possessions multiply, and greed-driven appetites are whetted, especially in the urban centers. In concert, these societal transformations decrease the effectiveness of informal networks of social control while at the same time increase the motivation and opportunity to commit crime. Kin police (clan members) and citizen police (vigilantes, watchmen, parish constables, thief takers, etc.) are no longer able to provide adequate protection as crime control becomes a full-time, twenty-four-hour-a-day job. Society experiments with different forms of protection until it is realized that the formal responsibility of policing needs to be vested in an organized police force.

The particular "type" of organized police force that emerges depends on a country's special mix of history, culture, and social structure. The personal influence of individual leaders is also quite important. Individuals such as

POLICE HISTORY AT A GLANCE: THE DEVELOPMENT OF PUBLIC POLICE

B.C.

Prehistory	Kin policing and private retribution dominates
4241	First recorded date in history
4000–1500	Egypt and Mesopotamia experience high crime
2000	Code of Hammurabi
1200	Mosaic Code
600	Pisistratus, ruler of Athens, develops guard system to protect the tower, the highways, and the men of the crown
27	Augustus, first emperor of Rome, creates the Praetorian Guard (to protect Caesar and the palace), the Urban Cohorts (to keep peace in the city), and the Vigiles of Rome (combined police and fire fighters)

A.D.

455	The Vandals sack Rome and terrorize Europe
700	The beginning of English feudal society; early roots of the tithing system of police
1066	Norman invasion of England replace localized tithing system of policing with centralized frankpledge system
1285	Statute of Winchester establishes the office of parish constable
1361	The passage of the Justice of the Peace Act
1500–1800	Crime soars in Europe
1692	Highwaymen Act creates new breed of crime fighters called thief takers
1829	British Parliament passes Metropolitan Police Act creating the New Police.
1833	Successful deployment of the New Police at Cold Bath Fields
1845	New York becomes first city in U.S. to make complete transition from citizen police to public police

Robert Peel have had the opportunity to shape the direction of modern police in lasting ways.

U.S. COPS VERSUS BRITISH BOBBIES

The United States borrowed selectively from the British when searching for its own model of police. Many of the central features of the early British police were retained and account for the unmistakable resemblance between the British and U.S. police. But there are unmistakable differences as well. In this section we highlight the important similarities and differences between the cops of the United States and the bobbies of Britain.

From our earlier discussion, we can identify a number of important similarities between cops and bobbies:

- Common legal/historical tradition;
- Civilian police for domestic order (not soldiers);
- Military-style command structure;
- Main mission—crime prevention;
- Main strategy—random patrol over fixed beats;
- Twenty-four hours a day, seven days a week availability;
- Restrained police powers;
- Combined crime control and order maintenance duties;
- Paid, uniformed, public police.

These features are still central to the British and U.S. police more than a century and a half after their formation. In the global family of international police, U.S. cops and British bobbies are close cousins.

But identical cousins they are not. The two police may share a common heritage, but U.S. police have developed in a way that is quite unlike their

---

ORIGIN OF "COP"

The origin of the word "cop" to refer to a United States police officer is not as clear as the origin of the word "bobby" (after founder Sir Robert Peel) used to describe a British police officer. *Webster's New Collegiate Dictionary* suggests the word "cop" is short for *copper,* meaning to "swipe," "capture," or to "get hold of." The use of this term is apparently in reference to catching a thief. DeSola's *Crime Dictionary* notes that the word "cop" emerged as a nickname for police in the mid-nineteenth century because they wore large copper stars on their uniforms. Another popular version is that the word comes from the acronym constable *on patrol.* Unlike the term "bobby" which is normally used with affection and respect, the term cop is slang and often used in a semi-derogatory manner. Regardless of the origin of the term, the U.S. "cop" is part of our common vocabulary.

Sources: *Webster's New Collegiate Dictionary* (Springfield, MA: G. and C. Merriam Company, 1980). Ralph DeSola, *Crime Dictionary* (New York: Facts on File, Inc., 1982), p. 31.

British counterpart. The social and political forces at play during the formation of each country's police were so diverse that the cops and bobbies have evolved as different social institutions. We shall discuss three critical features that distinguish U.S. cops from British bobbies: *centralization*, *professionalism*, and *authority*.

Centralization

The organizational structure of British police is highly centralized. The British maintain a tight reign over its police forces and police officers. The British do not have a *national* police system, but the government does have a considerable amount of control over how individual police agencies operate. Major policies and procedures are set by the central authorities which then apply to all departments. In other words, there is a "top" to the organizational structure of British policing—the British Home Secretary is the person ultimately responsible for Her Majesty's police.

By comparison, the organizational structure of U.S. police is extremely decentralized. Police agencies across the United States are scattered, overlapping, and disjointed. There has never been an overall "plan" to U.S. police; police departments developed haphazardly and without coordination. There is also no "top" to U.S. police. Instead what we have are thousands and thousands of independent agencies. This makes it nearly impossible to establish consistent policies and procedures throughout all police departments. For instance, one department may handle loud, off-campus student parties by "coming down hard" and making many arrests while another department in another college-town may have orders to disperse the young crowd with minimal force. Individual departments are free to establish their own policies in accordance with community standards as long as they remain within the broad constraints of the law.

Local autonomy and local control of governmental services (police, fire, sanitation, education, etc.) is the surviving legacy of Thomas Jefferson. Jefferson fought for the creation of many "little republics" that would be free from the excessive interference of a strong federal government. The highly decentralized nature of the police is evident by the sheer number of departments; the United States has approximately 20,000 agencies that serve 250 million people. This compares to forty-three agencies serving the approximately 50 million people of England and Wales.[57] No other country in the world comes close to having the number of police agencies as the United States. (The advantages and disadvantages of fragmented law enforcement is discussed thoroughly in chapter 13.)

Professionalism

A careful reading of the history of U.S. police reveals there is not much of which to be proud. The pages of U.S. police reek of scandal, corruption, brutality, and political meddling. Police administrators have lacked vision and experience. Street officers have been scorned, mocked, ridiculed, and held in utter contempt by citizens who have had every reason not to trust them. Throughout most of their history, the police of the United States have been thoroughly unprofessional. The people learned long ago to expect little from the police, and this is exactly what they have received.

A very different image emerges when we examine the police of Britain. The British police have always maintained a serious commitment to professionalism. Ever since the day that Peel's officers hit the streets there have been noticeably few scandals involving British police. Charges of brutality and corruption are rarely made, and powerful political machines have never been able to gain a foothold in British policing. The people of Britain have always had a deep abiding faith in their police. Public opinion polls consistently show that the people of Britain place a higher level of trust in their bobbies than in any other occupational group.[58] One writer even suggests that the average bobbie has represented the idealized male character for English males since the middle of the last century.[59] Americans may support their local police, but the British love their bobbies.

It is important to note that this difference between the U.S. and British police has been decreasing in recent years. On the one hand, U.S. police have made commendable strides toward professionalism, far beyond where they were a few decades ago. On the other hand, the shining image of the British police has been seriously tarnished by repeated scandals. With increasing regularity British police officers are being caught committing perjury, abusing prisoners, and engaging in corruption. Public opinion of the British police is at an all time low.

Authority

All organized systems of police derive their authority from the state (i.e., government) which, in turn, gives the police the legitimate right to do police work (make arrests, investigate crimes, search and seize, issue tickets, etc.). The police of Britain and the police of the U.S. have the authority of the state to back them when they perform their assigned duties. Beyond this basic commonality, however, there is a fundamental difference between the British and U.S. police. The authority (and, hence, legitimacy) of the British police is based almost exclusively on the *institutional* authority of the British government; but the authority of U.S. police is a combination of *institutional* authority plus *individual* authority.[60] Individual authority may be any combination of personal charm, wit, wisdom, charisma, knowledge, experience, physical size, individual strength, nightstick, and/or gun. The difference in authority between British and U.S. police may seem trivial on paper, but it has powerful implications on the streets as explained below.

It is a common observation that the authority of the British officer is rarely questioned by the public. The police have a historical, institutional legitimacy that has become a natural part of the public perception of them. Since the time of Peel, the police have been severely restricted in their use of physical force and, in fact, they seldom have had to use it. Although the criminals they arrest and the drunks they escort off the streets may not be

BRITISH POLICING UNDER FIRE

Policing in England and Wales is in crisis. Even the Police Federation has conceded this. Public surveys are critical of police behavior and police policy. Scandals crop up repeatedly, many if not all relating to the fabrication of evidence.

A *National Opinion Poll* survey recently showed that four out of 10 people think that there is a "great deal" or "a fair amount" of violence and corruption in the police. Although 45 percent of respondents thought that cases such as the West Midlands Force and the circumstances leading to the release of the "Guilford Four" were "isolated examples" of police malpractice, 40 percent took the contrary view—that they are "just the tip of the iceberg."

What is going on? What has brought about this shift from one of the most respected policing bodies in the world to a group typified recently by a writer in the *Sunday Times* as a "tribe apart." Although "the gulf between the police and the public has never been wider," theoretical examination has dwelt upon a plethora of reasons ranging from inadequate selection and training, through insufficient minority recruiting, to the need to transform public areas of police stations to "arm chair and pot plant spaces."

The reality is far more prosaic. There has been a fundamental and almost unrecognized shift in the nature of the criminal justice system in the U.K.—a shift from a traditional crime control model to that of due process, and movement from a British to an American style of policing and criminal justice. And it is this that police in England and Wales find so hard to stomach.

It has been suggested that there has been slow but identifiable movement of the traditional British model of policing towards that of the American. The Judicial System has been typified as "Due Process" oriented in the United States, but based on a "Crime Control" model in the U.K.. And in this context, the changes engendered in England and Wales by the Police and Criminal Evidence Act 1984, particularly in the provision of written rights, may have moved those two divergent models closer together.

The Police and Criminal Evidence Act 1984 was introduced with the intention of striking a balance between the powers of police on one hand and the rights of those arrested on the other and is a historic benchmark against which all future changes and past occurrences must be interpreted.

It is entirely likely that, in strictly quantitative terms, the effects of the Police and Criminal Evidence Act 1984 will be that crime, detection, and clearance rates will be unaffected, but the nature of policing and the relationship of the police with the rest of the criminal justice system will have been pushed in an unanticipated direction.

CRIME UP IN 1990

The number of offenses recorded in the first quarter of this year was 1,081,000—a 15 percent increase on the first three months of 1989, according to Home Office figures for England and Wales published in July.

Crimes against property accounted for 94 percent of the total. Crimes against the person—violence, sex attacks and robbery—amounted to 5 percent.

The figures for the 12 months to the end of March were also up, by 323,000 offenses, reflecting rises in all but three police force areas—Merseyside, where crime fell by 1.4 percent; North Wales, 2.3 percent; and Dyfed-Powys, 1.7 percent.

Among the biggest rises in the year ending March 1990 were Northumbria, 14 percent, West Yorkshire, 12 percent, and London, 8 percent.

Car crime represented the biggest portion of total offenses—about 100,000—and a quarter occurred when drivers left their doors unlocked.

Home Office Minister John Patten asked chief constables to give reasons for the crime rise; their explanations included more use of bail by courts, and lack of discipline in the home and schools.

Sources: Ian McKenzie, "Unexpected Consequences: Crime Control vs. Due Process," *C. J. International*, vol. 6, no. 4 (July–August), 1990: pp. 1–12; *C. J. International*, vol. 6, no. 5 (September–October), 1990: p. 7.

appreciative of the officer's efforts at that particular time, the basic legitimacy of the officer to act is never seriously challenged.

The institutional authority to which we are referring was the orchestrated effort of the early leaders of British police. They wanted their officers to look and act nonthreatening to the public. Peel specifically instructed his early recruits to be "civil and attentive to all persons, of every rank and class; insolence or incivility will not be passed over. . . . there is no qualification more indispensable to a Police Officer than a perfect command of temper."[61] This basic philosophy has meant that "muscle men" and "major muscle enhancers" (guns) have never been a part of the British police tradition. To this day the wooden truncheon (only a "minor" muscle enhancer) remains hidden under the officer's coat so as not to alarm the public, and women have patrolled the streets of London since 1914.[62] About all the bobbie needs to perform his duty is the authority of the state and the *occasional* use of the truncheon:

> The baton may be a very ineffective weapon of offence, but it is backed by the combined power of the Crown, the Government, and the Constituencies. Armed with it alone, the constable will usually be found ready, in obedience to orders, to face any mob, or brave any danger. The mob quails before the simple baton of the police officer, and flies before it, well knowing the moral as well as physical force of the Nation whose will, as embodied in law, it represents. And take any man from that mob, place a baton in his hand and a blue coat on his back, put him forward as the representative of the law, and he too will be found equally ready to face the mob from which he was taken, and exhibit the same steadfastness and courage in defense of constituted order.[63]

In stark contrast to the "gentleman bobbie" is the U.S. cop. The cop is rough, tough, predominately male, and decidedly macho. Examine the cop's uniform. It appears to be covered with badges and buttons and patches and emblems. Conspicuously attached to the basic uniform are an assortment of eye-catching appendages: keys, whistle, radio, flashlight, handcuffs, nightstick, ticket book, shiny bullets and, of course, the gun—the ultimate muscle enhancer. The cop's attire helps embellish the officer's commanding presence. The uniforms were designed to evoke an immediate sense of awe and respect from the public, which is quite the opposite of the cultivated underdog image of British officers.

The argument being made is that the contrasting uniforms are a reflection of the different sources of authority backing British and U.S. police officers. British officers overwhelmingly derive their legitimacy from the profound institutional authority of the state and therefore rarely have to rely on their own personal authority to maintain social order. However, U.S. officers frequently have to rely on their own individual style, their closeness to the community, and informal social control to maintain order in situations when their state authority is not enough. Far more often than their British counterparts, U.S. cops have had to rely on harsh words and intimidating weapons to maintain social order.

American police have experienced many difficult periods in the past. The last one hundred years have been a continuing struggle to right what is seriously wrong with the police and to enhance their relationship with the public. Three major challenges have persistently plagued the police: (1) to free local police departments from the control of political machines (known as *police reform*); (2) to improve the overall quality, character, and competence of police officers and to increase the effectiveness of police departments (*police professionalism*); and (3) to enhance the relationship of the police with the public, especially in high-crime, minority neighborhoods (*police-community relations*).

As we approach the year 2000, it becomes useful to look back to assess the progress made by the U.S. police in the twentieth century. While there are many qualifications and reservations, one can argue that the police have made significant improvements in the areas of police reform and police professionalism; today most police departments are "relatively" free of partisan politics and many are performing at "relatively" high levels of effectiveness. Important progress in the realm of police-community relations also has been made. As we shall see in later sections of the book, however, the police still need to make a great many improvements in each of these areas.

By most standards commonly applied, *American police are doing as good or better today than in any time in the past.* One reason there continues to be many criticisms of the police is because the American public has come to expect so much from the police, much more than they did a century ago. However, it is important to realize heightened public expectation of the police is a measure of their progress. The increased reliance on the police is but another indication of the elevated stature of the police in modern American society.

CONCLUSION

This chapter summarized several thousand years of developments that have shaped the modern role of U.S. police. Starting with the earliest known civilizations of ancient Egypt and Mesopotamia, we traveled through time taking note of significant developments along the way. Because many of our legal principles and practices may be traced to the British, we paid close attention to the evolution of the British police. We found that in many ways the U.S. police mirror the British model. We even argued that in the international family of police, British bobbies and American cops are close cousins. Nonetheless, there are fundamental differences between the British and U.S. police that cannot be masked. Consequently, the police of the United States have evolved in a way that is distinctly American.

An important lesson woven throughout the chapter is that as society modernizes and becomes increasingly complex, the simplistic forms of kin police and citizen police eventually fail to provide adequate protection. In the end, some type of paid, full-time police system must be created. We have seen how Britain and the United States were forced to make the transition from citizen police to public police, and so too have all modern societies. Every modern society must decide how it is going to organize and administer its police. Most liberal democratic societies like the United States and Britain have chosen some variation of *civilian police* that respects the political, economic, and social freedoms of its citizens. The *military police* model was only briefly considered and immediately rejected by Peel because "it was ill-equipped to meet the enduring needs of a policed society."[64] On the other hand, most autocratically ruled countries deploy a branch of the military to

THE LAST ONE HUNDRED YEARS

The last hundred years of American policing present a most interesting panorama, with operations that have ranged from the most sordid to the most splendid, and with practitioners whose capacity and character have spanned a continuum from the most incompetent and corrupt to the most brilliant and edifying.

NEGATIVE ASPECTS:

1. *Ugly Early Customs*—such as the third-degree, curbstone court for vagrants, and extra-judicial punishment of offenders.
2. *Damages Due to World War II Manpower Shortages*—when the scarcity of qualified manpower resulted in the admission to police ranks of individuals of lesser abilities and motivations.
3. *Bad Housekeeping*—inadequate facilities and equipment often resulted in physically dirty, noisy, crowded, shoddy buildings, and antiquated, shabby, inadequate, grotesque uniforms and equipment.
4. *Incompetent and Immoral Personnel*—who fail to keep informed, to care properly for equipment, to patrol efficiently, to investigate properly, to advise correctly, to report adequately, to interview and interrogate properly, to search and seize legally; and who engage in mooching, chiseling, theft, perjury, extortion, favoritism, prejudice, illegal violence, and lechery.
5. *Obstinate Refusal to Change Attitudes and Habits*—marred the sixties as rigid and me-

chanical police Neanderthals of all ages and ranks sought to solve all criminal justice problems with tons of hardware and immediate massive applications of force.

POSITIVE ASPECTS:

1. *Civil Service Merit System Processes*—have aided greatly in combatting the evil aspects of spoils-era operations, by positing merit and ability as an alternative to political sponsorship, and by providing disciplinary machinery with which to deal with the problem of graft and corruption.
2. *World War II Veterans*—by the hundreds, mature, seasoned, used to uniform and discipline, entered the police service.
3. *Expanded Education and Training*—marks the current scene, with over [1,000] colleges and universities offering Associate and Bachelor degrees in law enforcement. . . . no longer is the educated person an anomaly in the police agency.
4. *Personnel of Ability and Character*—there has been an ever-increasing attention given to the selection, payment, development, regulation, and motivation of police manpower during the past one hundred years.
5. *Changes in Role Perception*—sensitive and aware police professionals of all ages and ranks begin to reject the repressive orientation of the past.

Source: A. C. Germann, Frank D. Day, and Robert R. J. Gallati, *Introduction to Law Enforcement and Criminal Justice* (Springfield, IL: Charles C. Thomas, Publisher, 1973), pp. 69–72.

police the people. In these countries, individual rights are considered to be of secondary importance to the right of the state.

A rather interesting paradox has emerged from our conclusions from the first two chapters. Recall that we ended chapter 1 by saying that about all the police can realistically do in the "war on crime" is to help control crime; alone they cannot eliminate it. Here we are saying that a full-time public police has become a necessary agency of social control in modern society because the system of citizen police is too amateurish. To state this paradox more succinctly, it appears that we need the police even though they can't do much. How can this be?

The reason is that the police are not the only ones who police. (What?) Ordinary citizens like you and me, multiplied by the millions, do more policing than the police. What we are referring to here is something called *informal social control*, which is a subtle but powerful deterrent to most forms of deviance (we thoroughly discuss social control in chapter 4). For 99.9 percent of human history we managed to survive without a formal police system because ordinary people had no choice but to assume their share of the crime control burden. Today we may think the police have assumed full responsibility for crime control, but this is far from the truth. Louis Radelet asserts that "in a democracy, every citizen has a serious *obligation to do police work*, and the existence of a paid police force does not alter this duty."[65] We are still the "eyes and ears" of the police—yes, we are still the police.

KEY TERMS

kin policing
Code of Hammurabi
Mosaic Code
feudal system
Magna Carta
tithing system
hue and cry
shire-reeve
obligatory avocational policing
parish constable

justice of the peace
dangerous classes
voluntary avocational policing
entrepreneurial avocational policing
thief takers
Sir Robert Peel
bobbies
crime prevention
Bow Street Runners
rattle watch

DISCUSSION QUESTIONS

1. Why is it important to understand the historical beginnings of public police? Try to summarize the *major* developments in ten sentences or less.
2. In what ways have we developed our government to ensure that our benevolent policed society does not turn into a malevolent police state? Do you think our police have become more benevolent or less benevolent in the past century?
3. Discuss the uniform of the British police officer. How is it different from the uniform of a typical U.S. officer? Why?
4. Stretch your imagination. It is the year 2500 in the United States. How has policing changed?

CHAPTER THREE

CONTEMPORARY POLICE SYSTEMS IN AMERICAN SOCIETY

Policemen are soldiers who act alone; soldiers are policemen who act in unison.

—*Herbert Spencer*

Like all social institutions, American policing is strongly tied to its past. Contemporary police work is an interesting mix of the past and the present. In many ways old problems and practices resemble new problems and new practices; little seems to have changed since the inception of public police.

There is a popular saying that "the more things change, the more they remain the same." Although this folksy wisdom may be partially true with regard to police work, one cannot help being amazed by how much policing has really changed. American police are now in the latter stages of a transition from the "old" to the "new," a positive transition that is radically altering the very foundations of police work. Recent technological advances in computer applications and forensic science are changing how the police process information and conduct investigations. The research explosion of the 1970s and 1980s has resulted in the close examination of the very meaning of public policing, and it has altered basic patrol techniques, organizational principles, and management strategies. And, career-oriented, college-educated recruits are entering police work in increasing numbers, many of them women and minorities. These new recruits have a healthy spirit of professionalism and are dedicated to serving their communities. In short, virtually no aspect of police work has been unaffected by the transition. These changes are already benefitting the police and the communities they serve.

This chapter examines contemporary police systems in American society. We begin with a general overview of the criminal justice system as it relates to the police, focusing especially on the size and scope of the police industry. The main body of our discussion is a close look at the various types of U.S. police agencies that operate at the local, state and federal levels.

POLICE AND THE CRIMINAL JUSTICE SYSTEM

The criminal justice system serves millions of "clients" annually. Some clients are brought into the system during the year for criminal processing; others are already in the system and are being prosecuted by the courts or dealt with by corrections personnel. The justice system is additionally responsible for attending to the needs of victims, witnesses, and jurors who also have contact with the system.

There are three major components of the criminal justice system. The police are the first and largest component and serve as the "gatekeeper" to the criminal justice system. Criminal courts and corrections are the remaining two components. There is nothing unusual about this particular organization of the U.S. criminal justice system. Virtually every country in the world also has a police, a court system, and a corrections system. However, there are major cross-cultural differences in legal principles and procedural operations within the criminal justice system.

Numerous subcomponents of the criminal justice system exist as well. The office of prosecutor, public defenders, probation, parole, diversionary programs, diagnostic evaluation centers, and drug treatment programs are all subcomponents. Taken in its entirety, our system of criminal justice is a complex web of agencies and personnel.

Table 3.1   Total Government Expenditures (Federal, State, and Local),
             Fiscal Year 1988

Expenditure	Percent	Per Capita
Social Insurance Payments	20.2	$1,581
National Defense and International Relations	17.2	1,342
Education	13.6	1,061
Interest on Debt	10.5	824
Housing and the Environment	8.0	621
Public Welfare	6.0	468
Hospitals and Health	4.1	321
Transportion	3.7	287
Justice System	3.2	248
Space Research and Technology	0.5	36
All Other Spending	13.0	1,014

Source: U.S. Department of Justice, Bureau of Justice Statistics Bulletin, *Justice Expenditures and Employment, 1988* (Washington, DC: U.S. Government Printing Office, July 1990).

The Cost of Justice

The criminal justice system of the United States is a massive apparatus. There were 1.6 million persons actively employed in the justice field (civil and criminal) with a payroll over $3.5 billion in 1988.[1] Add to this amount the cost of operating expenses and capital improvements, and the total justice system expenditure for fiscal year 1988 exceeded $60 billion. This was equivalent to $248 for every man, woman and child in the country. Relative to other government outlays, however, the cost of operating the justice system is fairly modest. Total expenditures on the justice system consumed only 3.2 percent of all government spending in 1988 (see table 3.1).

Spending for criminal justice services varies considerably by level of government. State and local units of government absorb much more of the expense than the federal government. This reflects the important fact that the administration of justice is primarily a state and local responsibility. As shown in table 3.2, local units of government (cities and counties) shoulder the greatest cost of justice, followed by state government and then federal government. Furthermore, a far greater percentage of government expenditures at the state and local level go toward justice activities than at the federal level. Less than 1 percent of total federal government expenditures are allocated to justice activities while 6 percent of all state level expenditures and nearly 7 percent of all local expenditures are allocated to the justice system.[2]

The Cost of Police

The police are the largest component of the criminal justice system and therefore the most expensive to operate. American taxpayers spent $28 billion on police protection in 1988. This compares to $13 billion on the courts and $19 billion on corrections.[3] Of each criminal justice dollar spent roughly fifty cents goes to the police, twenty cents to the courts and thirty cents to corrections.[4]

Table 3.2   Distribution of Justice System Expenditures by Level of
Government, Fiscal Year 1988

Level of Government	Percent Distribution
Total local	55
City	31
County	24
State	33
Federal	12

Source: U.S. Department of Justice, Bureau of Justice Statistics Bulletin, *Justice Expenditures and Employment, 1988* (Washington, DC: U.S. Government Printing Office, July 1990).

Not every state spends as much on police protection as other states, just as not every state spends as much on education, transportation, health care, and so forth. Expenditure on the police is the lowest in the traditionally poor states like Arkansas and West Virginia. The per capita cost in both of these states in 1988 was less than $50 (compared to the national state average of $99). The District of Columbia spent the most on police protection in 1988, topping the list at $314 per capita, followed by Alaska ($222), New York ($181), New Jersey ($134), and California ($128).[5] Regionally, the Northeast has the highest per capita spending rate for police followed by the West, the Midwest, and then the South.[6]

Trends in Police Expenditures

Expenditures on police services increased steadily from the 1940s to the 1970s but tapered off in the 1980s. According to a Bureau of Justice Statistics report, between 1938 and 1982 spending for police services increased nearly six-fold after adjustments are made for inflation.[7] This growth reflects four different periods of expenditures:

- Between 1938 and the early 1950s, there was little growth in police expenditures (adjusted to the 1967 dollar value);
- Spending increased constantly from the mid-1950s through the mid-1960s;
- Beginning around 1967, police expenditures rose significantly and remained high for a decade;
- Since the late 1970s, spending for police protection has actually declined in constant dollars.

By comparison, spending for courts has remained fairly constant since the late 1970s and spending for corrections has increased.[8]

Number of Police Agencies

The exact number of police agencies in the United States is a debatable issue. Varying estimates are found in the literature. There are two reasons for the controversy: (1) the lack of complete and reliable data makes enumeration difficult; and (2) confusion exists over what constitutes a "police agency." The majority consensus is that there are around 20,000 independent police agencies in the United States. This is an exceptionally large number when compared to other countries. It is interesting to note that this estimate is only half of the 40,000 figure reported in the prestigious Task Force Report: The Police, prepared by the 1967 President's Commission on Law Enforcement. There are many contemporary scholars who continue to use the 40,000 figure.

Number of Police Officers

Working in the 20,000 police agencies across the country are approximately 800,000 employees (784,371 in fiscal year 1988).[9] Approximately 77 percent of police personnel are employed at the local level. The states employ approximately 15 percent of all police personnel while the federal system employs only around 8 percent (see right-hand column of table 3.3).

Police personnel may be classified as full-time or part-time employees. The vast majority of police personnel are full-time employees. This is shown in table 3.3. Nationwide, approximately 93 percent of all police personnel are full-time workers with the remaining 7 percent of employees working on a part-time basis. The only exception to this pattern is at the federal level where 100 percent of police personnel are classified as full-time employees.

Full-time equivalent (FTE) employment is a statistical estimate of the number of full-time employees there would be if all the hours worked by part-time personnel were actually worked by full-time employees. For example, two part-time employees working twenty hours a week would be considered the statistical equivalent of one full-time worker. The FTEs for fiscal year 1988 are shown in column 4 of table 3.3. Obviously part-time workers increase

Table 3.3   Police Employment by Level of Government, 1988

Level of Government	Total	Employment			
		Full-time (%)	Part-time (%)	Full-time Equivalent	(%)
Total	784,371	728,018 (93%)	56,353 (7%)	745,935	100
Federal	65,297	65,297 (100%)	0 (0%)	65,297	8
State	115,121	105,103 (91%)	10,018 (9%)	108,005	15
Local	603,953	557,619 (92%)	46,334 (8%)	572,633	77
City	459,241	421,606 (92%)	37,635 (8%)	433,615	—
County	144,710	136,009 (94%)	8,701 (6%)	139,018	—

Source: Adapted from U.S. Department of Justice, Bureau of Justice Statistics Bulletin, *Justice Expenditures and Employment, 1988* (Washington, DC: U.S. Government Printing Office, July 1990).

the number of police personnel considerably. The greatest utilization of part-time employees is found in rural and small-town police departments where limited funds prohibit hiring more expensive full-time help (with the associated fringe benefits). *As a general rule, the heavy use of part-time employees is an indication of a lower level of professionalism.*[10]

Another important distinction is between **sworn officers** and nonsworn **civilians**. Civilian personnel are not sworn officers of the law and therefore do not possess special police powers. Civilians are generally hired to perform the many "secondary" tasks of a police agency (e.g., records keeping, data processing, evidence technician, dispatch) that do not require the attention of a sworn police officer. Civilians are often employed in police agencies because they do not have to be paid as much as sworn officers. They are also not as expensive to train. However, as police work becomes increasingly computerized and complex, police administrators are finding it necessary to hire civilians to provide the technical expertise that is not ordinarily possessed by regular officers. The trend over the past two decades has been toward the increased utilization of civilians in police agencies (see figure 3.1). Civilians comprised 27 percent of the police employee force in the U.S. in 1990.[11] Contrary to our previous observation that the heavy use of part-time employees in police

FIGURE 3.1
Trends in Civilian Employment in Police Agencies, 1970–1990

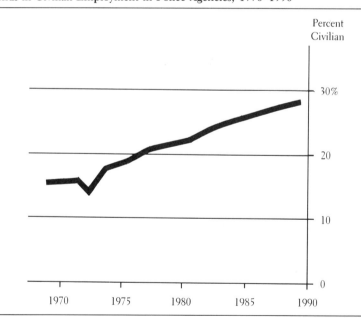

Sources: U.S. Department of Justice, Bureau of Justice Statistics, *Report to the Nation on Crime and Justice* (Washington, DC: U.S. Government Printing Office, March 1988), p. 62; U.S. Department of Justice, *Uniform Crime Reports for the United States, 1990* (Washington, DC: U.S. Government Printing Office, August 1991), p. 237.

agencies is a sign of a lower level of professionalism, *the "civilianization" of policing is often considered to be an indication of a higher level of professionalism.* Increased civilian employment has changed police agencies. The increase results from the desire to free up sworn officers for patrol duties as well as the need for technical expertise such as data processing.

Police Strength

Police strength is a term used to describe the degree of police protection that is available in a jurisdiction. The more comprehensive the protection of citizens, the greater the police strength. An important distinction is between *absolute* and *relative* police strength. Absolute strength refers to the size of the department and the number of officers. The absolute size of a police agency has an important impact on (1) the complexity of the organization; (2) the intensity of administrative functions; and (3) the division of labor necessary to accomplish basic police tasks.[12] In larger departments the police manager has added flexibility to cover momentary personnel shortages. This is because there is a greater number of officers to draw from, even though the officers will have to be taken from other assignments. Greater flexibility in assigning personnel is useful when there is a rapidly developing problem (e.g., a labor strike at the local factory that is becoming increasingly volatile) or when a regular but chronic problem requires additional police attention (e.g., steady drug trafficking near an inner-city high school). Furthermore, because of the vast pool of police officers in a large department, one usually finds a greater concentration of police expertise (sharpshooters, hostage negotiators, forensic investigators, etc.) than can be found—or developed—in smaller departments.

While "absolute" strength has important consequences for a department, a more meaningful indicator of police strength is the "relative" number of police employees to citizens in a given jurisdiction. The interest in relative police strength is based on the assumption that as the number of police officers increases in relation to the number of citizens, police services and police protection increase as well. (As we shall see in chapter 11, however, an increase in the relative number of police officers does not necessarily result in greater protection of citizens.)

Relative police strength is typically expressed in numerical form as the **police-to-population ratio**. The ratio is based on the total FTE count, thus including part-time and civilian employees in the estimates. Although there is no standard level of police protection, the ratio generally hovers between one to four police employees per one thousand residents. In 1990 there was an average of 2.8 police employees for every one thousand residents for the entire nation. Regionally, the highest police employee rate was 3.1 in the South. The Northeast averaged 3.0, the Midwest had 2.6, and the West had 2.5.[13]

An alternative measure of relative police strength is the number of police employees in a given geographical area (normally one hundred square miles). This is known as the **density index**. The density of officers in a given area varies in direct proportion to the density of residents. The number of police employees per one hundred square miles ranges from 8,667 in New York City to zero in some remote spots in Alaska.[14] Most jurisdictions have fewer than five police employees per one hundred square miles.

Research in the realm of relative police strength has produced rather interesting results. David Jacobs' early study of nearly one hundred metropolitan areas revealed inequality of income to be a major determinant of the relative number of police officers in a given department.[15] That is, the greater the income inequality among city residents, the higher the relative police strength. Other important determinants of relative police strength were crime rate, city size, number of drug and liquor stores, number of black residents, and level of unemployment. Jacobs interpreted his study results as being best explained by a *conflict theory* of policing. This theory attributes the higher number of police officers to an attempt by the political and economic elites within the community to pressure law enforcement agencies to increase the visual presence of police, thereby controlling the less powerful community members. In a more recent study, Jeffrey Slovak also found many of the same community variables originally used by Jacobs to be predictive of relative police strength in at least one of the three departments he studied.[16]

In the absence of any other information, assessments of police strength— either absolute strength or relative strength—fail to provide valid comparisons across jurisdictions regarding the level of police protection. The reason is because the numerical strength of the police tell us nothing about *effectiveness* or *efficiency*. The District of Columbia, for example, has more officers relative to number of residents than any other jurisdiction in the country, but it also has one of the highest crime rates. Once a minimum level of police strength is obtained—which appears to be around two officers per one thousand residents in a typical jurisdiction—"throwing additional police at the problem" is not likely to benefit the community to any appreciable degree.

POLICE AGENCIES

Police agencies in the United States are organized at the *local*, *state*, and *federal* level. This is because the local, state, and federal levels of government have their own laws to enforce. A common misunderstanding exists among citizens regarding the nature of the relationship among the three levels of police. Contrary to popular belief, federal police like the FBI are not the "bosses" of state police, nor are state police the "bosses" of local police. Individual police departments are their own bosses (with the courts serving as their immediate "supervisors" and the community serving as their ultimate "master").

There are substantial differences across the three levels of police in the laws enforced, services provided, and jurisdictions covered. There are also substantial differences in their visibility and closeness to the people. It is therefore necessary to discuss each level of police separately.

Local Agencies: City Police

Police at the local level are the workhorses of U.S. law enforcement. When people hear the word "police" they often think of the uniformed police officer or the marked squad car patrolling city streets. Local police handle a complex assortment of responsibilities that have been assigned to them over the years. The local police are required to maintain domestic order, render social services, and enforce the law. In short, *policing American society is primarily a local responsibility*.

According to the 1990 Law Enforcement Management and Administrative Statistics (LEMAS) survey, 83 percent of all sworn officers at the local level were white, 10.5 percent were black, 5.2 percent were Hispanic, and 1.3 percent were members of other minority groups.[17] The LEMAS survey further noted that 92 percent of local police were males and 8 percent were females. Interestingly, officers in larger jurisdictions were less likely to be white males than in smaller jurisdictions.

At the local level, there are two types of police agencies: city (or municipal) police departments and county sheriffs' departments. City police are the largest component in American law enforcement, accounting for nearly three-quarters of all police departments. Most police officers are employed by a city department and the great majority of people receive their primary police service from a city department.

Police officers kept a close eye on demonstrators and pedestrians near a Korean-American fruit and vegetable store in Brooklyn for months after the alleged beating of a Haitian woman there prompted black Americans to boycott the store. The group presence of police in low-income, black communities lends credence to the conflict theory of policing.

The size of city police departments varies tremendously. New York City is a giant in the police world, standing alone with 26,844 sworn officers in 1990.[18] This is more than the number of officers found in some entire states. New York City employs an additional 9,563 civilians for a total police employee count of 36,407. Next in line is Chicago with 13,535 total employees, Los Angeles with 11,190 and Philadelphia with 7,586. The ten largest municipal police departments in the United States are listed in table 3.4.

The contrast between the largest police departments in the country and the average department is striking. More than one-half of all police departments in the U.S. have fewer than ten officers, and nearly one thousand departments have only one officer.[19] At the other end of the scale is the largest two hundred police agencies in the United States (1 percent of the 20,000 U.S. police agencies), which employ over one-half of all police officers. The remarkable dissimilarity in the size of police departments is a reflection of the size of the population the department must serve. Nonetheless, the contrasting numbers raise an interesting paradox: *the typical police agency in the United States is a small-town department, but the typical police officer works for a big-city department.*

Small-Town versus Big-City Policing

The difference between police work in small towns and in big cities is in many ways like the difference between night and day. In most small towns across the United States, crime is not a serious social problem. Take a look at Brookfield Township, Ohio, a small midwestern city situated in the northeast section of Ohio that boasts of a population of around 10,000 people. Brookfield Township is a fairly typical example of small-town policing in America. In 1990 the Brookfield Township Police Department employed a total of eleven people—nine sworn officers and two civilians. Brookfield Township seldom has a murder, and only a few rapes and robberies are committed each year. Among the 150 to two hundred index crimes reported to the police annually, larceny-theft accounts for more than half of the total.

Table 3.4   Ten Largest City Police Departments in the United States, 1990

Department	Total Employees	Officers	Civilians
New York City	36,407	26,844	9,563
Chicago	13,535	12,048	1,487
Los Angeles	11,190	8,381	2,809
Philadelphia	7,586	6,651	935
Houston	5,653	4,104	1,549
Washington, DC	5,521	4,740	781
Detroit	5,113	4,508	605
Dallas	3,592	2,747	845
Baltimore	3,390	2,839	551
Boston	2,662	1,979	683

Source: Adapted from U.S. Department of Justice, *Uniform Crime Reports for the United States, 1990* (Washington, DC: U.S. Government Printing Office, August 1991), Table 72.

Located 220 miles northwest of Brookfield Township is Detroit, Michigan. Detroit is a large midwestern city with over 1 million people. It has a 5,113 member police force (4,508 officers and 605 civilians). Unlike Brookfield Township, crime is a serious problem in Detroit. In 1990 Detroit had 125,325 index crimes reported to the police department. There were 582 murders in Detroit in 1990, an average of 1.5 killings a day. There were 1,657 reported rapes (an average of 4.5 per day), 13,010 robberies (35 per day) and 26,063 burglaries (71 per day) reported to the police.[20]

The difference between police work in small towns and big cities does not end with the crime problem. City size has a bearing on the type of officer who would want to work in a smaller (or bigger) town, salary, fringe benefits, job development programs, job assignments, promotion opportunities, bureaucratic structure, administrative style, and police-community relations.

City size also influences the amount of outside attention the department receives. Newspapers and magazines seem to publish an unending stream of crime stories that occur in the larger cities. Scholarly research into American policing also has shown a big-city preference. This bias is explained in part because researchers find big-city police work inherently more interesting to study than small-town policing. In addition, universities are generally close to large urban centers, thus making the big-city department more accessible to researchers. The result is that we know more about policing in big cities than we know about policing in small towns. Even the entertainment industry has a distinct interest in big-city police shows, undoubtedly because the television viewers of America prefer these types of programs. It is unlikely that a show like *Brookfield Township Vice* would be nearly as successful as *Miami Vice*.

The Brookfield Township chief of police takes down information about a 9mm handgun being dusted for fingerprints. The gun was found on the premises after an attempted robbery. During the week this photo was taken, no major crimes were reported in the small Ohio community.

The effect of city size on the police is not always predictable. Varying social, demographic, and geographic characteristics of cities place different demands on police departments. A "college town" is quite unlike a "bedroom community," just as a small town in the shadows of a large city is unlike a small town in the middle of nowhere. Sam Walker describes what policing is like in one small town in Nebraska called Gordon. Gordon has a population of 2,268 and a police force of six members. It also has a problem:

> . . . Gordon is located a few miles south of the Rosebud Indian Reservation in South Dakota, and it has a serious problem in police-community relations involving Native Americans. In 1974 the Gordon police made 578 arrests, most of whom were Indians. Most of the arrests were alcohol-related: 411 for drunkenness, 30 for liquor-law violations, and 71 for driving under the influence.
>
> Tensions between the Gordon police and the Indian community reached crisis proportions in 1979 when Joanne Yellow Bird won a damage settlement of $300,000 for being beaten in the Gordon jail. She was pregnant at the time of the beating and lost the child as a result.[21]

Many areas experience seasonal fluctuations in population that cause significant short-term shifts in the police workload. For example, migrant farm workers who roam the countryside during harvest time in search of work have been known to cause the police a few problems, and college students who swamp the beaches of Fort Lauderdale every spring have become an annual police nightmare.

In short, there are two main conclusions to derive from this section: (1) there is considerable variation in police work between small towns and big cities; and (2) police work is not the same in all towns of similar size. Indeed, there are often stark differences in police work in cities of the same size—*not all small towns are tame and not all big cities are tigers.* There is such substantial variation in police work from department to department that broad generalizations are very difficult to make.

Local Agencies: County Sheriff

Sheriff's departments are the second major type of local police. The office of sheriff typically provides the rural and unincorporated areas of the county (i.e., outside city limits) with the full array of basic police services. The sheriff is responsible for maintaining the peace, providing a variety of social services, and enforcing the law in the county. To most residents in the rural areas of the country—and to some urban residents as well—the sheriff is their primary provider of police protection.

There are approximately 3,100 sheriff's departments nationwide, representing roughly one-fifth the total number of local police agencies.[22] The office of sheriff may be found in every state except Alaska. Hawaii has only one sheriff, who is appointed by the State Attorney General. The Hawaiian sheriff, however, is a state and not a local official.[23]

Sheriff's departments employ one-third of all local law enforcement officers (two-thirds are city police). Most departments tend to be fairly small but somewhat larger than the typical city police department. Based on the 1990 LEMAS survey, the typical sheriff's department employed a total of sixty-six persons—forty-six sworn officers and twenty civilians. Only an estimated seventeen departments employed only one officer, and less than 1 percent of the departments in the United States employed over one thousand officers.[24] Los Angeles County in California has the nation's largest sheriff's department with 7,640 sworn officers and 3,168 civilians.[25]

The proportion of civilians employed by sheriff's departments nationwide is higher than the proportion working in city police agencies (31 percent compared to 21 percent respectively).[26] The difference is due mainly to the greater need for civilian employment to operate the jail, a responsibility that generally falls on the county sheriff. It is estimated that approximately one-third of sheriff's department employees work in jail operations.[27]

The Role of Sheriff

The role of the county sheriff's department is more complex than the role of city police. While there is considerable divergence from the basic form—as discussed below—the county sheriff typically serves the criminal justice system in its three major capacities: *law enforcement, courts,* and *corrections.* As an officer of the law, the county sheriff is responsible for serving and protecting the public; as an officer of the court, the sheriff must ensure courtroom security, transport defendants to and from court, and serve civil documents including subpoenas, eviction notices, foreclosure rulings, divorce papers, and court-ordered liens; as a corrections officer, the sheriff is responsible for the administration and operation of the county jail. The county jail sometimes houses hundreds of prisoners who are anywhere in the pre-trial to post-conviction stages of the criminal process. In six states—Vermont, Rhode Island, Connecticut, Delaware, Alaska and Hawaii—jail operations are the responsibility of the state government rather than the local government.[28]

While most sheriff's departments are assigned law enforcement, judicial, and corrections responsibilities, what Lee Brown calls the *full service model,*[29] this does not apply to all departments. Three alternative models exist. The *law enforcement model* refers to departments that have only law enforcement duties; the responsibility of serving the court and running the jail are handled by other agencies. The Multnomah County Sheriff's Office in Oregon is an example of a law enforcement model. The Multnomah County sheriff is responsible for providing basic police services to county residents, but a separate Division of Corrections within the county assumes responsibility for serving the court and operating the jail. The *civil-judicial model* refers to departments whose duty is limited to the courts with no obligation for law enforcement or corrections. The office of sheriff in Rhode Island and several offices of the sheriff in Connecticut only serve civil-judicial functions. Finally, the *correctional-judicial model* applies to departments like the San Francisco County Sheriff's Department that operate the county jail and services the needs of the court. The San Francisco City Police Department provides law enforcement services for all county residents because the boundary lines of the city and the county are the same.[30]

More than any other segment of American police, county sheriffs have been the target of sharp criticism. The office of sheriff has been described as the eternal "weak link" in the chain of American law enforcement. This is a reputation that has been earned over the years because of the relative lack of professional standards in sheriff's departments, the employment of poorly educated and inadequately trained officers, and the abundance of corrupt, self-serving sheriffs. While these same criticisms may be just as appropriately lodged against other segments of American law enforcement, on balance the problems have been much worse in sheriff's departments.

The principal reason why sheriff's departments face so many problems is because of the prominent role partisan politics play in these agencies. As a general rule, sheriffs are *elected* to office by county voters. Of the more than three thousand sheriffs' agencies in the United States, it is estimated that only eight of the sheriffs are *appointed* to their position.[31] The political nature of the office has several negative consequences. First, sheriffs must learn to be effective "politicians" because their careers depend on it. The sometimes subtle, sometimes violently shifting winds of community sentiment force the politically savvy sheriff to shift his or her sails in response. For example, a politically wise decision by a sheriff who faces a local election in two weeks may not necessarily be the best law enforcement decision. Certainly appointed police chiefs must also be attuned to local political pressures, but normally not to the extent as county sheriffs.

A second problem created by the political nature of the office is that once elected, the sheriff is not directly answerable to any individual or group. Contrary to the local police chief who is hired by the city (city council, city manager, or the mayor) and can be fired at any time, the sheriff is only accountable to his or her amorphous constituency. In practice this means that an incompetent sheriff cannot be "fired" until the next election, and even then a standing sheriff has a good chance of being reelected.

A third problem with the office of sheriff is that the election process does not guarantee the sheriff is particularly good at—or even knowledgeable about—police work. Many sheriff's departments have been infused with self-serving political figures who have used and abused the office for personal gain.

The Office of Sheriff: Remedies

There are a number of potential remedies that could help improve the competency, professionalism, and accountability of the office of sheriff. Among the recommendations found in the literature, four seem most plausible: (1) minimal eligibility standards should be established to become a sheriff; (2) educational and training requirements should be increased for all officers in the agency; (3) partisan politics should be phased out in favor of an appointed sheriff system; and (4) **civil service** should be ushered into all sheriffs' departments. This final recommendation is to ensure that appropriate standards regarding the hiring and firing of personnel are maintained.

Implementing positive changes in sheriffs' departments is not easily accomplished. Sheriffs have traditionally resisted alterations of their office that would encroach on their authority. And the political clout of sheriffs throughout our history has been substantial. Southern sheriffs in particular have constituted a powerful political force. Since the office of sheriff exists by constitutional authority in thirty-five states (the remaining sheriffs derive their authority by statutory provisions), any alteration in the office of sheriff—such as making the position appointive rather than elective—would require making changes in the state's constitution. This is an extremely difficult, time-consuming, and volatile political process.

On a positive note, the United States has many exemplary departments that are truly showcases of professionalism. Several states have initiated legislative changes to improve the office of sheriff. In 1972 Oregon became the first state to enact minimal standards to qualify as a county sheriff. Other states such as Ohio have set similar standards. Moreover, the **National Sheriff's Association** (NSA) has recently emerged as a progressive force. Founded in 1940 to protect the power of local sheriffs, NSA has since broadened its focus. Today NSA is a leading voice advocating the growth of professionalism and accountability in the office of sheriff.[32]

Jurisdiction of Local Police

Officers in sheriff's departments and city police departments have the authority to enforce the law within their respective geographical jurisdictions. Generally speaking, the sheriff and his or her officers relinquish their enforcement authority as they exit the county line; city police officers lose their enforcement authority once they leave the city limits. This implies that in a neighboring county, the legal powers of a sheriff are roughly equivalent to that of an ordinary citizen, just as the city police officer becomes an ordinary citizen in the unincorporated area of the county or in any other city.

By constitutional authority in many states, the sheriff is the chief law enforcement officer of the county. The sheriff and his or her deputies have legal enforcement authority everywhere in the county and can arrest for any crime inside or outside city limits. In practice, however, an agreement is generally reached between the city police and the county sheriff's department whereby the city department provides all enforcement services inside the city while the sheriff's department covers the rest of the county. These city-county agreements usually stipulate that sheriff deputies can be mobilized within city limits if the city police department requests the county's help. In addition, sheriff deputies can take initiative on their own to enter the city in the event of serious civil strife, or in cases of suspected police corruption in the city police department. Because of the high mobility of criminals and the cross-jurisdictional nature of many types of crime, city and county police agencies are increasingly consolidating functional units such as city-county vice squads to better combat crime.[33] These cross-jurisdictional units have enforcement authority throughout the entire county.

The geographical confinement of sheriff's departments and city police is a distinguishing characteristic of local police. By comparison, the geographical authority of state law enforcement officers and especially federal agents covers a much larger area. The geographical confinement of local police is more than "compensated," however, by the immense variety and intensity of police work that is performed at the local level.

There are a few legal extensions to the geographical authority of local police. In many states across the United States the local police have a buffer zone that surrounds the normal boundary lines. In these buffer zones officers have full legal authority. North Carolina, for example, grants local officers legal authority up to one mile beyond their normal jurisdiction. There are two reasons for extending the normal enforcement boundaries: (1) because it is not always possible for an officer to know when he or she has crossed city or county lines, especially where the boundaries are not clearly marked; and (2) criminals should not be allowed to use arbitrary boundaries within a state to avoid criminal prosecution when they have violated a general state statute. The major exception to the extended legal boundary is in the enforcement of local ordinances (e.g., a city code regulating excessive noise) that are not applicable statewide.

Another extension to the geographical authority of police is when an officer is in **hot pursuit** of a suspect. An officer in hot pursuit generally has the legal authority to cross city lines, county lines, and even state lines to stop the offender and to make an arrest. Hot pursuits apply to local, state, and federal police officers.

Once in hot pursuit an officer could theoretically travel hundreds of miles outside his or her normal jurisdiction and still make a legal arrest of the suspect. In reality, such long distance chases are unusual because it is not easy for suspects to "outrun" radio transmissions to area patrol cars. Departmental policy varies on the exact procedures expected of officers in hot pursuit who cross jurisdictions. Some departments specify that only certain types of felony suspects can be pursued by officers (for example, only suspects that are violent and an immediate threat to public safety). Other departments require that a hot pursuit be stopped if the officer loses eye contact with the suspect or if a neighboring police department takes over the chase.

In situations where a suspect crosses state lines and is subsequently arrested by an officer from the second state, formal *extradition* proceedings may be required to legally transfer the prisoner back to the state where the crime was originally committed. Hot pursuits that cross state lines frequently result in new crimes being committed in the second state as well. At minimum traffic laws may be violated, and very often more serious crimes are committed like drug possession or carrying an illegal firearm. In the event that the statutes in two states are violated during a single hot pursuit episode, the suspect can be independently charged with criminal offenses in both states.

Other Local Police

Existing alongside the two dominant forms of local police are several agencies or individuals that perform limited law enforcement duties. The county **coroner** is considered a local law enforcement agent by the Census Bureau and the Department of Justice.[34] The coroner has limited enforcement authority to investigate deaths in order to determine (1) whether the person died of natural or unnatural causes; and (2) what was the exact cause of death.

County coroners are either appointed to their position or are elected. In a number of states the county coroner derives his or her specific law enforcement authority from the state's constitution. Many jurisdictions even to this day do not require the coroner to be trained in the medical profession, nor is the coroner required to possess any special investigative skill.

A growing number of states are trying to improve the office of coroner. In states that still retain the office, many now require that the coroner be a trained medical doctor. Other states have drastically reduced the role of the coroner, and some have entirely eliminated it. State-run medical examiners' offices, with their teams of medical experts, trained support staff, and state of the art equipment, are increasingly replacing the local office of coroner.

Special district police are another type of local police agency.[35] There are numerous types of special district police that operate at the local level. Transit, housing, and park police are a few examples. Many **campus police** departments are also special district local police. Of the more than 450 campus police departments at U.S. colleges and universities,[36] some are classified as local police agencies, some are state agencies, and some are private security agencies. Diane Bordner and David Petersen comment on the importance of campus policing in the overall realm of American police work:

> Local law enforcement agencies, such as county and municipal agencies, simply are not in an adequate position to provide police protection for the nation's college and university campuses. Their other responsibilities preclude them from giving institutions of higher education the special attention they need. There are over 3,000 colleges, universities and branch campuses in the United States today. They serve approximately 11.5 million students, employ approximately two million people, and represent more than 78 billion dollars of investment in property, facilities and equipment. . . . On any given campus, campus police are responsible for the safety and security of thousands of people and a multi-million dollar investment in plant and equipment in their daily work. They complement local police by providing a greater degree of protection and enforcement in an area largely overlooked by local police. Given the masses of humanity either passing through or economically dependent upon educational institutions, the sizeable investment in physical plant, and increases in crime, the campus police occupy a more pivotal position today than was the case in the past.[37]

State Police Agencies

In developmental sequence, state agencies of police appeared long after local police were already established. In the early colonial days, night watchmen, town constables, and county sheriffs provided law enforcement at the local level. Not until the mid-1800s were the earliest type of state police created, and the first modern-day state police agency was not established until 1905.

The slower beginning of state-level law enforcement is not apparent today. In many jurisdictions state-level law enforcement has outpaced local law enforcement in the important areas of professionalism, quality of recruits, technical expertise, and administrative competence. Without the long tradition of corruption and inefficiency that is difficult to change, state law enforcement has been able to start fresh and mature quickly. State police agencies have "come of age" in the twentieth century.

The earliest forerunner of the modern-day state police was the famous **Texas Rangers**. At the time of its creation in 1835, Texas was still an independent republic. The original Rangers were strictly a military group used to fight Indians and to protect the southern borders of Texas along the Rio Grande from the frequent attacks of Mexican armies. After Texas joined the United States in 1846, the military duties of the Rangers diminished while their law enforcement and investigative responsibilities expanded.

The reputation of the Texas Rangers expanded as well. In the eyes of nostalgic admirers, the Rangers were bigger-than-life legends unmatched in their crime-fighting skills. No problem was too big for the Rangers. Ranger folklore tells the story of the Texas town torn apart by riot and disorder; shots were fired, stores were looted, and the God-fearing good citizens of the town were in hiding. Town leaders dispatched a wire to the Ranger's central headquarters for immediate help. In a return wire, Ranger command assured the town that help would arrive the next day. As the noon train came to a stop the following day, town leaders waited anxiously for the regiment of Rangers to disembark. Only one Ranger stepped off the train. Gravely disheartened, the mayor challenged the new arrival: "What!—only *one* Ranger?" Unabashed, the Ranger replied: "There's only *one* riot, ain't there?"[38]

Texas has retained its legendary Rangers. Today the force is fairly small with fewer than one hundred officers.[39] The activities of the modern-day Rangers focus on criminal investigations and providing assistance to other law enforcement agencies in Texas. Although less glamorous in real life than in legend, the Texas Rangers continue to attract praise and respect from the law enforcement community.

Connecticut and Massachusetts experimented with state-level constables in 1865, but neither state constable system had wide-ranging police powers.[40] Credit for being the first *modern* state police agency goes to the Pennsylvania State Police, which was started in 1905. The Pennsylvania State Police was created primarily in the wake of a political crisis: local police were unable to contain the violent riots caused by striking coal miners. This was not an auspicious beginning for the first professional state police agency. They were viewed by many as a throwback to the abusive *Coal and Iron Police*, created in 1900 by the Commonwealth of Pennsylvania to break strikes. Fortunately for the Pennsylvania State Police, the strikes were short-lived and its reputation was not permanently tarnished.

Need for State Police

Other states began to realize that they too needed state-level police during the first half of this century for several reasons. First, there was a growing intolerance among the people during the reform era (the late nineteenth and early twentieth century) toward poor government and corrupt police. Local police agencies were often unwilling to investigate charges of corruption at the local level. Therefore, a state-level agency with authority to investigate local corruption was needed. Second, the growth of state government generated additional statutes that required enforcement. Third, the proliferation of highways and automobiles created massive problems of traffic enforcement. And fourth, governors found themselves without an enforcement arm of the state to carry out state laws. Governor Pennypacker of Pennsylvania faced this very dilemma in 1905 when he created the first state police. As Pennypacker wrote at the time:

> In the year 1903 when I assumed the office of chief executive of the state, I found myself thereby invested with supreme executive authority. I found that no power existed to interfere with me in my duty to enforce the laws of the state, and that by the same token, no condition could release me from my duty to do so. I then looked about me to see what instruments I possessed wherewith to accomplish this bounded obligation—what instruments on whose loyalty and obedience I could truly rely. I perceived three such instruments—my private secretary, a very small man; my woman stenographer; and the janitor. So, I made the state police. [41]

The idea of state police had its share of critics. The strongest argument against developing a state police was that it would put too much power into the hands of the governor, who might be tempted to abuse the privilege. Sheriffs also resented the encroachment of state police into their territory. Eventually, the resistance faded as the need for state police became more obvious.

Primary State Police

There are forty-nine primary state police agencies in the U.S.; Hawaii is the only state without one. Primary agencies refer to the uniformed divisions of state law enforcement that provide police services in marked patrol cars throughout the state. Some agencies operate independently and report directly to the governor (e.g., Michigan, New York, Rhode Island, Virginia), while others operate under an umbrella organization such as the North Carolina Department of Crime Control and Public Safety.[42] Nationwide approximately 70 percent of the employees of primary state agencies are sworn officers while the remaining 30 percent are civilians.[43]

Not all of the forty-nine primary state law enforcement agencies are alike. There are two distinct types: **state highway patrol** and **state police**. Twenty-six states have a state highway patrol (SHP) whose duties are centered on traffic enforcement and accident investigation. The legal authority of highway patrol officers extends statewide. They have full power to arrest for any crime committed in their presence and to assist other local, state, or federal officers in the enforcement of the law. As a general rule, highway patrol officers limit their activities to uniformed traffic enforcement; they normally do not have a plainclothes investigation division. Also as a general rule, the state highway patrol will leave the enforcement of traffic regulations inside city limits to the local police, even though they usually have the legal authority to enforce traffic laws anywhere in the state. The largest and perhaps best known state highway patrol is the California Highway Patrol (CHP). The

Table 3.5   Primary State Law Enforcement Agencies

State	Type*	State	Type*
Alabama	SHP	Nebraska	SHP
Alaska	SP	Nevada	SHP
Arizona	SHP	New Hampshire	SP
Arkansas	SP	New Jersey	SP
California	SHP	New Mexico	SP
Colorado	SHP	New York	SP
Connecticut	SP	North Carolina	SHP
Delaware	SP	North Dakota	SHP
Florida	SHP	Ohio	SHP
Georgia	SHP	Oklahoma	SHP
Idaho	SP	Oregon	SP
Illinois	SP	Pennsylvania	SP
Indiana	SP	Rhode Island	SP
Iowa	SHP	South Carolina	SHP
Kansas	SHP	South Dakota	SHP
Kentucky	SP	Tennessee	SHP
Louisiana	SP	Texas	SHP
Maine	SP	Utah	SHP
Maryland	SP	Vermont	SP
Massachusetts	SP	Virginia	SP
Michigan	SP	Washington	SHP
Minnesota	SHP	West Virginia	SP
Mississippi	SHP	Wisconsin	SHP
Missouri	SHP	Wyoming	SHP
Montana	SHP		

*SHP = State Highway Patrol; SP = State Police
Source: Adapted from U.S. Department of Justice, *Uniform Crime Reports for the United States, 1990* (Washington, DC: U.S. Government Printing Office, August 1991), Table 71.

CHP employed 6,129 officers and 2,481 civilians in 1990. The smallest highway patrol is in Wyoming with only 156 officers and fifty-five civilians.[44]

State police (SP) are found in twenty-three states (see table 3.5). While state highway patrols are generally limited to traffic enforcement on state roads in the unincorporated areas, state police have greater enforcement authority. State police have geographical jurisdiction throughout the state and have the authority to arrest for any violation of state statute. It is not uncommon to see the state police inside city limits writing traffic tickets and making arrests alongside the local police. State police provide both uniformed patrols and plainclothes criminal investigations. The organizational structure of most state police agencies resembles that of a large metropolitan police department with its many divisions (e.g., patrol, traffic, investigations) and functional units (burglary, theft, juvenile, forensics, etc.). In 1990, Pennsylvania had the largest state police with 5,226 total employees. Rhode Island had the smallest with 220 employees.[45]

Other State Police

The forty-nine combined state highway patrols and state police are the primary law enforcement agencies that operate at the state level. There are other investigative agencies that have statewide authority to investigate and arrest for specified offenses (all offenses in some states), such as alcohol beverage control, fish and wildlife, Department of Motor Vehicles (DMV), State Bureau of Investigation (SBI), and the state revenue commission. State investigative agencies vary tremendously from state to state in organization, jurisdiction, and authority so that it is difficult to harness them all in our brief discussion.

Federal Police Agencies

Just as there are state laws and municipal ordinances that require enforcement, there are laws at the federal level that need enforcement as well. Federal agencies generally have very specific enforcement duties that are clearly specified by federal statute. The United States *does not* have a **national police system** as do some countries like France or Italy. This is to say that we do not have a centralized federal agency endowed with wide-ranging police authority to enforce criminal laws anywhere in the country.

The *U.S. Marshals Office* is the oldest federal enforcement agency and is part of the Department of Justice. U.S. Marshals were assigned to remote federal districts during the frontier days. The geographical jurisdiction of the marshals was often immense, and they often had to cover the territory on horseback and sleep under the open stars. In the early heyday of the U.S. Marshals, the so-called "Western" areas that now constitute such states as Kansas, Missouri, and the Dakotas were not then states; they were federal districts. The marshal and his appointed deputy marshals were often the only

A "last-ditch" attempt by felons to elude police may lead to a car chase across state lines.

form of law enforcement available, barring of course the periodic lynch mob or posse.

The *Secret Service* was established in 1865 following the Civil War as part of the Department of Treasury. The major task of the Secret Service—then and now—is to combat counterfeiting. The Secret Service also protects the president and his family from political assassination. At the time the secret service was initially established, counterfeit currency posed a serious problem for the United States. It is estimated that as much as one-fourth of all currency in circulation during the Civil War was bogus. The treasury officers of the secret service were the first truly *investigative* agents of the federal government.

Clearly the best known and most prestigious law enforcement agency in the United States, if not the entire world, is the *Federal Bureau of Investiga-*

THE SPECIAL CASE OF THE NATIONAL GUARD

The historical roots of the National Guard date back to colonial days when all early settlements had some form of militia to protect their interests. The Uniform Militia Law of 1792 required every male between the ages of eighteen and forty-five to serve at least three months duty; however, the law was seldom enforced. The term "National Guard" was first used as the title of the Seventh Regiment of the New York State Militia in 1824. The founding of the National Guard Association in 1878 popularized the term, and the 1903 Dick Act made the National Guard the official reserve force of the country. Today's National Guard is comprised of fifty-two state-organized units of the Army and Air Force that are available for service in each state, the District of Columbia, and Puerto Rico. Men and women civilian volunteers who have met the minimum army training are eligible to join. There are approximately 500,000 National Guard officers available for duty.

The National Guard serves an unusual and complex role. Depending on the circumstances in which the Guard may be called into duty, it may be either a *military unit* under federal control or a *domestic police agency* under the authority of the state. As a military unit, the Guard may be "called up" from the states under conscription orders by the president to fight alongside the regular Army and Air Force in times of international conflict. This civilian force has been acti-vated into military service several times (during the two World Wars, the Korean Conflict, the Berlin crisis in 1961, and the 1991 Persian Gulf War). The National Guard is distinct from the Organized Reserve Corps (ORC). The ORC also serves as a large trained addition to the Army and Air Force in times of emergencies, but it is entirely administered by the federal military establishment with no direct link to the states. There are no National Guard units to serve the Navy or Marine Corps.

As a domestic police force, the National Guard may be activated by governor's orders to provide aid to victims of natural disasters like floods, forest fires, hurricanes, tornados, and earthquakes. The governor may also activate the Guard to help enforce the law in times Of pervasive civil disorder. An important point to be made regarding the peacetime emergency duty of the National Guard is that when activated, the Guard becomes a functional police agency with recognized legal enforcement authority.

The tragic incident at Kent State University in May of 1970 forced a reexamination of the National Guard system. Four unarmed students protesting U.S. policies in Indochina were killed by the Ohio National Guard Unit. Because of the Kent State incident, National Guard standards have been upgraded and training programs intensified.

Source: *The Encyclopedia Americana* (Danbury, CT: Grolier Inc., 1986), p. 762.

tion—the FBI, or G-men (for "Government" men) as Machine Gun Kelly called them. The FBI was originally created in 1908 under another name (Bureau of Investigation) and possessed limited clout. The name was changed to the FBI in 1935. The political future of the FBI was redirected in 1924. In that year the FBI was given a new enforcement mandate and a new leader. **J. Edgar Hoover** (1895–1972) was appointed director of the FBI at the young age of twenty-nine, and ruled the Bureau for forty-eight years. Hoover's uncanny ability to survive successive presidential administrations and to weather one political crisis after another enabled him to hold onto the reins of the FBI until his death in 1972.

The reputation of the FBI grew tremendously under Hoover's direction. (Interestingly, the size of the agency did not grow as quickly as its reputation. Hoover purposely kept the Bureau small so that he could maintain better control of his agents.) Hoover and his agency claimed credit for ridding the country of several notorious gangsters during the Depression era. The massive FBI manhunt of **John Dillinger**, Public Enemy Number One, which ended on a warm July evening when agents shot Dillinger to death on a Chicago street, was one of the FBI's proudest and most celebrated moments.

Recent years have thrown light on the many dubious practices of Hoover's FBI. The FBI is known to have committed outlandish violations of the civil rights of individuals and suspected radical groups (e.g., the New Left, the Black Nationalist movement, Socialist Workers party, Southern Christian Leadership Conference). Hoover justified the actions of the FBI by arguing that such violations were necessary to keep America safe. Hoover's intelligence network kept secret dossiers on thousands of people suspected of being sympathetic toward radical causes. Many leftist politicians and outspoken Hollywood celebrities were tailed by Hoover's agents. Hoover had no tolerance for communists, who he believed capable of destroying an overly complacent U.S. government, and he passionately hated Dr. Martin Luther King. Hoover thought that Dr. King was a communist and a threat to the national security of the United States. In 1962, the FBI placed Dr. King's name on the *Reserve Index* as someone who should be rounded up and detained during a national crisis.[46] Hoover was quoted as saying that King "is one of the lowest characters in the country," an "evil beast" and a "fraud."[47] Following Hoover's orders, the FBI went so far as to secretly wiretap Dr. King's hotel room to record romantic moments with a woman—not his wife—in an effort to irreparably embarrass King.

The public and personal life of J. Edgar Hoover is a fascinating story. In so many ways Hoover's story is also the story of the early FBI.

Federal Law Enforcement Today

The system of federal law enforcement has developed in a rather sporadic fashion. As Congress passes new regulations that require enforcement, either an existing agency assumes enforcement responsibility or a new regulatory agency must be created. Many of the enforcement agencies of the federal government, like the small U.S. Supreme Court Police Force, receive fairly little public attention; other agencies such as the FBI, Drug Enforcement

FEDERAL LAW ENFORCEMENT AGENCIES

DEPARTMENT OF JUSTICE

Federal Bureau of Investigation

The FBI is the premier enforcement agency of the Department of Justice. Its nearly eight thousand agents have jurisdiction over any federal crime not the specific responsibility of another federal enforcement agency. There are over two hundred offenses that come under the enforcement duty of the FBI with bank robbery, theft or embezzlement of federal property, kidnapping, political corruption, espionage, and air piracy receiving high priority. The geographical jurisdiction of the FBI extends throughout the United States and its territories. The FBI has the authority to make arrests in other countries when backed by a court order. The director of the FBI is an appointed official who reports directly to the Attorney General of the United States.

Drug Enforcement Administration

The Drug Enforcement Administration, or DEA, was formed in 1973 following the consolidation of other agencies assigned to drug enforcement. There are approximately two-thousand DEA agents who enforce federal drug laws nationwide. The DEA was formally merged with the FBI in 1982 and continues to serve in that capacity as a semiautonomous agency. The head of the DEA now reports directly to the FBI director.

Immigration and Naturalization Service

The INS was created in 1891 as part of the Justice Department to enforce immigration regulations of the United States. Its well-known Border Patrol protects U.S. borders, apprehending illegal aliens and assisting in deportation proceedings.

U.S. Marshals Service

The oldest federal enforcement agency, U.S. Marshals have broad enforcement authority covering all federal crimes that are not the specific duty of another federal agency. The U.S. Marshals Service actively seeks from federal fugitives the law, transports prisoners, renders emergency services in cases of civil disturbances, assists INTERPOL with the apprehension of foreign fugitives on U.S. soil, and provides witness protection and relocation services in high-risk trials. The Marshals Service plays a particularly close role with the federal courts. The ninety-five U.S. Marshals—one for each federal district—are appointed by the president with consent of the Senate to four-year terms (Deputy U.S. Marshals, the line agents of the Marshals Service, are hired through regular federal personnel procedures). The Director of the U.S. Marshals Service reports directly to the Attorney General.

DEPARTMENT OF TREASURY

Secret Service

The Secret Service was established in 1865 to investigate counterfeiting and government check forgery. The fifteen hundred agents of today's Secret Service continue to perform the same primary mission. The Secret Service is best known for its highly visible role of providing round-the-clock protection for our country's past and present presidential leaders.

Bureau of Alcohol, Tobacco and Firearms

Officers of ATF are treasury agents with responsibility to enforce federal tax law regulations related to the manufacture of alcohol and tobacco. ATF also enforces federal gun control laws.

Customs Service

Customs inspectors and investigators are responsible for enforcing U.S. laws regulating the importation of foreign goods into this country and collecting import duties and fees. Customs officers have the authority to search and seize illegal items located in cars, boats, planes, luggage, and baggage. They have the powers of arrests for customs violations. In recent years the Customs Service has assumed a larger role in interdicting narcotic drugs entering the United States.

Administration, and the U.S. Customs Service receive considerably more publicity. Generally speaking, federal law enforcement agencies have fairly limited albeit well-defined enforcement responsibilities. The geographical jurisdiction of federal agents usually extends throughout the United States and its territories. What is more, the FBI has limited authority to make arrests of people wanted by U.S. courts in other countries.

The United States has over sixty federal enforcement agencies.[48] This number includes (1) agencies whose *primary mission* is the enforcement of specific federal statutes (e.g., FBI, DEA, ATF); and (2) other agencies that have a special enforcement division within its overall structure. Thus, for example, while the Internal Revenue Service and the U.S. Postal Service are not law enforcement agencies by role or mission (the main mission of the IRS is to collect taxes and the main mission of the Postal Service is to deliver mail), a separate enforcement division exists within each of these federal agencies. Hence, there are IRS agents and Postal Inspectors who are responsible for ensuring compliance with the nation's tax and postal laws.

Other Federal Police

The *U.S. Coast Guard* performs both military and domestic law enforcement duties. In times of war, the Coast Guard can be conscripted by presidential orders to serve under the Department of Navy (similar to the National Guard); in times of peace, the Coast Guard operates under the Department of Transportation, becoming the main maritime law enforcement agency of the federal government. In its peacetime role the Coast Guard is responsible for enforcing boating regulations, ensuring safe navigation of merchant ships, preventing customs and immigration violations, and protecting fish, game, and wildlife.

As part of the nation's military establishment, **Military Police** (MPs) are not formally classified as a domestic police force. Military Police are the security forces of the Army and Marine Corps (the security forces of the Navy and the Air Force are called *Shore Patrol* and *Security Police*, respectively). MPs are soldiers who guard military property, enforce federal laws and military regulations, arrest offenders, and attend to other duties assigned by the military. Regardless of their military designation, MPs perform many of the same duties on military bases as civilian police forces provide in the community.

There are a dozen or so organizations collectively referred to as the *intelligence community* that are not considered to be domestic police agencies. The *Central Intelligence Agency* (CIA), the super secret *National Security Agency* (NSA), and the intelligence branches of the Army, Navy, Air Force, and Marines are among the federal agencies that provide for the security of the United States in national and international affairs.

CONCLUSION

The goal of this chapter was to provide an accurate examination of modern-day police agencies in the United States. Given the amazing complexity and disjointedness of the 20,000 police agencies operating at the local, state, and federal levels, we clearly could not begin to cover them all. By necessity our discussion was more selective than thorough. We concentrated mostly on local police agencies because of their greater numbers, longer tradition, wide-ranging responsibilities, and closeness to the people. The important contribution of state and federal law enforcement was also discussed although our coverage of the various types of state and especially federal law enforcement agencies was less comprehensive.

It is important to underscore the point once again that American policing is mainly a local phenomenon. City police and county sheriffs' departments are the heart of our nation's police system. They are the major providers of basic police services for most citizens, and they employ over 75 percent of all police officers. From small towns to big cities, from the east coast to the west, policing American society is primarily a local responsibility.

KEY TERMS

full-time equivalent (FTE)	coroner
sworn officer	campus police
civilian	Texas Rangers
police strength	state highway patrol
police-to-population ratio	state police
density index	national police system
civil service	J. Edgar Hoover
National Sheriffs' Association	John Dillinger
hot pursuit	Military Police

DISCUSSION QUESTIONS

1. Discuss the trends in police expenditures over the past fifty years. (Has the proportion of state and local spending on the police changed much over time? Why or why not?)
2. Discuss the difference between *absolute* and *relative* police strength. Why is it that increases in police strength do not automatically result in greater police protection?
3. We made the argument that policing American society is predominantly a local responsibility. What do we mean by this?
4. In what ways is police work in small towns different from police work in big cities? In what ways is it similar?
5. Explain the ways in which the office of sheriff is different from most city police departments?
6. Explain the differences between state highway patrols and state police.

PART II
Police and Society

In the first section of the book we began drawing a portrait of police work in America by etching in the basic outline. We defined its overall size, scope, and some essential features but left much of the canvas blank. In this section, Police and Society, essential detail to the portrait is added. Chapter 4 focuses directly on the main role of police in modern society. This is a critical chapter in our study of American police and, as such, forms the "heart" of the book. Chapter 5 addresses the important area of police-community relations. We shall learn how citizen attitudes toward the police, particularly local police, are an important driving force in how the police respond to community problems. Chapter 5 also closely examines a popular philosophy in policing today known as "community policing." Chapter 6 concludes this section by taking a closer look at what police work is really like. Topics in this chapter include the police socialization process, domestic disputes, police stress, and line-of-duty deaths.

CHAPTER FOUR

THE POLICE CHARGE

Law is order, and good law is good order.

—Aristotle

The terms *police agency* and *law enforcement agency* are used interchangeably in daily discussions of the police and even in formal written works. No harm is done because the two phrases have about the same meaning in everyday language; one can refer to the police department in New York City as a police agency or a law enforcement agency with equal accuracy. The reader may have noticed both terms have been used in our discussions thus far.

This book generally refers to what most state and federal agencies do as **law enforcement** and to what most local agencies do as **policing**. The different terms draw attention to an important distinction between the activities of investigative agencies (e.g., FBI, DEA, Postal Inspection Service), and "general" duty police (most city police and county sheriff's departments). Policing involves far more than just enforcing the law; it also entails rendering services to the community and maintaining order in local neighborhoods. When you lock your keys in the car, when your child is bitten by the neighbor's dog, or when you are approached by a panhandler on a city street, who are you going to call? The FBI? The DEA? The Postal Inspection Service? Obviously not. If you think about calling the police at all you would think first of calling the local police.

This chapter examines the police largely from a sociological perspective. The central question we address is, "What do the police contribute to society?" Sociologists refer to the special contribution of the police as their *role* or *function*. We capture the same idea in our chapter heading—The Police Charge.

SOCIAL CONTROL

At the center of all police systems is the process of **social control**. We shall temporarily define social control as "trying to keep society running smoothly." The police are not the only mechanism of social control. In fact, they are not even the most important. The police are only one of many control mechanisms that help to keep order in society.

Public policing as we recognize it today may be a recent historical development, but social control is as old as human societies. Social control is a fundamental requisite for the survival of any society, whether the society is one from the past, present, or future. Although human beings are by nature social creatures and choose to congregate with others for mutual protection and emotional satisfaction, eons of evolution have demonstrated how social living requires considerable compromise, adaptation, and forced civil behavior. Large prehistoric clans living in small caves found this true 20,000 years ago just as large families living in one bathroom homes find it true today; it is necessary to learn to share with others and to forego one's immediate yearnings for the benefit of everyone. Without this measure of civility, tempers rise and pandemonium flourishes.

If a human collectivity is to survive, a sufficient degree of social control must be established. Control is accomplished through an elaborate system of social rules or **norms**. These norms are the beginning of social structure. When the essential norms of a society are well known, and when there is consensus among people that the dominant norms are desirable, then the necessary ingredients for social harmony are at hand. In the absence of widespread consensus of the fundamental norms, social structure begins to weaken, role relationships become ambiguous, and people become increasingly alienated from the world around them. If the breakdown of norms occurs on a large scale and over an extended period of time, society experiences what Robert Merton calls **anomie**.[1] Merton argued that as anomie increases (in other words, when social rules become more alien and meaningless to the people), crime and deviance increase as well.

In practical terms, the greatest value of social norms is that they enable members of society to get along with one another. Norms lend stability and predictability to social actions, thus avoiding mass chaos when people come into contact with each other. Imagine the confusion that would reign in social life if we had no rules to follow, or if only minimal agreement existed on which rules to obey. This is perhaps no better illustrated than when we take to the roads in our automobiles. The predictable movement of other drivers makes it possible to whiz by cars only a few feet away at fifty-five miles per hour without screaming in horror or taking evasive action. We assume other cars are going to stay on their side of the road, and thus we are able to anticipate their movement in advance. Without the predictable ebb and flow of automobiles produced by traffic regulations, only the bravest of souls would dare drive on a busy city street.

Whereas the "rules of the road" help ensure the patterned regularity of automobile traffic, the myriad "rules of social living" promote the patterned regularity of human behavior in most—but certainly not all—social situations. As humans beings we thrive on predictability in our social world! Whether walking down the street, ordering a hamburger, or going on an important first date, we expect people to act and react to us in certain ways. When the norms governing social encounters are violated (e.g., if you were mugged on the street or your date repeatedly belched during dinner), social situations begin to lose their predictability. At minimum, the loss of predictability is unsettling and at times it is traumatic.

Social control may be thought of as a way of maximizing the predictability of social behavior. Effective social control results in few norm violations; ineffective social control jeopardizes the very basis of social life. Yet social control is not an *all or nothing* thing—people are not straight-jacketed into inflexible robot-like behaviors. All societies must be able to tolerate a certain amount of deviation from the norms. Moreover, not all social norms are as important as others. William Graham Sumner (1840–1910), a highly respected early sociologist, identified three different types of norms. **Folkways** are norms that are useful but not essential. Rules regarding proper etiquette and other social pleasantries are examples of folkways. **Mores** are essential norms that reflect society's fundamental moral values. Rules prohibiting murder, incest, and theft are examples of mores because these behaviors violate the basic moral sentiments of society. **Laws** are special norms. Through the political process society selects certain behaviors to formally prohibit, and then assigns the enforcement of these norms to the police. Please note that the police are not the only enforcers of the law; parents, teachers, and numerous regulatory agencies—like the county health department—also help enforce the law. The important point to be made here is that out of the incredible array of norms guiding almost every conceivable social interaction, only a few are made into law. Stated another way, the police are responsible for enforcing only a tiny portion of all the rules of social living.

Defining Social Control

At this juncture we need a better definition of social control than our earlier one of "trying to keep society running smoothly." The following definition will suit our purposes well: social control refers to *all those social arrangements that either motivate or compel people to conform to society's rules.*[2] On the one hand, the new definition is quite general, including "all those social arrangements" that help regulate human behavior. On the other hand, the definition is quite specific; it points to how social control is a dual process—it is one of "motivating" people to conform and/or "compelling" them to conform. But we need to probe further. Now that we know what social control is, how do we achieve it?

Achieving Social Control

For the most part, society has a way of cunningly tricking people into social control.[3] The major part of the "trick" is to arrange society in such a way that individuals do not even want to violate the rules. We can call this the **first line of defense** against deviance. This first line of defense encompasses many different processes, yet it essentially boils down to the proper socialization of children to the values and customs of their society. Most children are taught the difference between right and wrong, or between good and bad. Largely through the nurturing praises of parents and other adults, most children learn to feel good about themselves when they do good things. When socialization is working properly, the important values and moral judgments of society are deeply instilled in a person. This occurs at a young age and remains relatively intact throughout a person's life. The major test of the first line of defense is when individuals refuse to violate the rules of society even if they have the opportunity to do so. Fortunately, the great majority of people refuse to commit crimes even when the opportunities exist.

But of course not everyone is honest. Many people are not adequately restrained by the first line of defense. So what can we do to control the deviant motivations of people who break through our first line of defense?[4] Society's **second line of defense** is to make it difficult or impossible for people to violate the rules even if they want to. Innumerable arrangements exist in society as part of this second line of defense. These arrangements function either as *formal* or *informal* mechanisms of social control. The police are the best example of a "formal" social control agency. The major reason police exist is to regulate the social activity of people. Depending on the situation, parents, teachers, neighbors, employers, and priests—in fact, just about any person in a position of authority over another—also serve in the capacity of a formal social control agent.

"Informal" mechanisms of social control refer to social arrangements that inadvertently prevent crime and disorder, even though this is not their main purpose. For example, our role relationships with friends, family, and coworkers all indirectly serve to monitor our behavior. So does the time we spend pursuing conventional activities like attending school, studying, working, watching television, going to religious services, having dinner with our folks, and so on. Indeed, most of our lives are so consumed with conventional activities and everyday responsibilities that little time remains for being bad.

An alternative way of viewing social control is to consider *internal* and *external* sources of deviance control. Criminologist Walter Reckless calls them **inner** and **outer containments**.[5] A person who has effective inner containments is able to regulate, monitor, and govern his or her own inclinations toward deviance. Effective inner containments result from the proper internalization of society's norms and values. They are also aided by certain personality characteristics like a good self-concept and a high level of tolerance to frustration. Outer containments are complementary "external" processes that also produce conforming behavior. Parental supervision, police patrol, and the watchful eyes of neighbors are a few of the many types of outer containments. According to Reckless' containment theory, insufficient controls—whether the weakness is internal, external, or both—increase the likelihood of deviance. Research has demonstrated how inner containments (our "first line of defense") are more important for the control of criminal behavior than outer containments (our "second line of defense").

This brings us to a crucial lesson regarding the role of police as social control agents: assuming that someone wants to break the law, there is not a great deal the police can do to stop them. We commonly view the police as an important source of deterrence, who stand strong between lawful and lawless behavior. This is the so-called **blue curtain** metaphor used to describe the social control capability of the police. However, this is somewhat misleading—the police are more like a thin **blue veil** than a thick blue curtain. Granted the police apprehend thousands of serious offenders every year who commit criminal violations. The police also issue millions of tickets annually to traffic violators. Yet as we discussed back in chapter 1, the police can catch only a small fraction of all violators. And more to the point, if the police have to catch a crook or stop a speeder, it means they were unable to prevent the crime from occurring in the first place—the police merely reacted to the situation after it already occurred.

If a person breaks through the first line of defense by wanting to commit a crime, and then breaks through the second line of defense by actually committing a crime, what can we do now? Our **final line of defense** is to take formal steps to prevent further crime. Modern society provides three remedies: (1) punish the offender (to deter him or her); (2) incarcerate the offender (to segregate the offender from society); and (3) rehabilitate the offender (to cure him or her). Although rehabilitation is often the most difficult and expensive of the three remedies to do effectively, from a theoretical standpoint it is perhaps the most rational remedy. The reason is because rehabilitation attempts to go back to the first line of defense and make it so the person does not even want to commit additional crime. In other words, rehabilitation tries to strengthen a person's inner containments. This reduces the need to rely solely on outer containments like the police to control crime.

ROLE OF THE POLICE

There is consensus among many scholars that general duty police agencies perform three essential functions (we are excluding purely investigative agencies from this discussion). Ranked in order of their importance as suggested in the literature, the major functions of the police are **order maintenance** (the peacekeeper role), **social service** (the social worker role), and **law enforcement** (the crime fighter role). Please note that the order in which the three functions are listed should not automatically be taken as an indication of their relative importance to society. For reasons that are outlined later, the common practice of ranking the importance of the three functions can cloud the reality of police work.

Order Maintenance

Students are frequently amazed to learn how much of everyday police work involves order maintenance (i.e., "peacekeeping") activities. Yet maintaining social order in the community consumes a large part of a typical patrol officer's time and energy. Quite often when citizens call the police for help, they are not calling about a crime in progress. They call the police to intervene in a situation that is out of order. Some of the more common types of order maintenance calls are "rowdy youth," "loud stereo," "domestic disturbance," "landlord-tenant dispute," "barking dog," and "drunk and disorderly."

The officer answering the call is normally able to resolve the problem without having it escalate into a serious disturbance. The officer may make a simple request (e.g., "please turn the volume down on your radio"), try gentle persuasion ("I don't want to be called back here tonight"), or give a direct order ("turn that radio down now or I will write you up"). Since disturbance calls seldom result in an arrest, the attending officer is cast more in the role of *mediator* than enforcer.

Social Service

Providing aid and assistance to the public is another major role of the police. Historically, the police were given responsibility for rendering social services largely by default because there was no other public agency open twenty-four hours a day, seven days a week, to take care of immediate problems. In colonial times and up to the mid-nineteenth century, it was common for the night watchman to report fires, catch runaway animals, light street lamps, and stand ready to serve the public in any way he could.[6] In modern times, the social service function of the police incorporates a wide variety of activities: for example, giving directions to lost tourists, helping inebriated people get home safely, counseling and referring people with problems to appropriate social agencies, opening car doors when the keys have been accidently locked inside, aiding fire fighters and paramedics during emergencies, and notifying next of kin of a tragic death are a few of the many social services general duty police typically provide.

In this capacity, the police are cast into the role of *social worker*, a role the police have not always eagerly accepted. Nonetheless, the social service function is deeply ingrained in the tradition of local police agencies.

Law Enforcement

Law enforcement is another major function of the police. Activities that are considered to be law enforcement include responding to crimes in progress

Police offer assistance to all kinds of citizens. Here, an officer calms a three-year-old child in the aftermath of a traffic accident.

(burglary, robbery, rape, assault, etc.), taking a report from a crime victim, investigating a crime, checking on a prowler, questioning a suspect, and making an arrest. Crime fighting may be thought of as the *core mission* of the police, one that harnesses wide public support and serves as a basic strategy of policing.[7] The crime fighting mission is central to the self-definition of most police officers, and is the dominant view of the police held by the majority of citizens.

Despite the centrality of crime fighting in the overall strategy of policing, this image of the police is at odds with the day-to-day reality of police work. One of the oldest and most popular myths about police work is that patrol officers are continuously engaged in law enforcement action. The entertainment industry is largely to blame for this false impression, but so are the news media and even the police. Research conducted in the 1960s began to raise questions about how often police were actively engaged in enforcing the law. Not only did research document how much "dead" time is spent in a typical eight hour shift with officers just driving around the streets (what the police refer to as "preventive patrol"); now for the first time research authoritatively demonstrated that real police work entails a "bundle of tasks," not all of which are crime related.[8]

In one of the earliest studies, James Q. Wilson examined citizen complaints called into the Syracuse (New York) police department in June of 1966. Only around 10 percent of the calls were for law enforcement.[9] A full two-thirds of the calls were a combination of order maintenance and service requests from the citizens, and approximately one out of every five calls (22 percent) dispatched to patrol cars were classified as "information gathering." Other researchers monitoring citizen complaints radioed to patrol cars have found similar results as Wilson, even though the percentage of order mainte-

---

ARE POLICE SOCIAL WORKERS?

After three months on the street, I began to realize that it's not what I expected. The big thing that hit me is I'm a social worker. That just blew my mind. I was looking for car chases and shoot-'em-ups, all the things I saw on every cop show for twenty years of my life. Now I come on the street and they expect me to fill out a bunch of forms and mediate family fights, child abuse, people OD'ing on the street.

You never see a guy handle an aid case on a cop show—pick up some psycho that's stepped in front of a bus and get him registered in the local hospital mental health ward—but you do that more than shoot your gun at people.

At twenty I'd hung around with teenagers all my life. Now I'm dealing with forty- to fifty-year-old people who have problems which I didn't even know then what the problem was made of. I didn't know what a family fight was or a child abuser. I was brought up in an all-white neighborhood. Suddenly I'm in the ghetto and a woman comes up to me and says, "My husband took the check and the kids can't eat and he's going to come back and beat me up." People come up to you and explain things to you and you felt stupid. You wanted to help them, but you didn't really know what to say to them.

Source: Mark Baker, *Cops: Their Lives in Their Own Words* (New York: Simon and Schuster, 1985), pp. 29–30.

	Type of Department					
Activity	Midwest City Urban Department	Smithville Suburban Department	Pinewood Suburban Department	East Coast State Police Station	Township Department	Grand Totals
Information Gathering	8	6	5	19	12	9
Service	13	23	10	12	5	13
Order Maintenance	24	29	16	13	26	24
Law Enforcement	33	19	13	19	27	30
Traffic	18	21	52	29	30	21
Other	3	3	4	8	0	3
Totals	99	101	100	100	100	100
	(2,835)	(264)	(214)	(150)	(168)	(3,631)

Source: Richard J. Lundman, "Police Patrol Work: A Comparative Perspective," in *Police Behavior*, Richard J. Lundman ed. (New York: Oxford University Press, Copyright 1980), p. 56, Table 1.1. Reprinted by permission.

nance, service, and law enforcement calls varies somewhat from one study location to another. For instance the Police Services Study, perhaps the most comprehensive study of its kind to date, found only 19 percent of over 26,000 calls for police service involved crime, and only 2 percent involved violent crime.[10] In summarizing this entire body of research, Joel Samaha notes "the results show that officers spend less than 25 percent of their time enforcing the law."[11]

However, not all research demonstrates such a limited role of law enforcement. Richard Lundman's investigation of police activity in five different departments is one such study.[12] Instead of simply monitoring citizen calls dispatched to radio patrol cars as most studies have done, Lundman made careful observations of actual police activities over a fifteen-month period. Thus, Lundman's study was a much larger and more representative sampling of real police work because it included situations when the police initiated a police-citizen encounter on their own (officer-initiated encounters accounted for about one-third of all observed activities). Table 4.1 reports Lundman's findings. When comparing percentages across the columns, we can see that patrol activities vary from one police department to another. Although the traditional order maintenance and service calls represented a substantial portion of the total number of calls in each town, Lundman found that "the single most frequent type of activity overall was law enforcement."[13] And if one adds to the total the large number of traffic enforcement activities from table 4.1 as well, law enforcement accounted for over 50 percent of all patrol activities.

The relative frequency of various types of police activity fluctuates across police departments and even within departments. As a consequence, it is not always accurate to say that one police function dominates the other two in all communities. In one department law enforcement might assume a high priority while in another department the social service function may be emphasized. The same can be said within a single department; high-crime and continuous citizen demand may force a police manager to initiate a "vigorous enforcement agenda" in one part of town (i.e., heavy coverage mixed with aggressive patrol) while social service and/or order maintenance is emphasized in another part of town. An important point to make here is that the three major functions of police work may be separated at the conceptual level for analytic purposes, such as we have done here. In reality, however, their differences often lose clarity and meaning because the three functions are so closely interwoven. Wilson argues a similar point:

> Even in a routine law-enforcement situation (for example, arresting a fleeing purse snatcher), how the officer deals with the victim and the onlookers at the scene is often as important as how he handles the suspect. The victim and onlookers, after all, are potential witnesses who may have to testify in court; assuring their cooperation is as necessary as catching the person against whom they will testify. The argument about whether "cops" should be turned into "social workers" is a false one, for it implies that society can exercise some meaningful choice over the role the officer should play. Except at the margin, it cannot; what it can do is attempt to prepare them for the complex role they now perform.[14]

What can we conclude about the three major functions of the police? First, just as it is inaccurate to define the police simply in terms of crime fighting, it is also inaccurate to define them exclusively as social workers or keepers of the peace. The police perform all of these roles, often simultaneously, everyday on the streets. Second, while it is possible to quantify the number of law enforcement, social service, and order maintenance calls handled by officers through research, such "counting" invokes an artificial separation of activities that are often inseparable in real life. For example, a routine domestic disturbance requires an officer to act as peacekeeper (getting the disputants to quiet down, breaking up an angry crowd, requesting curious neighbors to return to their homes, etc.), as social worker (offering counsel and advice, listening to an emotionally upset victim, referring victim to a local shelter), and as law enforcer (using the authority of the state to give orders and occasionally make arrests). In summary, the various roles of the police are multifaceted and highly complex. As agents of social control, the police serve the public's momentary and persistent needs in many ways.

NON-NEGOTIABLE COERCIVE FORCE

As agents of social control the police strive to maintain community order, render services to the people, and enforce the law. Yet identifying these three areas does not necessarily distinguish the police from other social actors who also perform some of these same functions (e.g., parents, school teachers, building inspectors, trash collectors). So then, what is the special contribution of the police? One of the most useful and cogent answers to this question is given by sociologist Egon Bittner.[15]

Bittner argues that what distinguishes modern police from the average person is their ability to resolve problem situations that ordinary people can-not—or refuse to—resolve by themselves. Bittner refers to this as the authority of the police to use **non-negotiable coercive force**.

The authority to use non-negotiable coercive force gets to the very heart of policing. It is uppermost in the minds of citizens when they "call the cops" for some problem or predicament that is beyond their ability to resolve. Imagine yourself in the following situation:

It is 3:30 in the morning. For the past several hours you have been toss-ing and turning in bed unable to sleep because the new tenants in the apart-ment above you are playing their stereo too loud. This is not the first night they have bothered you and a few of the other tenants in the building. Yes-terday you spoke with the apartment manager, Mr. Sophtee, who was al-ready aware of the problem. It seems that Mr. Sophtee has tried on two occa-sions to get the new tenants to turn down their music, but the tenants are unwilling to comply. When you suggested he ought to throw them out of the building, Mr. Sophtee agreed but informed you that it was not easy get-ting rid of bad tenants. He said he was already doing all that the law allowed him to do at this time. Now you lie awake in anger. You have to be at work in a few hours and need to get some rest. Deciding that direct action is needed, you put on your clothes and head upstairs to ask your neighbors to be more considerate. After you pound loudly several times, the tenant finally hears you and opens the door. In the most disarming voice that you can mus-ter given your anger, you kindly request the young male neighbor to turn down the volume. He carefully squints at you through bloodshot eyes, scratches his head, and then tells you to "buzz-off." Before you have a chance to respond to the abrasive young man, he shuts the door in your face.

Now you are confronted with an unruly neighbor. What can you do to resolve the situation? Actually, your options are quite limited. Appealing to the neighbor's sense of fair play by speaking calmly to him is out of the question—both you and the apartment manager have already tried but the guy will not listen. Calling him on the phone probably would not work either. Perhaps you become so mad that you decide to threaten the noisy neighbor with your fists or a baseball bat. But "communicating threats," which is what you would be doing, is a more serious crime than "disturbance of the peace," which is what he is doing. And of course physically forcing the neighbor to be quiet will end in your arrest, not his. So what can you do? *Call the cops*!

What the police have that allows them to resolve the situation is the *authority* (meaning the explicit legal right to intervene backed by the laws of the state) to use *non-negotiable* (no bargaining or trade-offs necessary) *coercive force* (e.g., give a direct order, write a ticket, cite to court, or make an arrest). Granted the young stereo player may not be any more pleasant to the police when they knock on his door, but if he tells the police to "buzz-off" and refuses to turn down the music, he stands a very good chance of spending the remainder of the night in jail. In short, the police have the legal authority to at least temporarily resolve most problem situations (the noisy neighbor may crank up his stereo the next night) when you and I, as ordinary citizens, do not.

Yet to argue that the police never "negotiate" a settlement is to lose sight of reality. The fact is they often do. The police cannot ticket or arrest everyone who does not readily comply to their wishes. There are times when the police must adjust their position in order to keep a situation from getting out of hand, such as backing away from an angry crowd. Indeed, the interaction process requires some give-and-take—i.e., negotiation—by both citizen and police officer. Sometimes the negotiation is subtle (e.g., accepting a motorist's excuse for speeding), and sometimes it is not (fighting with a suspect who is resisting arrest). We return to the interactional interplay of police-citizen encounters in a more thorough manner in chapter 6.

POLICING: A CONSERVATIVE TASK

Another dimension of the social control responsibility of the police is their **power maintenance** function.[16] As enforcers of the law and protectors of the peace, the police are society's guardians of the existing social, political, and economic order. The occupational task of police work is inherently conservative because it nearly always involves the preservation of the status quo—i.e., enforcing the dominant rules of society, protecting existing institutions, upholding contemporary morality, and maintaining domestic peace. Rarely are the police vanguards of social change. Whether it is the riot police in South Korea (known as the "grabbers" because of their open-fingered gloves used for grabbing demonstrators and breaking their wrists), the abusive Republican Guard in Peru, or the patrol unit of any police department in the U.S., they are all employees of the established government system and therefore must work to preserve the established order.

NON-NEGOTIABLE COERCIVE FORCE?

(AP) Douglas, Wyo.—Giving new meaning to the phrase "the long arm of the law," a Douglas policeman provided spectators with a taste of the Old West when he used his rodeo roping experience to arrest a man on disorderly conduct charges at the Wyoming State Fair.

The officer was on mounted patrol at the State Fair grounds when he received a call Thursday night about a disorderly person at the fair, police Chief Larry Majerus said.

The suspect, who had been drinking, was difficult to arrest, so the mounted patrolman hauled out his rope and "caught the man by the heels," Majerus said.

Witnesses said the patrolman then handcuffed the suspect and raised his arms, yelling "Time," as calf and steer ropers do in rodeos.

Majerus declined to identify the patrolman or suspect, saying he didn't want to blow the incident out of proportion. But he said the officer has been with the force for about four years and had previous experience as a bull rider and team roper in rodeos.

Roping disruptive suspects "is definitely an effective method but is not used as an attention getter," Majerus said. "Those ropes can be dangerous, and it's a last resort technique."

Source: *Wilmington Morning Star*, Wilmington, NC, August, 1984.

POWER-MAINTENANCE: BLACK ENFORCEMENT OF WHITE MINORITY RULE

In a world complicated by divisive forces, hostility, and misunderstanding, the black police officers in South Africa are truly people "caught in the middle." In many quarters there is little sympathy for them, from black and white alike, but they carry out complex roles in helping to try and calm the turbulence in this troubled country.

Contrary to popular belief, the black South African police officer enjoys many of the same benefits of his or her white counterparts, including equal pay and benefits. The training curriculum is the same as for white officers, and the six month recruit school offers a rigorous mental and physical program which turns out classes ranging between one and two thousand officers. The graduation ceremonies bring the families of the new police officers from throughout the country to witness with pride what is obviously viewed by the recruits as a significant accomplishment in their lives.

To their detractors, they are viewed as turncoats, who have abandoned their people to help support the concept of apartheid, which maintains separation of the races. At the recruit level the schools remain separate, with separate institutions for whites, Indians, colored, and black officers. "It is only a matter of time," said one high ranking police official, before there will be integration in training," pointing out that other advanced courses for ranking police officials are integrated.

Black police officers have also begun to move through the ranks of the South African Police, and currently the highest rank achieved is that of colonel. In 1974 a decision was made by the police hierarchy to move toward a single force concept in terms of preparation. In 1975 uniforms were made the same, the difference in color and style were eliminated. There are black instructors in the training schools, working alongside white officers.

Currently, the South African police force consists of 29,394 white officers, 19,750 black officers, 2,300 Indian officers, and 4,137 colored officers. (A colored officer, in this country's unusual lexicon, means an individual of mixed blood).

With crime increasing, (7.3 percent in murder, 14 percent in robberies, 18 percent in auto thefts, 15 percent in burglaries), and an increase in drug abuse, expansion of the police is viewed as a high priority by the financially pressed government. Black officers from all tribal groups are drawn from the various provinces after completing an examination and background investigation. According to several police sources, there are about four or five applicants for every available job.

This is in a time when 48 black officers have been killed over the past two years, largely as a result of disorder in connection with demonstrations against apartheid or acts of terrorism committed by the African National Congress. During this time period three white police officers have been killed.

Among senior officials, who are candid, there is also the realization that South Africa is changing. "We've come a long way in ten years," he said, "and there are many who see the need for change. But it will take time. After all, it took us three hundred years to get here."

Meanwhile, on a lonely stretch of road, a black police officer and his white counterpart stand alongside a land rover. Two people caught in the middle.

Source: "The Black Police Officer in a Troubled World," *C. J. International*, vol. 3, no. 2 (March–April), 1987: 3–4.

The following hypothetical situation demonstrates the power maintenance function at work:

> Imagine that you are a police officer assigned to the fourteenth precinct,
> a high-crime, inner-city neighborhood populated mostly by lower-class resi-
> dents. It is a warm, late summer's afternoon when you receive a call over
> the car radio to respond to a "disturbance" at a local grocery store. As you
> pull your cruiser to the curb in front of the store you observe a group of
> eight to ten teenagers "hanging out." A couple of the boys are sitting on the
> curb, a few are leaning against the brick wall of the store smoking cigarettes,
> and a boy and girl are dancing to the music coming from a large "boom
> box." You make a mental note to yourself that the youth are seemingly well
> behaved and not too loud. Before you can completely exit your car, a white
> middle-aged man approaches you. He informs you that the youth have been
> in front of his store all afternoon and this has inconvenienced his customers.
> The owner insists a few customers have been scared away by the youth's pres-
> ence and that he cannot afford to lose any more business. The owner ap-
> pears highly frustrated by the whole situation. Although the youth have not
> been accused of committing any crime or of overtly harassing any customers,
> the owner still requests that you move them along. *What do you do?*

Perhaps the better question would be "What else could you do?" If you
are like most officers and wish to stay out of trouble with your superiors, you
will honor the store owner's request by dispersing the youth. After all, as most
"respectable" people would argue, the store owner has a right to conduct his
business and earn a living just as paying customers have a right to patronize
local merchants without being intimidated by a group of youth. This is
the power maintenance function at work. The police are an entrenched
conservative social institution that preserves the status quo. It enforces the will
of the powerful over the powerless, or at least the will of the more powerful
over the less powerful. It does these things with the consent and even blessing
of the majority of people. John Galliher makes a similar point in his critical
review of the police literature:

> Much of police behavior seems most easily explained if one considers that
> whenever there is a conflict of interests between the dominant classes in a society
> and less powerful groups, the police protect the interests of the former and
> regulate the behavior of the latter.[17]

Remember that the police are the most visible representative of the
"justice" system. Yet one sometimes wonders who suffers the greater "injustice"
from the very efforts of the police to preserve community order. Drawing from
the above case, is it the middle-class store owner who may lose some business
because the youth are hanging around his store, or is it the lower-class youth?
Chances are good that the youth have no jobs, no summer camp, no spacious
green back yards to play in and no car with which to escape to the malls, the
movies, or the beaches. Faced with limited means of geographical mobility,
inner-city youth find themselves trapped in a concrete jungle. With no area
of their own, they are forced to use public places as private spaces. And when

the lifestyle of one group clashes with the rights of another, the police generally establish social order by enforcing the will of the more powerful against the will of the less powerful.

As the reader has surely noticed, we have introduced two terms in sequential sections of this chapter that appear to be conceptually similar. In the last section the term *order maintenance* was introduced and described as one of the three major roles of American police. In this section the term *power maintenance* was discussed. To a significant degree the two terms are conceptually similar. Both terms emerge from the same social control responsibilities of the police and both reflect the conservative, status quo orientation of police work. The important difference between order maintenance and power maintenance is the level of analysis on which each term is properly conceptualized. As portrayed in figure 4.1, our use of the term order maintenance is on the *micro* (momentary, situational) level of analysis; power maintenance is conceptualized on the *macro* (institutional, historical) level. Referring again to the above hypothetical situation, the police were called in to "maintain order," yet over the long haul the cumulative effect of this type of police action is the "maintenance of the power structure" of society. The ultimate conclusion here is that if racism or sexism (or any other discriminatory "ism") exists in the formal social, political, and economic structure of a society, then racism and sexism will be an inevitable consequence in the actions of the police.

FIGURE 4.1
The Order Maintenance/Power Maintenance Connection

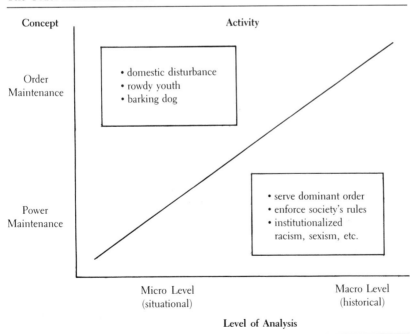

Do the police exist because they are truly needed, because they protect all of society and serve the greater good? Or do the police exist mainly to protect the rights and privileges of the wealthy? These questions are derived from a continuing debate in the literature regarding the true purpose of police in society.

Advocates of **functionalist theory** assume the police exist because they serve the interests of the most people. Functionalists argue that the police do not just protect the property and lives of the wealthy—everyone receives police protection. Indeed, the heaviest consumers of police services and protection are the poor, not the wealthy. But supporters of **conflict theory** disagree. Conflict theorists contend the functionalist notion about the police is a myth, conceived and perpetuated by those who stand to gain the most from the status quo, namely the political and economic elite. The argument that the poor receive the greatest benefit from the police is also a myth—the poor receive the greatest attention from the police, but this is because they are more violent and predatory and present a potential threat to existing social order that serves the wealthy so well.

The functionalist versus conflict debate cannot be resolved here, nor perhaps can it ever be resolved in the sense that one is proven true and the other false. Advocates of each can marshal data to support their stance. To a large extent, both functionalist theory and conflict theory offer important insights into the role of the police. For example, our study of the historical development of the police in chapter 2 was couched primarily in the functionalist perspective as we took note of the rise of the police in response to increased crime and disorder and the need for public protection. Yet the above discussion on the power maintenance function of the police is clearly within the realm of conflict theory. In short, our study of American police does not consciously strive to promote one theory over the other. We shall continue to draw from the best available literature regardless of the theoretical stance.

THE DILEMMA OVER DIRECTION

Public policing in the 1990s is at a crossroads. Police administrators, policymakers, and academicians are debating the appropriate direction for police work in the twenty-first century. The explicit crime fighting role of the police, which has dominated American police work during the latter two-thirds of this century, has not fulfilled our expectations. Crime and fear of crime is a more serious problem today than sixty years ago when we first embarked on the crime fighting mission. The burning question being asked by police scholars today is, "What now?"

The police have always been crime fighters, just as they have always been service providers and keepers of the peace. But they have not always been good crime fighters—poor leadership, minimal education and training of officers, political meddling, and widespread corruption have assured criminals they have little to fear from the police.

Beginning in the 1930s, police departments across the United States started focusing their energies almost exclusively on fighting crime. The police still handled the routine order maintenance and service calls, but with little sincerity or sense of commitment. Anything less than a call for a serious crime in progress was considered a nuisance. Requests for social service or order maintenance momentarily took the police away from their "main job," which they defined as law enforcement. Professors Moore and Kelling, two leading thinkers of modern American police, suggest a similar theme:

> To a great extent, the professional "crime fighting" strategy of policing that emerged after World War II is the current dominant police strategy. Its explicit goal is the control of crime, not maintaining public order or providing constabulary services. It depends on even-handed, non-intrusive enforcement of the laws, but only those laws with widespread public support.[18]

This new crime fighting strategy called for: (1) a highly mobile, motorized patrol force to create a sense of police omnipresence in the area; (2) rapid response (four minutes or less) to calls for help to increase the chances of apprehending offenders; and (3) vigorous retrospective investigation by highly trained detectives to solve crimes already committed.[19] As even-handed, corruption-resistant law enforcers, these "new and improved" professional crime fighters were not only presumed to be better at controlling crime, they were

Los Angeles police stand over a group of looting suspects in the midst of the 1992 riots.

also removed from the daily meddling of the powerfully intrusive political machines.

The police pursued a policy of keeping their relationship with the community from becoming overly warm and friendly. Past experience taught them that excessive familiarity between the police and the public breeds lax enforcement. The frosty personality and rigid repartee of T.V.'s Sergeant Joe Friday ("Just the facts, Ma'am") illustrates the professional prototype of the times.

Currently we realize the exclusive crime fighting strategy that has dominated policing in recent decades has failed. Research convincingly establishes three sobering facts.[20] First, increasing the number of police officers and heightening the visibility of patrol cars does not have an appreciable effect on the crime rate. Even with today's improved technology and administrative efficiency, the police are not much better at fighting crime than they were fifty years ago. Second, high mobility and rapid response to most calls does not significantly improve the apprehension rate (although rapid response to emergency calls and "crime in progress" calls is important). The reason why rapid response has limited benefits is because many crime victims and witnesses wait a considerable amount of time (out of shock, disbelief, or initial indecision) before calling the police. This means that the strategy of keeping the entire patrol force ready in their cars for a four minute response to every call is not necessary. And third, without the active cooperation of victims and witnesses, the solvability of many crimes is greatly diminished. The tailored aloofness generated by the autonomous, professional crime fighting strategy of the past half century has fostered a sterile and largely uncooperative relationship between the police and the public, a relationship that is hardly conducive to the good-faith exchange of information.

It is critically important to understand the overall argument being presented. We are not suggesting that the police are so impotent as crime fighters that the entire crime fighting mission ought to be scrapped; on the contrary, the amount of crime in our society is deeply troubling and we desperately need the police to help contain it. The argument here is that the particular crime fighting strategy the police have chosen to pursue—one of overemphasizing their crime fighting role while simultaneously minimizing their order maintenance and social service roles—is seriously flawed. Remember that officers spend tremendous time and energy keeping the peace and rendering assistance to citizens. Regardless of how annoying some calls may seem to officers (e.g., "drunk down," "fender-bender," "barking dog"), citizens who request the help of the police take these problems seriously. Moreover, if these service and peacekeeping duties are done properly, the police can go a long way toward improving their relations with the public and allaying citizen fear of crime. As Moore and Kelling declare, "The bitter irony . . . is that it is probably these constabulary functions, properly performed, that make people feel safer in their neighborhoods than a drop in the 'crime rate' as measured in the *Uniform Crime Reports.*"[21]

The crossroads we spoke of at the beginning of this section refers to the direction American police should pursue in the near future. This "evolving

POLICE AT THE CROSSROADS

The core mission of the police is to control crime. No one disputes this. Indeed, professional crime fighting enjoys wide public support as the basic strategy of policing precisely because it embodies a deep commitment to this objective. In contrast, other proposed strategies such as problem-solving or community policing appear on the surface to blur this focus. If these strategies were to leave the community more vulnerable to criminal victimization, they would be undesirable alternatives. In judging the value of alternative police strategies in controlling crime, however, one should not be misled by rhetoric or mere expressed commitment to the goal; one must keep one's eye on demonstrated effectiveness in achieving the goal.

Professional crime-fighting now relies predominantly on three tactics: (1) motorized patrol; (2) rapid response to calls for service; and (3) retrospective investigation of crimes. Over the past few decades, police responsiveness has been enhanced by connecting police to citizens by telephones, radios, and cars, and by matching police officer schedules and locations to anticipated calls for service. The police focus on serious crime has also been sharpened by screening calls for service, targeting patrol, and developing forensic technology (e.g., automated fingerprint systems, computerized criminal record files, etc.)

Although these tactics have scored their successes, they have been criticized within and outside policing for being reactive rather than proactive. They have also been criticized for failing to prevent crime.

Reactive tactics have some virtues, of course. The police go where crimes have occurred and when citizens have summoned them; otherwise, they do not intrude. The police keep their distance from the community, and thereby retain their impartiality. They do not develop the sorts of relationships with citizens that could bias their responses to crime incidents. These are virtues insofar as they protect citizens from an overly intrusive, too familiar police.

Moreover, the reactive tactics do have preventive effects—at least in theory. The prospect of the police arriving at a crime in progress as a result of a call or a chance observation is thought to deter crimes. The successful prosecution of offenders (made possible by retrospective investigation) is also thought to deter offenders. And even if it does not deter, a successfully prosecuted investigation incapacitates criminals who might otherwise go on to commit other crimes.

Finally, many police forces have developed proactive tactics to deal with crime problems that could not be handled through conventional reactive methods. In drug dealing, organized crime, and vice enforcement, for example, where no immediate victims exist to mobilize the police, the police have developed special units which rely on informants, covert surveillance, and undercover investigations rather than responses to calls for service. In the area of juvenile offenses where society's stake in preventing crimes seems particularly great, the police have created athletic leagues, formed partnerships with schools to deal with drug abuse and truancy, and so on. It is not strictly accurate, then, to characterize modern policing as entirely reactive.

Still, the criticism of the police as being too reactive has some force. It is possible that the police could do more to control serious crime than they now achieve. Perhaps research will yield technological breakthroughs that will dramatically improve the productivity of police investigation. For now, however, the greatest potential for improved crime control may not lie in the continued enhancement of response times, patrol tactics, and investigative techniques. Rather, improved crime control can be achieved by (1) diagnosing and managing problems in the community that produce serious crimes; (2) fostering closer relations with the community to facilitate crime solving; and (3) building self-defense capabilities within the community itself. Among the results may be increased apprehension of criminals. To the extent that problem-solving or community strategies of policing direct attention to and prepare the police to exploit local knowledge and capacity to control crime, they will be useful to the future of policing.

Source: Mark H. Moore, Robert C. Trojanowicz, and George L. Kelling, "Crime and Policing," *Perspectives on Policing*, no. 2., U.S. Department of Justice, National Institute of Justice (Washington, DC: U.S. Government Printing Office, June 1988), pp. 1–2.

strategy of policing" is a decision which cuts to the heart of policing.[22] According to current thinking, what is needed is a better balance among the three major police roles and a driving commitment by police leaders to reintegrate the police back into the community. The evolving police strategy taking shape today is something called **community policing**. Community policing is actually more than a simple technique for the police to follow— it is a philosophy that demands a closer, almost intimate relationship between the police and the community.[23] (Community policing is discussed more thoroughly in chapter 5.) The evolving strategy of policing is the main reason why *foot patrol* is making such a strong come-back today. This is an attempt to get officers out of their cars and back into the neighborhoods they serve.

CONCLUSION

The central question this chapter addressed is "What is policing?" In other words, what is the special contribution that general duty public police make to modern society. The answer turned out to be rather involved. Policing American society is multifaceted and quite complex. The literature on police work suggests the police serve three primary roles: order maintenance, social service, and law enforcement. As we discovered, however, these separate functions often converge on the streets. Any one radio call for service may require the officer to simultaneously perform all three roles (peacekeeper, social worker, law enforcer). In rapidly deteriorating situations, the officer must learn to quickly recognize the cues and switch from one role (perhaps the helpful civil servant) to another.

What appears to be uppermost in the minds of citizens when they "call the cops" is the authority of the police to use coercive force. Citizens frequently find themselves powerless to resolve everyday annoyances like loud parties or roughhousing youth, so they request police intervention to bring the problem to an end. Egon Bittner suggests that the authority of the police to use coercive force is non-negotiable, which is to say that the police have the wherewithal to ultimately "win" any police-citizen confrontation even if the police have to make an arrest on a minor charge to establish an end to the disturbance. The police may arrest for disorderly conduct, interfering with an officer's duty, public intoxication, or some other chargeable violation of the law. Carl Klockars has expanded upon Bittner's idea. Klockars suggests the police are *"individuals given the general right to use coercive force by the state within the state's domestic territory."*[24] While others are given the right by the state to use coercive force at certain times and specified places (parents, school teachers, prize fighters), their authority to use coercive force is not general. Parents usually can only spank their own children, school teachers can only discipline their own students (and only during the school day when the teacher is directly in charge of them), and prize fighters can only commit assault and battery in the ring. The police are not so limited.

law enforcement
policing
social control
norms
anomie
folkways, mores, laws
first line of defense
second line of defense
inner and outer containments
blue curtain

blue veil
final line of defense
order maintenance
social service
law enforcement
non-negotiable coercive force
power maintenance
functionalist theory
conflict theory
community policing

DISCUSSION QUESTIONS ──────────────────────────

1. Do we need the police? Could we get along without them?
2. If you answered "yes, we do need the police," and "no, we could not get along without them," as I am pretty sure you did, please remember that we did get along without the police for 99.9 percent of human history. If you respond to this fact by saying, "but things have changed," then what has changed? Have people changed? Has evolution turned us into vile creatures and predatory monsters, or has something about our civilization changed? If so, then what?
3. Discuss the major roles of the police. In what ways does the entertainment industry alter the public's perception of the police?
4. What do we mean when we say the police have the authority to use non-negotiable coercive force? Do the police ever have to "negotiate"?
5. Differentiate the order maintenance function of the police from the power maintenance function. Why is police work inherently a conservative task?

CHAPTER FIVE

POLICE AND THE PUBLIC

The police are the public and
the public are the police.
  —*Sir Robert Peel*

In Western liberal-democratic societies such as ours, there has always been a certain amount of distrust of the police. After all, the police are highly visible representatives of the state, symbolizing state power and control over the lives of people. While nearly two centuries of "successful" public policing has allayed most of the deeply felt skepticism toward the police, a residual distrust still lingers.

In a society that has never known freedom, a society where individual rights are sacrificed in favor of state control, people accept the rule of the police as being tolerable, if not natural. By way of contrast, we carefully control the authority of the police in our society. We do so in a number of ways. For example, the Constitution of the United States, statutory laws, and court decisions all serve as an important check on the activities of the police.

There is another important check over the police that is the focus of this chapter. The police are also controlled by the close scrutiny of the public. Public opinion is a powerful political force that deeply affects all police departments. Given sufficient community consternation, negative public opinion can bend the back of any police department; if properly managed, the collective will of the people can fundamentally shape the police in positive and lasting ways.

POLICE AND COMMUNITY RELATIONS

What has been the relationship between the police and the community over the past century? Depending on the specific period being considered, and keeping in mind the many qualifications that should be made, the relationship might be described as being good, bad, or very bad. Currently the relationship might be described as being fairly "good" in the sense that the nation seems to be firmly behind the police in an effort to control crime and restore order to our communities. Nearly two decades of a national *get tough* attitude toward crime has paid handsome dividends for police in terms of their relations with the community; surprisingly, even the inability of the police to stem the wave of crime has produced a groundswell of support for our beleaguered police.

Certainly there are "hot spots" of contention that occasionally flare up to test the patience of the police and the public with each other. The riots that swept across many cities in the spring of 1992 following the Los Angeles police brutality trial in the Rodney King case is evidence of the continuing tension between the police and certain communities, particularly in black and minority neighborhoods. Indeed, the image of the police in many lower-class minority neighborhoods is seriously, if not permanently, tarnished. However, the relationship between the police and mainstream, middle class America in general appears to be positive.

We do not have to travel far back in time to witness widespread disenchantment with the police. As recently as the 1960s the relationship between the police and many communities progressed from "bad" to "very bad." The decade of the 1960s was an extremely important period for American police in terms of their public relations—it was a time of intense public scrutiny and frequent critical lashings from numerous sectors of society. In particular, blacks, the poor, and the young voiced their grievances against the police, voices that were significantly amplified by a sympathetic media and a watchful court system. With their backs to the wall, the police found it imperative to reevaluate their longstanding policies and practices in an effort to appease the public. Perhaps the greatest lesson to be learned from the police-community relations crisis of the 1960s is that, in the end, the will of a united community prevails.

Prelude to Trouble

In the "long hot summer" of 1967, Americans stood in shock as riots flared up in cities across the nation. In Watts, Newark, and Detroit the riots were especially bloody. It was during this heated time that the police found themselves in a very unenviable position. They were called to the front to fight in a battle—a battle being waged on the streets of their own towns and among their own people. Dressed in riot gear, lobbing tear gas canisters at approaching mobs, it is hard to imagine a time when the police seemed further removed from the communities they served and the people they protected.

There were plenty of signs prior to the "long hot summer" that social tensions were fast approaching the boiling point. Increased crime, heightened

Police officers search black youths in 1966 after a bloody afternoon of lootings, shootings, burnings, and beatings in Watts.

publicity of police scandals and corruption, the rebellious baby boom generation, campus unrest, and a growing sentiment against the Vietnam war were
all partly responsible for the general social unease.[1] The most pressing issue
of the times, however, and the one that produced the deepest cleavage between
the police and the community, was the **civil rights movement.**

The civil rights *era* marked its formal beginning with the 1954 racial
desegregation case of ***Brown v. Board of Education.***[2] Prior to Brown, in *Plessy
v. Ferguson* (1896), the Supreme Court ruled that the doctrine of "separate
but equal" for blacks and whites was constitutionally permissible.[3] The *Plessy*
case placed the court's stamp of approval on so-called Jim Crow laws. Jim
Crow laws allowed the practice of racial segregation to exist virtually everywhere; eating and drinking establishments, residential neighborhoods,
churches, schools, public parks, and even prisons were racially segregated.
The *Brown* case overturned the earlier *Plessy* decision. Speaking for a unani-
mous court in the *Brown* case, Chief Justice Earl Warren ruled that segregated
schools for blacks and whites, regardless of how equivalent the two systems
may appear, were a violation of the "equal protection" clause of the Fourteenth
Amendment and henceforth unconstitutional.

The civil rights *movement* marked its formal beginning in early February
of 1960. Inspired by the nonviolent, sit-in style of protest popularized by
Mahatma Gandhi in the 1930s, four university freshmen at the all-black North
Carolina Agricultural and Technical School sat at a segregated lunch counter
at the Woolworth's store in Greensboro, North Carolina. One of the black
youths ordered a doughnut and coffee, but the waitress refused to serve him.
The waitress pointed to a sign on the wall to remind the youths that "Negroes"
were allowed to purchase snacks in the store, but they were not permitted to
sit next to whites at the counter and eat. Determined to proceed with their
demands, the four black students refused to leave. The store manager instructed the waitress to ignore them.

During the entire ordeal, a Greensboro police officer stood a menacing
watch behind the four youths with nightstick in hand, yet he never intervened.
The nonviolent nature of the protest kept the situation from becoming disorderly. Finally, out of utter exasperation by the youths' refusal to leave, the
manager closed the lunch counter early.

Word of the youths' daring deed spread quickly across the college campus. By the next morning more than a dozen fellow students perched themselves at the Woolworth's lunch counter, and two days later more than a
thousand protesters, black and white, demonstrated outside the Greensboro
Woolworth's store.[4] Over the ensuing months, nonviolent public demonstrations and sit-ins became commonplace throughout the South.

The sit-in by the "Greensboro Four" was not the first act of defiance by
Southern blacks. Previous public protests sponsored by the National Association for the Advancement of Colored People (NAACP) and Southern Christian
Leadership Conference (SCLC) were staged, but the timing was premature to
ignite a widespread social movement. Rosa Parks' bold refusal to give up her
seat on a bus for a white man in Montgomery, Alabama in 1955 received
national attention, but this too was premature and did not spark a major

movement. Even the periodic riots of the 1950s could not mobilize the masses. But by the early 1960s, the time had come. The Greensboro sit-in was the spark that ignited the civil rights movement.

Most of the civil rights victories of the 1950s were won in the courts.[5] The landmark *Brown* case and several less famous lower court decisions were gradually eroding the laws allowing racial segregation. Yet the courts were limited in what they could accomplish on their own. In particular, the "equal protection" clause under the Fourteenth Amendment allowed the courts to ban *state sponsored discrimination in public places* (e.g., in schools and public facilities), but the courts were unable to outlaw discrimination in places not operated by the government (restaurants, stores, movie houses, the workplace, etc.). In other words, merchants who wanted to operate a segregated establishment or employers who preferred to hire only whites could continue to do so.

Congress gave the courts and the civil rights movement a major boost with the passage of the **Civil Rights Act of 1964.** The 1964 act significantly expanded the court's ability to outlaw racial, religious, and ethnic discrimination in the private sector.[6] With the backing of the federal courts and now Congress, the civil rights movement had leaped to the forefront on the public agenda. The impressive victories gave the civil rights movement increased visibility, a higher level of legitimacy, *and a new urgency*—just as racial and ethnic barriers in society began to crumble, expectations for immediate change began to soar. Blacks and other minority groups were no longer dreaming of social equality, they were now demanding it!

As the decade of the 1960s wore on, the struggle for equal rights and equal opportunities became more intense. The number of public demonstrations increased as did their volatility. As a result, the police were ordered to intervene more often. Although the police were not ultimately responsible for what the blacks were fighting against (institutionalized racism is deeply ingrained in American society), as the most visible symbols of "the system," the police were literally drawn into the middle of the conflict. They were also the target of frequent charges of brutality, harassment, and unequal protection of blacks. As the demonstrations became more violent, the police had to intervene with force; when the demonstrations turned into riots, the police went to riot gear and tear gas.

The Crisis: Conflict and Confrontation

To many observers, what is most astonishing about the urban disorders (e.g., Chicago, Detroit, Newark, and Watts) and campus uprisings (Columbia, Harvard, Berkeley, and Kent State) of the late 1960s and early 1970s was the small, seemingly insignificant events that ignited entire riots. Quite often the events that incited the mobs to action were linked to the police. An ordinary arrest, a routine raid, or even an unconfirmed rumor can engulf an entire town in rage when tension and hostility are already running high.

Perhaps no American city has experienced more racial tension and hostility in this century than Detroit, Michigan. In the past half century Detroit has had two major riots, one in 1943 and another in 1967. The riot of 1947 was started by the false rumor that "a Negro woman and her baby had been thrown into the river" following a fight on a bridge with some whites.[7] Within hours, over four hundred stores owned by whites were looted or destroyed by the black rioters, and many blacks and whites were injured in scuffles when the whites began to retaliate. The Detroit riot of 1967, which escalated into the deadliest and most destructive riot of the turbulent sixties, was set off by a routine police raid of an after-hours night club on Twelfth Street.[8] Forty-three people in all were killed and a half billion dollars worth of property was destroyed. Robert Trojanowicz details the event:

> That same after-hours club had been raided twice before in the recent past, but what the police did not know was that on Saturday night, July 22, the establishment was hosting a party for several veterans, including two servicemen recently back from Vietnam. This meant that it took the police far longer than anticipated, about two hours, to remove the 82 patrons with what some people on the street viewed as excessive force.
>
> The raid started at 3 a.m. At about 5 a.m., someone threw a bottle through the window of a patrol car; then, like a scene in the Spike Lee movie about a race riot, someone threw a litter basket through a store window. At some point, a young man in a shirt with green sleeves galvanized the crowd by shouting, "We're going to have a riot," and within an hour, thousands of people had spilled into the street. By the end of the week, the police and the National Guard had picked up 7,200 people.[9]

According to one Detroit journalist, the riot of 1967 has never really ended; today it is a "riot in slow motion," as deadly racial violence continues on the streets of Detroit. Other U.S. cities are experiencing the same problem.

Discontented crowds transform into violent mobs with amazing quickness. Once mobilized in collective behavior, the psychology of group dynamics can motivate even nonviolent people to action. Lost in the crowd and intoxicated by the rush of emotions, cowards become brave, the weak become mighty. The police can be easily caught off guard.

The basic crowd control strategy of the police is to try to reduce the level of tension in the group. Specific techniques such as diverting the crowd's attention away from their common goal, dividing the crowd psychologically, and minimizing the influence of the leaders are typically recommended. However, when semi-orderly *crowds* transform into disorderly *mobs*, communication links between the police and the group rapidly disintegrate. The basic mob control strategy at this point normally requires direct police action in order to protect people and property. For example, shortly after the start of the 1992 Los Angeles riot, Governor Pete Wilson activated the National Guard and notified President Bush that federal troops might be needed. Within a few days, 8,500 combined Marines, Army, and National Guard troops were stationed inside the riot areas helping to restore order. One week after the riots began, the police had recorded over 15,000 arrests.

POLICE-COMMUNITY RELATIONS PROGRAMS

The upheaval of the 1960s spawned a major crisis in police-community relations. Charges of police brutality, harassment, and unequal protection of the law were common—and true in many cases! The crisis in relations was not with middle-class, middle-age mainstream society, for this sizable group of Americans was appalled by the pervasive social unrest. Indeed, much of "middle America" stood firmly behind the police and relied heavily on them to restore order.

The crisis in police-community relations was concentrated among the lower class black population. The *National Advisory Commission on Civil Disorders* (better known as the Kerner Commission) called attention to the dismal quality of relations between the police and the black community in its 1968 report:

> The police are not merely a "spark" factor. To some Negroes police have come to symbolize white power, white racism, and white repression. And the fact is that many police do reflect and express these white attitudes. The atmosphere of hostility and cynicism is reinforced by a widespread belief among Negroes in the existence of police brutality and in a "double standard" of justice and protection—one for Negroes and one for whites.[10]

In response to the crisis of the 1960s, a variety of **police-community relations** (PCR) programs were developed. PCR units are comprised of police

---

MIAMI—RIOT IN SLOW MOTION

Miami—A police officer was sentenced Wednesday to seven years in prison for the deaths of two black men in an incident that ignited three days of racial violence a year ago.

William Lozano, 31, was convicted last month on two counts of manslaughter for fatally shooting an unarmed black motorcyclist on a street in the Overtown section, sending the vehicle crashing into a car and killing the motorcycle's passenger.

"This court cannot do perfect justice in this case," said Dade Circuit Judge Joseph Farina, who called the deaths and resultant trial a "tragic incident."

The January 16, 1989, deaths led to the city's fourth round of racial unrest in the 1980s, all linked to the killings of blacks by white officers. In two of those cases, acquittals of the policemen had sparked racial violence, and police braced for renewed rioting as Lozano's trial neared an end last month. But on December 7, a racially mixed jury convicted Lozano.

Police said the city was quiet after Wednesday's sentencing.

"Everything is good, there's no disturbance, no nothing," said police spokesman George Law.

Outside the courtroom, Patricia Lloyd, sister of slain motorcyclist Clement Lloyd, 23, said only: "I wish it had been longer."

Ray Fauntroy, head of the Southern Christian Leadership Conference here, said he was disappointed with the sentence.

Blacks "get seven years just for stealing a loaf of bread," Fauntroy said. "This officer . . . will be out in two or three years."

Hogan, who had recommended a 12-year sentence, said he was satisfied.

"It's a just sentence," he said.

Lozano could have faced a punishment of 12 to 17 years under state sentencing guidelines.

Defense attorneys from the beginning bitterly criticized the case as an effort to ease racial tensions in Miami rather than give their client a fair trial.

"If Officer Lozano was black, he never would have been charged with a crime. If the two people on the motorcycle were white, he never would have been charged with a crime," defense attorney Mark Seiden told the judge.

Source: *Wilmington Morning Star*, Wilmington, NC, Thursday, January 15, 1990.

officers who are assigned as "community relations specialists." These officers have the specific task of enhancing the quality of relations between the police and the community. PCR officers actively seek out opportunities for community contact as a means to open channels of communication. The common methods for increasing community contact include attending civic meetings, speaking to different community groups, giving crime prevention tips to local businesses, and going into the schools to talk with children.

The number of officers assigned to a PCR unit depends mostly on department size and the existing quality of relations with the community. Smaller departments may be able to spare no more than one officer on a part-time basis; larger departments may be able to assign several officers to PCR units in each precinct. PCR units normally operate as autonomous units and report directly to a division commander.[11]

The idea of police-community relations did not originate in the sixties. University of Chicago Professor Joseph Lohman and Harvard Professor Gordon W. Allport were teaching courses in police-minority group relations as early as 1942.[12] The first official PCR unit was formed in 1957 in St. Louis, Missouri, due mainly to the lobbying efforts of the National Conference of Christians and Jews (NCCJ).[13] Jack Greene has traced the changing style and emphases of PCR programs since the original St. Louis program:

> The ebb and flow of PCR programs has changed over the years. Prior to the mid-1960s these programs emphasized open communication and a dialogue between the police and community residents. Many were directed at the issue of race relations. The urban turmoil of the 1960s resulted in the development of many action-oriented programs that emphasized some form of community participation often through team policing strategies. Throughout the 1970s PCR changed direction stressing community crime prevention rather than police and community relations. Programs aimed at reducing the opportunity to commit crime flourished. In the 1980s community crime prevention has given way to a raft of programs aimed at improving community social cohesion, many of which fall under the rubric of "community policing."[14]

Public Relations versus Community Relations

A close examination of the many types of PCR programs suggests there is little agreement on what police-community relations actually mean.[15] Scores of ill-conceived programs have been initiated by police professionals with good intentions, yet eventually abandoned because of the absence of an organized and accepted body of knowledge to guide their development.

A basic source of confusion in many programs has been the failure to distinguish **public relations** from **community relations**. Let's take a closer look at each concept.

Public Relations

Public relations, or PR, is concerned largely with *image building* and *looking good* in the eyes of the public. Madison Avenue is best known for its PR and "hype," where high-paid marketing executives peddle products to

American consumers through sleek packaging and sexy advertising. Similarly, PCR programs that only emphasize PR are attempting to "sell" the police to the public. Prearranged photo opportunities, voluntary press releases, safety lectures, citizen-ride-alongs in patrol cars, tours of the police station, and an active speakers bureau are all in the realm of PR.

The effective use of PR is a powerful management tool. Most organizations utilize PR to some degree (e.g., businesses, the military, schools and universities). Police departments are no exception. A properly managed PR program can generate benefits for both the department and the community. As important information about the department is routinely communicated to citizens—including information that may be negative—the public becomes more knowledgeable of department affairs. The public also becomes more trusting of its police since the department harbors few secrets. Although an "informed" public is not always a "supportive" one, the frequent exchange of information is an essential first step in developing positive police-community relations.

But the exclusive use of public relations is not sufficient to substantiate a meaningful PCR program. Whenever PR programs are disguised as bona fide PCR programs, a critical one-third of the equation is left out—i.e., the "C," meaning community. Police PR is characterized by a one-way flow of information from the police to the community. The lack of community involvement is notable. Because there are actually many "communities" within the jurisdiction of a single police department (i.e., neighborhoods separated by socioeconomic status, religion, ethnicity, race, business sectors, college campuses, retirement enclaves, etc.), PR efforts often target the wrong "community."[16] Business and civic groups welcome police speakers and generally provide an appreciative, nonthreatening audience. Yet these are hardly the "communities" the police need to reach the most. As a result, a pure PR approach may unintentionally alienate certain community residents who feel the police are not addressing their needs. Finally, PR is wholly inadequate as a preventive, problem-solving mechanism. Public relations is more of a management tool to build the department's image while defending their current policies. It is not a mechanism for making genuine improvements.

Community Relations

Community relations, or CR, goes beyond public relations. In its ideal form, CR combines an administrative philosophy with the sincere commitment of the entire department to create a good-faith, two-way flow of information between the police and the public. Unlike PR, community relations welcomes citizen participation. As partners in the ongoing struggle against crime, the community helps the police identify problem areas and establish enforcement priorities. Community input is also solicited for proposed remedies. PCR programs based on community relations emphasize a preventive approach; the idea is that it is better to resolve problems before they occur than to react to a community crisis that already exists.

Police managers also must be aware of potential problems of CR programs. By the very nature of their close contact with community residents, community relations officers are often privy to sensitive information. For instance, they may hear through the rumor mill that "Bobby the Bookie" is back in town, or that a local youth gang is out to get a member of a rival gang. Community relations specialists may also hear about the misdeeds of fellow officers. How should this intelligence-type information be used?

Obviously the sensitive information is of vital interest to the department. As a fully sworn officer of the law, the community relations specialist has an enforcement responsibility that precludes him or her from simply ignoring the facts. But if the community relations officer is routinely used as a "spy" to gather intelligence information, word will quickly hit the streets. Community residents who are already skeptical of the police will become even more suspicious.[17] Conversely, the morale of the department will suffer greatly if officers on regular assignment believe that CR officers work closely with "internal affairs." Whisenand and Ferguson offer police managers some sound advice on how to avoid such dilemmas:

> While the PCR unit is the source of a great deal of information that should not be ignored, the information should be primarily utilized for training and

J. EDGAR HOOVER—PR GENIUS?

(*FBI Most Wanted*)—America has always been a nation of superlatives. We thrive on recognition of the best and brightest, eager to know everything about the fastest car or tallest building, anxious to discover for ourselves which movie star or athlete is the highest paid. We publish lists and books of lists, recording every detail of the largest, smallest, best, or worst in every field of human enterprise or natural phenomena. From the ridiculous to the sublime, we dote on categories, ranks, and ratings.

What, therefore, could be more natural—and more American—than an official list of outlaws who are deemed the worst and most notorious in our society?

Throughout the 1930s, "public enemies" were named and numbered by the press, contenders moving up the ladder as their predecessors were consigned to prison or the grave. With notoriety came nicknames—Scarface, Mad Dog, Pretty Boy—designed to make the headlines sing, surrounding thieves and killers with an air of romance and adventure, elevating some to the undeserved status of folk heroes before they were finally cut down. And yet, for all the fanfare, there existed no official list of public enemies until the decade after World War II.

As 1949 was drawing to a close, a feature writer for the International News Service—predecessor of United Press International—asked the FBI to name the "toughest guys" whom Bureau agents were pursuing at the moment. The resultant story proved so popular and generated so much positive publicity that FBI Director J. Edgar Hoover officially inaugurated the Bureau's "Ten Most Wanted Fugitives" program a few weeks later, on March 14, 1950.

Criteria for the selection of a "Top Ten" fugitive is specialized, befitting designation as among the worst of several hundred thousand criminals at large on any given day. For openers, the individual must have a lengthy history of conflict with the law or, if a new offender, must be counted as a special danger to society because of pending charges. Sheer ferocity is not enough, however. It must also be determined that publicity afforded by the program, coast to coast, will be of positive assistance in the apprehension of a fugitive. Accordingly, the candidate should not already be notorious from prior publicity—like Patty Hearst and her abductors in the 1970s—as this defeats the purpose of the "Top Ten" list.

The single purpose of the "Ten Most Wanted" list, like other "top ten" programs, is the genera-

bringing about understanding and change in the broadest, most positive sense. The PCR officer must not be placed in a compromising situation with the community. It is only reasonable that he or she likewise should not be compromised in his or her own department. [18]

Undoubtedly, delicate situations are bound to occasionally arise as a result of having a PCR program. However, the advantages of having an effective, proactive PCR program greatly outweigh the disadvantages of not having one.

Evaluating PCR Programs

It is not easy to judge the overall effectiveness of PCR programs. The great variety of programs, varying levels of administrative support, and different program objectives makes evaluation difficult. Complicating the task is the problem that most programs have never been critically evaluated. Surely there are many disappointing PCR programs that have fallen short of their stated goals, just as there have been a number of well-designed and well-run pro-

---

tion of publicity. Unlike the other lists, however, ego and commercialism play no part in execution of the Bureau's program. In the case of wanted fugitives, publicity becomes a searing spotlight, stripping them of precious anonymity, applying heat that leads directly to their capture and confinement.

How effective is the program? In the past four decades, 420 fugitives have been named to the FBI's list. Of those, 391 have been apprehended by authorities; process was dismissed against another fifteen . . . and four were ultimately dropped because they no longer fit "Top Ten" criteria in some manner. Of the fugitives arrested, some 115—29 percent—were caught as a direct result of citizen cooperation; many others were corraled by local officers who memorized the information on their federal WANTED bulletins.

In short, the program works.

Critics of the Bureau's "Top Ten" program emphasize three main concerns. For some, the program is a mere "publicity event," and so a waste of time and money. Others criticize the list for the attention paid to "small-time" criminals,

while leaders of the Mafia and major traffickers in drugs remain at large. A final criticism deals with brief expansion of the program in the 1970s, with emphasis on left-wing radicals, asserting that the list was thereby made "political."

Imitation, we are told, is the sincerest form of flattery. With that in mind, it is significant to note that many other law enforcement agencies have borrowed freely from the Bureau in the past four decades, publishing their own "Most Wanted" lists of desperate fugitives. The Royal Canadian Mounted Police inaugurated the "Canadian Top Ten" in January 1952, and other agencies have followed suit. Kentucky's state police created a "Top Five" list in June 1965, followed closely by Ohio. United States marshals stalk their own "Top Fifteen," and the concept has filtered down to a number of big-city police departments, as well. A weekly television program on "America's Most Wanted" has been credited with more than one arrest per week since its debut in February 1988 (including three of the FBI's own "Top Ten" felons).

Source: Michael Newton and Judy Ann Newton, *The FBI Most Wanted: An Encyclopedia* (New York: Garland Publishing, 1989), pp. xiii–xvi.

grams. Among the successful PCR programs, all have had at least one crucial element in common: a police leadership that is sincere about police-community relations and willing to commit department resources and personnel to the program. Anything less than the complete effort of the entire department to developing an ongoing, good-faith relationship with the community is wasted effort. Radelet refers to this as the *total orientation* of the department. He describes this as "an attitude and an emphasis for all phases of police work, not merely for a specialized unit in the department."[19]

The unfortunate fact is that the goal of "total orientation" is seldom achieved. For instance, when community tensions peaked in the late 1960s and early 1970s, a large number of police departments rushed to develop some type of PCR program to help avert a crisis. Not surprisingly, many of these programs were little more than half-hearted PR ploys to try to improve the police image. While one or two of the more personable and articulate officers would serve as the department's "community relations specialist" at business luncheons, school assemblies, and so forth, extolling the virtues of the police department, it was "work as usual" for the remaining officers. Street cops did not think PR or CR was their job. Residents living in lower-class, high-crime neighborhoods where police and community tensions were high quickly realized that little had changed. For them, PCR was only cheap "lip service," a smoke screen to hide the real intentions of the police. Interestingly, many of these PCR programs were eliminated once the turbulent times ended. This supports the argument that many of these earlier PCR programs were more PR than CR.

Mixed PCR Programs

Many observers of the police recognize that benefits may be gained from both public relations and community relations. Thus, police managers have developed a variety of mixed PCR programs.[20] These programs blend the central elements of public relations with community relations. We shall briefly examine a few of the more prominent mixed programs.

Mini-Stations

Police mini-stations (also called substations or storefront centers) operate as miniature police stations. Mini-stations are similar to the well-known Japanese *kobans*, or "police boxes," which are staffed by one or two officers. Located primarily in lower-class, high-crime areas, mini-stations are used for a variety of purposes such as meeting places, information centers, and for fielding citizen complaints. Because mini-stations help make the department more accessible to residents, they serve as a useful bridge between the police and the community.

Despite the advantages mini-stations offer the department and community, a common problem is that the officers who work them are often "looked down upon" by regular patrol officers as doing "soft" police work, not "hard" police work. Skolnick and Bailey describe the tension that existed between mini-station officers and regular patrol officers in Detroit.[21] They report how patrol officers seldom consulted with mini-station officers on crime-related matters. Even patrol commanders showed disdain for the mini-stations. Skolnick and Bailey quote one commander as saying, "Shiiit, we don't even know they're there."[22] Given the relatively low status of mini-stations in American policing, they are often the first area to be cut when department funds are scarce.

Neighborhood Watch Programs

One of the most popular PCR program emulated nationwide is the neighborhood watch. The key to the neighborhood watch is that community residents become the "eyes and ears" of the police. With the training and support of the local police, residents assume an active crime prevention role in their neighborhoods. At the outset of establishing a neighborhood watch program, a crime prevention officer from the police department meets with concerned residents at one of the neighbor's homes. The officer explains to the residents how the neighborhood watch program works and advises them on useful crime prevention tips. The first meeting is intended to galvanize the support of residents and to break the ice among neighbors; as is often the case, neighbors who live close by may not even know each other. The better neighbors know one another, the better they can monitor suspicious strangers and peculiar events.

Whether or not neighborhood watch programs are successful at preventing crime is unclear. There is some argument that neighborhoods organized enough to establish a watch are not likely to have a serious crime problem in the first place. Others contend that neighborhood watches simply displace crime to other neighborhoods. Perhaps the major advantage of a watch program is that it helps improve citizens' feelings of safety in their neighborhoods because they are personally involved in controlling the problem.

Operation Identification

This program was started in Monterey Park, California in the early 1960s. As with the neighborhood watch program, Operation Identification has spread nationwide. An identification number is inconspicuously etched into a person's valuable property. Stereos, televisions, home computers, and other items easily taken in a burglary are marked. The person's unique identification number (usually their driver's license number) is then filed with the local police department. In the event the property is stolen and later recovered, the identification number helps the police locate the rightful owner. As an added deterrent, homeowners receive stickers to place on their doors and windows warning potential burglars that their property is properly tagged and recorded with the police.

Departments that have implemented an Operation Identification program report varying levels of success. As with the neighborhood watch program, the greatest benefit from such a program is that it provides an opportunity for the police and the average citizen to work together toward some common goal, thus enhancing police-community relations.

Educational Programs

A great number of police departments actively conduct educational programs for youth and adults. For example, *McGruff the crime dog* is a favorite among children. McGruff tries to "take a bite out of crime" by teaching children about the dangers of crime and the importance of avoiding alcohol, drugs, and strangers. *Project D.A.R.E.* (Drug Abuse Resistance Education) is another highly acclaimed educational program intended for youth. First developed by the Los Angeles Police Department to teach youth how to resist drugs, D.A.R.E. programs have been implemented in school systems nationwide.

POLICE ATTITUDES TOWARD CITIZENS

Do police officers dislike citizens? The question is often raised and is based on the all-too-common observation that the police seem to act and talk as if they do. Many officers come across to the public as being short tempered and irritable, even in the most routine situations. In fact some officers are downright nasty in their contacts with ordinary citizens, like those who are caught violating minor traffic ordinances. Of course policing has its share of good-natured police officers with winning smiles and disarming personalities, but the irritable cops seem to stand out most in our minds.

Citizens are not the only ones to detect an "attitude problem" among police—scholars and researchers have too. According to police experts, seasoned streetcops have a tendency to develop something called the **we/they syndrome:**

- We the police, they the public;
- We the good guys, they the bad guys;
- We the saints, they the scum;
- We the island of heroes, they the sea of villains.

James Q. Wilson refers to this syndrome as the *war theory of police-community relations.*[23]

Research suggests the reason why many officers develop the we/they syndrome is because they think the general public does not support them. Police frequently feel isolated from the people. They sense that citizens will not help them in times of trouble. Wilson cites several early studies showing that the majority of officers believe the public attitude toward them is typically apathetic and at times hostile. The feeling of isolation is most pronounced in the larger cities.

In one important study conducted by Peter Rossi and his associates for the Kerner Commission report, over four hundred police officers working in predominately black neighborhoods in eleven major cities were asked what they viewed as the most serious problem confronting them in their work.[24] More than any other response, the "lack of public support" was mentioned. Additionally, one out of every two officers questioned were dissatisfied with

CRIME PREVENTION PROGRAM: HOME SECURITY CHECKS

In dealing with residential burglaries, traditional law enforcement practices tend to be strictly reactive and do little to deter future crime. Additionally, due to fiscal constraints in many jurisdictions, this problem is compounded by the limited number of police officers available to patrol neighborhoods. And, while neighborhood watch programs are important, they can be difficult to maintain due to the high mobility of our society.

The problems of residential burglaries confront every law enforcement agency in the country. And the Downers Grove, Illinois, Police Department, with a sworn and civilian staff of 92, is no different. However, even with a crime prevention program in place, local residents did not request any crime prevention assistance.

HOME SECURITY SURVEY

The police department determined that the best service it could provide to deter residential burglary was to offer a home security survey. The home security survey, performed by members of the department's Crime Prevention Unit, is a proactive program aimed at reducing the number of residential burglaries.

In the past, however, the Crime Prevention Unit performed home security surveys when requested by citizens. Unfortunately, this method resulted in only 30–40 home surveys being conducted annually, despite an area population of 46,000. It was clear that in order for the program to be more effective, it needed to reach more residents.

REACHING THE PUBLIC

As a result, in October 1988, the unit began having messages printed on all water bills forwarded to Downers Grove residents. These messages encouraged residents to call the police department to make appointments for free home security surveys. This initiative was met with a very positive response from the community and resulted in 258 home security surveys being conducted during 1989.

TELEMARKETING

Encouraged by the success of this initiative, the unit thought that a more aggressive marketing campaign would deliver even better results. Therefore, in early 1990, the unit began a telemarketing program using the city telephone directory as a source for contacts.

Under this program, the Crime Prevention Unit's community support assistant telephones residents to explain the free home security survey and to make appointments to conduct the survey at a time and date convenient to the resident. During the survey, which takes approximately one hour, a crime prevention practitioner evaluates home security risks, such as exterior lighting and landscaping, doors, windows, and locks, and gives advice to homeowners that would make their property and possessions less vulnerable to burglars.

RESULTS

The telemarketing of home security surveys in Downers Grove, Illinois, has not only proved successful but has also paid big community relations dividends for the police department and the village of Downers Grove. In 1990, the Crime Prevention Unit completed 380 surveys and expects to perform over 400 during 1991.

CONCLUSION

Unfortunately, the importance of adequate crime prevention is oftentimes difficult to instill in the general public until it is too late. However, if law enforcement agencies want successful crime prevention programs, they need to reach out to the citizens before the unfortunate occurrence takes place. Programs of this type are especially appropriate for departments with small crime prevention components, because instead of expensive equipment or capital outlay, they require only time and dedication.

Source: David I. Rechenmacher, *F.B.I. Law Enforcement Bulletin* (Washington, DC: U.S. Government Printing Office, October 1991), pp. 8–9.

the amount of respect citizens gave them, and three out of every ten felt that the average citizen held them in contempt!

The Rossi study further documented that the perceptions of black officers working in predominately black neighborhoods were really no different than the perceptions of white officers; both groups felt residents were generally unsupportive of the police.[25] This finding questioned the conventional wisdom of assigning black officers to patrol black neighborhoods as a way to defuse racial tension. It also suggests that the occupational role of police work is more salient in shaping officers' perceptions and attitudes than their racial identity. In the language of sociologist Everett Hughes, the role of the police officer becomes a **master status**. Being a police officer significantly influences how others see them and, ultimately, how officers come to view themselves and the world around them.[26] Other social statuses like gender, religion, ethnicity, social class, and race are certainly important in the formation of an officer's total self-identity, yet each of these tends to become a **subordinate status** on the streets. Citizens and crooks alike interact with police officers as police officers, not as black police officers, female police officers, Jewish police officers, etc. The police may be black or white, male or female, Irish or Italian, Protestant or Jewish, but they are police officers first.

The we/they syndrome has an ironic twist. Public opinion polls demonstrate convincingly that the majority of all citizens have a favorable image of the police and rate the performance of the police highly. In other words, most citizens support their local police. (We will examine some of these opinion polls in the following section.) So the question arises: if many police officers believe deeply that the average citizen does not care, yet we know from survey studies that the great majority of the people do care, why are the police misreading the level of citizen support in their communities?

The best answer seems to be because the average police officer does not have regular, positive contact with average citizens.[27] Instead, the police spend most of their time and energy dealing with the smaller problem populations—the heavy consumers of police service. Teenagers, the poor, minorities, and repeat petty criminals are disproportionately on the receiving end of police attention. The individuals the police deal with the most are the same ones who tend to give the police the most trouble.

Unfortunately when the police occasionally have contact with the average, middle-class supporter of the police, the encounter is often negative. The person may have been a crime victim or the unsuspecting target of a police radar gun. Police-citizen encounters such as these are emotionally intense; it is not surprising that they frequently end in harsh words and bitter feelings.

CITIZEN ATTITUDES TOWARD POLICE

In an earlier chapter we alluded to the fact that the police are symbolic figures. A symbol is something that stands for or represents something other than its essence. For example, the U.S. flag, an Olympic gold medal, a wedding ring, a Mother's Day card and an Ivy League diploma all have important symbolic value.

Police officers represent something other than themselves as well; they symbolize state authority and state control. When you see a man or woman "in blue," what do you really see? Chances are you focus on the uniform with its accompanying badges, patches, emblems, gun, bullets, nightstick, walkie-talkie, whistle, and handcuffs. But what about the person underneath the uniform? Do you see him or her as an individual, a human being?

Police have been called "a **Rorschach test** in uniform."[28] This phrase is in reference to the standard "ink block" quiz used by psychological evaluators to assess people's perceptions. Most people have been culturally conditioned to see the police predominately in their occupational role as police officers, as if they were wearing "sociological blinders." These blinders make it difficult to view police officers as everyday people, just as it is difficult to relate to certain other persons outside the role they perform viz-à-viz ourselves (e.g., mom, dad, doctor, or priest).

The late **August Vollmer** (1876–1955), known respectfully as "Dean of American Chiefs of Police" because of his efforts to improve the quality of police training and education, once sarcastically reflected on how the public views the police. According to Vollmer, citizens expect police officers

> . . . to have the wisdom of Solomon, the courage of David, the strength of Samson, the patience of Job, the leadership of Moses, the kindness of the Good Samaritan, the strategy of Alexander, the faith of Daniel, the diplomacy of Lincoln, the tolerance of the Carpenter of Nazareth, and finally, an intimate knowledge of every branch of the natural, biological, and social sciences. If he had all these he might be a good policeman.[29]

While Vollmer was never known for his subtlety, he did have a valid point: citizens expect a great deal from the police and there is no way the police can satisfy everyone. There are so many competing interests in a community that it is difficult for the police to do anything that does not irritate some group somewhere. For instance, increasing patrol coverage in an area following complaints from neighbors that there is too much crime will almost certainly result in complaints from other residents about selective enforcement and police harassment. The police often feel they are "damned if we do and damned if we don't." However, as we noted previously, most citizens think highly of the police most of the time.

Public Opinion Polls

Public opinion polls are our main source of information about attitudes toward police. Citizen surveys use a variety of sampling strategies and measurement techniques. Some surveys are more methodologically rigorous than others. Mervin White and Ben Menke wrote a very critical paper in the late 1970s on the state of social survey research to assess citizen attitudes. They concluded that:

> We have seen in the past several decades a burgeoning effort to apply social science methodologies to criminal justice concerns, particularly to determine

consumer satisfaction with these services. . . . *The vast majority of the empirical literature assessing the mood of the public toward criminal justice agencies is not useful for informing policy decisions.*[30]

Not all public opinion polls produce the same findings, and some findings are open to alternative interpretations. Raymond Momboise, another police authority writing over two decades ago, maintained:

> That the police are disliked throughout America there can be no doubt. Many polls have proven conclusively the existence of that dislike. The public, with some justification, has come to think of the policeman in terms of some very unflattering stereotypes.[31]

This claim has since been refuted. Contrary to Mombosie's critical remark, and duly recognizing White and Menke's warning about the blind acceptance of public opinion polls, the current state of research leaves us with one unmistakable conclusion—survey research overwhelmingly demonstrates citizen support for the police. Of course not everyone is pleased with the police, and police ratings tend to fluctuate from one sociodemographic group to another. Below we examine public ratings of the police on two important criteria: (1) honesty and ethical standards of the police; and (2) job performance.

Honesty and Ethical Standards

One of the most impressive findings from citizen surveys is how well the police compare with other professions in ratings of honesty and ethical standards. Table 5.1 shows the police ranked seventh highest out of the twenty-five occupations surveyed by the Gallup organization in 1990. While the police are among the lowest paid occupations represented on the list, citizens rank them in the upper one-third of the group. If we combine the percentage of citizens who rank the honesty and ethical standards as "very high" or "high," the range of these *above average* ratings extends from 62 percent for druggists and pharmacists to 6 percent for car salesmen. Approximately one out of every two Americans (49 percent) rated the police as above average. Conversely, less than one out of ten respondents (9 percent) rated the police as *below average* ("low" or "very low"). Forty-one percent thought the honesty and ethical standards of the police was about "average."

It appears that respondents' race accounts for the most pronounced differences in ratings of honesty and ethical standards of the police. According to the 1990 Gallup poll, only 33 percent of blacks and 33 percent of nonwhites rated the police as above average (very high or high) compared to 49 percent of the white respondents. Thus, while only one out of every three minority respondents gave the police high marks on these criteria, approximately one out of every two whites thought the police were above average. It is instructive to look more closely at how different groups of people rate the honesty and ethical standards of the police. From the same 1990 Gallup survey described above, the data revealed the following results:

- Whites rate the honesty and ethical standards of the police higher than do blacks and other members of minority groups;
- Young adults rate the police higher than do older adults;
- Residents in the Midwest, East, and West rate the police higher than do residents in the South;
- Catholics rate the police higher than do Protestants, and especially higher than do Jews;
- There is no appreciable difference in ratings between Republicans and Democrats;
- There is no appreciable difference between males and females in rating the police.

Finally, table 5.2 reports the results of the same question asked by Gallup interviewers at different points in time. The data demonstrate a fairly steady

Table 5.1   Citizen Ratings of Honesty and Ethical Standards of Various Occupations, 1990

Question: How would you rate the honesty and ethical standards of the people in these different fields—very high, high, average, low, or very low?

	Very High	High	Average	Low	Very Low	No Opinion
Druggists/Pharmacists	12%	50%	31%	5%	(0)%*	2%
Clergy	12	43	35	6	1	3
Medical Doctors	9	43	38	7	2	1
Dentists	8	44	41	3	1	3
College Teachers	8	43	36	4	1	8
Engineers	8	42	36	3	1	10
Policemen	9	40	41	7	2	1
Funeral Directors	6	29	44	9	2	10
Bankers	4	28	52	12	1	3
TV Reporters/Commentators	4	28	46	16	4	2
Journalists	4	26	51	13	2	4
Business Executives	3	22	55	12	2	6
Newspaper Reporters	2	22	54	15	3	4
Senators	4	20	52	17	3	4
Lawyers	4	18	43	22	9	4
Local Office Holders	2	19	56	16	4	3
Building Contractors	3	17	50	18	3	9
Congressmen	3	17	52	20	4	4
State Office Holders	2	15	55	20	4	4
Real Estate Agents	2	14	54	21	4	5
Labor Union Leaders	2	13	37	28	11	9
Stockbrokers	2	12	50	19	3	14
Insurance Salesmen	2	11	47	28	8	4
Ad Practitioners	1	11	48	25	6	9
Car Salesmen	1	5	36	37	16	5

*(0) Less than 1%

Source: George Gallup, Jr., *The Gallup Poll Monthly*, Report No. 293 (Princeton, NJ: The Gallup Poll, February 1990), p. 23.

increase over time in the percentage of respondents who rate the honesty and ethical standards of the police as above average. In 1990, 49 percent of the respondents rated the police as above average compared to only 37 percent in 1977. The improvement in citizen ratings likely reflects the significant strides toward police professionalism made in recent years. It also coincides with the growth of the "get tough attitude" during the 1980s.

Job Performance

The general public is of the opinion that law enforcement agencies do an adequate job of policing. According to a 1986 Associated Press poll, 59 percent of the people questioned said the police in their community did a "good" job against crime, and 31 percent said they did a "fair" job.[32] Only 8 percent evaluated the job performance of the police as "poor" (the remaining 2 percent had no answer). The greatest disparity among citizens in their ratings of the police existed between blacks and whites. Sixty percent of the white

Table 5.2   Citizen Ratings of Honesty and Ethical Standards of Various Occupations by Selected Years, 1977–1990

Question: How would you rate the honesty and ethical standards of the people in these different fields—very high, high, average, low, or very low?

	Percent Saying Very High or High—Trend					
	1977	1981	1983	1985	1988	1990
Druggists/Pharmacists	NA	59	61	65	66	62
Clergy	61	63	64	67	60	55
Medical Doctors	51	50	52	58	53	52
Dentists	NA	52	51	56	51	52
College Teachers	46	45	47	53	54	51
Engineers	46	48	45	53	48	50
Policemen	37	44	41	47	47	49
Funeral Directors	26	30	29	32	24	35
Bankers	39	39	38	38	26	32
TV reporters/Commentators	NA	36	33	33	22	32
Journalists	33	32	28	31	23	30
Business Executives	19	19	18	23	16	25
Newspaper Reporters	NA	30	26	29	22	24
Senators	19	20	16	23	19	24
Lawyers	26	25	24	27	18	22
Local Office Holders	14	14	16	18	14	21
Building Contractors	18	19	18	21	22	20
Congressmen	16	15	14	20	16	20
State Office Holders	11	12	13	15	11	17
Real Estate Agents	13	14	13	15	13	16
Labor Union Leaders	13	14	12	13	14	15
Stockbrokers	NA	21	19	20	13	14
Insurance Salesmen	15	11	13	10	10	13
Advertising Practitioners	10	9	9	12	7	12
Car Salesmen	8	6	6	5	6	6

Source: *The Gallup Poll News Service*, vol. 54, no. 40, (Princeton, NJ: The Gallup Poll, February 28, 1990).

respondents said the police did a "good" (i.e., above average) job compared to only 39 percent of the blacks; 44 percent of the hispanics and 52 percent of the "other" nonwhites said the police did a good job.

Interestingly, while younger adults are more likely to rate the honesty and ethical standards of the police as above average (as noted above), the Associated Press poll revealed that older adults are more likely to rate the job performance of the police as above average. While age differences are quite small in both surveys (probably too small to have much practical implication), the contradiction in findings between the two similar types of questions is intriguing. The literature generally reports a direct positive relationship between age of respondents and their evaluations of the police—that is, older people tend to have better opinions of the police.[33] According to the survey data we have examined, however, older people may rate the job performance of the police higher than younger people, but they tend to rate the honesty and ethical standards of police lower.

Pollsters have asked citizens to rate the job performance of police at the local, state, and federal levels. The results are intriguing. People tend to rate the job performance of local police the highest, followed in order by state and then federal law enforcement.[34] Americans have shared a closeness with their local police ever since the frontier days. We regularly see the local officer serving our community residents and fighting our crime problem; we are much less familiar with the activities of state and federal law enforcement. While it is sometimes true that "familiarity breeds contempt," particularly when the police department is poorly run, there have been innumerable instances when community residents have gone to great lengths to support their local police.

As a final observation, it is important to note how public opinion of the police can quickly change, especially following a major police scandal. For example, a March 1991 Gallup poll asked citizens across the United States, "In some places in the nation, there have been charges of police brutality. Do you think there is any police brutality in your area, or not?" This poll was conducted two weeks following the police beating of Rodney King in Los Angeles, which was caught on videotape by an amateur photographer and shown repeatedly on television to a shocked American public.[35]

The survey found that more than one out of three respondents felt that police brutality existed in their area. Although responses to the same survey question are not available from just prior to the Rodney King beating, a 1965 Gallup poll found that only one in ten respondents believed police brutality existed in their area. In other words, public opinion of the police is in a continual state of flux—the police can generally rely on public support, but they cannot always count on it.

COMMUNITY POLICING

In the last chapter we noted that the evolving strategy of policing today is a concept called **community policing**.[36] At this point in time community policing is far from being the dominant police strategy, but it is the preferred approach in a growing number of cities. It is estimated that two-thirds of departments serving over 50,000 residents have already moved to community policing or plan to do so in the near future.[37] Community policing is more than another new patrol tactic or technique; it is a general police philosophy. Community policing blends together new empirical and theoretical knowledge about police work with some old patrol practices.

The ultimate aim of community policing is to bring the police and citizens together in a close working relationship. Of course there is nothing new about this idea. As you recall from our earlier discussion, the main rationale for developing police-community relations units in the late 1960s was to bring the police and the community close together again. However, today's community policing is more than simple PR (public relations) or CR (community relations). Unlike PR and CR, improved police-community relations is a by-product of an effective community policing program, not its main objective. The police and the community become genuine partners in the maintenance of social order. Under this arrangement, the police continue to provide the personnel, equipment, and administrative expertise while the community provides much needed information, encouragement, and support.

To state it simply, community policing is the basic strategy of *walking, talking, and consulting with the community*. The following components are all within the realm of community policing:

- *Foot patrol*—assignment of Community Policing Officers (CPO) to permanent foot patrol in densely populated urban neighborhoods and business districts;
- *Park and walk*—combined patrol strategy of cruiser and foot patrol;
- *Decentralized decision making*—regular consultation with citizens and neighborhood organizations about problem solving and maintaining order;
- *"Open-door" administrative philosophy*—police leadership actively solicits input from lower police managers and rank-and-file officers;
- *Reprioritizing police mission*—rendering services and maintaining order assume a much greater role in community policing than the predominant crime control strategy of the past;
- *Accentuating role of street-level patrol officer*—recognition that the uniform patrol division, not the detective squad, is the most crucial to the police role;
- *Focus on victims*—making a serious attempt to attend to the emotional, physical, and financial needs of crime victims.

Background

Properly understood, the community policing era is the most recent of three periods of police reform that began in the middle of the last century.[38] The first was the *Political Era*, lasting from the middle 1800s through 1920s. The Political Era was characterized by the close relationship between the police and the community and by the relative importance of order maintenance and social service functions. In these important respects, policing during the political era was similar to community policing of today. The main difference, however, was the tangled web of political ties to local police departments commonly found a hundred years ago. All too often the invasive political ties resulted in police favoritism, outside meddling in departmental affairs, and corruption.

The *Reform Era* lasted from the 1920s through the 1970s. It represented a 180-degree turn from the organizational strategy of policing during the political era. Political ties to local party machines were deliberately severed during the reform era in an effort to professionalize police departments. The definition of the police role was narrowed to "crime fighting." Fighting crime was exalted by police leaders as the only worthy mission of the police. The advances in criminalistics and computer applications significantly enhanced the ability of the police to solve crimes. Naturally, the role of the professional detective as a crime fighting specialist was glorified over the role of the generalist uniformed officer.

The Reform Era succeeded in reducing the extent of local political interference in police departments. It also curtailed the prevalence of police corruption. Unfortunately, these improvements came at a substantial cost to the quality of community life. Research conducted during the 1970s and early 1980s demonstrated that the guiding organizational strategy of the reform era—car patrol, quick response, and criminal investigations—was not working well. Police officers in random motorized patrol were removed from daily, intimate contact with community residents. Moreover, crime was flourishing as was citizens' fear of crime.

The *Community Policing Era* was born in the early 1980s, largely out

A street patrol officer holds his carefully recorded notes as he surveys a crime scene.

of the startling research findings of a patrol experiment conducted in Newark, New Jersey. Newark reinstituted the old style foot patrol by taking a large number of officers out of their patrol cars and placing them on permanent walking beats. The critics argued that the foot patrol in Newark (and other cities of the time) did not solve the problem of crime in the past so they saw little reason to return to that practice now. Critics further argued that foot patrol increases response time to crimes and weakens headquarter's control over officers. It is also hard work—police leaders have used foot patrol as a disciplinary measure for decades.

The carefully controlled foot patrol experiment in Newark did not produce a drop in crime. This finding was hardly surprising to most people. What *is* surprising is that residents in the foot patrolled sectors reported they felt safer in their neighborhoods because of the presence of the officers. Residents appeared to be using the streets more frequently than before and taking fewer precautionary measures. According to most accounts, Newark's foot patrol program substantially enhanced the quality of community life for its residents. The foot patrol program had two added benefits: (1) community residents reported a more favorable opinion of the police; and (2) the foot patrol officers themselves had higher morale and greater job satisfaction than officers on regular assignment.

The "Broken Window" Theory

Advocates of community policing draw support from what is known as the **broken window theory**.[39] The theory makes an analogy between a broken window in a building and the allowance of certain "harmless" (but fear-inducing) activities on the streets. It is generally understood that once a window in an unattended house or building is broken or left unrepaired, then there is a tendency for the remaining windows to be broken. This is especially true in rundown neighborhoods with large numbers of unsupervised youth. Similarly, once a few "social windows" are broken (e.g., vagrancy, vandalism, littering, loitering, drinking), there is a tendency for more and more social windows to be smashed. Left unchecked, a once peaceful and prosperous area can quickly change:

> We suggest that 'untended' behavior also leads to the breakdown of community controls. A stable neighborhood of families who care for their homes, mind each other's children, and confidently frown on unwanted intruders can change, in a few years or even a few months, to an inhospitable and frightening jungle. A piece of property is abandoned, weeds grow up, a window is smashed. Adults stop scolding rowdy children; the children, emboldened, become more rowdy. Families move out, unattached adults move in. Teenagers gather in front of the corner store. The merchant asks them to move; they refuse. Fights occur. Litter accumulates. People start drinking in front of the grocery store; in time, an inebriate slumps to the sidewalk and is allowed to sleep it off. Pedestrians are approached by panhandlers.[40]

Community policing protects these "social windows" from becoming broken in the first place. The community policing strategy is concerned with the overall quality of community life and not just with serious crimes. *Physical incivilities* (trash, litter, graffiti, abandoned cars, vacant houses, unkept lots) and *social incivilities* (stray dogs, disruptive neighbors, unsupervised youth, excessive noise, public drunks, and drug addicts) greatly diminish the quality of community life. The CPO identifies these sources of incivility and attempts to eradicate them. The literature commonly describes this type of policing as "aggressive order maintenance."[41] The CPO also serves as community liaison officer to public and private agencies that may serve the needs of local residents. To the extent that community policing can protect additional social windows from breaking, and can help fix those that are already broken, the quality of community life is enhanced.

Evaluating Community Policing

Community policing has its share of supporters and detractors. We have already mentioned several of the more prominent benefits community policing is suppose to deliver:

- Reduced fear of crime;
- Greater citizen satisfaction and involvement;
- Improved officer morale;
- Improved police-community relations;
- Increased social cohesion;
- Improved flow of information from citizens;
- Enhanced quality of community life.

However, community policing is in its early stages, thus leaving most of its basic assumptions and presumed benefits untested. The major community policing programs that have been evaluated (Houston, New York, Boston, Newark, and Flint, Michigan) have produced mixed results.[42]

One of the problems of evaluating community policing is the conceptual cloudiness inherent in the concept of "community." As mentioned earlier in this chapter, the term community represents a vast array of people and places. These become undifferentiated under the community policing concept. Class, race, and neighborhood variables are often overlooked by advocates of community policing. Not all residents desire visible police response,[43] and not all "communities" can benefit from a community policing program. For example, rural areas and typical middle-class suburban neighborhoods do not need aggressive order maintenance to preserve their quality of community life.

Some critics claim that community policing is ideologically nostalgic, lonesome for a time in policing's past that never was. Others contend that community policing is (1) soft on crime; (2) more rhetoric than real; (3) glorified foot patrol; and (4) another PR gimmick. Yet advocates assure us that community policing is none of these things.[44]

On balance it appears that community policing has much to offer urban communities that are densely populated. It has already made a mark in a number of major cities, and communities across the country are making plans for their own community policing program. What remains to be seen is if this evolving strategy of policing will weather the test of time.

CONCLUSION

This chapter has focused on the relationship between the police and the public over the past few decades, with special attention given to the 1960s. It is clear

---

DEBATING NEW YORK CITY'S COMMUNITY POLICING PROGRAM

In 1991, lawmakers and taxpayers in New York City authorized a $1.8 billion expenditure, to be raised by new taxes and a special lottery, to fund Mayor David N. Dinkins's ambitious crime control program entitled "Safe Streets, Safe City." A central feature of the safe city program is to increase the size of the NYPD by 23 percent (an additional 6,000 officers) over a six-year period in an effort to implement community policing city-wide. Enthusiastically endorsing Mayor Dinkins's safe city program is New York City Police Commissioner Lee P. Brown. Brown is one of the nation's most avid and articulate supporters of community policing. In an interview with *Law Enforcement News,* Commissioner Brown expressed some of his thoughts on community policing:

> I view community policing not as a program, but, rather, as the way you deliver police services, as a management philosophy. . . . We define community policing here in New York as a partnership between the police and the law-abiding citizens to prevent crime; to arrest those who choose to violate the law; to solve reoccurring problems where we tend to go back to the same places over and over again; and to evaluate the results of our efforts. The whole objective is to improve the quality of life in the neighborhoods throughout our city.
> Policing New York City, in our estimation, calls for bringing the old beat cop back, where we have a visible presence of officers on the streets of New York City. When I came here in 1990, we had approximately 750 officers on

foot patrol—10 for each of our 75 precincts. Now we have over 3,000 officers out there on foot patrol in the neighborhoods, whereas we've only hired 5 perent more officers than we had when I started.

Not everyone is as enamored with community policing as Commissioner Brown, nor does everyone endorse the $1.8 billion safe city program. Criminal justice professor Angelo Pisani asks whether this is the wisest use of taxpayers' money during fiscally troubled times, to which he answers a resounding "no." While Pisani agrees that the "concept, philosophy, and aspirations of community policing are unquestionably good," the research literature cannot convincingly show that community policing, even with additional officers, can reduce serious crime:

> Why then spend all this money on policing, when a more appropriate use of the funds would be on the social (and economic) agenda? If research and experience in other cities show that it is unlikely that these efforts will have a significant impact on serious crime (crime rose in Houston after community policing was implemented), why doesn't the Mayor seek funds for social and economic programs instead of policing? . . . Can you imagine a scenario where an executive in a major corporation requests and receives approval for a $1.8 billion program without providing a projected return on the investment?

Where do you stand on the debate?

Source: *Law Enforcement News,* John Jay College of Criminal Justice, New York, May 15, 1992.

that the relationship between the police and the community is dynamic and ever changing, just as are relationships between husband and wife, student and teacher, nation A and nation B, and so on. Relationships seem to have a natural, almost rhythmic flow, between periods of warmth and trust to periods of tension and distrust. Sometimes the pendulum swings almost imperceptibly as the relationship adjusts accordingly. At other times the swings are wildly erratic and relationships become damaged or even destroyed—husbands and wives divorce, students drop out, nations go to war.

An inherent difficulty in assessing the quality of police-community relations in the United States is that there are thousands of police agencies and tens of thousands of communities. In addition, there are three quarters of a million public police officers and a quarter of a billion citizens. Think for a moment about your attitude toward the police. What factors do you think have shaped your view? Undoubtedly your family background, economic position, residential area, age, period in history, what you read or watch on TV, the opinions of your parents and friends, and your own experiences with the police have all shaped your opinion in various ways.

Researchers have found that even middle-class college students often harbor negative feelings against the police following the issuance of a traffic ticket. Terry Cox and Mervin White note that it is not so much the receipt of the ticket that produces the poor attitude as it is the negative interaction that frequently occurs between the officer and the student.[45] The more arrogant and verbally abusive the officer appears to the student (or vice versa), the more negative the student's attitude is toward the officer (also vice versa). What is unclear from the Cox and White study is how long the negative attitude lasts following the incident and whether the same findings are generalizable to older adults.

The community policing concept is generating a tremendous amount of attention in the United States and in Europe as well. Communities large and small have already adopted the community policing approach either in whole or in part. Many departments recognize a need to retain the traditional tripod of policing—motorized patrol, rapid response, and retrospective criminal investigation—as the mainstay of their patrol strategy. This traditional patrol strategy is then supplemented with community policing in neighborhoods most likely to benefit. Community policing requires substantial restructuring of the department's organization and a reworking of the administrative philosophy. What remains to be seen is if today's community policing will be any more successful than yesterday's foot patrol.

KEY TERMS

civil rights movement
Brown v. Board of Education
Civil Rights Act of 1964
police-community relations
public relations
community relations

we/they syndrome
master and subordinate status
Rorschach test
August Vollmer
community policing
"broken window" theory

DISCUSSION QUESTIONS

1. Discuss the nature of police-community relations from the early 1950s through the late 1960s in the United States. What factors helped shape the public's perception of the police?

2. How would you describe the nature of police-community relations in the United States today? What about in your community?

3. Discuss the relative advantages and disadvantages of a pure PR (public relations) approach versus a pure CR (community relations) approach to police-community relations programs.

4. Do you think the goals of community policing are realistically obtainable, or is it "pie-in-the-sky" idealism? Will the police and the community ever be genuine partners in the maintenance of social order? Do citizens really want an intimate relationship with the police?

CHAPTER SIX

WORKING THE STREETS

Don't tell me what the textbooks say—they don't apply out here.
                    —*anonymous police officer*

The title of this chapter—Working the Streets—signifies the assorted menu of people, problems, and situations police encounter daily. In the pages that follow we examine the work-a-day world of policing and how it shapes the behavior and attitudes of police officers. Throughout the chapter our focus is on the multitude of street-level problems that comprise the major part of public policing. Topics range from the early police socialization process of learning to think and act like a "cop," to the long-term career consequences of being a cop. As will be apparent by the chapter's end, police work is a difficult occupation. At its worst, police work can literally kill an officer. At its best, police work can be exciting, challenging, and deeply rewarding.

POLICE-CITIZEN ENCOUNTERS

Routine patrol brings police officers and citizens together in a variety of situations, so many in fact that it is nearly impossible to characterize the "typical" police-citizen encounter. This is true because no two encounters are exactly alike. Some encounters are initiated by officers while others—in fact most—are initiated by citizens; some encounters require the enforcement of the law while others require order maintenance or social service; some encounters are warm and cordial while others are tense and distant. Thus, a friendly conversation with a dedicated fan at the ballpark is quite different from having to escort an intoxicated, bellicose fan out of the stadium. Similarly, giving a motorist directions sets the stage for a different type of encounter than giving a motorist a ticket. As we shall soon discover, what transpires during a police-citizen encounter is contingent on a multitude of factors.

A major theoretical perspective in sociology relies on face-to-face interactions and the immediate situation at hand to understand human behavior. This is known as the **interactionist perspective** and is useful for our study of police-citizen encounters. The interactionist perspective is distinguished from other major sociological perspectives in that it specifically focuses on the micro, social-psychological level of human behavior. Other major sociological perspectives focus on the macro, historical, structural level. In other words, social interactionists rely on the momentary mix of sociology, psychology, and the immediate situation to explain many types of human interaction.

To begin with, all police-citizen encounters are a form of *social interaction*. Social interaction is defined as "action that mutually affects two or more individuals,"[1] such as coffee counter chit-chat or a phone order for a pizza. A community-relations officer showing a young girl or boy how the police radio in the squad car works is engaged in social interaction; so is an arresting vice officer reading a pornographer his or her rights. Police-citizen encounters may be fleeting, not taking more than a few minutes or even seconds, or they may be lasting. Encounters that assume a regular and continuing pattern of social interaction become a *social relationship*. One of the advantages of community policing as discussed in chapter 5 is that it nurtures personal, lasting relationships with citizens where only fleeting interactions existed before.

What develops during a police-citizen encounter is in large part contingent on the interactional interplay between the police officer and the citizen.

How does the officer "read" the citizen? How does the citizen "read" the officer? What does the officer do and say? How does the citizen respond? All of this feeds into a complex interaction process. The interaction evolves as the encounter continues. The outcome of the encounter is never known at the outset—the interaction is flexible, fluid and ever changing.

But social interaction never exists in a vacuum! There are always conditions external to the interacting parties that affect the interaction. These outside conditions are part of the *situational context* of the interaction. There are an infinite number of conditions that can affect the nature of a police-citizen encounter. For example, the length of conversation between a traffic officer and a motorist may be affected by something as mundane as the weather. On extremely hot days or cold nights or when it is raining especially hard, an officer may wish to terminate an encounter as quickly as possible (or avoid it altogether). Likewise, a patrol officer advising a teenager to "move along" may face a major test of wills if the youth is surrounded by friends who are encouraging defiance.

Noted police authority Richard Lundman has carefully detailed the chain of events that occur during police-citizen encounters.[2] Lundman dissects encounters into three parts: (1) problem, (2) encounter, and (3) decision. We shall examine each of these below.

After three days of clashes with police in 1991, officers assigned to the Crown Heights section of Brooklyn toured the neighborhoods, playing with children and chatting with residents.

The *problem* refers to the kinds of situations that police are asked to resolve. Problems run the gamut from barking dogs to bank robbery. Citizens generally are the ones who determine the kinds of problems police must handle by calling in complaints to the department. Lundman suggests that approximately 75 percent of all police-citizen encounters are initiated by citizens, and up to 90 percent are initiated by citizens if traffic offenses are

A RAPIDLY DETERIORATING ENCOUNTER

"I've already explained to you twice that your signature on this traffic citation is merely a promise to appear. You are not admitting guilt. Understand?" said Rantlee, with a glance at the group of onlookers that suddenly formed.

"Well, I still ain't signin' nothin'," said the tow truck driver, slouched back against his white truck, brown muscular arms folded across his chest. He raised his face to the setting sun at the conclusion of a sentence and cast triumphant looks at the bystanders who now numbered about twenty, and Gus wondered if now were the time to saunter to the radio car and put in a call for assistance.

Why wait until it started? They could be killed quickly by a mob. But should he wait a few more minutes? Would it seem cowardly to put in a call for backup units at this moment, because the truck driver was merely arguing, putting up a bluff for the onlookers? He would probably sign the ticket in a moment or so.

"If you refuse to sign, we have no choice but to arrest you," said Rantlee. "If you sign, it's like putting up a bond. Your word is the bond and we can let you go. You have the right to a trial, a jury trial if you want one."

"That's what I'm going to ask for too. A jury trial."

"Fine. Now, please sign the ticket."

"I'm goin' to make you spend all day in court on your day off."

"Fine!"

"You jist like to drive around givin' tickets to Negroes, don't you?"

"Look around, Mister," said Rantlee, his face crimson now. "There ain't nobody on the streets around here, *but* Negroes. Now why do you suppose I picked on you and not somebody else?"

"Any nigger would do, wouldn't it? I jist happened to be the one you picked."

"You just happened to be the one that ran the red light. Now, are you going to sign this ticket?"

"You specially like to pick on wildcat tow truckers, don't you? Always chasin' us away from accident scenes so the truckers that contract with the PO-lice Department can git the tow."

"Lock up your truck, if you're not going to sign. Let's get going to the station."

"You don't even got my real name on that ticket. My name ain't Wilfred Sentley."

"That's what your license says."

"My real name is Wilfred 3X, whitey. Gave to me by the prophet himself."

"That's fine. But for our purposes, you can sign your slave name to this ticket. Just sign Wilfred Sentley."

"You jist love workin' down here, don't you? You jist soil your shorts I bet, when you think about comin' here every day and fuckin' all the black people you can."

"Yeah, get it up in there real tight, whitey," said a voice at the rear of the crowd of teen-agers, "so it feels real good when you come."

This brought peals of laughter from the high school crowd who had run across from the hot dog stand on the opposite corner.

"Yes, I just love working down here," said Rantlee in a toneless voice, but his red face betrayed him and he stopped. "Lock your truck," he said finally.

"See how they treats black people, brothers and sisters," the man shouted, turning to the crowd on the sidewalk, which had doubled in the last minute and now blocked access to the police car, and Gus's jaw was trembling so that he clamped his teeth shut tight. It's gone too far, thought Gus.

"See how they is?" shouted the man, and several children in the front of the crowd joined a tall belligerent drunk in his early twenties who

omitted.[3] The fact that citizens set the pace of work for officers is to say that policing is largely a *reactive*—not *proactive*—enterprise. Once a problem is identified, the police must judge the relative importance of the problem and set enforcement priorities.

The *encounter* refers to face-to-face interaction between the officer and citizen. While citizens are largely in control of the types of problems police

---

lurched into the street from the Easy Time Shine Parlor and announced that he could kill any motherfuckin' white cop that ever lived with his two black hands, which brought a whoop and cheer from the younger children who urged him on.

Rantlee pushed through the crowd suddenly and Gus knew he was going to the radio, and for an agonizing moment Gus was alone in the center of the ring of faces, some of which he told himself, would surely help him. If anything happened someone would help him. He told himself it was not hate he saw in every face because his imagination was rampant now and the fear subsided only slightly when Rantlee pushed his way back through the crowd.

"Okay, there're five cars on the way," Rantlee said to Gus and turned to the truck driver. "Now, you sign or if you want to start something, we got enough help that'll be here in two minutes to take care of you and anybody else that decides to be froggy and leap."

"You got your quota to write, don't you?" the man sneered.

"No, we used to have a quota, now I can write every goddamn ticket I want to," Rantlee said, and held the pencil up to the driver's face. "And this is your last chance to sign, 'cause when the first police car gets here, you go to jail, whether you sign or not."

The man took a step forward and stared in the young policeman's gray eyes for a long moment. Gus saw that he was as tall as Rantlee and just as well built. Then Gus looked at the three young men in black Russian peasant hats and white tunics who whispered together on the curb, watching Gus. He knew it would be them that he would have to contend with if anything happened.

"Your day is comin'," said the driver, ripping the pencil from Rantlee's hand and scrawling his name across the face of the citation. "You ain't goin' to be top dog much longer."

While Rantlee tore the white violator's copy from the ticket book, the driver let Rantlee's pencil fall to the ground and Rantlee pretended not to notice. He gave the ticket to the driver who snatched it from the policeman's hand and was still talking to the dispersing crowd when Gus and Rantlee were back in the car, pulling slowly from the curb while several young Negroes grudgingly stepped from their path. They both ignored a loud thump and knew that one of the ones in the peasant caps had kicked their fender, to the delight of the children.

They stopped for a few seconds and Gus locked his door while a boy in a yellow shirt in a last show of bravado sauntered out of the path of the bumper. Gus recoiled when he turned to the right and saw a brown face only a few inches from his, but it was only a boy of about nine years and he studied Gus while Rantlee impatiently revved the engine. Gus saw only childlike curiosity in the face and all but the three in the peasant caps were now walking away. Gus smiled at the little face and the black eyes which never left his.

"Hello, young man," said Gus, but his voice was weak.

"Why do you like to shoot black people?" asked the boy.

"Who told you that? That's not. . . ." The lurching police car threw him back in his seat and Rantlee was roaring south on Broadway and west on Fifty-fourth Street back to their area. Gus turned and saw the little boy still standing in the street looking after the speeding radio car.

Source: Joseph Wambaugh, *The New Centurions* (Boston: Little, Brown and Company, 1970), pp. 129–32. By Permission of Publishers.

respond to, the police are primarily in control of the actual encounter. Cox and White make this point clear in their study of interaction dynamics: "it must be noted that the officer is the dominant factor in police-citizen contacts and as such bears a greater share of responsibility for the interaction that takes place."[4]

Police are taught to quickly take control of encounters with citizens, particularly when they are performing a formal police duty such as enforcing a law or maintaining social order. Lundman suggests there are three sequential steps in establishing control in an encounter. First, police seek to establish their safety. This is an ongoing concern of an officer throughout the entire encounter. Jonathan Rubenstein notes how officers learn to position themselves in a way that assures them the greatest control and safety:

> Policemen act as though all people are right-handed. If he has any choice in the matter, the patrolman tries to move in a leftward direction toward a person in order to control his fighting arm. This allows him to stand at the person's right, at a slight angle, when he is facing him, which keeps his gun away from the man he is seeking to dominate. He consistently violates the normal distances which people seek to maintain when they are engaged in friendly conversation, causing discomfort and nervousness when he does not mean to. . . . By constantly crowding people, he reduces their opportunities for kicking and punching him effectively. When he can, the patrolman stands slightly at an angle to the person he is confronting to avoid a crippling blow to the groin. Naturally he can be grabbed and wrestled with; this is the main reason why most policemen wear clip-on ties and hate any gear that offers someone a handhold on them.[5]

Once a minimal level of safety is assured, the police seek to establish their authority and then normalize the situation. This latter strategy, normalization, does not mean to correct the problem, although this may be a desired end. Rather, normalization allows the officer to "categorize" the problem by recognizing it as similar to other problems he or she has experienced in the past. Ultimately, normalizing a situation implies the encounter has a degree of predictability to it. Once adequately normalized, the officer has a **recipe for action** to help resolve the problem.

Lundman's third stage of police-citizen encounters is the *decision*. During this stage the officer is forced to resolve the problem in a manner he or she thinks is most appropriate. The decision must be consistent with the law and with departmental expectations, but these broad restraints frequently leave much room for individual judgment. Oftentimes the decision involves a discretionary choice by the officer—to warn, cite, ticket, arrest, or ignore. Here again, as in the interaction itself, the decision of the officer is not made in a vacuum. The many determinants of police discretion are fully discussed in chapter 7.

In an unusual application of the interactionist perspective to study police-citizen encounters, Wiley and Hudik conducted a field test of *exchange theory*.[6] The researchers reasoned that the social exchange between citizens and police officers could be understood in terms of the "costs" and "rewards" of human interaction. It was presumed that the more rewarding the interaction was to the citizen, the more willing the citizen would be to reciprocate the reward by cooperating with the police. The authors found this to be true. When officers did not explain to subjects why they were stopped on the street for brief questioning, the subjects were less cooperative and more eager to end the encounter. However, when officers took the time to explain to subjects why they were momentarily detained (e.g., "had a call about a burglary"), subjects were likely to reciprocate the positive gesture and cooperate with the police for a longer period of time. Moreover, the length of willing cooperation of citizens increased as the severity of the offense increased, apparently because serious crimes give the police greater legitimacy to act.[7]

The implication from the Wiley and Hudik study is that even though police-citizen encounters are a two-way exchange, it is the police officer who sets the tone for social interaction. Thus, police may improve the quality of interaction by increasing the tangible rewards (i.e., information) given to citizens.

Maintaining the Edge

The typical police-citizen encounter is characterized by a mutual show of respect. This keeps the interaction both civilized and short-lived. In ideal situations, the police officer is even-handed, restrained, and professional; in turn, the citizen is polite and respectful. Indeed, most average citizens—and a surprising percentage of criminal suspects—are outwardly polite to the police.

Richard Sykes and John Clark argue that the **deference exchange** in police-citizen encounters is normally *asymmetrical* whereby the police display deference (i.e., courtesy and respect) at a level just below the level of deference shown by citizens.[8] Officers come to expect citizens to be deferent toward them, and they may react negatively when citizens are not. Occasionally, the acceptable or expected exchange of deference is not always asymmetrical. This may occur when the encounter is with a law-abiding citizen rather than a criminal suspect, or when the officer is interacting with someone who is much older or who is of a higher social status than the officer. In cases like these, the deference exchange may become symmetrical or even asymmetrical in the opposite direction.[9]

As long as the interaction has a sufficient exchange of deference, there is little likelihood the officer will lose control of the situation. Police refer to this as **maintaining the edge.** Just as school teachers must establish control in the classrooms in order to teach, the police must establish control on the streets to perform their duty. As soon as an officer loses the "edge," he or she has lost the ability to control the encounter. What is often worse, the officer may have lost "face" in front of citizens or fellow officers.

In striving to maintain control of citizen encounters, the police carefully monitor citizens' actions and attitudes. The degree of deference that is exchanged is continually assessed. With experience, police learn to sense when the balance of power is shifting. They also develop techniques to regain control of the situation. For instance, officers may rely on their personal charisma, natural leadership, or ability to physically intimidate when their control is jeopardized. Other officers with less powerful personalities or intimidating physiques may have to rely more on their ability to talk. And on the streets, talk is essential; it is an officer's most powerful tool, not only for maintaining control on the streets but also for interacting with and influencing other officers in the department. William Muir's seminal study of the police as "Streetcorner Politicians" assessed the importance of verbal ability: "Policing demanded eloquence. . . . There were many uses of eloquence—it was the key to taking charge in public. . . . Lacking a ready and capable ability to talk, an individual policeman simply could not make professional responses and accept the risks inherent in them."[10] Simply put, a good officer is also a good talker.

The police are often challenged to semi-playful exchanges of verbal insults by streetwise youth, more commonly known as "doing the dozens." The aim of this frisky repartee is to outsmart the other person through "ingenuity, hair-trigger responsiveness, inventiveness, and the acute exercise of mental faculties."[11] Most verbal jabs of this nature are innocuous and do not seriously threaten the control of the police. Actually, many seasoned officers enjoy these playful exchanges and view them as an opportunity to improve their relations with youth.

Playful, nonthreatening challenges aside, what happens when an individual simply refuses to respect the authority of an officer? How does an officer handle a situation when someone is uncooperative or verbally abusive? To a large extent, the actions of an officer depend on whether the troublemaker is a criminal suspect or not. Surprisingly, maintaining the edge is far simpler when the troublemaker is a suspect to a crime. This is because the officer always has the power of the law to regain control. If the suspect gets too far out of line, he or she may be placed under immediate arrest and the officer maintains the undisputed edge. Even if the suspect continues to challenge the officer after the arrest is made, or if the suspect is later released without further prosecution, the police officer was still able to keep the immediate situation under control.

Retaining control of a police-citizen encounter is greatly complicated when the troublemaker is not a suspect. The "creep-in-the-crowd" is especially problematic because the officer does not have the leverage of arrest unless the citizen substantially hinders the officer's duty. Police find these types of troublemakers difficult to tolerate and frequently devise clever names to call them. For example, the police in Houston are fond of the label "turd" to describe the assorted wiseguys, bigmouths, creeps and jerks of the streets,[12] and John Van Maanen heard the word "asshole" a lot in his study of the Union City police:

> I guess what our job really boils down to is not letting the assholes take over the city. Now I'm not talking about your regular crooks . . . they're bound to wind up in the joint anyway. What I'm talking about are those shitheads out to prove they can push everybody around. Those are the assholes we gotta deal with and take care of on patrol. . . . They're the ones that make it tough on the decent

people out here. You take the majority of what we do and it's nothing more than asshole control.[13]

Van Maanen suggests that assholes are candidates for several remedies from which the officer can choose. Depending on the situation and the actions of the troublemaker, the police officer may alternatively castigate, teach, ignore, or isolate the person. Assholes are also candidates for arrest on charges of "disorderly conduct" or "disturbing the peace."

It matters little which derogatory anatomical term for a troublemaker is used—what matters is the considerable aggravation they cause the police. "Asshole control" is a frustrating yet unavoidable part of police work. When it comes to dealing with antagonistic people on the street, there are few simple solutions.

STYLES OF POLICING

Recall from chapter 3 that the United States houses thousands of police departments and hundreds of thousands of public police officers. We find large departments in urban centers and small departments in suburban and rural areas; there are young and old officers, experienced and inexperienced officers, introverted and extroverted officers, high school drop-outs and college educated officers. The list could continue at length.

With such incredible diversity, would one expect that police departments and individual police officers across the country police the same way? Do they respond alike to crime, make the same number of arrests, issue the same number of traffic tickets and interact identically with citizens? Obviously not.

Police departments and police officers perform their duties in a variety of ways—what the literature refers to as **styles of policing.** We may speak of different "department styles," which focuses on the *group* level of analysis, or "officer styles" at the *individual* level. While in everyday police work a department's style and an officer's style are closely woven together, we shall separate them here for the purpose of discussion.

Department Styles

James Q. Wilson's *Varieties of Police Behavior* is perhaps the best study of department styles of policing.[14] During the 1960s, Wilson and his assistants visited eight different departments for periods of three weeks to two months. The researchers carefully observed each agency and its officers, taking extensive notes. Six of the communities were in the state of New York (Albany, Amsterdam, Brighton, Nassau County, Newburgh, and Syracuse). The other two were in Highland Park, Illinois, and Oakland, California. The communities were selected "because of their differences, not their similarities" in order to maximize diversity.[15]

From his observations, Wilson was able to identify three department styles—the **watch, legalistic** and **service** styles. Wilson was careful to note that although none of the departments he studied operated exclusively as one style, each department tended toward one style over the others most of the time.

Watch Style

The watch style of policing was found in Albany, Amsterdam, and Newburgh. Under the watch style, order maintenance is the dominant operating strategy, not law enforcement. Watch-style communities emphasize a caretaker approach to policing where the main duty of the police is to keep the peace. The department allows officers wide discretionary authority to handle minor infractions. This typically results in the underenforcement of the law; few traffic tickets are handed out and few minor offenders are arrested. Watch-style departments seem willing to tolerate discreet immorality. What is more, there is a tendency to handle some types of people differently, as if community standards varied by neighborhood or social group. For example, respectable middle-class citizens are often excused for minor infractions while many lower-class citizens, particularly blacks, are either ignored altogether or arrested. In short, the major order of business in the watch style of policing is to keep things running smoothly without ruffling too many feathers.

Legalistic Style

Legalistic departments are in many ways the opposite of watch-style departments. Law enforcement is the dominant operating strategy. Even though officers in legalistic departments perform order maintenance and social service duties when necessary, their primary obligation to the community is perceived as crime control. As a consequence, the enforcement style is more to the "letter" of the law than in the "spirit" of the law; speeders are ticketed and minor offenders are arrested, regardless of social class position or racial membership. Legalistic departments project a professional image. Furthermore, the evenhanded enforcement of the law and the close scrutiny of officer behavior minimizes the problem of police corruption. Wilson classified the police departments in Oakland, Highland Park, and Syracuse as legalistic.

Service Style

Wilson described the police agencies in Brighton and Nassau County as service-style departments. With watch- and legalistic-style departments at near opposite ends of the continuum, service-style departments fall somewhere in the middle. For the most part, the service style combines the advantages of the watch and legalistic styles with few of the disadvantages. For example, police in service-style departments patrol actively and intervene frequently (as in legalistic departments), but often handle encounters informally (as in watch departments). Also, service-style departments emphasize professionalism and the absence of corruption, but are committed to maintaining good rapport with the community. Finally, service-style departments are not sloppy nor discriminatory, and project a relaxed attitude toward the people.

If we recognize that not all departments police in a similar fashion, what accounts for the differing police styles? There are numerous factors both inside and outside the department that shape the style of policing. The more important of these are listed here:

Inside Influences:
• Size of department;
• Police leadership
• Management philosophy;
• Composition of officers;
• Informal power structures and peer groups;
• Departmental politics and history.

Outside Influences:
• Crime problem;
• Applicable laws and legal restrictions;
• Demographic and geographic composition of community;
• Citizen expectations;
• Media coverage;
• Local politics and local history.

A reading of the police literature on community influences gives the impression that a community gets the kind of policing it either wants or deserves—as if there is a conscious collective decision on the matter. Donald Black argues that this idea is greatly mistaken.[16] Black notes how the police serve an unorganized mass of complainants far more than they serve an organized constituency. Police work is a potpourri of case-by-case, isolated contacts between police and citizens. As Black suggests, "Their field work evades planned change, but as shifts occur in the desires of the atomized citizenry who call and direct the police, changes ripple into policemen's routine behavior."[17] In this sense, the police serve a phantom master more than a real one.

Officer Styles

While Wilson concentrated on department styles of policing, other police scholars have focused on individual officer styles. In one of the early writings on this subject, Jerome Skolnick described the **working personality** of police officers in his study of Oakland, California (one of the eight cities in Wilson's study).[18] Working personality refers to the sum total of values, attitudes, and behavior patterns of a police officer. Skolnick settled on the term "working personality" to distinguish the officer's *on-the-job* personality from his or her *total* personality. The implication is that police think and act differently when working the streets than when off duty with friends and family.

Since the time of Skolnick's publication, the notion that police officers develop similar working personalities has been challenged. Observational studies and common sense impressions suggest that individual police officers,

Table 6.1   Working Personalities of Police Officers

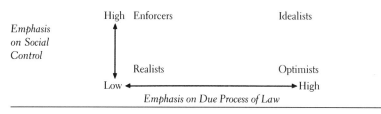

Source: John J. Broderick, *Police in a Time of Change*, 2nd. ed. (Prospect Heights, IL: Waveland Press, 1987), p. 5. Reprinted by permission.

just like departments, have different styles. The literature is now replete with varying typologies of officer styles. One of the most useful typologies is John Broderick's four-fold classification: (1) enforcers, (2) idealists, (3) realists, and (4) optimists.[19]

Enforcers are officers who place a high value on keeping the streets safe for law-abiding citizens, making good arrests and occasionally helping people. Enforcers have compassion for the elderly, the poor, and the homeless, who the officer sees as basically good people down on their luck. Enforcers often try to help these unfortunate people make good. However, enforcers have little patience with habitual drug users, homosexuals, and people who show no respect for the police. As revealed in table 6.1, enforcers place a high value on the need for social order but a low value on individual rights and due process of law.

Idealists also place a high value on maintaining social order. But unlike enforcers, they feel the need to carefully protect the procedural rights of all citizens. Idealists generally subscribe to the Law Enforcement Code of Ethics, although the inability of policing to live up to the professional goals often leaves these officers highly frustrated. The average age of idealists is slightly lower than the average age of all officers, and idealists are more likely to have a college education.

The final two types of officers described by Broderick, *realists* and *optimists*, are similar in that they do not define their jobs simply as "keeping society safe." Both realists and optimists agree that preserving social order is essential to the job, but unlike the typical enforcer or idealist they recognize that most of police work is not spent fighting crime. Where the realists and optimists differ is that optimists place higher reward value on due process considerations than the realist (see table 6.1). In other words, optimists still get enjoyment out of helping people and by doing what they can to better the community—realists are less enthralled with police work.

While it is true that not all police officers exhibit similar on-the-job styles, and that by identifying these styles we can gain a deeper understanding of what working the streets is really like, we must be careful not to overlook important similarities among officers. In fact, many observers of the police are more struck by the *convergence* of style than by the *divergence*. As we shall discover in the next section, the process of learning to be a police officer assures a fair degree of continuity of style from one generation of officers to the next.

POLICE SOCIALIZATION

Socialization is a concept used by social scientists to refer to the process of learning the manners and customs of society and developing a personality. In formal language, socialization is defined as "the process whereby one internalizes the norms of the groups among whom one lives so that a distinct 'self' emerges, unique to this individual."[20] Informally, socialization may be defined as the process of taking uncivilized, alien creatures to our world (i.e., newborns) and slowly molding them into acceptable, civil members of society. The family is the main socializing agency in society as it has profound early influence over children. However, socialization is a lifelong process, meaning it is never fully complete. Once children's experiences begin to extend beyond the immediate family, other socializing agents and agencies (neighbors, schools, teachers, church groups, boy scouts, little league, etc.) assume an important role in shaping young people.

Sociologists frequently apply the concept of socialization in a more specific way to refer to the learning process that occurs within various occupations. This is called "occupational" socialization. Medical doctors, lawyers, teachers, auto mechanics—in fact all occupations to a greater or lesser extent—must be appropriately socialized to meet the expectations of their work. Police officers are no exception. **Police socialization** is the process by which new recruits learn how to be police officers. Similar to socialization in general, police socialization is a "process" that never really ends. Just as with young children, however, the socialization experiences that occur early in one's police career are the most potent and lasting.

The "making of a police officer" occurs over a period of time as the young officer gains experience on the streets and develops working relationships with police colleagues and other criminal justice practitioners. Old values and attitudes from "civilian" life gradually lose meaning as new values and attitudes assume priority. The world somehow looks different through the eyes of a police officer, more seedy and more hostile. New recruits listen carefully to the teachings of veteran officers, whom they admire and respect, and often take these lessons to heart.

It is vitally important to understand that police socialization is more than simply learning how to act and interact with others. It is also more than learning the techniques of policing. Police socialization goes much deeper. *Police socialization shapes in fundamental ways an officer's values, attitudes, perceptions and beliefs that are appropriate and necessary for police work.* In short, the recruit must learn how to think like a cop.

Police socialization has a powerful influence over new recruits. Some observers believe that it does not really matter what type of recruits you hire—be they liberal or conservative, accommodating or assertive, passive or aggressive—after a short while on the force they too will walk and talk and think like cops.

A Beechwood, Ohio, senior officer instructs a rookie patrol officer.

This line of reasoning raises a fundamental sociological question: Do social roles shape the individual (called *role taking*), or does the individual shape the social role (*role making*)?[21] While it is true that we are all "role makers" to some extent in our lives and our occupations, the truth is that we are all "role takers" to a far greater extent. Whether we realize it or not, we tend to accept the roles and duties that have been already defined for us, and we strive to satisfy the expectations of others. We do this as students, teachers, spouses, and parents. The point being made is essential—just as society shapes the individual far more than the individual shapes society, police work shapes the officer far more than the officer shapes police work.

Subculture of Policing

Much has been written about the close, special bond officers develop among themselves. The intimacy, camaraderie, and loyalty among officers, particularly between partners, is also dramatized in television police shows and popular police novels. Most occupations develop an inclusiveness or solidarity among fellow workers, yet police are thought to develop an unusually high degree of occupational solidarity.[22] The following passage is one author's view of what the "brotherhood" of police officers really means:

> *Brotherhood.* It means a fraternity of legally frustrated men with clean-cut hair, large coffee-ridden stomachs and impaired social lives who show up in embarrassing numbers to give blood to their wounded and race to 10–13's (assist officers) with their 38's loosened and the adrenalin shifting extra blood to the stomach and other vital organs, making them breathe faster. Men who stand at

massive cop funerals in stricken lines and socialize with each other and look at
clocks that have 13, 14, 15, etc., written over the normal hours; men who are
linked always to each other by $700 walkie-talkies and their Bad-News car radio;
men who feel despite societies for ethnic cops, "We are all blue." The department
is the family; the precinct is "the House."[23]

139

CHAPTER 6:
Working the
Streets

It is sometimes argued that police officers develop such close working
relationships with fellow officers because the life-and-death situations and ever
present danger instinctively draw them close together, just as life-and-death
situations draw soldiers close together.[24] What is more, the job of policing
marks them as being different from ordinary citizens. Officers complain that
other people do not understand them, that they no longer "fit in." So they
begin to associate more with other officers both on and off duty. Officers often
joke that they know their partners better than their spouses.

This special society of police officers is known as the **subculture of
policing**. William Westley was the first police scholar to closely describe the
police subculture,[25] and other writers have since filled in the missing details.[26]
Writing four decades ago, Westley concluded from his study of the Gary,
Indiana Police Department that a police subculture did exist with a distinctive
set of customs, rules, morality, and special language. The basic elements of
the subculture were secrecy, silence, and loyalty to the group, elements to
which all officers were expected to adhere. Those who did not subscribe to the
subculture's dictates were disdained by other officers and ostracized. Westley
characterized the subculture of policing as having a powerful, conforming
influence over police officers. As a result, being socialized into the police
subculture provided the major frame of reference for young officers.

Department Code versus Street Code

The first real contact with the police subculture for most officers occurs at the
training academy,[27] and subsequently continues in the police department as the

---

⌐ MY HUSBAND THE COP ───────

"My husband, the cop. Always has to be the big
man. One of the neighbors gets a ticket, they
show up on our doorstep. 'Hey, Jimmy, old
buddy, can you fix this for me? I swear the light
was yellow. Can you fix it?'

" 'Don't worry about it,' he says. 'No problem.' "

The wife of a police officer, a thin, conservatively well-dressed woman in her fifties, was trying
to explain to me the gulf between illusion and
reality in her neighbors' perception of her husband, as well as in his perception of himself. He
is a patrolman in a large metropolitan area and
has worked in the same precinct on the same
assignment for fifteen years.

"The big, important policeman. Do you know
how he fixes tickets? He goes downtown and he
pays them, that's how he fixes tickets."

She was angry about his behavior, but in telling me this story she wasn't trying to belittle her
husband. She wanted to give me a glimpse of the
man inside the uniform—not a hero or a Fascist,
a gunslinger, or a centurion, just a mere mortal
like everyone else.

Source: Mark Baker, *Cops: Their Lives in Their Own Words* (Simon and Schuster, 1985), p. 5.

newly sworn officer begins patrol duty. Each new recruit must quickly learn two sets of rules. First there are the written formal rules of the job that require sufficient knowledge of the standard operating policies and procedures of the department. These formal rules include all of the "do's" and "don'ts" of the department, like "do" groom appropriately and "don't" wander out of your district. We refer to these formal rules of the agency as the **department code.**

The second set of rules existing alongside the department code are the unwritten informal rules, or what we can call the **street code.** In many ways the street code is more salient to the working world of the police officer than is the department code.[28] The street code cannot be learned by studying the department's procedure manual or by reading the chief's memos; it is learned by watching, listening, and interacting with other police officers. Oftentimes the street code augments the formal department code, thereby furthering the goals of the police agency. At other times, the street code works directly against the formal wishes of the department, such as when new recruits are told to "take it easy" and "not work too hard," or when patrol officers keep silent about the misbehaviors of fellow officers. Given the shrouded secrecy of policing, the strong group loyalty, and the immense pressure to conform, when the street code comes into conflict with the department code it is usually the latter that is either conveniently circumvented or blatantly violated.

Police Suspicion and Cynicism

It is commonly taught in rookie school and on the streets that because of the nature of police work, its frequent danger and unpredictability, an officer must be continually prepared for the unexpected. The potential for trouble is always there—one just never knows. An officer must be ready in the event that "all hell breaks loose."

Police suspicion is a part of the working personality of police officers.[29] Trained officers scan city streets and alleys in search of the unusual, out-of-the-ordinary person or situation. Many observers argue that good officers develop a *gut feeling* when something is wrong, as if they had a sixth sense to detect trouble. Officers themselves may not be able to articulate the specific reasons for their suspicions, other than to say that "something" is giving them a bad feeling. However, they swear they develop these feelings.

Skolnick suggests that seasoned street officers develop a *perceptual shorthand* for identifying certain kinds of people as troublemakers. He refers to this shorthand device as the **symbolic assailant,** meaning an individual who dresses or behaves in a way that police come to recognize as a prelude to trouble.[30] Neighborhood gang members, men in long trench coats on a warm summer's day, and strangers in a quiet neighborhood are all obvious examples of symbolic assailants. They are so obvious in fact that they would likely arouse the suspicions of ordinary people. But police officers are trained to be far more vigilant than the average citizen.

We can extend Skolnick's reasoning to include **symbolic situations** that also signal trouble to the officer. Examples of symbolic situations that would ordinarily elevate an officer's suspicions include:

- Store lights on at odd hours;
- A moving van at a house with no "For Sale" sign;
- A car in a school parking lot on a weekend night;
- Cars with mismatched hubcaps;
- Clean cars with dirty license plates (or vice versa);
- Cars with out-of-state plates in a known drug area;
- A barking dog late at night;
- The sound of breaking glass.

Related to the concept of police suspicion is **police cynicism.** Suspicion and cynicism are similar in that they both make reference to the negative view of certain people and situations that is characteristic of the police. The difference between the two concepts is that police suspicion is a normal, healthy awareness of potential trouble resulting from identifiable symbolic assailants or situations; police cynicism, on the other hand, is an unhealthy, gnawingly pessimistic view of the world. The police officer justifies his or her

---

SYMBOLIC ASSAILANTS

A. Be suspicious. This is a healthy police attitude, but it should be controlled and not too obvious.
B. Look for the unusual.
C. Subjects who should be subjected to field interrogations.
   1. Suspicious persons known to the officer from previous arrests, field interrogations, and observations.
   2. Emaciated-appearing alcoholics and narcotics users who invariably turn to crime to pay for cost of habit.
   3. Person who fits description of wanted suspect as described by radio, teletype, daily bulletins.
   4. Any person observed in the immediate vicinity of a crime very recently committed or reported as "in progress."
   5. Known troublemakers near large gatherings.
   6. Persons who attempt to avoid or evade the officer.
   7. Exaggerated unconcern over contact with the officer.
   8. Visibly "rattled" when near the policeman.
   9. Unescorted women or young girls in public places, particularly at night in such places as cafes, bars, bus and train depots, or street corners.
   10. "Lovers" in an industrial area (make good lookouts).
   11. Persons who loiter about places where children play.
   12. Solicitors or peddlers in a residential neighborhood.
   13. Loiterers around public rest rooms.
   14. Lone male sitting in car adjacent to schoolground with newspaper or book in his lap.
   15. Lone male sitting in car near shopping center who pays unusual amount of attention to women, sometimes continuously manipulating rearview mirror to avoid direct eye contact.
   16. Hitchhikers.
   17. Person wearing coat on hot days.
   18. Uniformed "deliverymen" with no merchandise or truck.

Source: Thomas F. Adams, "Field Interrogation," *Police* (March–April, 1963), p. 28.

cynical philosophy by "having seen the real world" and "knowing what the score is."[31] In this sense, police cynicism serves as a *cognitive lens* that casts a dark shadow over police officers' lives and their relationships with others.

The concept of police cynicism is most associated with the late Arthur Niederhoffer, a one-time police officer and training academy instructor who became a noted police scholar later in his career.[32] Niederhoffer claimed there were two different levels of police cynicism. The first type of cynicism is against the criminal justice system. Cynicism of this type is most prevalent among patrol officers who have witnessed firsthand the flaws in the system. James Hernandez captures this view well by describing the **Custer syndrome** in police work—"the belief that not losing ground can be counted as success."[33] In other words, simply maintaining reasonable control over our communities is all we can ask of the police. By way of contrast, professionally committed police officers normally do not have an overly cynical view of their jobs or of the system.

The second type of cynicism is directed against all of humanity and, according to Niederhoffer, is endemic to police officers of all ranks regardless of professional orientation.[34] To drive home his point, Niederhoffer retells the answer that William Parker, the late chief of the Los Angeles Police Department, gave when asked the question "Are you inclined to be pessimistic about the future of our society?":

> I look back over almost thirty-five years in the police service, thirty-five years of dealing with the worst that humanity has to offer. I meet the failures of humanity daily, and I meet them in the worst possible context. It is hard to keep an objective viewpoint. But it is also hard for me to believe that our society can continue to violate all the fundamental rules of human conduct and expect to survive. I think I have to conclude that this civilization will destroy itself, as others have before it. That leaves, then, only one question—when?[35]

Cynicism tends to vary over a police career. Niederhoffer found that cynicism begins developing as early as the training academy. It reaches the point of greatest intensity somewhere around the seventh to tenth year, then gradually diminishes for the duration of the police career (see figure 6.1). Niederhoffer described four stages leading to cynicism:

- *Stage One—Professionalism and Commitment:* New recruits tend to be more idealistic than the average person: "I truly want to help people";
- *Stage Two—Occasional Frustration:* Failures occur periodically but are viewed as part of the job: "They won't get me down";
- *Stage Three—Chronic Disenchantment:* Failures and frustrations are unrelenting: "They are getting me down";
- *Stage Four—Cynicism:* Changes in officer attitude are evident: "This job sucks, the criminal justice system is a farce, and people are slime."

Many researchers have tackled the issue of police cynicism since Niederhoffer's 1967 study. Some of their findings have revised our thinking. For instance, the study by Rafky, Lawley, and Ingram at a regional training

FIGURE 6.1
Police Cynicism

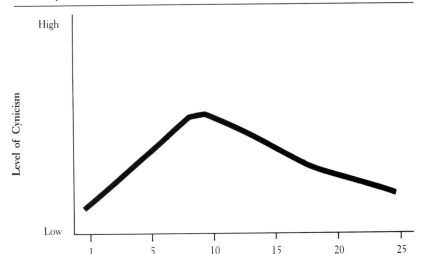

academy in the Southeastern section of the U.S. found no evidence of cynicism in academy recruits, a finding that contradicts Niederhoffer's claim. The authors conclude: ". . . if experienced police officers are indeed cynical, this cannot be traced to the academy, which produces officers leaning toward a neutral, common sense orientation to their occupation."[36] Another study has been able to connect police cynicism with work alienation, a relationship Niederhoffer suggested but never empirically established.[37]

The existing research still leaves unanswered many questions regarding police cynicism. For instance, do all officers experience cynicism to the same level? Is it different for male officers than female officers, or for white officers than black officers? Does officer education affect cynicism? Is "small-town" cynicism different from "big-city" cynicism? Is police cynicism qualitatively different than "doctor cynicism," "sales clerk cynicism" or "professor cynicism?" Is police cynicism necessarily a bad thing, or does it serve some positive function? Clearly there is much more we need to learn about this important topic.

From Professor To Police Officer

Several selections in the police literature describe the personal experiences of criminal justice professors who became sworn law enforcement officers. Their rationale for doing so was to learn more about police work from the "inside." For instance, in an article entitled "I'm Not the Man I Used to Be," Professor William Doerner reflects on his transition from professor to rookie police officer: "Changes, which I thought were subtle and only partially visible to others, have altered me to such a degree that I am an entirely different person with a completely different set of values, beliefs, and attitudes."[38] Doerner reports how his personality turned more cold and calloused and cynical as a police officer, and how these negative changes affected his marriage.

Professor George Kirkham also made the transition from the classroom to the streets.[39] Kirkham was a young criminology professor at Florida State University in the early 1970s. He was troubled by the fact that most of the experts who write books and articles on the police have never themselves been police officers. What was more, Kirkham's frequent criticisms of the police were resented by students in his class, many of who were police officers. These officers argued that Kirkham "should not judge the worth of another man's actions until he walked a mile in his shoes." So Kirkham decided to accept their challenge.

Kirkham contacted the sheriff in Jacksonville, Florida, and told him about his idea of doing police work. Note that this was in the early 1970s and the idea of a professor doing police work was a complete novelty. So in a way, Kirkham was proposing the idea on a lark. To Kirkham's surprise, the sheriff was not only willing to let Kirkham become an officer, he was also enthusiastic. The sheriff thought it was time to get the so-called academic expert out of the safe classroom and behind a badge.

Kirkham became a fully sworn member of the department. He passed the same requirements as all officers. This meant completing the four month, twenty hours per week training academy while still teaching. Finally, Kirkham was ready for the streets.

The Jacksonville Sheriff's Department was responsible for patrolling the unincorporated area of the county as well as the city of Jacksonville. At the time, the city of Jacksonville had a population of about 500,000 with the typical inner-city slum and high-crime area. This is where Kirkham was assigned! Needless to say, the professor-turned-cop went through a profound change of heart similar to the change that Doerner describes. Kirkham's ivory tower orientation took a cold slap in the face with the reality of policing.

Stories like Doerner's and Kirkham's are interesting because they are dramatic and contain vivid, gruesome descriptors of the unpleasant things in life. We get a "voyeuristic charge" reading about these sordid things—like a man sticking a knife in the face of his best drinking buddy over some poker game squabble or brains spilling out on the sidewalk after a gang member has his head blown apart by a shotgun.

A potential pitfall to these types of "insider" studies is the ease with which a researcher can lose his or her objectivity and, in the process, "go native." Field researchers must guard against becoming the *intellectual apologists* for police by consciously striving to be objective social scientists.

SPECIAL POLICE PROBLEMS

Police are responsible for handling an immense variety of tasks. A listing of the many street-level activities to which patrol officers respond would be extremely long and no doubt incomplete. Veteran patrol officers marvel at the fact that no two days on the street are ever alike. Each eight hour "tour of duty" brings some unique experience, some new encounter.

While there are a wide variety of problems that challenge the police, there are also numerous recurring and especially difficult tasks that become special police problems. In the paragraphs that follow, we discuss three special police problems: (1) problem populations, (2) domestic disputes, and (3) line of duty deaths.

Problem Populations

Certain segments of the population greatly increase the work load of police. Teenage gang members, drug users, and prostitutes, for example, burden the

---

FROM PROF TO COP

STREET LESSON 1: SCHOOL OF HARD KNOCKS

Several hours into my first evening on the streets, my partner and I were dispatched to a bar in the downtown area to handle a disturbance complaint. Inside, we encountered a large and boisterous drunk who was arguing with the bartender and loudly refusing to leave. As someone with considerable experience as a correctional counselor and mental health worker, I hastened to take charge of the situation. "Excuse me, Sir," I smiled pleasantly at the drunk, "but I wonder if I could ask you to step outside and talk with me for just a minute?" The man stared at me through bloodshot eyes in disbelief for a second, raising one hand to scratch the stubble of several days' growth of beard. Then suddenly, without warning, it happened. He swung at me, luckily missing my face and striking me on the right shoulder. I couldn't believe it. What on earth had I done to provoke such a reaction? Before I could recover from my startled condition, he swung again— this time tearing my whistle chain from a shoulder epaulet. After a brief struggle, we had the still shouting, cursing man locked in the back of our cruiser. I stood there, breathing heavily with my hair in my eyes as I surveyed the damage to my new uniform and looked in bewilderment at my partner, who only smiled and clapped me affectionately on the back.

STREET LESSON 2: THE LESSON OF FEAR

I recall particularly a dramatic lesson in the meaning of fear which took place shortly after I joined the force. My partner and I were on routine patrol one Saturday evening in a deteriorated area of cheap bars and pool halls when we observed a young male double-parked in the middle of the street. I pulled alongside and asked him in a civil manner to either park or drive on, whereupon he began loudly cursing us and shouting that we couldn't make him go anywhere. An angry crowd began to gather as we got out of our patrol car and approached the man, who by this time was shouting that we were harassing him and calling to bystanders for assistance. As a criminology professor, some months earlier I would have urged that the police officer who was now myself simply leave the car double-parked and move on rather than risk an incident. As a policeman, however, I had come to realize that an officer can never back down from his responsibility to enforce the law. Whatever the risk to himself, every police officer understands that his ability to back up the lawful authority which he represents is the only thing which stands between civilization and the jungle of lawlessness.

Source: George L. Kirkham, *FBI Law Enforcement Bulletin* (U.S. Department of Justice, U.S. Government Printing Office, March 1974), pp. 14–22.

police by their frequent criminal behavior. This forces the police to respond predominately in a law enforcement capacity. The arrests police make and the subsequent prosecutions place heavy demands on the entire criminal justice system. The overloaded court dockets and overcrowded prisons and jails are creating pressure to find alternative ways of dealing with these problem people.

There are other special population groups that are less of a criminal problem than a social order problem. But these people also burden the police. Three main groups fall into this category: (1) the mentally ill, (2) the public inebriate, and (3) the homeless.[40] Individuals in these groups are heavy consumers of police services because they require a large amount of police officer time and energy. Handling the mentally ill is an especially difficult task for the police. One study of over one thousand police-citizen encounters in an urban area found that 8 percent of the contacts involved a mentally disordered person.[41] The same study found that the police handled the encounter informally over 70 percent of the time; approximately 12 percent of the situations resulted in psychiatric hospitalization, and nearly 17 percent ended in arrest.

The public inebriate and the homeless are also difficult problems for the police. The difficulty in handling these people is exacerbated by the lack of available facilities to help them. For the homeless, space at shelters is limited and many shelters refuse to accept homeless people who are mentally unstable or alcoholic; for the public inebriate, beds at detoxification centers are in short supply, jails are crowded, and the police station is not the best place to "sleep it off."[42]

Domestic Disputes

Domestic disturbance calls are notoriously disliked by the police. To many officers the "domestic" is the hardest call to answer. It showcases the worst that humanity has to offer. Domestic violence accounts for one out of every four homicides and serious assaults in the United States, an appalling statistic but one that says nothing of the number of marriages destroyed or children devastated by its impact. Family fights are unpredictable situations and potentially dangerous to officers. The ear-shattering screaming, hysterical crying, angry actions, and frequent bloodshed easily overwhelms the senses. As in all police-citizen encounters, the officer's first order of business is to take charge of the situation, but the chaotic nature of most domestic disturbances seems to defy officer control. The best the police can usually hope for is to stabilize the situation, and even then perhaps only for the night. In too many cases the violence will continue, and the police will return.

Past practices dictated that police calm domestic disturbances as best they could with what little formal training they had. In many departments patrol officers subscribed to the unwritten policy of responding slowly to domestic complaints in the hope that the combatants would make up before they arrived.[43] The practice of "slow response" has backfired for a few departments because of recent civil suits brought by victims of domestic disputes. The **Thurman case** illustrates this point. In June of 1983, Tracy Thurman was stabbed thirteen times in her neck, arms, and throat by her estranged husband. The attack left Thurman partially paralyzed on the right side of her body. She claimed all this happened while a police officer from the city of Torrington, Connecticut, witnessed the attack from outside the house as he waited for backup. Thurman took the city of Torrington and twenty-nine of its officers to federal court in a multi-million dollar law suit *and won!* The court ruled that by failing to act, the department was negligent of its duty to protect Thurman, thereby violating her Constitutional rights. The *Thurman* case has profound implications for police everywhere, and similar cases are pending. The message is unmistakably clear: the courts are increasingly willing to hold the police accountable for their actions—or nonactions—in domestic disturbances.

The police will normally make an arrest in a domestic disturbance if any of the following apply: (1) someone is seriously injured; (2) the officer witnesses the attack; (3) the victim is willing to press charges; or (4) the officer is assaulted.[44] (The laws of arrest are more thoroughly covered in chapter 8.) However, the normal tendency is for the police to make few arrests in domestic disturbance calls, even in situations when someone is injured. There are several reasons why. First, the police are reluctant to arrest because experience

Growing militancy among the homeless creates further problems for police. Here, a group of Philadelphians protest the arrest of several members of the homeless community who, in a demonstration against city budget cuts, tried to force their way into a City Hall office.

teaches them that once the rage of the moment or the alcohol of the night dissipates, disputing parties often change their minds. The typical scenario is when a wife has her drunk and abusive husband arrested for the night, only to drop the charges against him the next day.

A second reason why some officers prefer not to arrest is because they believe the arrested party will become even more angry and, once released, return to avenge their arrest on the victim.

A third reason why the police do not make more arrests in cases of domestic violence is because the law does not encourage them to arrest. Historically, the criminal law has been unsympathetic to the plight of abused spouses and children. The pervasive legal view has been that domestic fights are a private matter and should be resolved without state interference. It was only little more than a hundred years ago in some communities that the law prohibited a man from beating his wife past 10:00 p.m., or on Sundays—a law purely for the convenience of neighbors. In many states today, domestic violence is classified as a criminal misdemeanor which requires the officer to witness the attack before they can initiate an arrest. The only option is to encourage the victim to go to the local magistrate and take out an arrest warrant on their abuser. The arrest warrant gives the officer the legal authority to return and arrest the abuser, but not without the considerable effort from the victim.[45]

States are beginning to modify their arrest laws in cases of domestic violence, thus making it easier for the police to initiate arrests on their own. The **Minneapolis Experiment** tested the proposition that arresting offenders in domestic assault cases and jailing them overnight works better at reducing future violence against the victim than traditional police strategies like counseling or trying to separate the parties.[46] Officers who participated in the experiment relinquished their discretionary authority and agreed to: (1) arrest, (2) counsel, or (3) separate the disputant parties based on random assignment. Data from the experiment show that while 18 percent of all offenders repeated their violence, only 10 percent of the arrested offenders were subsequently abusive.[47] The results of the study suggest that in most situations, arresting offenders in domestic disputes deters subsequent violence better than counselling or short-term separation.

The experiment in Minneapolis attracted widespread attention and praise from the law enforcement community. Police departments nationwide responded with aggressive arrest polices of their own as the preferred method of handling cases of domestic violence. Unfortunately, the shift to a discretionary or even mandatory arrest policy for incidents of misdemeanor domestic assault may be premature. A recent study in Omaha designed to replicate the Minneapolis Experiment failed to do so.[48] The Omaha study found that arresting offenders did not reduce subsequent domestic conflict any more than counselling or separating disputants. This puts us in an awkward bind considering the conflicting findings from two very similar experiments. In other words, policymakers currently have few clear guidelines to follow in domestic assault cases. Policymakers will have to proceed cautiously until additional research becomes available.

The physical dangers of police work are well known. Unlike ordinary citizens who avoid the dangers of social living and who flee life-threatening situations, the police are drawn into the middle of trouble. Thus, it is not surprising that the homicide rate for police officers is more than twice the rate for the general population, and the rate of assault is more than six times higher.[49]

In a typical year, anywhere from sixty-five to seventy-five police officers are murdered while on duty. The number of officers slain in the line of duty has decreased appreciably in the past two decades. The deadliest year for police officers was 1974 when 132 officers were feloniously killed. In 1990, only sixty-five officers were slain in the line of duty, the lowest number killed since the FBI began collecting data in the early 1960s. The reduction of officer deaths appears to be due to two factors: (1) improved training methods for police officers; and (2) the availability of bullet proof vests. Kevlar, a lightweight synthetic material developed by DuPont as an alternative to steel belts in tires, has revolutionized the body armor industry. Worn "relatively" comfortably under one's shirt, Kevlar is credited with saving the lives of hundreds of police officers.[50]

Victoria Major has tallied the number of officers killed in the line of duty during the 1980s.[51] From 1980 through 1989 a total of 801 officers were feloniously killed (783 males and eighteen females). Firearms claimed the lives of 92 percent (735) of the fallen officers—15 percent (120) were killed with their own weapons. The following identifies the types of weapons used:

- 70 percent by handguns;
- 13 percent by rifles;
- 9 percent by shotguns;
- 4 percent intentionally struck by vehicles;
- 2 percent stabbed to death;
- 2 percent "other" (blunt object; hands or feet; burned; drowned; asphyxiated).

Southern states tend to be the most dangerous for officers. Of the 801 officers murdered during the 1980s, 47 percent were from the South. Western states claimed 18 percent of the deaths; Midwestern states, 17 percent; Northern states, 13 percent; and U.S. territories, 5 percent. One hundred and fifty-seven officers were wearing body armor at the time of death. Of this number, ninety-four officers were killed when bullets struck their heads; thirty-two when bullets entered through arm openings or the panels of the vest; twenty-five when bullets struck the torso above or below the vest; and six when bullets penetrated the vest.

A problem of nearly equal magnitude is the number of police officers who die accidental deaths while performing their official duties. During the 1980s, accidental line of duty deaths took the lives of 713 officers. The leading cause of accidental deaths was automobile accidents, which claimed 312 officers. An additional 160 officers were accidentally killed when struck by a vehicle. Of the remaining fatalities, eighty-nine were aircraft accidents; sixty were accidental shootings; forty-nine were motorcycle accidents; and forty-three were from falls, drownings, etc.[52]

Occasionally an officer is slain by ambush or when performing a routine task like investigating an auto accident, but usually officers lose their lives answering calls known to be dangerous. Armed robberies, burglaries in progress, apprehending violent offenders, and domestic disturbances are all potentially dangerous.

Domestic disturbances are known to be highly dangerous. For years police trainers have preached that more officers are killed while answering domestic disturbance calls than any other type of call. As evidence of the dangerousness of domestic calls, the FBI's yearly report to the nation on the number of police officers feloniously killed is commonly cited. The FBI annual statistics reveal disturbance calls to be among the most—or *the* most depending on the year—dangerous police activity.

However, startling new evidence is debunking the conventional wisdom about the dangers of domestic disturbances.[53] The traditional FBI category of "domestic disturbance" was an amalgamation of an assortment of disturbance complaints. Family quarrels were classified as domestic disturbances, but so were situations like a man brandishing a gun, bar fights, and gang disorders. Starting in 1982, the FBI began separating the standard "domestic" category into two different categories: "family disturbances" (family quarrels exclusively) and "other domestics" (bar fights, gang calls, man with gun, etc.). As revealed in figure 6.2, when disturbance calls are reclassified, the true family style

FIGURE 6.2
Officer Deaths: Separating "Family" from "Other" Disturbances

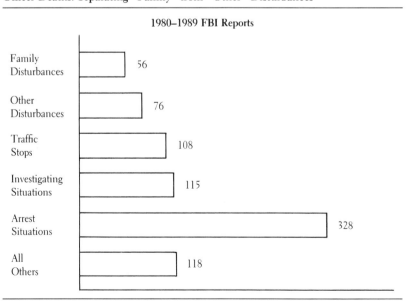

Source: U.S. Department of Justice, *Law Enforcement Officers Killed and Assaulted*, 1989, FBI Uniform Crime Reports (Washington, DC: U.S. Government Printing Office, 1990), p. 19.

domestic disturbance is far less likely to result in an officer death than previously thought. From 1980 to 1989, only fifty-six officers were killed responding to "family" disturbances compared to seventy-six officers killed responding
to "other" disturbances. Even standard traffic stops and routine investigations
of suspicious persons or situations have ended the lives of more officers than
family quarrels. The policy implication from this new research suggests that
training considerations should be revised to more accurately reflect the relative
danger of handling family disturbances.

Notification of family members that a police officer has been killed in
the line of duty is never easy. Few departments are adequately prepared for
such an occasion, and few have formal death notification policies. A group
known as **C.O.P.S.** (Concerns Of Police Survivors) was created in 1984 as a
national networking organization. C.O.P.S. provides peer support to police
survivors and assists departments in developing plans to handle the trauma
suffered by family members.

POLICING: A STRESSFUL OCCUPATION

Police officers do not have to be the victim of a line of duty death or debilitating
injury to become a *career casualty*. **Police stress** is another major hazard of
policing that takes its toll on officers. Police stress is a quiet hazard that works
slowly, almost imperceptibly. In its mildest form, excess stress can affect
officers' psychological and emotional well-being, causing them to be periodically depressed or easily agitated. In moderate form, excess stress can lead to
lethargic behavior (reduced alertness and stamina) or unhealthy physiological
symptoms (high blood pressure, headaches, backaches, heartburn, ulcers,
gastric disorders). At its worse, the cumulative effect of too much stress over
the course of a career can lead to severe clinical depression, alcoholism,
substance abuse, suicidal behavior, heart disease, and even death. Police
officers can literally become victims of their careers.

Experts agree that police work is a highly stressful occupation.[54] Police
officers feel the pressure placed on them by the multiple and often conflicting
demands of the job. There are numerous stressors inherent in police work.
One group of researchers identifies the following sources of stress:

- Erratic work schedules and shift assignments;
- Role conflict—law enforcer versus public servant;
- Constant threat to officer's safety;
- Drastic emotional shifts from boredom to need for sudden alertness and
  mobilized energy;
- Responsible for protecting lives of others;
- Continual exposure to people in pain or distress;
- Presence of gun, even during off-duty hours;
- Fragmented nature of police work, with rare opportunities to follow case
  to its logical conclusion.[55]

To this list the same researchers note the additional stress that female
(and some minority) police officers face. Not only do female officers have to

contend with the same stresses of police work as male officers, women have the additional burden of continually having to "prove" themselves on the job. They also meet with greater disapproval from family and friends about their decision to become a police officer. Moreover, females and many minority recruits do not receive the same level of friendship or tutelage from fellow officers,[56] both of which are important ingredients for minimizing the effects of stress.

A traditional observation about police work is that the long-term effect of excess stress leads to high levels of suicide, divorce, alcoholism, emotional instability, and physical disorders. Assorted studies over the years place the likelihood of these types of disorders among the police anywhere from one to three times higher than the general population. However, research findings are not consistent from one study to another, and several studies actually refute the notion that the police are any more susceptible to destructive behaviors like suicide or alcoholism than the average person.[57] Nonetheless, the overwhelming weight of evidence at this time still supports the argument that the stress of policing takes a heavy toll on employees and their families, often in highly destructive ways.

DEATH NOTIFICATION

"I had just finished grocery shopping when I heard the chilling report of a police shoot-out on the car radio. The reporter was the one who informed me that it was my husband that had been killed. My neighbors found me, crying hysterically, parked in the middle of the road several blocks from home."—A police widow from Texas

1. The name of the deceased officer *MUST NEVER* be released by the media before immediate survivors living in the area are notified.
2. If there is knowledge of a medical problem with an immediate survivor, medical personnel should be dispatched to the residence to coincide with the death notification.
3. Notification *MUST ALWAYS* be made in person and never alone. The public safety chaplain, psychologist, the head of the agency (or his representative), or another public safety survivor could appropriately accompany the informing officer.

"When I got to the hospital, he had already died. He had been at the hospital for two hours. The department waited for the chap-lain to arrive before coming to tell me. I could have seen him before he died."—A police widow from Pennsylvania

Keep in mind, however, that if the above-suggested persons are not readily accessible, notification should not be held up until these people can gather. If the opportunity to get the family to the hospital prior to the demise of the officer presents itself, *DON'T* wait for the appropriate delegation to gather.

As soon as most public safety families see you, they will know something is wrong. Ask to be admitted to the house. *NEVER* make a death notification on the doorstep. Gather everyone in the home and ask them to sit down. Inform them slowly and clearly of the information you have on the incident. Make sure you use the officer's name during the notification.

If the officer has already died, relay that information. *NEVER* give the family a false sense of hope. Use words like 'died' and 'dead' rather than 'gone away' or 'passed away.'

"We drove for what seemed like hours with the escorting officer saying repeatedly, 'He's

Police officers are especially susceptible to the condition known as **post-shooting trauma.** Police officers are only human with feelings and emotions just like everyone else. When an officer wounds or kills another person, the officer must deal with an immense emotional burden, even if the shooting was justified on legal grounds. Guilt, fear, flashbacks, nightmares, and depression are common symptoms that may last for an extended period of time. The officer's family, friends, and co-workers also frequently experience emotional shock following a shooting. Of course some officers are affected by post-shooting trauma more than others, meaning that not all officers experience severe or prolonged stress. To keep the problem of post-shooting trauma in proper perspective, however, one must realize that the typical police officer will never shoot at a criminal suspect over the course of an entire career.

Law enforcement professionals are becoming increasingly aware of the negative career consequences of police work. Since the 1970s, the concept of "stress management" has become popular in the police community.[58] In 1979, for instance, the National Institute of Justice published a bibliography listing 113 references and thirty-three training films on stress reduction and management techniques.[59] Stress management programs are sometimes formal and

---

going to be all right.' When we got to the hospital, I was told he was dead on the scene."—An east coast police widow of 1981

If the person responsible for the death notification has been seriously affected by the death, he (she) should understand that showing emotions is perfectly acceptable.

If specifics of the incident are known, the officer should relay as much information as possible to the family.

NOTE: Reactions of the family may include hysteria, anger, fainting, physical violence, shock, etc.

4. If the family wants to go to the hospital, they should be transported via department vehicle. It is highly recommended that the family *NOT* drive themselves to the hospital. Should there be serious resistance and the family insists on driving, please have an officer accompany them in the car.

The department should know if there are young children in the home. The survivor may wish to leave the children at home. The department should be prepared to handle immediate babysitting needs. This is where co-workers' spouses or a spouse support group can be used.

Because of the nature of possible radio transmissions, the officer making the transport should notify the OIC at the hospital that the family is enroute.

Keep in mind that the surviving parents should also be afforded this courtesy of personal notification if they live in the same geographic area.

5. If immediate survivors are from out of town, request personal death notification from the public safety agency in that area. Logistical arrangements should enable simultaneous telephone contact with the fallen officer's department.

6. It is most reassuring to the family when the Chief or another high-ranking designee responds to the home or hospital. (In some cases, the absence was viewed by both the family and fellow officers as not only insensitive but poor leadership as well.)

Source: C.O.P.S., *Support Services to Surviving Families of Line-of-Duty Death,* 1989.

FIGURE 6.3
The Broken Badge

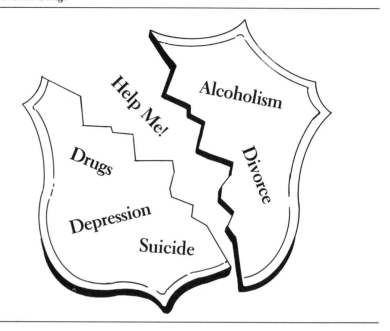

highly involved, such as programs that utilize a team of police psychiatrists, psychologists, and other trained professional counselors. Other stress management programs are less formal and far less expensive. For example, some departments encourage officers to engage in physical exercise as a way to reduce the effects of job stress. A few departments encourage officers to act as a support group for fellow officers to talk out their problems. Former Boston police officer Raymond Donovan has traveled the country counseling police officers and serving as a consultant to police agencies that want to develop a stress management program. The success of Donovan's approach is built on the belief that the only people who can truly understand what a police officer thinks and feels are other police officers.

There is little doubt that a stressed-out, emotionally unstable, and physically unhealthy work force is a severe detriment to the police department. To the extent that we are able to help officers and their families deal with the multiple and sometimes debilitating stresses of police work, we will be promoting the well-being of the police profession.

CONCLUSION

This chapter focused on the working world of patrol officers as they go about their daily routines on the streets. We devoted considerable attention to police-citizen encounters, noting that the typical interaction pattern is one where the police exchange deference and respect at a level just below that which they receive from citizens. A major consideration of the police is to maintaining the edge (control) in all police-citizen encounters. In the absence of a controlling edge, the police lose the ability to quickly resolve a troublesome situation. We noted that the legal capacity to arrest an unruly suspect of a crime provides the police with a state-sanctioned tool to maintain the edge in difficult encounters; regardless of how raunchy the suspect's language toward the police may be, if he or she is in handcuffs the police are in control. However, a disrespectful citizen who is not suspected of any crime—our so-called "creep-in-the-crowd"—is not as easily controlled. The typical "turd" or "asshole" can be a tremendous hassle to the police.

What is it really like to be a patrol officer working the streets? One would imagine that the entertainment industry has given us some idea of what it is like. Or has it? Has the American viewing public, as outsiders to the real world of police work, learned any more about the police after watching some vindictive cop blast away a dozen criminals in a two hour movie? Or what about when a TV detective gets in a gun battle in nearly every episode? Even the more "realistic" police shows are exaggerated theatrics designed to entertain viewers.

Real life policing falls somewhere between silly cop shows and killer cop shows. And real life policing is different in small towns than it is in big cities. After reading this chapter you should now have a deeper understanding of everyday police work, and perhaps a greater appreciation for those who work the streets.

KEY TERMS

interactionist perspective
recipe for action
deference exchange
maintaining the edge
styles of policing
watch, legalistic, service
working personality
police socialization
subculture of policing
department code versus street code

police suspicion
symbolic assailant
symbolic situation
police cynicism
Custer syndrome
Thurman case
Minneapolis Experiment
C.O.P.S.
police stress
post-shooting trauma

DISCUSSION QUESTIONS

1. What is an "asshole" and why is "asshole control" a difficult challenge to the police?
2. Think about your local police department. Would you describe it as a watch, legalistic, or service-style department? Why?
3. What personal style of policing do you think would best describe you if you were a police officer (enforcer, idealist, realist, optimist)? If you were a police administrator, which type of individual would you prefer to have on the force?
4. Explain the concept of "police cynicism." Is police cynicism really any more of a problem than "social worker cynicism" or "school teacher cynicism"?
5. Discuss the significance of the Tracy Thurman case. What are your views regarding police responses to family fights?

Legal Parameters of Policing

Here in Part III we carefully examine the legal parameters of American policing. This is a critical juncture in our study as we establish the legal boundaries separating lawful from unlawful police behavior. Chapter 7 on police discretion concentrates on police behavior which falls on "this side" of the law. We note that police discretion is part of the job responsibility of officers and, if properly used and adequately controlled, can benefit society in many ways. Chapter 8 takes a close look at the rights of citizens in relation to the authority of the police. The evolution of citizen rights, particularly with regard to search and seizure and self-incrimination, is traced through important Supreme Court cases. Finally, the material in chapter 9 draws our attention to police behavior which falls on the "other side" of the law. This chapter shows only too clearly that the police are not always honest or tame.

CHAPTER SEVEN

POLICE DISCRETION

That the police exercise broad discretion in carrying out their multiple functions should, by now, be patently clear.

—Herman Goldstein

Have you ever witnessed an incident when the police did not arrest a criminal suspect when they had the legal right to, or when the police did not issue a traffic citation when they could have written one? Maybe you know of a case where the police caught an adolescent engaged in mischievous behavior, but only scolded the youth without further action. Or perhaps you have knowledge of an incident when the police made an arrest for "disorderly conduct" or "disturbance of the peace" when the public peace was not seriously endangered. Many of us know of situations like these when the police appear to act on their own accord. At times it seems as if the police set the rules of social living and decide who is selected for legal sanction. To a large extent this is true. The police have much freedom to make up their own minds how best to handle problem situations. The decision-making ability of the police is referred to as **police discretion**, and is the central topic of this chapter.

Citizens are often surprised to discover that police officers make many important discretionary decisions in the performance of their daily duties. In fact, the practice of police discretion was openly recognized only a few decades ago.[1] A common but naive conception about the police is that statutory laws and/or departmental policies guide nearly every move of the officer, whether it is the enforcement of a law, maintaining social order, or rendering community service. And there are police leaders today who publicly claim that their officers go strictly "by the book," not because these police leaders believe their statements to be accurate, which they do not, but because it helps to ally criticisms that the police act as if they were above the law. In private, of course, police leaders are well aware that discretion exists.

The major assumption from which this chapter begins is that police discretion is a necessary and unavoidable result of police work. All police officers regardless of rank, division, or department have occasion to use their personal judgment to resolve problem situations. Discretionary decisions may be called for if the department policy is unclear or out of date, if the criminal law has minimal relevance to a particular situation, or if the ends of justice might be better served by not fully applying the written law.

Once we recognize the existence of police discretion, we can state the major premise of the chapter. *Police discretion can result in either a positive or negative police action depending on how it is used and how it is controlled.* If discretionary decisions emanate from an officer's personal experience, common sense, and devotion to fair play, and if discretionary decisions are carefully monitored by the department, police discretion can be an effective tool for achieving social justice. Coming to terms with police discretion is a necessary prerequisite to establishing police work as a true profession.

DEFINING POLICE DISCRETION

Discretion is a relatively simple concept to understand. Webster's New Collegiate Dictionary defines discretion as the "ability to make responsible decisions—the power of individual choice or judgment." Discretion refers to the choice-making ability we all have in various facets of our lives. Of the multitude of discretionary decisions we make daily, most are uneventful (e.g.,

Should I eat Brand Flakes or Sugar Crunchies for breakfast?). Other discretionary decisions are more stressful (Do I hang onto the dependable old Ford or buy a slick new sports car?), and some are critically important (Maybe I should quit college and get a job). A distinguishing feature of being an adult is that parents, teachers, and other significant persons no longer make our important decisions; they may continue to influence our thinking and provide us with advice, but we make the decisions. As adults we use our own discretion—common sense mixed with personal judgment—to decide what is best for us.

Police discretion is a special application of this freedom to make decisions. The only difference is that the individual making the decision is a police officer in the performance of his or her duty. Thus we can define police discretion as *the job-related decisions of the police made within the limits of the authority given to them.* Police generally have the discretionary authority to determine how to spend uncommitted time, which situations to intervene in, and how to resolve a problem once intervention is made (e.g., scold, warn, educate, ticket, or arrest).[2] However, an officer's discretionary latitude varies depending on such factors as the seriousness of the offense, the demands made by citizens, and department policy. This we shall see as the chapter progresses.

ESTABLISHING THE PARAMETERS OF DISCRETION

In nearly every occupation workers must make choices about what they do and how they do it. As a general rule, the most far-reaching discretionary decisions are made at the level of upper management. These important decisions filter down through the organization. For example, if the corporate bosses decide to set higher production standards for the next fiscal quarter, middle managers, foremen, and line workers are forced to work harder. Of course, even line workers may find it necessary to make an occasional judgment call in the performance of their work, but these decisions are not as far-reaching as the decisions of their superiors.

Normally police leaders do not set "production standards" as in the corporate world, but they do establish policies and procedures that affect every employee in the department. The sum total of written and verbalized commands of police leaders become the *blueprint* from which the department conducts its business. Whether it is by design or by accident, police leaders establish enforcement priorities for the entire department. They also set performance expectations for the various divisions in the department and for individual officers.

A special organizational feature of the police is the wide latitude for making discretionary decisions by the lowest ranking officers in the department.[3] Unlike most other bureaucratic organizations where the decisions of the lowest workers are highly routinized and tightly controlled, patrol officers make important discretionary decisions every day. Wilson maintains that police work is one of the few occupations where discretion actually increases as one moves down the police hierarchy.[4] Moreover, patrol officers dispersed throughout the streets of a city cannot be closely monitored by supervisors the way office workers or factory workers can be monitored by their bosses. The result is that many of the discretionary decisions made by patrol officers never come to the attention of their superiors and, therefore, are not subject to review.

Discretionary authority varies from one department to another. Some departments carefully control officer discretion while others do not. For instance, the watch-style department described in the last chapter encouraged police officers to use their discretionary judgment for most routine problems, but the legalistic department normally discouraged officer discretion.[5] Moreover, the use of discretion varies from one officer to another. Some officers seldom stray from the legal guidelines while others do, relying on their common sense and personal judgment.

Discretion exists in every operating division of the department (patrol, traffic, juvenile, vice, narcotics, investigation, etc.) and applies to many types of police decisions (e.g., intervention strategy, investigation technique, field method, equipment acquisition, personnel allocation).[6] In short, there is really no escaping the fact that police discretion is widespread and unavoidable.

WHY IS POLICE DISCRETION AN IMPORTANT TOPIC?

The practice of police discretion waves a cautionary flag to all of society. Unlike routine job-related decisions of most other occupations, discretionary decisions by police officers invariably raise difficult questions regarding law, morality, ethics, and justice. The following discussion highlights five important reasons why we should pay close attention to police discretion.

Power of Intrusion

One reason why the issue of police discretion is so important is because the police wield great authority to intrude in the lives of ordinary citizens without the citizens' consent. Police discretionary decisions have the potential to powerfully affect the people they touch. Take the common speeding ticket as a classic example. Most drivers stopped by the police are loyal Americans and law-abiding citizens (when not in their cars). The typical traffic officer writes several tickets a day and dozens a week. The officer may not think twice about it. But what effect does the ticket have on a careless driver? For a minor offense the ticket probably has little effect, but if the ticket is for a serious offense it may end up costing the driver hundreds of dollars. There may be a fine to pay, court costs, attorney fees, and increases in automobile insurance carried over several years. And the economic hardship to the driver says nothing of the driver's embarrassment and inconvenience.

Similarly, imagine what effect an arrest would have on a basically good youth who used poor judgment one night and broke a window at the neighborhood school. Or what about a civic-minded, church-going elderly woman who is arrested for driving under the influence after leaving a charitable social function. In either case, the consequences for the person arrested could be tremendous.

According to one view, in cases like these the police are not using discretion. They are not using discretion because the arresting officers are simply doing what the law says they should. In other words, it is only when an officer decides to handle a situation informally (warn and release) or not at all (ignore) that discretion is being used. If citizens are warned and released instead of ticketed or arrested, the police would be using their personal judgment rather than the written law to resolve the encounter. The written law gives the police authority to intervene in the situation, but personal judgment is used to resolve the situation.

On a theoretical level, this view of discretion is quite narrow but it has some merit. On a more practical level, however, it is less useful. The reason why is because the police are given the implicit authority not to enforce the law if, in the officer's professional judgment, such action is in the best interest of both the offender and the community, and as long as the criminal offense is minor. As a general rule, police officers are obligated to fully enforce the law only when (1) they have witnessed a serious felony offense; or (2) they have probable cause that a serious felony offense has been committed. Failure to arrest a felony suspect would be, under normal circumstances, dereliction of duty.

Unequal Justice

A second reason why police discretion is an important topic of study is because discretion often runs counter to equal justice under law. Whenever the police make a judgment call, it necessarily follows that different individuals are subject to different forms of justice. If one person receives a ticket and another does not for essentially the same offense, then justice is not being dispensed equally. The same can be said when the police decide who to select from a crowd to question, who to interrogate, who to arrest, and so on. The only way to enforce the law equally is for the police to either (1) enforce all laws fully, or (2) enforce no law.

But society can still have "justice" under law even if it is not equal justice. The fact is, the police can contribute more to maintaining an orderly society by the underenforcement of the law than by its full enforcement.

When the police exercise their discretion conscientiously and judiciously, meaning that not everyone the police discover to have broken the law is dealt with formally, we say the officers are policing in the **spirit of the law**. For example, not every youth who behaves mischievously—albeit illegally—needs to be arrested. Using their experience and common sense, officers learn to "read" offenders and attendant circumstances to determine what would be most beneficial in a given situation. If an officer decides formal action is required after considering the nature of the offense and/or the feasibility of alternative dispositions, the officer would still be policing in the spirit of the law.

Policing to the **letter of the law** is a very different proposition. Here, police discretion is all but eliminated—all traffic offenders the police catch are ticketed, and all criminal offenders the police identify are arrested. Policing to the "letter" of the law means that justice is being dispensed equally and as

FIGURE 7.1
Letter versus Spirit of Law

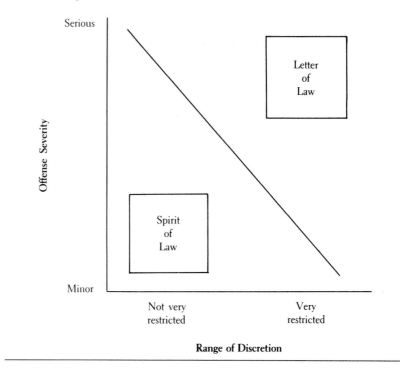

fully as possible. As mentioned earlier, many police leaders maintain that their officers stick closely to the letter of the law. One police leader voiced it this way:

> A police officer does not have the discretion to arrest or not to arrest any more than a judge has the discretion to judge or not to judge. . . . When some people advocate the philosophy that a police officer has discretion in the field to arrest an individual or to take him home, they are talking about *discriminatory law enforcement* which is *police corruption.*[7]

The freedom to make discretionary decisions is in large part contingent on the seriousness of the offense. As shown in figure 7.1, the use of police discretion is tightly restricted for serious offenses (i.e., letter of law) and less restricted for minor offenses (spirit of law).

Police as Legislative and Judicial Officials

If the police always enforced the law to the letter, then their role would be limited strictly to law enforcement. But this is not the case. For the most part, police regulate society in the spirit of the law. This places the police in the position to make important legislative and judicial decisions, not just law enforcement decisions. This greatly complicates the role of police.

Street-level decisions regarding which laws to enforce and when to enforce them allow the police to breathe life into the laws. On paper the laws are fixed, unbending, and sometimes vague. Laws only "come to life" when the police apply them in everyday situations. In this sense, the police are the real legislators since they are the ones who make the laws what they are. And, to the extent that the police decide who to scold, warn, admonish, educate, ticket, or arrest, they are cast into the role of street-level judge. Police use their discretion to decide who deserves what. This entails shifting attention away from the criminal offense and focusing on the offender and/or attendant circumstances.

Absence of Control

When a police officer decides to arrest someone the arrest is subject to review on several levels. Assuming the shift supervisor supports the officer's arrest, it must pass the subsequent review of the prosecutor and the courts. The odds are overwhelming that an unwise arrest eventually will result in a case dismissal.

On the other hand, when an officer decides not to ticket or arrest, the decision is not subject to routine review. An officer may make an unwise discretionary decision by not acting formally. The problem here is that we have no way of knowing how many unwise, overly lenient discretionary decisions police officers make since there is no easy way to monitor their every activity. What is more, when the police fail to ticket or arrest someone who should be ticketed or arrested—let's say someone whose behavior is excessively reckless—it follows that the police are falling short of their responsibility to protect society.

Discretion, Selective Enforcement, and Discrimination

There are far more laws on the books and criminals on the streets than the police can possibly handle. This means that enforcement priorities must be established. The traditional strategy for prioritizing work load has been to concentrate on "street crime," particularly serious offenses like assault, robbery, and drug trafficking, but also less serious offenses like prostitution and panhandling. There are at least two reasons why the police tend to concentrate on street crime. First, these crimes normally occur in public or semi-public places. This makes them more visible to the police and relatively easy to control. More sophisticated types of crime like embezzlement, fraud, or antitrust violations are less visible, thus making them more difficult to detect and investigate. Second, police historically have concentrated on street crimes because the public demands that they do so. The public mandate to control street crime lends legitimacy to the enforcement priorities the police have established.

Few would deny that the police enforce some laws more aggressively than others. This is known as **selective enforcement**, and it is a major bone of contention in policing. On more than one occasion enforcement practices of a department have been ruled unconstitutional because they violated the equal protection clause of the Fourteenth Amendment. Furthermore, the majority of states subscribe to the legal principle of *full enforcement*, thus making it illegal for police not to enforce the law.[8]

The term "selective enforcement" is normally associated with the discretionary decisions made in the higher police ranks where enforcement priorities are established. J. Edgar Hoover was notorious for going after bank robbers, kidnappers, and communists while practically ignoring other federal crimes that fell under his jurisdiction (e.g., organized crime and white-collar crime).[9] While Hoover's selective enforcement policies were more blatant than most, every police leader must set enforcement priorities. For example, a chief who orders patrol officers to "crack down" on a drug-infested street corner, or a sheriff who directs deputies to establish constant radar surveillance in a neighborhood speed zone, are both "selectively" enforcing the law. As long as officers are concentrating their efforts in one area for a particular type of crime, it follows that they cannot be somewhere else to enforce other crimes.

A plainclothes officer nabs a suspect in a purse-snatching incident. Street crimes, because of their visible, public nature, receive considerable police attention.

Minorities often resent what they perceive as the wholesale abuse of police discretion. Racial and ethnic groups claim they are disproportionately subjected to field interrogations and arrests by the police and are more likely to be the recipients of excess force than middle-class whites. This perception leads to frequent charges of harassment, unfair treatment, and discrimination. The charges are usually unfounded when "officially" investigated, but this does little to allay feelings of distrust. The past and recent history of policing teaches us all too well that the police sometimes abuse their discretionary power. Police discretion does not affect us all equally.

SOURCES OF POLICE DISCRETION

More research has been conducted on the determinants of police discretion than perhaps any other topic in policing. The volume of data on the subject is now enormous. For nearly three decades investigators have searched for the many sources of police behavior and the discretionary decisions they make. We know that the police officers' decisions are contingent on many different factors that often act simultaneously. The saliency of these factors varies depending on the attendant circumstances.[10]

At least four major sources of police discretion are currently identified in the literature: (1) the reality of criminal law, (2) the police department, (3) the police officer, and (4) the situation. In the discussion that follows, we describe these major sources of police discretion in detail.

OFFICE-LEVEL DISCRETION

FBI TARGETS VIOLENT CRIME

(AP) Washington—The FBI is making violent crime a nationwide investigative priority to counter a 40 percent increase in such offenses in the 1980s, Director William S. Sessions said Wednesday.

Sessions told reporters that violent crime will rank with foreign counterintelligence, terrorism, drugs, organized crime and white collar crime as major priorities of the FBI.

"With the acknowledged 40 percent increase in violent crime, the American public is understandably outraged by the growing disregard for human life by criminals," Sessions said.

While state and local police still have jurisdiction to investigate the vast majority of violent crimes, Sessions said the FBI can expand its role in this area.

For example, recently enacted legislation gives the FBI expanded jurisdiction to investigate the killings of all state and local law police officers. The FBI also has new jurisdiction under the drug law passed by Congress last year to investigate murders related to drug trafficking.

In the past, violent crime "did not receive, as I believe, the kind of emphasis it should receive," Sessions said.

The amount of time agents have spent investigating violent crime has dropped "because of the other priorities that we have established. I anticipate this will hold the line in any reduction in those numbers," Sessions said.

President Bush has asked Congress to appropriate $19.5 million to hire 300 new FBI agents as part of his anti-crime package.

Source: *Wilmington Star News*, Wilmington, NC, June 23, 1989.

Several features inherent in the American criminal justice system encourage the use of police officer discretion. Two features in particular stand out as having special relevance: the ambiguity of criminal law and the overreach of the criminal law.[11]

Ambiguity of Criminal Law

Regulating human behavior through criminal law is a painstaking task. Legislators struggle to write laws that are clear and precise, laws that apply only to a specific behavior, and to every incident of the undesired behavior. But it is not always easy or even possible to write exacting laws. Wayne LaFave suggests that "no legislature has succeeded in formulating a substantive criminal code which clearly encompasses all conduct intended to be made criminal and which clearly excludes all other conduct."[12]

Consequently, the legal statutes in every state have their share of vague, ambiguous criminal laws. As the front line of the criminal justice system, the police are required to use their discretionary judgement *to interpret these laws and apply them to real-life situations*. The more ambiguous the criminal law, the more freedom an officer has to use discretion.

"Disorderly conduct" is an example of an ambiguous statute that leaves individual officers wide discretionary authority. Every state code has a disorderly conduct statute. Disorderly conduct can be thought of as a *residual* offense. This is because police officers can charge an "unruly" or "disruptive" person with disorderly conduct in the absence of a clear violation of another criminal law (e.g., criminal assault or theft). To a great extent, disorderly conduct is in the eyes of the beholder—it is whatever a police officer says it is.

Overreach of Criminal Law

Another feature of American criminal law that fosters police officer discretion is its **overreach**. By overreach we refer to modern society's increasing propensity to regulate human behavior through an astounding variety of formally enacted rules. Sam Walker describes the overreach of the law this way:

> American society has had a tendency to deal with social and medical problems, as well as questions of morality, through criminal sanctions. 'Bad' conduct is made criminal. Many of these laws, however, are virtually unenforceable. In some cases, legislators have no realistic expectations that the laws will be enforced.[13]

The criminal law overreaches in two ways. First, there are literally hundreds of written criminal laws that come under the authority of the police, far too many for the police to fully regulate. We identify this as the *widening of the criminal justice net*. This type of overreach of the criminal law places a huge strain on the limited police resources (i.e., time, money, equipment, and personnel).[14] As a consequence, it is not possible for the police to do all that is expected of them. A single officer can regulate only so many people and so many crimes. For example, a routine call for help may keep a patrol unit out of service for thirty minutes or more, and an arrest may take an officer out of patrol for several hours. The overreach of the law requires the police to establish enforcement priorities—some crimes are highly regulated while other crimes are largely ignored.

The second way the criminal law overreaches is by its broad language, which frequently defines actions as a criminal when, because of special cir-

---

NORTH CAROLINA'S DISORDERLY CONDUCT LAW

(a) Disorderly conduct is a public disturbance intentionally caused by any person who:

(1) Engages in fighting or other violent conduct or in conduct creating the threat of imminent fighting or other violence; or

(2) Makes or uses any utterance, gesture, display or abusive language which is intended and plainly likely to provoke violent retaliation and thereby cause a breach of the peace; or

(3) Takes possession of, exercises control over, or seizes any building or facility of any public or private educational institution without the specific authority of the chief administrative officer of the institution, or his authorized representative; or

(4) Refuses to vacate any building or facility of any public or private educational institution in obedience to:

   a. An order of the chief administrative officer of the institution, or his authorized representative; or

   b. An order given by any fireman or public health officer acting within the scope of his authority; or

   c. If a state of emergency is occurring or is imminent within the institution, an order given by any law-enforcement officer acting within the scope of his authority; or

(5) Shall, after being forbidden to do so by the chief administrative officer, or his authorized representative, of any public or private educational institution:

   a. Engage in any sitting, kneeling, lying down, or inclining so as to obstruct the ingress or egress of any person entitled to the use of any building or facility of the institution in its normal and intended use; or

   b. Congregate, assemble, form groups or formations (whether organized or not), block, or in any manner otherwise interfere with the operation or functioning of any building or facility of the institution so as to interfere with the customary or normal use of the building or facility; or

(6) Disrupts, disturbs or interferes with the teaching of students at any public or private educational institution or engages in conduct which disturbs the peace, order or discipline at any public or private educational institution or on the grounds adjacent thereto.

(7) Disrupts, disturbs, or interferes with a religious service or assembly or engages in conduct which disturbs the peace or order at any religious service or assembly.

As used in this section the term "building or facility" includes the surrounding grounds and premises of any building or facility used in connection with the operation or functioning of such building or facility.

(b) Any person who willfully engages in disorderly conduct is guilty of a misdemeanor punishable by a fine not to exceed five hundred dollars ($500.00) or imprisonment for not more than six months.

Source: North Carolina Statute 14-288.4.

cumstances, they should not be criminal. Even when an officer has all the legal evidence necessary to charge someone with a crime, there are times when doing so clearly would be an unnecessary application of the law. For example, Klockars offers ten witty reasons why someone clocked going fifty miles per hour in a thirty-five mile per hour zone should not be ticketed by a *reasonable* police officer:

> Officer: "Where's the fire?"
> Driver: (1) I am a volunteer fireman responding to a fire alarm.
> (2) I am a volunteer ambulance driver responding to a call.
> (3) I am an undercover cop tailing the car ahead which you did not stop.
> (4) My wife just called and told me to rush home. She is starting to have her baby.
> (5) I am having a baby.
> (6) I am on my way to the hospital. There has been an accident. My child was hurt.
> (7) I am on my way home. I left for work a short while ago, but halfway there I remembered that I left a steam iron burning on the kitchen table.
> (8) I am on my way home. I left for work a short while ago, but halfway there I discovered that I have a serious case of diarrhea.
> (9) I am a school crossing guard. I am late for work because I just had a flat tire. If I don't get to my post right away, the children will try to cross a dangerous intersection by themselves.
> (10) I am part of a funeral entourage on its way to the cemetery. I do not know the way to get there and a few blocks back I got separated. Unless I catch up I will miss the burial.[15]

The important point here is that all criminal laws, not just traffic violations, have the potential to overreach. Kenneth Davis suggests that a positive contribution of police discretion is the ability to set more realistic enforcement expectations than the legislators established.[16]

The horizontal or vertical overreach of criminal laws widens the entire criminal justice net. The result is that more and more "offenders" are brought under the official scrutiny of the system.

The Police Department

Many characteristics at the department level influence discretionary behavior. Specifically, police researchers have identified the bureaucratic organization, supervisory control, and stability of patrol assignment as important factors.[17]

Bureaucratic Organization

The degree of bureaucracy refers to the level of complexity in a police organization. A highly bureaucratic organization is one with a high degree of vertical differentiation between the lowest and highest ranks, also known as a "tall rank structure."[18] The bureaucratic model of organization that police departments follow is the military model. The military model stresses rules, regulations, discipline, and a commitment to the rank structure. Police departments vary in the extent to which they adhere to strict military organizational principles. Skolnick argues that officers from highly militaristic departments have a more rigid view of their duties and are more likely to follow the department code to avoid being disciplined.[19]

As a general rule, officers perceive less freedom to make discretionary decisions in highly bureaucratic police departments; hence, the probability of being ticketed or arrested is greater in highly bureaucratic departments.[20] Departments with an intensive bureaucratic structure are usually more formal, with many layers of supervisory personnel ensuring administrative control. This creates the appearance—but not necessarily the reality—of close supervisory control over officers. Contrary to the informal, more intimate relationships between officers of superior and subordinate rank in less bureaucratic departments, role relationships between officers of different rank in highly bureaucratic departments tend to be more rigid.[21] Oftentimes officers in bureaucratic departments feel like they cannot rely on their superiors in times of trouble, so they employ defensive maneuvers (also known as "CYA" for "cover your ass") to minimize their risk of being disciplined.

Supervisory Control

Discretion tends to increase as the degree of supervisory control decreases. Researchers typically examine the ratio of patrol officers to supervisory personnel to measure the **span of control**. "Top heavy" departments are normally able to monitor the actions of patrol officers better because the span of control (i.e., number of underlings to supervise) is reduced. In departments with a wide span of control, or in departments where officers know that they are not closely supervised (regardless of the number of supervisors), there is more freedom to make discretionary decisions. In addition, there is evidence that supervisory control is related to department size. Larger departments tend to have less effective supervisory control and more discretion because there are more officers to monitor.[22]

Stability of Patrol Assignment

The extent to which police officers rotate shifts and beat assignments is likely to influence discretion. Police officers who maintain regular patrol hours and who are assigned to one beat over an extended period of time tend to develop close ties with local residents. This fosters a "service style" of policing where officers understand the problems of the area and can easily empathize with members of the community. Under this arrangement, the police enforce the laws less rigorously and are more willing to consider alternative solutions to a problem.[23]

By comparison, officers who frequently rotate hours or beat assignments do not have the opportunity to develop similar levels of trust with residents. This lends itself to a more legalistic or "professional" posture with citizens— hence, reduced discretion. Indeed, the rotation of shift and beat assignments is sometimes a calculated management strategy to prevent officers from getting too close to any one community.

The Police Officer

Researchers have studied numerous personal characteristics of police officers to try to explain their behavior. Although the empirical evidence is not particularly strong nor entirely consistent, at least five characteristics appear to be predictive of officer behavior: officer age, length of service, gender, education, and race. These five characteristics are described below.

Officer Age

It is a common observation that younger police officers lack the wisdom, patience and perspective of older officers. They are thought to be more aggressive than older officers and more likely to initiate citizen encounters to enforce minor infractions. The relative immaturity of younger officers affects the way these officers perform their job and the quality of their interaction with citizens, fellow officers, and superiors.

Several studies support the notion that officer age affects job performance. One study found that officers become less aggressive and less punitive in their crime control philosophy as they age.[24] Another study discovered that older officers were less likely to have citizen complaints filed against them for being discourteous, making racial slurs, or using excessive force.[25] This is supported by a study in Miami which found younger officers to be more likely to fire their weapons (both intentionally and unintentionally) while on duty.[26] Another study of thirteen southeastern cities found that younger officers were more likely to be assaulted. However, this later finding may be due to the tendency to assign younger officers to high-crime areas where the risk of assault is greater.[27]

Length of Service

An officer's biological age and his or her length of service as a police officer are strongly correlated—that is, older officers tend to have more job experience. It is not altogether clear given the available evidence whether the effect of age on officer performance is independent of the effect of job experience.[28] Similar to the findings on officer age, officers with less experience tend to be more active on the streets. Less experienced officers do more preventive patrol work, initiate more citizen contacts, and keep more thorough records of their activities than experienced police officers.[29] Several studies demonstrate that although less experienced officers make more arrests, the arrests made by experienced officers are more likely to end in conviction.[30] In other words, less experienced officers tend to work "harder" by making more contacts and more arrests, but experienced officers work "better."

Gender

Researchers have carefully studied male and female officers and have found a few minor differences. Specifically, female officers initiate fewer citizen contacts and make fewer misdemeanor and felony arrests than male officers.[31] However, the arrests that female officers make are just as likely to end in conviction as the arrests of male officers. Unfortunately, the studies comparing male and female officers have looked predominantly at inexperienced male and female officers. It is not clear the extent to which gender differences grow or diminish as officers gain experience. (The topic of women patrol officers is discussed more thoroughly in chapter 13.)

Education

Lawrence Sherman speculates that police officer education is related in some way to officer performance, yet we cannot be completely sure whether education is a causal factor.[32] The reason is because while numerous studies demonstrate that officers with a college education perform differently than officers without college experience, the studies do not control for confounding factors such as motivation or I.Q. In other words, the relationship between education and performance might be a spurious relationship caused by the correlation between education and a third causal variable. Moreover, if we only count the years of higher education, this does not tell us anything about the quality of the education or how much the officer actually learned.

Nonetheless, if we accept at face value the findings of existing research it appears that officers with a college education are active in their patrol work. They stop more cars, check more businesses, initiate more citizen contact, and make more arrests than non-college educated officers.[33] College-educated officers also receive fewer formal complaints from citizens,[34] and are charged less with using excessive force.[35]

Race

Finally, many observers of the police contend that black and white officers behave differently. The available evidence supports this contention, although most of the research on racial differences is seriously dated. In particular, researchers have found black officers to patrol more aggressively than white officers. Friedrich, for example, found that black police officers initiated more citizens contacts, filed more reports, and made more arrests.[36] Black police officers have a reputation for being more strict with black suspects than with white suspects,[37] a reputation that has received some empirical support.

Black police officers have been found to use deadly force more often than white officers. Surprisingly, research on racial differences reveal that black police officers are overrepresented in shootings of citizens, especially shootings of black citizens.[38] It is likely that this finding is spurious due to the more frequent assignment of black officers to high-crime areas.[39]

The Situation

Encounters between police officers and citizens never exist in a vacuum. The outcome of an encounter is never fully determined at its outset. Encounters evolve as the interaction takes shape. There are a variety of situational factors in every police-citizen encounter, and these factors have the potential to influence officer behavior.

Researchers have tested numerous situational factors to assess their relative effects. This section focuses on four situational factors known to influence officer behavior: the type of police entry, characteristics of the complainant, suspect characteristics, and the "human side" of policing.

Police Entry

Two questions dealing with the type of police entry may be raised. First, do officers behave differently when they initiate a citizen encounter than when they are radioed to a call? Second, does the number of police officers at the scene affect officer behavior?[40] The answer to both questions appears to be "yes." Regarding the first question, when officers are called to a scene at the request of a citizen—namely, *reactive* police work—they normally are granted more legitimacy than when they initiate an encounter on their own (*proactive* police work). Oftentimes when police proactively engage themselves, citizens respond antagonistically. This prompts the police, in return, to respond more harshly.[41] At least one study shows the police are more likely to make arrests in proactive encounters.[42]

The number of officers at a scene also appears to influence officer behavior. However, research findings are not consistent so we are not sure in what way the presence of other officers affects behavior. For instance, several studies report that lone officers are more likely to file a report or make an arrest because of the pressing need to establish control. But other studies suggest that as the number of other officers at a scene increases, so does the likelihood of harsher sanctions.[43] There is also evidence that the presence of supervisory personnel increases the probability of filing a crime report and arrest.[44]

Complainant Characteristics

In general, police decisions are strongly influenced by the wishes of complainants. This is known as **citizen discretion** and is a potent predictor of officer behavior. The major part of citizen discretion is their private decision to report, or not to report, an incident to the police. A citizen who prefers not to get involved—or who does not want the police to get involved—may prevent the police from discovering a problem, and the incident may pass without police intervention.

The discretionary power of citizens carries into police-citizen encounters as well. Police officers often consider the wishes of complainants when deciding how to resolve a problem. For example, if a homeowner requests that the menacing kid from next door be warned rather than arrested for maliciously burning his prized azalea bush, chances are good the youth will not be arrested. Conversely, the youth might very well face criminal charges if the homeowner requests formal action.

Officers tend to be less accommodating to complainants if they are antagonistic or disrespectful to the police. Conversely, polite and respectful complainants are more likely to have their wishes granted. Race, social class, age, and relational distance between suspect and complainant influence the discretionary decisions of officers.[45] In particular, the preferences of whites, members of the middle and upper classes, and mature adults (middle-age and senior citizens) are assigned greater weight. Moreover, police are generally less likely to make an arrest if the suspect and complainant are close acquaintances than if they are strangers. This is because the police often view squabbles between close acquaintances as a private matter that does not need formal intervention.

Suspect Characteristics

Race, social class, and age of criminal suspects are known to influence police discretion. There is a large body of research showing that nonwhites, members of lower classes, and teenagers are treated more harshly than their counterparts.[46] Police officers tend to spend less time, show less empathy and respond more punitively when the suspects are nonwhite, lower class, or young.[47]

The suspect's gender raises important questions regarding differential police response. In an article entitled "Is Chivalry Dead?," Marvin Krohn and his associates examined whether there has been a change over time in the way police handle male and female youths who are in trouble.[48] In the past, police had a tendency to handle girls in a paternalistic (fatherly) manner. This normally meant that girls caught committing a delinquent act would be sent home to their parents while boys were likely to be arrested (presumably because the boys were the "leaders" while the girls were the "followers"). For certain offenses, however, like running away, curfew violations, or sexual promiscuity,

During an interview, an officer may make discretionary decisions regarding the weight of a complainant's testimony.

police would handle girls more formally than boys—"boys will be boys, but girls must be little ladies."

Krohn and his colleagues found that over time, the police have become more egalitarian in their treatment of boys and girls in trouble—namely, they have become less paternalistic toward girls. Other research supports this claim. Two reasons exist for the shift in police treatment: (1) girls are getting into more trouble than before, and (2) the police are not immune to the narrowing of the gender gap in American society. The Krohn research group concludes that although chivalry may not be entirely dead among police officers, there are strong signs that it is dying.[49]

A final characteristic of the criminal suspect to be discussed here, one that has received a great deal of research attention, is *demeanor*. Demeanor refers to the manners, attitude, and deference of the criminal suspect, or what has been called **situational etiquette**.[50] The evidence overwhelmingly demonstrates the influence of demeanor in swaying an officer's decision. Specifically, suspects with a "bad attitude" increase their chances of being ticketed or arrested; suspects with a "good attitude" are less likely to receive formal sanctioning, assuming they are not suspected of a serious crime.

Piliavin and Briar conducted an important early study of police discretion in the handling of juvenile cases.[51] The researchers conducted a nine-month observational study of police encounters with juveniles on the streets. They found that in 50 to 60 percent of the encounters, the demeanor of the youth was predictive of the police response. Youths who were contrite about their

A young boy is led away after being arrested for looting a toy store along with a group of adults.

FIGURE 7.2

177

CHAPTER 7:
Police Discretion

Relationship between Level of Respect and Likelihood of Formal Sanction

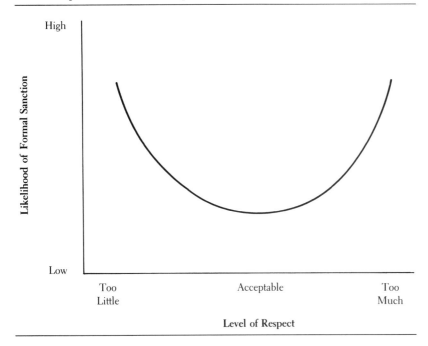

behavior, respectful to the officers, and genuinely afraid about what was going to happen to them were viewed as "good" kids. The police were likely to handle these juveniles informally (outright release, warn, or take home to parents). However, youths who did not show adequate respect toward the officer or who appeared to have little remorse for their behavior were viewed as "bad" kids in need of formal sanctions (arrest or cite to juvenile court).

Other researchers have since noticed something that Piliavin and Briar did not detect—*overly* deferent youths may talk themselves into trouble.[52] The reason for this is because most police officers know when they are being "snowed" or "conned." The motivations of the overly deferent youths are transparent. This not only irritates the police but also increases police suspicion. Figure 7.2 shows this relationship between level of respect and likelihood of formal sanction (assuming all other factors we have already discussed are held constant).

The Human Side of Policing

The human side of policing is the last situational factor to be discussed. Police officers are only human. They experience mood swings and varying levels of physical comfort just like everyone else. Emotionally, police might be happy, excited, upbeat, and jovial one day (or even one moment) and sad or angry the next; physically, they may feel terrific or they may feel exhausted, sleepy, hungry, hot, cold, achy, or nauseated. While police officers often joke about how these things can affect their behavior (e.g., "If I didn't have to take a leak I would have stopped that speeder"), researchers have shown only a passing interest in them, preferring instead to examine more easily observable and quantifiable factors like those already discussed. The limited research that is available, however, demonstrates the "human side" of policing does affect officer behavior.[53] This issue raises many questions that cannot be answered until additional research has been conducted.

To briefly summarize this lengthy section on the sources of police discretion, it can be said that the decisions of police officers are influenced by many factors. Some of these factors are more powerful than others, some factors only operate in the presence or absence of other factors, and some officers are more easily influenced by these factors than other officers. The sum total of all these sources of discretion creates an extremely complex and confusing pattern, not only for students but for police scholars as well. Unraveling the empirical relationships is complicated by the relative absence of recent data. Clearly we have learned much in the last three decades about police discretion, but there is much more we need to know.

THE MANAGEMENT OF DISCRETION

The police find themselves in an awkward bind. On the one hand, the very nature of their work places them right in the middle of complex human problems, problems that defy simple solution. The police are expected to be more than *regulatory robots* when handling human dilemmas; we expect them to use their professional knowledge and sound judgment to resolve dilemmas in the best possible way. On the other hand, the police are expected to be full and equal enforcers of the law, to apply the law as written, and to shun arbitrary police behavior. Goldstein expresses a similar thought: "So the police really suffer the worst of all worlds: they must exercise broad discretion behind a facade of performing in a ministerial fashion."[54]

At their extremes, these dual expectations imposed on the police are impossible to achieve. To have full and equal enforcement of the law means to sacrifice discretion, and to allow police discretion means to sacrifice full and equal enforcement. One needs to realize that this bind is, to a great extent, unavoidable—the multiple and sometimes conflicting roles of the police as law enforcers, service providers and keepers of the peace often conflict. The stubborn refusal of some police leaders to step out from behind the mask of full enforcement only exacerbates the problem.[55]

The conclusion we are driving to is this: *we will never entirely eliminate police discretion, nor would we want to.* Compared to other actors in the criminal justice system, the police are usually in the best position to "judge" a situation. Why wait for a case to get to court before dropping the charges or divert the case to another agency if the police can immediately perform the same function?

But to recognize the existence of discretion is to go only halfway. Most police experts agree that discretion—although inevitable and frequently beneficial—needs more effective control. This is known as **discretion manage-**

ment. Discretion management entails the formulation of written guidelines and policy directives by the department to give officers of various rank and assignment a clear understanding of what is expected of them. In the past, police departments often had few if any formal policy statements to guide officer behavior. Or, if they had formal policies, the department did not adequately disseminate the information to officers. However, with the increased accountability and civil liability of police departments today, such poor administrative procedure can no longer be justified.

There are several reasons why the management of police discretion is important. First, closer control would clear the often fuzzy boundary between *authorized police discretion* and *unauthorized police indiscretion*. Police officers would have a better feel for how much discretionary authority they have, what alternative choices are open to them, under what conditions they are allowed to use their discretion, and when their decisions would be subject to department review. Second, discretion management would help to dispel citizen perception that the police establish their own rules and engage in discriminatory selective enforcement. Third, discretion management would increase administrative control over police action. And fourth, it may improve the working atmosphere within the department. Goldstein views this last reason as the most promising rationale for tightening control over police discretion:

> Perhaps most important, the police would be provided with a more realistic and healthier atmosphere in which to function. It would no longer be necessary for a police administrator to dodge issues, to maintain an image that is unsupported by practice, or to be less than forthright in his dealings with the public. Openly structuring discretion should encourage greater integrity on the part of the administrator and make it possible for police agencies to realize a much higher level of credibility in the community. Both the community and the police should recognize that the police must make difficult choices, that the police must take risks, and that the police will occasionally make mistakes.[56]

The more professional police departments have clearly written and well-disseminated policies and procedures. These departmental rules are established at the upper administrative levels and made binding on all personnel. Normally, policy statements are contained in the department's **standard operating procedure (SOP) manual**. All employees are expected to read and understand the manual. While some manuals are more useful than others, SOPs generally offer the following advantages:

- They increase consistency of officer performance;
- They decrease ambiguity when making difficult decisions;
- They enhance supervisory capability;
- They minimize department liability if an officer makes a mistake.

But SOPs are not an administrative panacea. First, standard operating procedure manuals are extremely difficult and time consuming to formulate properly, especially if starting from scratch. Second, they force administrators to be explicit about where the department stands on contentious issues such as accepting gratuities, crowd control tactics, and the use of deadly force. And third, it is not possible to have a written policy for every type of situation the police must face. Nonetheless, SOPs serve their purpose if they help reduce officer uncertainty and provide guidance when making important police decisions.

CONCLUSION

Police discretion refers to the job-related decisions made by the police within the limits of the authority given to them. (Decisions of the police *outside* the limits of the authority given to them is *police indiscretion*. This is the subject of chapter 9 on police misconduct.) Important discretionary decisions are made throughout the police hierarchy and in every operating division. Yet the discretionary decisions of the uniformed street officer have the most direct impact on ordinary citizens. People are scolded, warned, ticketed, cited to court, and arrested by the police, and sometimes they are simply ignored. Depending on attendant circumstances and the seriousness of the criminal offense, any one of these options might fall under the proper discretionary judgment of the police.

By now the reader should realize why the topic of police discretion is critically important to our study of the police. Indeed, the significance of police discretion explains our devoting an entire chapter to it, which surely would not have been the case if this were a textbook on almost any other occupation. Police discretion raises profound questions regarding law, morality, ethics, and justice. The history of policing teaches us that the police sometimes flaunt and even abuse their discretionary authority. The result is unequal treatment by the police. The bottom line is that police discretion does not affect us all the same way.

KEY TERMS

police discretion
spirit of the law
letter of the law
selective enforcement
overreach
span of control

citizen discretion
situational etiquette
discretion management
standard operating procedure (SOP)
  manual

DISCUSSION QUESTIONS

1. Discuss the reasons why police discretion is important. What are the advantages and disadvantages to society resulting from police discretion?
2. The alternative to policing in the spirit of the law is to police to the letter of the law. Is policing to the letter of the law possible? Practical? Desirable? Imagine a town where the police did not use discretion. What would it be like?

3. Discuss the major sources of police discretion. Which do you believe is important and why?
4. Imagine you are a police administrator responsible for formulating a new department policy for issuing traffic citations. How much discretion do you think officers should have in these types of situation? What are the issues surrounding the policy?

CHAPTER EIGHT

CITIZEN RIGHTS AND DUE PROCESS OF LAW

It is a fair summary of history to say that the safeguards of liberty have been forged in controversies involving not very nice people.

—Justice Felix Frankfurter

Perhaps in no other realm of U.S. policing is the relationship between the police and the public more delicately balanced than in the realm of citizen rights versus police restraints. An interesting paradox exists as a result of this balance: it is the role of the police, in part, to protect our constitutional rights, and it is the role of the Constitution, in part, to protect us from the police. To argue that we need "protection from our protectors" is to argue that we need the Constitution.

Americans have become sophisticated consumers of police services. This is especially true since the 1960s. Many Americans know their legal rights because they routinely see them in action—mostly on TV. How many times have we seen or heard of an otherwise good case thrown out of court because of some procedural flaw in the state's case, what we disparagingly call a "technicality"? Usually the technical error is due to some inappropriate police action, such as an illegal search and seizure or the failure to interrogate a suspect properly. Of course, there are many *pedestrian lawyers* who think they know their legal rights, but who in actuality are woefully misinformed.

Constitutional law and criminal procedure is a highly complex area of study. It is also continually evolving. Modern-day police officers must be well-versed in the latest legal developments in criminal law, court decisions, legislative enactments, and executive actions. This task is by no means easy, but it is a necessary one.

This chapter walks us through the tangled legal landscape. We begin with a discussion of the U.S. Constitution, the Bill of Rights, due process of law, and the important role of the courts. Subsequent sections examine the search and seizure protection of the Fourth Amendment and the self-incrimination protection of the Fifth Amendment.

THE U.S. CONSTITUTION

The **U.S. Constitution** is truly one of civilization's greatest documents. Conceived during the tumultuous early years of our nation, the founding fathers were determined to protect our basic civil liberties and to limit the powers of government. The Constitution of the United States achieved final adoption in 1789 after years of heated debate, controversy, and compromise. The new Congress convened in March of that year, and George Washington was inaugurated as the first president on April 30, 1789. The U.S. Constitution has survived for over two hundred years entirely intact, and has been amended only twenty-seven times. This qualifies the government of the "new world" as one of the oldest in the world.

The U.S. Constitution is divided into seven major sections known as *Articles*. The first three Articles create the three branches of government:

Article I establishes the structure and function of the federal legislature, known as Congress, consisting of a House of Representatives and a Senate.

Article II establishes executive power that rests in the hands of a president, who is designated as commander-in-chief.

Article III vests judicial power of the United States in the Supreme Court and such inferior courts to be established when deemed necessary.

The fourth, fifth, and seventh Articles are of minimal significance to the present discussion: *Article IV* deals with duties of the states, *Article V* establishes the procedures for amending the Constitution, and *Article VII* describes the method for ratifying the Constitution. *Article VI*, however, is of major importance—it contains the **supremacy clause**, a doctrine that makes the Constitution of the United States the supreme law of the land. Even judges at the state level are bound to the U.S. Constitution. If the laws or constitution of a state run counter to the U.S. Constitution, they are held to be *unconstitutional*.

The constitutional framers feared governmental power, especially concentrated power in a national government. In a stroke of genius they drafted the Constitution in such a way that provides for individual liberty on the one hand, but also grants the national government adequate authority to perform its duty on the other. The *separation of powers* and *checks and balances* among the three branches of government assures that no one government entity accumulates excessive power to the detriment of the other branches.

Because the legislative branch was comprised of a large number of elected state representatives, the founding fathers hoped this branch of government could serve as an important check on executive power (headed by a single elected person) and judicial power (comprised of nonelected, politically appointed, "lifetime" members). Yet in the past two hundred years, the executive and judicial branches of federal government have greatly expanded their spheres of influence. A pivotal point for the U.S. Supreme Court came as early as 1803 in *Marbury v. Madison*.[1] In the *Marbury* case the Supreme Court established for itself the power of **judicial review**. This power gave the Supreme Court authority to declare legislative and executive actions as "unconstitutional," and thus illegal. Over the years the Supreme Court has used its power of judicial review numerous times.

The Bill of Rights

An immediate complaint about the original Constitution was that it did not explicitly set forth the rights of individuals. Representatives from several states were concerned that a strong centralized government would be able to abuse individual rights unless those rights were formally stated. In response to the huge outcry, the first Congress adopted ten amendments to the Constitution that were ratified by the states in 1791.

These ten amendments are known as the **Bill of Rights**. The First Amendment establishes our *substantive rights* (freedom of speech, religion, and press) while the remaining amendments spell out our *procedural rights* (search and seizure, self-incrimination, double jeopardy, cross examination, bail, cruel and unusual punishment, etc.).[2] The Bill of Rights are more than just a statement of goals or ideals of what we expect from our federal government—the Bill of Rights are formal laws with the full weight and status given to the original Constitution itself.

It is important to understand that the Bill of Rights applied only to the national government when originally adopted; *the Bill of Rights did not limit the powers of the states.* Indeed, the states retained much of the power denied to the national government through the Tenth Amendment. This arrangement gave states far greater potential to abuse the rights of citizens than the national government. In actuality, however, the rights of citizens in their home states were at least partially protected by the separate state constitutions and state laws.

Due Process

The Fifth Amendment contains a number of constitutional protections that are guaranteed to the people. Embedded among the various protections in the Fifth Amendment is the **due process** clause, which reads: "no person shall be deprived of life, liberty, or property without due process of law." The principle of due process of law requires the government to treat every individual with a *fundamental fairness.* This, of course, applies directly to issues of criminal law and criminal justice.

The due process clause was written in general terms to provide expansive protection throughout the years. Federal and state courts have been reluctant to pin a precise definition on "due process" so as to allow the concept to gradually take shape over time, based on society's evolving notions of what is justice and unjust.[3]

As previously noted, the Bill of Rights did not apply to the states. This meant that citizens were guaranteed due process of law only in matters dealing with the national government (i.e., federal law enforcement, federal courts, and federal corrections). It was not until the passage of the Fourteenth Amendment in 1868 that citizens were granted due process of law at the state level. In part, the Fourteenth Amendment reads: "nor shall any state deprive any person of life, liberty, or property, without due process of law." The Fourteenth Amendment applies exclusively to the states and not to the federal government.

A major difference between the due process provision of the Fourteenth Amendment (state level) from the due process provision of the Fifth Amendment (federal level) is the more limited umbrella of protection. When the Fourteenth Amendment was passed in 1868, it was not intended to embrace the many protections of the Bill of Rights. In other words, the protection from illegal searches and seizures (Fourth Amendment), forced self-incrimination (Fifth Amendment), right to counsel (Sixth Amendment), and so on from the Bill of Rights were not immediately made applicable to the states. State courts and legislatures were left to decide what constituted "fundamental fairness" for their citizens, decisions that have been handed down gradually on a case-by-case basis rather than all at once. Many argue that the due process provision of the Fourteenth Amendment should cover all the same rights as enumerated in the Bill of Rights, the so-called **shorthand doctrine**, but the U.S. Supreme Court has never been willing to go that far.[4] Today, however, there is little practical difference in the due process protections at the federal and state level. Nearly all of the basic provisions of the Bill of Rights are also applicable at the state level. (see figure 8.1).

BILL OF RIGHTS

AMENDMENT I

Congress shall make no law respecting an establishment of religion, or prohibiting the free exercise thereof; or abridging the freedom of speech, or of the press; or the right of the people peaceably to assemble, and to petition the Government for a redress of grievances.

AMENDMENT II

A well regulated Militia, being necessary to the security of a free State, the right of the people to keep and bear Arms, shall not be infringed.

AMENDMENT III

No Soldier shall, in time of peace be quartered in any house, without the consent of the Owner, nor in time of war, but in a manner to be prescribed by law.

AMENDMENT IV

The right of the people to be secure in their persons, houses, papers, and effects, against unreasonable searches and seizures, shall not be violated, and no Warrants shall issue, but upon probable cause, supported by Oath or affirmation, and particularly describing the place to be searched, and the persons or things to be seized.

AMENDMENT V

No person shall be held to answer for a capital, or otherwise infamous crime, unless on a presentment or indictment of a Grand Jury, except in cases arising in the land or naval forces, or in the Militia, when in actual service in time of War or public danger; nor shall any person be subject for the same offence to be twice put in jeopardy of life or limb; nor shall be compelled in any criminal case to be a witness against himself, nor be deprived of life, liberty, or property, without due process of law; nor shall private property be taken for public use, without just compensation.

AMENDMENT VI

In all criminal prosecutions, the accused shall enjoy the right to a speedy and public trial, by an impartial jury of the State and district wherein the crime shall have been committed, which district shall have been previously ascertained by law, and to be informed of the nature and cause of the accusation; to be confronted with the witnesses against him; to have compulsory process for obtaining witnesses in his favor, and to have the Assistance of Counsel for his defense.

AMENDMENT VII

In suits at common law, where the value in controversy shall exceed twenty dollars, the right of trial by jury shall be preserved, and no fact tried by a jury, shall be otherwise reexamined in any Court of the United States, than according to the rules of the common law.

AMENDMENT VIII

Excessive bail shall not be required, nor excessive fines imposed, nor cruel and unusual punishments inflicted.

AMENDMENT IX

The enumeration in the Constitution, of certain rights, shall not be construed to deny or disparage others retained by the people.

AMENDMENT X

The powers not delegated to the United States by the Constitution, nor prohibited by it to the States, are reserved to the States respectively, or to the people.

FIGURE 8.1
Due Process Protection

	Federal	States
Amendment	5th	14th
Year Passed	1791	1868
Purpose	Fundamental Fairness	Fundamental Fairness
Protection at Time of Adoption	Expansive	Limited
Protection Today	Expansive	Expansive

The Role of the Courts

The courts have been persistent and powerful players in issues of constitutional law. The role of the courts—particularly the U.S. Supreme Court—in shaping constitutional law and influencing public policy has expanded over the years in tandem with the broadening scope of the Fourteenth Amendment's due process provision. Police officers are often affected by federal court decisions as well as court decisions handed down in their own states. State and local police officers are generally held accountable to the same minimum standards applicable at the federal level, standards that individual states may make more stringent than the federal requirements, but not less so.

The United States Supreme Court is the nation's highest court with final authority to interpret the Constitution. The court sets the tone for the entire country in matters of constitutional law and criminal procedure. The nine justices of the court are appointed by the president of the United States with Senate confirmation. The lifetime appointment of each member, the Court's isolation from partisan politics, and the endowed prestige of the Supreme Court gives the voice of each justice tremendous clout.

The **Warren Court** of the 1960s, named after Chief Justice Earl Warren, extended numerous due process rights to criminal defendants. This was known as a liberal and active Supreme Court, but has since given way to a more conservative bench. As president Ronald Reagan placed three new conservative justices on the Supreme Court (Justices O'Connor, Scalia, and Kennedy), and elevated William Rehnquist to Chief Justice to replace retiring Warren Burger. (Reagan also appointed over three hundred federal judges to district and appeals courts.) To date, President George Bush has appointed two new conservative justices to the court (David Souter and Clarence Thomas). The conservative majority of the Supreme Court has already scaled back some of the due process protections extended to criminal defendants by the Warren Court. Given the composition of the current Supreme Court, it is very likely the conservative "law and order" trend will continue into the near future.

THE FOURTH AMENDMENT—SEARCH AND SEIZURE

As citizens of the United States we have the right to be secure in our persons, houses, papers, and effects from unreasonable searches and seizures by the police. The police are forbidden from arbitrarily invading our homes and seizing our property unless they do so under the proper authority of the law. Usually, but not always, this means the police must have a valid search warrant. Today the restrictions against unreasonable searches and seizures are broadly interpreted and rigorously enforced. What is more, the law of search and seizure is now nearly identical for state and federal police, which as we shall see was not always true.

Many police officers complain bitterly that the Supreme Court has gone too far in protecting Fourth Amendment rights of criminal defendants. A common expression is that the police are the ones who are "handcuffed," not the crooks, thus interfering in their efforts to control crime. Indeed, the lion's share of "legal technicalities" aborting successful criminal prosecutions are in the realm of the Fourth Amendment. This is particularly true for drug offenses where the sheer volume of cases, coupled with the normal absence of a complaining victim as a prosecutorial witness, places added pressure on the police to stretch the legal limits of their authority. Yet there are many individuals who believe that the Fourth Amendment was intended to protect everyone from unwarranted police intrusion, not only law-abiding citizens; if the police (or prosecutor or courts) act illegally against someone who has broken the law, then that person should be free of criminal prosecution.

Herein lies the difficulty in a free society. We must strike a reasonable balance between protecting the procedural rights of criminals and protecting the lives and property of citizens.

The Exclusionary Rule

The cornerstone of search and seizure restrictions is the **exclusionary rule**. The exclusionary rule states that *no evidence obtained by the police through*

Service of a search warrant in Stark County, Ohio, in a case involving drug trafficking and stolen property.

an illegal search and seizure shall be admissible in court. Illegally obtained evidence is "excluded" from criminal trial. Hence, an illegal search that uncovers drugs, guns, or other evidence of a crime would ordinarily be inadmissable in court under the exclusionary rule. Defense attorneys vigilantly monitor the activities of the police for possible violations of the exclusionary rule. It should be noted that the exclusionary rule applies only to police officers—evidence unlawfully seized by a private individual, without police knowledge or approval, ordinarily is admissible in court. (The private individual who unlawfully seized the evidence may be open to criminal or civil charges.)

The exclusionary rule is a product of the criminal law in the United States and is not found in most other countries. Even in common law England where much of our legal tradition is rooted, there is no exclusionary rule. Evidence illegally gathered by the British police is generally allowed in court as long as the evidence is relevant to the case. This places the interest of the state above the rights of individuals.[5] As in one case involving the illegal possession of ammunition, the British court ruled that:

> In the Lordships' opinion the test to be applied in considering whether evidence is admissible is whether it is relevant to the matters in issue. If it is, it is admissible and the court is not concerned with how the evidence was obtained.[6]

This ruling, however, does not give British police officers free reign. In a more recent case, the British court held that "common law does not permit police officers . . . to ransack anyone's house . . . simply to see if he may have committed some crime or other."[7]

It is noteworthy that the exclusionary rule is not a specific provision in the Fourth Amendment. Rather, the exclusionary rule was created by the courts beginning in the early part of the twentieth century. Until this time, the Fourth Amendment was little more than a "paper tiger" without real teeth; the police routinely circumvented search and seizure restrictions with relative impunity. Two landmark U.S. Supreme Court decisions drastically altered police search and seizure procedures with the establishment of the exclusionary rule. The 1914 *Weeks* case created the exclusionary rule for all federal law enforcement officers, and the 1961 *Mapp* case extended the rule to all state (and local) law enforcement officers. Given the importance of these two cases, we will examine each more closely.

Weeks v. United States (1914)—Federal Exclusionary Rule[8]

Weeks was charged with the federal crime of using the U.S. postal system to defraud. A United States marshal, with the aid of local police, seized some letters and other articles from the home of Weeks without a search warrant. Weeks asserted his Fourth Amendment rights were violated by the federal agent and petitioned the federal district court to have the illegally seized evidence dismissed. The court refused. The materials seized from Weeks' home was used at his trial, and he was subsequently convicted. On appeal, the U.S. Supreme Court reversed the lower court's ruling, arguing that Weeks'

Fourth Amendment protections were seriously violated. Delivering the opinion of the court, Justice Day wrote:

> If letters and private documents can thus be seized and held and used in evidence against a citizen accused of an offense, the protection of the Fourth Amendment, declaring his right to be secure against such searches and seizures, is of no value, and, so far as those thus placed are concerned, might as well be stricken from the Constitution.

The Supreme Court used the opportunity in *Weeks* to establish the exclusionary rule at the federal level. Since 1914, all federal law enforcement officers (U.S. Marshals, FBI, DEA, etc.) have been barred from gathering incriminating evidence illegally and presenting it in federal court. In 1920, the Supreme Court further ruled that illegal evidence discovered by federal agents could not be used to uncover other evidence.[9] This extension of the exclusionary rule is known as the **fruits of the poisonous tree doctrine**, which states that *no evidence illegally gotten shall be admissible in court, nor shall fruits borne from this poisonous tree be admissible.* In effect the poisonous tree doctrine implies that investigatory leads developed as a result of an illegal search and seizure are as tainted as the original fruit.

The *Weeks* case did not apply to the states. The Supreme Court preferred to let individual states decide on appropriate criminal procedure rather than dictate it to them. Also, the *Weeks* case did not exclude illegally obtained evidence in federal courts as long as state law enforcement officers were the ones who originally seized the evidence. State officers could hand the tainted evidence over to federal prosecutors on the proverbial "silver platter" (called the **silver platter doctrine**). As recently as 1949, in *Wolf v. Colorado*,[10] the Court refused to extend the exclusionary rule to the states through the Fourteenth Amendment's due process clause (although a growing number of states had already adopted the exclusionary rule on their own). It was not until the 1961 *Mapp* case that the Supreme Court made the exclusionary rule binding in all states and for all police officers.

Mapp v. Ohio (1961)—State Exclusionary Rule[11]

On May 23, 1957, three Cleveland police officers arrived at the home of Dollree Mapp. The police suspected Mapp of harboring a man wanted for a bombing in the Cleveland area. They also thought Mapp had a large amount of illegal policy paraphernalia hidden at her residence. After telephoning her attorney, Mapp refused to permit the officers to enter her home without a search warrant. The officers advised headquarters about the situation and stationed themselves outside to watch the home.

Several hours later, four additional Cleveland police officers arrived at the home, a two-family dwelling where Mapp and her daughter lived on the second floor. When Mapp did not immediately answer her door, the officers made a forceful entry, meeting Mapp on the interior stairway leading up to her apartment. Mapp demanded to see the search warrant. One of the officers waved "a piece of paper" in front of her claiming it was the warrant, at which point Mapp grabbed the paper and stuffed it into her bosom. The officer quickly retrieved the paper and handcuffed Mapp because she was interfering with the officers. The paper in question was not a search warrant and, in fact, no search warrant was ever obtained.

A complete search of Mapp's apartment and the basement did not uncover the bombing suspect or other items the police were looking for, but they did find some "dirty pictures." Mapp was arrested, charged, and convicted for possessing obscene materials over the objections of her attorney that the search and seizure was unlawful.

Four years later, on June 19, 1961, the Supreme Court overturned Mapp's obscenity conviction on the grounds that the Cleveland police officers violated her constitutional rights. In so doing, the Supreme Court went the final mile in search and seizure rulings by holding that the Fourth Amendment, *by inference*, is incorporated in the "due process" clause of the Fourteenth Amendment. The Court stated that from this date forward, evidence illegally gathered by any police officer would be inadmissible in every court in the country. As Justice Clark wrote in the opinion of the Court:

> Because it is enforceable in the same manner and to the like effect as other basic rights secured by the Due Process Clause, we can no longer permit it to be revocable at the whim of any police officer, who, in the name of law enforcement itself, chooses to suspend its environment. *Our decision, founded on reason and truth, gives to the individual no more than that which the Constitution guarantees him, to the police officer no less than that to which honest law enforcement is entitled and, to the courts, that judicial integrity so necessary in the true administration of justice.* (emphasis added)

The significance of the *Mapp* ruling on American law enforcement is difficult to overstate. While state and local police were never permitted to violate the Fourth (and Fourteenth) Amendment rights of citizens, the easy admissibility of illegally obtained evidence in criminal courts allowed the police to get away with it. As one indication of the clear and strong signal sent to the law enforcement establishment, New York City police did not request a single search warrant in the year prior to *Mapp*, but requested over eight hundred search warrants the year after *Mapp*. In short, the *Mapp* ruling reduced the incentive for police officers to violate the Fourth Amendment by extending the exclusionary rule to all states.

Despite the emotional cries of many outspoken critics of *Mapp*, the *Mapp* ruling does not require police to "bend over backwards" to protect the rights of criminal defendants! *Mapp* simply forces police to be more careful and to abide by the fundamental protections guaranteed in the United States Constitution. If the police have very good reason to believe that someone has illegal contraband in their home, and there is no immediate threat that the evidence will be destroyed, it is little to ask of the police to take the extra step and secure a valid search warrant from a judicial officer before searching the property or seizing evidence. This is simply what the Constitution requires.

Retreat from *Mapp*

Since the time of the *Mapp* decision, the Supreme Court has "fine-tuned" its original position. Some Court observers see these more recent search and seizures rulings as a slight retreat from *Mapp*. In particular, the Court has been willing to permit limited **good faith exceptions** to the Fourth Amendment. This means that evidence seized by an officer who acts in "good faith" (i.e., subscribing to what the officer has reason to believe is proper procedural law), which is later called into question because of some minor technical mistake in the search, is not automatically excluded from court. For example, in *U.S. v. Leon* (1984), a search warrant was issued to a police officer without sufficient probable cause, but the U.S. Supreme Court let Leon's conviction stand, ruling that it would serve no useful purpose to exclude the evidence since the officer acted entirely in good faith when using the warrant.[12] Similarly, in *Massachusetts v. Sheppard* (1984), the Supreme Court let stand a conviction based on a search warrant that was filled out incorrectly and placed on the wrong form.[13]

The good faith exception applies directly to the **lucky find** doctrine. The lucky find doctrine states that in a lawful search, if an officer acting in good faith happens to find incriminating evidence not being searched for, the evidence is admissible in court. The key to getting evidence from a lucky find admitted into court is that the officer must be acting in good faith. For instance, if the officers in the *Mapp* case had a valid search warrant when they accidentally found the obscene materials, the original conviction of Mapp would have been fully justified.

The Court appears to have modified the exclusionary rule in other ways as well. Illegally seized evidence may be admitted into court if the judge decides the evidence would have been eventually discovered. This is known as **inevitable discovery**. In one case, the police used illegal tactics to talk a murder suspect into telling them where the body of a young girl was hidden.[14] The Supreme Court held that the evidence found when the suspect led the police to the body was still admissible because, with over two hundred people searching the immediate area, it was inevitable that the body would have been found.

To date, the Supreme Court has been unwilling to grant police the authority to make drastic intrusions into the human body. While "limited" cavity searches are permissible under appropriate circumstances (i.e., ears, nose, mouth, anus, and vagina), "probing" cavity searches requiring medical personnel are not. In *Rochin v. California* (1952), the Supreme Court ruled that pumping a suspect's stomach to make him vomit incriminating evidence was a "shocking performance" and in violation of the Fourteenth Amendment's due process clause.[15] Rochin had put two drug capsules into his mouth and swallowed them when sheriff deputies approached him. Rochin was taken to the hospital and, at the direction of the officers and against the will of Rochin, a doctor forced an emetic solution into his stomach. Rochin vomited revealing the evidence. The capsules were retrieved, cleaned off, and used at his trial where he was found guilty. The Supreme Court reversed the conviction on review, holding "this is conduct that shocks the conscience." More recently, the Supreme Court has ruled that forced surgery to remove a bullet from a suspect's body is constitutionally unacceptable. In this case, prosecutors wanted the bullet to place the suspect at the scene of a crime.

Search Warrant

The best method for police to conduct a legal search and seizure is to first obtain a valid **search warrant**. A search warrant is a written order, signed by a qualified judicial officer, that gives police the authority to search and seize evidence listed on the warrant and to bring the evidence before the court. A valid search warrant grants police the legal right to enter people's homes, look through their personal belongings, and seize items that may be evidence of a crime. Police searches can be extremely thorough depending on the nature of the evidence being sought. When drugs or other small items are listed on the warrant, there is virtually no limit to where the police can search (under carpeting, behind walls, inside plumbing, etc.). Evidence seized with a search warrant carries substantial legal weight and is more likely to be admitted into court than evidence seized without a warrant (there are limited exceptions to the search warrant to be discussed below). What is more, search warrants help protect the police from criminal charges and civil suits.

POCKETFUL OF GUFFAWS

The lawyer for an Oakland County, Mich., man charged with cocaine possession may have had his client's interests at heart when he tried to prove a claim that police had improperly searched his client, but during a pretrial hearing on a suppression motion, the judge examining the defendant's coat triggered a courtroom uproar when he pulled out more suspected cocaine from the defendant's pocket.

Circuit Court Judge Barry Howard had to order a five-minute recess to calm the guffaws and hysterical laughter that reverberated throughout the courtroom after the March 29 incident, the *Detroit Free Press* reported.

Defense attorney John Lazar had been trying to prove that police had improperly searched a denim coat belonging to Christopher Plovie, who was arrested in front of a suspected crack house in Detroit last October. During that search, said Assistant Prosecutor Brian Zubel, police found a bag that held about 19 grams of cocaine.

Judge Howard complied with Lazar's request to examine the coat in question, and promptly pulled a smaller bag of cocaine out of a pocket. The coat had been in police custody since October, and a 1½-inch square plastic bag that held about one gram of the substance apparently had gone unnoticed by police.

"I thought, 'This is something out of 'L.A. Law.' This just doesn't happen,'" said Howard.

But the "Great Coke Coat Defense," as the newspaper dubbed the incident, went unavailing because Howard ruled that the original search had been carried out properly by police.

"The funny thing is, even if I had dismissed the search, he could have been charged," Howard noted.

Plovie pleaded guilty to possession of a controlled substance and faces up to four years in prison.

Source: *Law Enforcement News*, John Jay College of Criminal Justice, New York, March 31, 1990.

The U.S. Constitution is quite specific regarding the requirements for obtaining a search warrant. The Fourth Amendment provides that "No warrants shall issue, but upon probable cause, supported by oath or affirmation, and particularly describing the place to be searched and the persons or things to be seized." Sheriffs, police chiefs, and prosecutors are not authorized to grant a search warrant; this responsibility is granted only to a judge or magistrate. Search warrants must be very specific, as the Constitution stipulates, describing precisely what evidence is being sought and where it is to be found. "Fish hunts" are not allowed, and blank warrants are not issued to the police only to be filled in later once something is found. Generally speaking, if an officer has sound reason to believe that illicit drugs are being distributed from someone's home, the search warrant would have to list the correct house number and street. Yet because drugs can be hidden in almost any location, the warrant would not have to identify exactly where in the house the drugs are kept.

Search warrants must be executed within a reasonable time period after they are issued. The time varies from state to state but is usually around forty-eight or seventy-two hours. Once the time period elapses the warrant becomes invalid. Occasionally the police have probable cause that illegal contraband will be at a location in the near future, but is not there now. For example, an officer may have reliable information that a package containing child pornography is to be dropped off in a bus station restroom sometime in the next two days. The **anticipatory warrant** allows the officer to obtain a search warrant before the evidence arrives rather than risk having the evidence removed or destroyed while the officer is attempting to secure a warrant. Anticipatory warrants are used most often to seize packages delivered by mail.[16]

To secure a search warrant, the police officer must be able to convince the judge that there is *very good reason to believe* (1) evidence of a crime exists, and (2) the officer knows where the evidence is located. This is known as the **probable cause** requirement. Since the 1925 case of *Dumbra v. United States*, the Supreme Court has held that probable cause is what a "reasonable, discreet and prudent man would be led to believe."[17] Probable cause refers to a level of awareness that is less than "certain" knowledge but more than mere "suspicion."

Exceptions to Search Warrant

The Constitution says nothing about search and seizures without a warrant, but there are occasions when a search warrant is not necessary or is impractical to obtain. The law specifies four major exceptions to the search warrant: (1) waiver of suspects rights, (2) plain view, (3) emergency circumstances, and (4) search incident to a lawful arrest. Each of these exceptions are discussed below.

Waiver of Rights by Suspect

Individuals have the authority to waive their constitutional right and allow an officer to conduct a search in the absence of a search warrant. It is amazing how often criminal suspects waive their rights even when they have something to hide. This is partly because they want to appear innocent to the police, and partly because they think they have carefully concealed the evidence. However, criminals are seldom clever in hiding evidence, and this allows the police to score numerous convictions each year from such "go ahead" searches.

Evidence seized from a waiver of rights will be closely examined by the courts. Police officers have to demonstrate that the waiver of rights was voluntarily and intelligently given by the defendant, without the use of force or intimidation by the officer. For example, an officer cannot interpret silence

WIRETAPPING AND EAVESDROPPING

Wiretapping and electronic eavesdropping fall under Fourth Amendment protection, meaning that certain safeguards apply when "searching and seizing" conversations. The development of electronic listening and surveillance devices in the twentieth century has provided the police with investigatory capability far beyond that which was anticipated in the Constitution. Advances in communication technology allow us to listen to private conversations with minimal or no physical intrusion onto a suspect's property. In what way does the Fourth Amendment's protection against unreasonable searches and seizures apply to wiretaps and electronic eavesdropping devices?

As early as 1928 in *Olmstead v. United States,* the Supreme Court gave its approval to police wiretaps of telephone lines. Olmstead headed a huge organized crime ring conspiring to violate the Prohibition Act. Police tapped the telephone lines of major figures in the liquor scheme, including Olmstead, which produced the evidence they needed for conviction. Although Olmstead contested that his rights were violated by the wiretaps, the Court ruled that the Fourth Amendment applied only to material things, not to intangible conversations. The Court affirmed Olmstead's conviction.

By 1967, however, in *Katz v. United States,* the Supreme Court had completely reversed the Olmstead ruling. The Court ruled that

FBI agents violated Katz's Fourth Amendment right to privacy when they tapped a public telephone they believed Katz was using to transmit gambling information.

Eavesdropping (e.g., "bugs" or "plants" inconspicuously placed) is similar to tapping telephone lines in the sense that one can surreptiously record private conversations, yet the legal establishment has treated eavesdropping slightly differently. The Court has allowed police to secretly listen to private conversations as long as there is no physical trespass onto the suspect's property. For instance, in *Goldman v. United States* (1942) the Court permitted the police use of a sensitive detectaphone placed against a wall to pick-up conversations in the next room. However, in the *Silverman* case two decades later, the Court held that placing a microphone on a spike going through a partition wall and touching the adjacent wall of the suspect's room was a physical trespass. It therefore fell under Fourth Amendment protection.

As long as one of the parties agrees, there is no restriction to secretly recording conversations. This applies regardless of whether the person with the hidden recorder is an informant, a regular citizen, or a police officer. The Court reasons that this is no different than making an accurate recording of what the person could later repeat from memory.

Sources: John C. Klotter and Jacqueline R. Kanovitz, *Constitutional Law For Police* (Cincinnati: The W. H. Anderson Company, 1973), p. 183; *Olmstead v. United States*, 277 US 438, 72 LEd 944, 48 SCt 564 (1928); *Katz v. United States*, 389 US 347, 19 LEd (2d) 576, 88 SCt 507 (1967); *Goldman v. United States*, 316 US 129, 62 SCt 993 (1942); *Silverman v. United States*, 365 US 505, 5 LEd (2d) 734, 81 SCt 679 (1961); *Lopez v. United States*, 373 US 427, 10 LEd (2d) 462, 83 Sct 1381 (1963).

to a question (e.g., "You don't mind if I take a little look-see, do ya?") as a waiver of rights. Suspects have the right to withdraw their waiver at anytime during the search. However, the police normally would be allowed to continue with the search if they had already identified incriminating evidence.

The person granting permission for a warrantless search must be authorized to do so. A homeowner clearly has authority to grant the police permission to search his or her dwelling, as does the spouse of the homeowner. As a general rule, landlords do not have the right to permit the search of a tenant's apartment, nor do temporary guests have the right to permit a search of another's home. Parents normally have the right to permit a warrantless search of a minor child's room and any common areas used by the entire family, but not the private room of an adult child. An adult child living in his or her parents' home may grant police permission to search common areas of the home and his or her own personal room, but not the private room of the parents. Under ordinary circumstances, children do not have proper authority to grant permission for a warrantless search of their parents' home.[18]

Plain View

A second exception to the search warrant is when evidence of crime is in **plain view** of the police. So long as the police are not trespassing, what is plainly visible is not considered to be a "search," and the constitutional guarantee does not apply.[19] Commenting on the plain view doctrine, the Supreme Court has held that "the police are not required to close their eyes and need not walk out and leave the article where they saw it."[20]

Yet what officers can plainly see is not always what they can immediately seize. It depends on where the evidence is located and one's constitutional right to privacy. For example, an officer standing on a public sidewalk can immediately seize a stolen bicycle found in an adjacent alley. The same officer standing on the same sidewalk, however, who sees a stolen bicycle through an open window of a first floor apartment would not be permitted to burst into the dwelling and seize the evidence. When evidence in plain view is on private property where the owner can claim an expectation to privacy (which certainly is true for one's home), the important rule is *look but don't touch* until you have a search warrant, unless the situation is an emergency and falls under the third exception to the search warrant (see below).[21] As one Maryland Appeals Court judge eloquently put it, "Light waves cross thresholds with a constitutional impunity not permitted arms and legs. Wherever the eye may go, the body of a policeman may not necessarily follow."[22]

The Supreme Court also has ruled that the police have the right to search a suspect's garbage that is placed near the curb for removal without a warrant because of the reduced expectation of privacy. In *California v. Greenwood* (1988), the Court held that the warrantless removal of trash by a Laguna Beach police officer that was near the curb ready for pickup was not a Fourth Amendment search and seizure because the garbage was fully accessible to the public.[23] However, the Court held that picking through someone's garbage that is near the porch or perhaps still behind the garage would not be legal without a warrant because of the greater expectation of privacy.

The Court has ruled that the use of "eye aiders" like binoculars, telescopes, or flashlights in the night are acceptable police tools that qualify under the plain view exception.[24] Moreover, aerial surveillance by plane or helicopter in the public air space above someone's property is not a violation of the Fourth Amendment, even if the property is hidden by a privacy fence.[25]

Emergency Circumstances

Search warrants are not required if the destruction of evidence is imminent, or if the evidence is likely to be moved by the time officers return with a warrant. For example, a suspected drug runner being chased by the police may not use his or her home as a refuge. An officer in *hot pursuit* may immediately enter the suspect's dwelling without a warrant before the evidence can be destroyed, usually by flushing it down the toilet, or before the suspect has the chance to become armed.

Warrantless emergency searches apply most often to cars on the road. Automobiles pose special problems for the police because of their high mobility. This is why the courts have been willing to relax Fourth Amendment restrictions in automobile searches. The **moving vehicle doctrine**, established in *Carroll v. United States* (1925), grants police officers the right to conduct warrantless searches, based on probable cause, if a suspected vehicle is moving or is soon likely to be moved.[26] However, the *Carroll* case left open the question of how thorough the search of the automobile may be without a warrant. In *United States v. Ross* (1982), the Supreme Court held that "If probable cause justifies the search of a lawfully stopped vehicle, *it justifies the search of every part of the vehicle and its contents that may conceal the object of the search.*"[27] While the *Ross* case granted officers the right to look into loose bags or pouches found in the trunk area, it was not clear if police were equally permitted to open sealed containers or closed briefcases. However, in *California v. Acevedo* (1991) the Supreme Court clarified its stance by ruling that if the police have the right to open the trunk of a car, they also have the right to search the contents sealed within containers.[28]

Search Incident to a Lawful Arrest

In conducting a lawful arrest of a suspect, the police have the right to search the area around the suspect without having to get a search warrant. The search incident to a lawful arrest produces a great many legal seizures of incriminating evidence every year for the police. In years past, the police stretched this privilege by using their power of arrest as a reason for searching one's entire home or place of business. In *Chimel v. California* (1969), the police searched Chimel's entire home, without his consent, following his arrest and seized some coins stolen from a coin store.[29] In overturning Chimel's conviction, the Supreme Court ruled that the police went far beyond that allowed by a search incident to an arrest. The Court limited the search following an arrest to that area under the *immediate* control of the suspect. This area is normally interpreted as within arms reach or lunging distance where the suspect might be able to destroy evidence or grab a weapon.

Normally we think about the Fourth Amendment when the police search and seize *things*, but the Fourth Amendment clearly protects "the right of the people to be secure in their *persons*, houses, papers, and effects" from unreasonable searches and seizures. When an officer seizes a person—that is, makes an arrest—his or her actions are in the realm of the Fourth Amendment.

An arrest is the process of taking someone into custody. Strictly speaking, taking a suspect to police headquarters for questioning is an arrest even though the officer intends to let the suspect go if the interrogation leads nowhere. In other words, an arrest does not require the person to be formally "booked" or charged with a crime. Simply inviting someone to the station to answer a few questions, or briefly stopping someone on the street to gather general information, does not constitute an arrest.

The law permits an officer to make an arrest under the following three conditions:

1. When an officer has an arrest warrant (for felony or misdemeanor);
2. When an officer witnesses a crime (felony or misdemeanor);
3. When an officer has probable cause to believe a felony has occurred.

As a general rule, probable cause of a misdemeanor is not sufficient to justify an arrest. The police officer must either have a warrant to make a misdemeanor arrest or have personally witnessed the offense. Because of this restriction, police often advise victims of misdemeanor crimes to take out an arrest warrant on the suspect, which then gives the police authority to make an arrest. Some states allow for limited misdemeanor arrests based only on probable cause, a growing trend particularly in spousal assault cases.

Stop and Frisk

In *Terry v. Ohio* (1968), the Supreme Court held that a Cleveland police officer acted appropriately when he detained and "patted down" three suspicious persons.[30] The officer observed the men (one being Terry) casing out a store to rob it. The suspects would walk along the sidewalk peering into the same store window each time they passed, then briefly confer at the corner. After witnessing the same routine for some time, the officer approached the men, identified himself, and asked for their names. Terry muttered something, at which time the officer spun Terry around and quickly patted down his outer coat. Feeling a gun inside the coat, the officer seized the weapon. A pat down of the second suspect also resulted in a gun seizure. The officer failed to identify a weapon when patting down the third suspect, and so he did not search inside the man's coat. The two men were charged with carrying a concealed weapon and convicted in court. On appeal, the Supreme Court upheld the conviction.

The Terry case approved the right of the police to **stop and frisk** suspicious persons even when there is not sufficient evidence (probable cause) to make an arrest. A "stop" is less than an arrest, and a "frisk" is less than a thorough search of the suspect. An officer who stops a suspicious person for further information must make the detention brief if the person appears innocent, and any frisk must be limited to a quick pat down of outer clothing for weapons. The frisk for weapons is allowed because of the potential danger to the officer or others. As a general rule, evidence of a crime other than a weapon (or something consistent with the shape of a weapon) confiscated by an officer during a routine stop and frisk would not be admissible in court.

A stop and frisk only requires the officer to have *reasonable suspicion* of the possibility of crime. Reasonable suspicion must be based on more than a "hunch" or "gut feeling." Some specific, articulable fact must exist which, combined with an officer's judgement and experience, qualifies as reasonable suspicion. In reality, the reasonable suspicion requirement to justify a stop and frisk is not difficult to satisfy in court.

Fourth Amendment Implications for Law Enforcement

Many critics contend that the Fourth Amendment, particularly the exclusionary rule, severely handcuffs the police. They argue that the courts pick cases apart looking for minor "technicalities," and then flush prosecutions down the drain to the delight of defendants and defense attorneys, but to the detriment of law-abiding citizens. No doubt this occasionally happens. Former Supreme Court Justice Warren Burger once complained that "thousands" of criminals are released every year because of minor procedural flaws.[31]

In reality, the effect of the exclusionary rule on case prosecution appears to be inconsequential in all but drug-related cases. According to a National Institute of Justice report of felony cases in California, less than 1 percent of the cases were dismissed by the courts because of the exclusionary rule (most of the questionable cases were previously screened out by the police or the prosecutor).[32] James Fyfe characterizes the effects of the exclusionary rule from the NIJ study as "minuscule" and "infinitesimal."[33] Only in the realm of drug-related cases can we document substantial numbers of dismissed cases. The NIJ study found that over two-thirds of all dismissed cases due to the exclusionary rule were drug cases, a finding readily explained by the normal lack of a complaining victim or witness in drug offenses. This places added pressure on the police to apply more "aggressive" investigatory techniques.

The exclusionary rule is not an unreasonable obstacle to effective law enforcement. It merely forces the police to be more professional when performing their duties by respecting the basic constitutional rights of citizens. In a free and democratic society such as ours, blatant violations of the Fourth Amendment cannot be tolerated.

THE FIFTH AMENDMENT—SELF-INCRIMINATION

The Fifth Amendment to the Constitution states that "No person . . . shall be compelled in any criminal case to be a witness against himself." This is widely known as our right against **self-incrimination**. The privilege against self-incrimination protects us from having to give testimony to the state. The belief that suspects should not have to testify against themselves dates back to English common law and practice. It is based on the idea that forcing someone to "contribute" to their own prosecution is repugnant and fundamentally unfair. Note that the privilege is against forced self-incrimination; we all have the right to incriminate ourselves if we wish to by confessing.

Scope of Privilege

Despite the language of the times (i.e., ". . . witness against *himself*"), the Fifth Amendment protection against self-incrimination applies equally to males and females. The privilege is also applicable in civil cases even though the amendment only mentions "criminal cases." Occasionally, during a civil proceeding, defendants will "take the fifth" (meaning not answer) a sensitive question that may implicate them in crime. Normally, this occurs on a question-by-question basis at the advice of an attorney and with the consent of the judge.

In criminal cases, the privilege against self-incrimination starts as soon as an individual becomes a suspect to a crime and it extends throughout the entire prosecution, including the trial. The protection can actually begin before an arrest. For instance, during the initial confrontation the police may not consider the person a suspect; the police may only wish to gather information. At this point, before the person is considered a suspect and when the police are only gathering general information, the Fifth Amendment protection does not apply—the officer may ask (nonaccusatory) questions freely. However, *if the investigation begins to target the person as a suspect, and when the questions become accusatory, the rules regarding self-incrimination apply.* Moreover, a suspect who at first voluntarily answers the questions of an interrogating officer has the right to stop at any time. The officer is required to respect this decision and cease interrogation.

The courts have ruled that the privilege against forced self-incrimination does not apply to having to give blood, urine, hair, breath, voice, fingerprint, or handwriting samples. The reason why the protection does not apply is because the Fifth Amendment only covers **testimonial evidence** (verbal utterances) while these items are **nontestimonial evidence**. The legal principle here is an intriguing one since blood, urine, breath, and so on can be involuntarily seized from someone's body and used in court. The result is a powerful law enforcement tool. For instance, the police have the right to pluck a few hairs from a suspected rapist to send to the crime lab, and they routinely force unwilling motorists to take a sobriety test.

Relatedly, individuals may be forced to participate in a *suspect identification* procedure even though their physical appearance may prove incriminating when the victim or witness recognizes them. The most common suspect identification procedure used by the police is the **lineup**. This is when an array of possible suspects is brought before the witness for identification. The **showup** is like a lineup, yet only the targeted suspect is brought before the witness for identification. Sometimes the police only show photographs (mug shots) to the witness, which is a type of showup. The Supreme Court has ruled that because the lineup is a critical stage in the investigation process, suspects have the right to have an attorney present.[34] The defense attorney may not prevent the police from placing the suspect into the lineup; the attorney may only watch to ensure the lineup is not biased or suggestive in any way (for example, placing a tall thin female suspect into a lineup with only short plump women).[35] The courts have not extended the right to counsel to on-the-street showups that occur shortly after a crime is committed or to the viewing of mug shots.[36]

Although the Fifth Amendment offers protection against forced self-incrimination, there is one effective mechanism for legally requiring a suspect to talk. The prosecutor may grant a suspect **immunity** from criminal prosecution—meaning that incriminating statements the suspect reveals during police questioning cannot be used in criminal court. Granting immunity is an excellent way to build cases against important yet insulated criminals by sacrificing the "small fish" for the "big fish." Please note that even if immunity is granted, it is still possible to prosecute the suspect if *independent evidence* is discovered that is unrelated to the coerced testimony. Such would be the case, for example, if an eyewitness to the crime emerged.

Major Court Decisions Regarding Self-Incrimination

Four landmark Supreme Court cases have laid the principal foundation for the Fifth Amendment protection against self incrimination: *Brown v. Mississippi* (1936); *Malloy v. Hogan* (1964); *Escobedo v. Illinois* (1964); and the famous *Miranda v. Arizona* (1966). We shall summarize the facts of each case and the Supreme Court's ruling below.

Brown v. Mississippi (1936)—No Forced Confessions[37]

Ed Brown, along with two other black men, were charged with the murder of a white man in March of 1934. On the evening of the murder, a deputy sheriff, accompanied by others, escorted one of the defendants to the home of the deceased where a number of white men had gathered. The defendant was accused of the crime but he maintained his innocence. Upon his denial, several white men, including the deputy, took a rope and hanged him by his neck to a tree, then let him down. Still protesting his innocence, the defendant was severely beaten and whipped by the men, then eventually released in great agony. The following day the same black man was again picked up by the deputy and a few other men and arrested for murder.

On the way to the county courthouse in Mississippi, they followed a route leading into the state of Alabama and, while in that state, the deputy and his accomplices resumed torturing the suspect. The deputy indicated the beating would continue until the suspect plead guilty. Unable to endure the pain any longer, the suspect agreed to confess and, with the coaching of the deputy, the suspect revealed important details of the crime. Once back at the courthouse, the "confession" was formally recorded. Complete confessions eventually were extracted from the other two black suspects after similar beatings.

Aside from the confessions, which were beaten and tortured out of the defendants, the state did not bother to produce any other evidence. Moreover, the deputy did not deny torturing the suspects, nor did he deny the fact that the confessions were physically coerced. Amazingly, the presiding judge permitted the confessions in his court. The three black men were convicted for murder and sentenced to die. Even the highest court in Mississippi affirmed the lower court's decision on appeal.

The United States Supreme Court agreed to hear the case. Outraged by the treatment of the defendants, the Court noted:

> Further details of the brutal treatment to which these helpless prisoners were subjected need not be pursued. It is sufficient to say that in pertinent respects the transcript reads more like pages torn from some medieval account, than a record made within the confines of a modern civilization which aspires to an enlightened constitutional government.

The Supreme Court overturned the convictions of Brown and the two other men because of the flagrant violations of their Fifth Amendment rights. More broadly, since the *Brown* decision was handed down all confessions that are physically forced out of suspects are inadmissible in criminal court.

Malloy v. Hogan (1964)—Protection Extended to All States[38]

Beginning with *Twining v. New Jersey* (1908), the Supreme Court refused to extend the Fifth Amendment protection against self-incrimination to the states through the Fourteenth Amendment.[39] State courts that permitted self-incriminating testimony to be entered as evidence were not overruled by the Supreme Court. The 1964 *Malloy* decision was a complete reversal of the *Twining* ruling. Malloy was arrested by Connecticut police in a gambling raid. He pleaded guilty to the misdemeanor crime and received a one-year sentence and $500 fine. Some months after Malloy was released from jail, he was required to testify before a judicial hearing on gambling in the local area. Malloy refused, claiming his statements would be self-incriminating. Malloy was placed in jail for contempt of court and ordered to stay there until he agreed to testify. Drawing form the earlier *Twining* case, the Connecticut court of last resort ruled that the Fifth Amendment protection against self-incrimination did not apply.

On review the U.S. Supreme Court reversed the decision of the Connecticut court, thus ruling in Malloy's favor. The Supreme Court also reversed the *Twining* decision. The Court held that "the Fifth Amendment's exception from compulsory self-incrimination is also protected by the Fourteenth Amendment against abridgment by the states." Similar to the *Mapp* decision just three years earlier regarding Fourth Amendment search and seizure protections, the *Malloy* decision extended the Fifth Amendment's protection against self-incrimination to all states.

Escobedo v. Illinois (1964)—Interrogation Critical Stage[40]

On January 19, 1960, Danny Escobedo's brother-in-law was fatally shot in the back. Escobedo was arrested several hours after the shooting without a warrant and interrogated for fifteen hours by Chicago police. During this time Escobedo made no incriminating statements to the police and was released once his lawyer obtained a writ of *habeas corpus*. Eleven days later Escobedo was again arrested and taken to police headquarters for further questioning. On several occasions during the interrogation Escobedo requested to speak with his attorney, but was told by police that he could not do so until they finished questioning him. At the same time, Escobedo's attorney requested to see his client and was also refused. It was during this second interrogation that Escobedo made certain incriminating statements that were later used at his trial to convict him.

On appeal to the Supreme Court, the defense argued that the incriminating statements made during the police interrogation should be suppressed because Escobedo's Sixth Amendment right to counsel had been denied. The Supreme Court agreed, holding that a police interrogation is a *critical stage* in a defendant's prosecution and that the right to counsel must be guaranteed. Incriminating statements made during a custodial interrogation when the right to counsel is withheld may not be used against the accused at trial.

Miranda v. Arizona (1966)—Advising Suspects of Rights[41]

Few criminal cases have attracted more attention and debate than the 1966 *Miranda* decision. On the evening of March 3, 1963, an eighteen-year-old Phoenix woman was abducted and forcibly raped. The Phoenix police arrested Ernesto Miranda ten days later. The victim identified Miranda from a police lineup. Miranda was questioned by the police for approximately two hours, during which time he signed a confession that he abducted the young woman and raped her. Miranda was convicted for kidnapping and rape over his counsel's objection that the police failed to advise Miranda of his right to remain silent and his right to speak with an attorney. Miranda received twenty to thirty years on each count to run concurrently. On appeal the Arizona Supreme Court affirmed the conviction.

The Supreme Court reversed the conviction on the grounds that Miranda's right against self-incrimination was violated by the Phoenix police. The Court ruled that custodial interrogations require the police to advise suspects of the following procedural rights: (1) the right to remain silent; (2) any statements made by the accused may be used against them in a criminal court; (3) the right to speak with their attorney; and (4) if they cannot afford an attorney one will be provided to them. These rules are better known as the **Miranda rights**.

The Erosion of *Miranda*

When *Miranda* was originally handed down, the courts seemed eager to comply with the new legal procedures. The rule of thumb was *no warning equals no confession*, a rule that fueled the wrath of police officers nationwide.

To many, the Supreme Court had simply gone too far by tipping the scales of justice in favor of the criminal. Critics called for the reversal of *Miranda*. A number of court watchers were searching for a "test case" to bring up from a lower court that would give the Supreme Court the opportunity to overturn *Miranda*. The shifting membership of the Supreme Court due to Reagan and Bush conservative appointees has given opponents of *Miranda* hope, although to date no single case has completely reversed *Miranda* nor does it appear likely that it will be overturned in the near future. Since the late 1970s, however, the *Miranda* ruling has suffered a number of minor reversals, the cumulative effect of which has been the erosion of *Miranda's* original impact.

The spirit of *Miranda* was left largely intact in *Brewer v. Williams* (1977) when the Supreme Court disallowed certain incriminating statements made by a murder suspect who was being transported by a police detective.[42] Robert Williams, a recent escapee from a mental hospital, surrendered to police in Davenport, Iowa, for the Christmas Eve abduction, rape, and murder of ten-year-old Pamela Powers of Des Moines, Iowa. Williams was to be driven back to Des Moines, a 160 mile trip, to answer to the charges. The attorney for Williams requested that no interrogation take place during the long drive. The detective agreed.

During the trip, however, the detective played on William's religious sentiments with what is referred to in the court record as the *Christian burial* speech. The detective requested Williams to observe the weather conditions; it was raining and cold, and they were predicting several inches of snow by the evening. On the way, the detective pleaded that they should stop where Williams had put the body before the snow made it difficult to find it. He told Williams that this would allow the parents of the poor child to have a proper Christian burial for their daughter, who was taken from them and murdered the night before Christ's birthday. Convinced that it was the "Christian" thing to do, Williams led the detective to the dead and frozen body.

Williams was convicted of murder even though the incriminating statements were made while in police custody. By a five to four decision, the Supreme Court ruled that Williams had not waived his right to counsel during the trip, and that the detective's speech constituted an illegal custodial interrogation in violation of *Miranda*.

In *New York v. Quarles* (1984), however, the Court upheld the permissibility of using incriminating statements made to a police officer without benefit of Miranda warnings.[43] Quarles was already in handcuffs when the officer asked where his guns were located. Quarles stated, "The gun is over there," and motioned to a nearby empty carton. The officer retrieved the gun, placed Quarles under arrest, and recited the Miranda warnings. The Supreme Court held that although the incriminating statement about the location of the gun was made before being read his rights, the danger of the concealed weapon justified a *public safety* exception to *Miranda*.

In another case, *Moran v. Burbine* (1986), Rhode Island police read Burbine his Miranda rights. Burbine waived his rights and signed a complete confession of murder.[44] In the meantime, Burbine's sister had contacted his attorney regarding another crime Burbine was suspected of committing.

Burbine's attorney called the police to offer his services to his client. The police lied to the attorney, saying that Burbine did not want to speak with him. Burbine was convicted but subsequently appealed the conviction, arguing that his right to have the assistance of counsel during police questioning as provided in *Miranda* was denied. Writing for the Court, Justice Sandra Day O'Connor held:

> The Constitutional right to request the presence of an attorney belongs solely to the defendant. Because the evidence is clear that [Burbine] never asked for the services of an attorney, the telephone call from the lawyer had no relevance to the validity of the waiver or the admissibility of the statements.

Fifth Amendment Implications for Law Enforcement

There is considerable confusion among citizens when the police need to read a criminal suspect his or her Miranda rights. The common perception is that the police have to read all criminal suspects their rights, particularly anyone they arrest, and if they do not it is sufficient grounds to dismiss the case. This popular view is in error. The police are often not required to read suspects their Miranda rights.

However, the best rule for the police is to "play it safe" by advising suspects of their rights whenever feasible, even if it is not legally required. This practice provides the greatest assurance that any willful or inadvertent statements made by a defendant will be admissible at trial. It also helps the police fulfill their professional responsibility of protecting our constitutional rights.

The police are required to advise suspects of their rights whenever they conduct a custodial interrogation, or any time their questions go from general information gathering (name, age, residence, place of employment, etc.) to accusatory (e.g., Why did you break into your neighbor's home? Who were you planning to sell the stolen merchandise to? Where did you get the burglary tools?). This Miranda requirement holds true regardless of whether the questions are asked at the police station after an arrest or on the street before an arrest.

The police are not legally required to advise suspects of their rights following arrest if they do not plan to interrogate the suspect. Herein lies much of the confusion surrounding *Miranda*. *Miranda* applies only to police custodial interrogations and is not necessitated by the mere act of an arrest. In fact, police often make arrests without advising suspects of their rights *because they do not need their confessions for a conviction.* A person caught "red-handed" by an officer may not have to be "Mirandized." For example, a hand-to-hand purchase of drugs by an undercover officer using marked money is sufficient evidence for conviction—the police officer is an eyewitness to the crime and the marked money is evidence of the illegal transaction. However, if the officer wants to question the arrested suspect about the crime, Miranda warnings must be given.

As stated above, the best policy for police is to Mirandize suspects whenever feasible just to be safe. Standard procedures in many departments require officers to advise all arrested offenders—for felonies and misdemeanors—of their rights. Some departments go so far as to print the Miranda warnings on a small card. The card is read verbatim by the arresting officer. The rationale for reading from a printed card is to assure the court that the police officer did not abbreviate the warnings or leave anything out, as occasionally happens when emotions run high. Reading from a printed card is going beyond the minimum requirements set by the Supreme Court in *Miranda*, but is nonetheless a good idea.

Any waiver of Miranda rights by a suspect must be *voluntary* and *intelligent*. Incriminating evidence obtained from a custodial interrogation based on an "involuntary" or "unknowing" waiver is inadmissible at trial. A useful police procedure is to have the suspect sign a waiver form before questioning begins. This way the police have a formal written record of the waiver in case the suspect later says he was not advised of his rights prior to police questioning.

Police usually readvise suspects of their Miranda rights after a significant delay in questioning, such as after stopping for the night and resuming the next morning. It is also important to repeat the warnings if an officer from a different law enforcement agency wishes to continue the questioning. This is especially important when state and federal agencies are conducting separate investigations. As always, suspects who agree to answer police questions may invoke their right not to incriminate themselves at any time during the interrogation. Furthermore, once a suspect requests counsel during an custodial

DEFENDANT	LOCATION

SPECIFIC WARNING REGARDING INTERROGATIONS

1. YOU HAVE THE RIGHT TO REMAIN SILENT.

2. ANYTHING YOU SAY CAN AND WILL BE USED AGAINST YOU IN A COURT OF LAW.

3. YOU HAVE THE RIGHT TO TALK TO A LAWYER AND HAVE HIM PRESENT WITH YOU WHILE YOU ARE BEING QUESTIONED.

4. IF YOU CANNOT AFFORD TO HIRE A LAWYER ONE WILL BE APPOINTED TO REPRESENT YOU BEFORE ANY QUESTIONING, IF YOU WISH ONE.

SIGNATURE OF DEFENDANT	DATE
WITNESS	TIME

☐ REFUSED SIGNATURE   SAN FRANCISCO POLICE DEPARTMENT   PR.9.1.4

A Miranda card, used by police departments to inform arrested persons of their rights.

interrogation, questioning may not resume later without the suspect's attorney present.

Additional precautions need to be taken before questioning certain types of people. Suspects who speak little or no English need to be interrogated by officers fluent in the language or through an interpreter. If at all possible, police should refrain from interrogating suspects who are mentally or emotionally distraught, intoxicated, or badly injured until a later time. Children normally should not be interrogated without the presence of a parent, guardian, or

INTERROGATION TECHNIQUES

Police interrogators develop a variety of methods for extracting information from criminal suspects. Which method they employ depends on their own experiences and personality, the nature of the crime under investigation, and who is being questioned. The police officer carefully monitors physiological symptoms of the suspect (e.g., sweating, breathing, fidgeting, voice quality, eye contact, dryness of mouth) as clues to truthfulness or deception. The following describes a few of the many different interrogation techniques used by the police.

NOT YOUR FAULT

The officer recognizes that the suspect is not the type of person who is normally in trouble. He is basically a good person, a family man and stable employee. However, he has a weakness or two that occasionally gets the better of him—perhaps he takes a drink now and then, likes to bet on the horses, or is particularly fond of women. The officer is understanding and not judgmental. In fact, he has a close friend, maybe even a brother, who has the same little weakness as the suspect. "I know it's not your fault that you are in trouble," he empathizes with the suspect, "and I can help you." "What you need to do, for yourself and for your family, is to confide in me. Now, start from the beginning. . . ."

THE BLUFF

For more hardened criminals who are less likely to "cave in" to emotional appeals, the officer might try to encourage the suspect to talk by bluffing. The officer can overwhelm the suspect by giving the impression that he has far more knowledge of the crime than he really does. The officer can confront the suspect with a few facts that he definitely knows and imply that he knows much more, in which case it would be foolish for the suspect to hold back information now. A related technique is used when there are two suspects in a crime. Each suspect is placed in a separate room for questioning. After an appropriate amount of time the interrogator goes into one of the rooms and gives the impression that the other suspect has "already told us everything we need to know" and that "he has placed all the blame on you." Most suspects find it difficult to remain quiet under these circumstances as they want to tell their side of the story.

MUTT AND JEFF

Two police officers are used in this familiar interrogation technique, one playing the role of Mutt the "bad cop," the other being Jeff the "good cop." Mutt is impatient because he knows the suspect is guilty and doesn't want to waste his time. Mutt becomes extremely angry at the suspect's unwillingness to talk. He paces about the room in a highly agitated state, trying hard to look menacing and unpredictable. Jeff, who is also in the room, is kindhearted and calm but greatly concerned over Mutt's actions. He tells Mutt to leave for a while to let off some steam. Mutt does so grudgingly, but says he will be back shortly. Once Mutt is gone, Jeff turns to the suspect and, in a comforting manner, encourages the suspect to confide in him before Mutt has a chance to return.

attorney. In North Carolina, for instance, if a youth is thirteen years of age or less, the right to have a parent, guardian, or attorney present is absolute and may not be waived; a youth fourteen or fifteen years old may waive this right, but a parent or guardian may not waive it for him.

It is clear from *Brown v. Mississippi* (1936) that confessions can no longer be physically forced out of suspects, nor can police threaten the suspect with physical force. What is less clear is whether police are on shaky constitutional grounds when they use "psychological tricks" to get a suspect to talk. Police interrogators use a variety of ploys to get a suspect to confess, such as the "good cop, bad cop" routine (better known as *Mutt and Jeff*). The Supreme Court voiced concern over such police tactics in the *Miranda* case, but never barred them. The use of psychological leverage to obtain confessions falls into the grey area of constitutionally permissible police practice; a practice perhaps not to be applauded, but also not to be abandoned.

CONCLUSION

This chapter carefully examined a very complex and ever changing area of police work, namely the constitutional rights of citizens and the corresponding restraints placed upon the police. Our focus was on the Fourth and Fifth Amendments since they have particular relevance to police work. The reader should fully realize that our coverage has been nowhere near exhaustive, and it by no means establishes a guideline for police behavior. Individual departments are free to set their own guidelines regarding procedural requirements for officers *as long as they satisfy the minimal standards as set forth by the Constitution, Supreme Court, and statutory law.* In the spirit of professionalism and evenhanded justice, police departments should strive to be protective of our constitutional rights.

Most of us are not naive. We know that the police are not always "boy scouts" when it comes to safeguarding our constitutional rights. The police learn certain tricks or shortcuts to their jobs that sometimes stretch the legal limits. For instance, most officers are able to find a "justifiable" reason for pulling over almost any car on the highway. Even for the most innocent of drivers the officer may say the car was "swerving" or did not use the turn indicator properly. Some patrol officers routinely stop and frisk "suspicious" persons on the streets when there is little legal authority to do so. A common police practice in some departments is to conduct a warrantless search and seizure when the officer knows that whatever they seize will not be admissible in court! This frequently occurs in minor drug cases when the police do not want to bother with a warrant or an arrest. For example, an officer who finds a small amount of marijuana on a suspect during a stop and frisk (which you recall is limited to a brief search of the outer clothing exclusively for a weapon) might confiscate the marijuana and let the suspect go. The officer would then either destroy the marijuana or take it to the evidence room at the police department. The fact that there is no arrest or prosecution is of little importance—the officer has taken the drug away from the suspect and, in so doing, has caused the suspect grief and misery.

KEY TERMS

U.S. Constitution
supremacy clause
judicial review
Bill of Rights
due process
shorthand doctrine
Warren Court
exclusionary rule
fruits of poisonous tree doctrine
silver platter doctrine
good faith exception
lucky find
inevitable discovery

search warrant
anticipatory warrant
probable cause
plain view
moving vehicle doctrine
stop and frisk
self-incrimination
testimonial evidence
nontestimonial evidence
lineup versus showup
immunity
Miranda rights

DISCUSSION QUESTIONS

1. Explain the connection between the Fourteenth Amendment and the Bill of Rights. How does this relate to the separation between the federal and state governments?
2. Do you think the exclusionary rule is necessary? Many crime control conservatives claim that we should abolish the exclusionary rule. What do you think? What were the police doing before we had the rule?
3. Are you willing to sacrifice some of your constitutional rights to allow the police to fight crime better? Think carefully about what this would entail.
4. What are your thoughts about the "psychological tricks" police play to get people to confess? Is it fair? If you were the police chief, how closely would you monitor the interrogations conducted by your police?

CHAPTER NINE

POLICE MISCONDUCT

But who is to guard the guards themselves?

—*Juvenal, 60* A.D.

Bad cops, brutal cops, cops on the take. These words cut to the heart of the darkest and most sinister side of policing—police misconduct. No other aspect of U.S. policing attracts more negative press and community consternation than the problem of police misconduct. Although many city officials and department leaders are reluctant to admit it, the reality of police misconduct is all too clear. Since the very beginning of public policing, society has had to wrangle with the pesky problem of dishonest and corrupt police. Few departments, large or small, have been spared the misfortune of a local police scandal, and many departments have felt the stinging wrath of outraged citizens time and time again. Police officers who violate the public trust and authority vested in them are a blot on the entire profession. Even a single bad cop in a precinct is one too many, because the pernicious effects of the officer's actions reverberate throughout the department. Just like crime erodes the social fabric of trust among people, police misconduct tears at the delicate threads of public confidence in the police. On a large scale, police misconduct can entirely destroy the faith citizens place in their police.

In an earlier chapter we studied police *discretion*. We argued that police discretion is both necessary and beneficial, provided it falls within accepted policy guidelines and is carefully monitored by the department. This chapter focuses on police *indiscretion*. Here we explore the darker side of policing American society.

POLICE MISCONDUCT

The history of policing is also the history of corruption, brutality, and incompetence. The police in America have a long reputation for being crooked and abusive, a reputation they have not yet outlived. Even in modern times, cases of police misconduct are not isolated events. The following cases of misconduct are only the tip of the iceberg.

Item. In the aftermath of *The French Connection*—the real-life story of two New York City police detectives who stumbled onto a multimillion dollar, international drug ring operating out of Marseilles, France—the New York City Police Department property room was put in charge of nearly a hundred pounds of confiscated heroin valued at over $30 million. Sometime between 1962 and 1972, eighty pounds of the heroin from the French Connection and approximately 125 additional pounds of heroin and cocaine from other cases were stolen from the property room and cleverly replaced with two hundred pounds of sugar. The person or persons responsible for the theft have never been caught. One thing is certain: someone within the police department must have been involved. Thus, for a period of time, the New York City Police Department was "one of New York's major suppliers of drugs."[1]

Item. Mark Davidson, a high school senior from South Ozone Park in Queens, New York, was arrested on Monday, April 22, 1985, as he and a young female friend were walking on a city street. Several police officers and one sergeant swooped down on Davidson, claiming that he had sold $10 worth of marijuana to undercover officers thirty minutes earlier. The officers searched both suspects and, finding nothing, let the woman go. However, Davidson was tortured by the officers when he refused to admit he sold the drugs. According to the charges, one officer held Davidson down while another applied shocks from an electric device for twenty minutes. A medical examination later revealed over fifty burn marks on Davidson's body. The officers also were charged with slamming Davidson's head against a wall and punching him the eye. The torture ended when the youth confessed. A police sergeant and a patrol officer were arrested and charged with beating and torturing the teenager. Mayor Edward Koch remarked, "The facts as alleged are horrendous. . . . We'll come down on them as best we can like a ton of bricks." Both officers were convicted of the criminal charges in May of 1986 and were sentenced to two to six years in prison for torturing the teenage drug suspect.

Item. Seven members of an elite drug squad of the Los Angeles County Sheriff's Department were convicted in December, 1990, on charges that they stole $1.4 million from drug dealers and other criminals. Following an eight week trial, a federal jury convicted the seven officers on twenty-five counts, including money laundering, conspiracy to commit thefts, filing false tax returns, and interstate travel in furtherance of racketeering.[2]

Item. On the night of March 3, 1991, an unarmed black motorist named Rodney King was brutally beaten by several white Los Angeles police officers after being stopped for speeding. Several officers took turns beating King, who lay helpless on the pavement in handcuffs, while a dozen or more officers, including a supervising sergeant, watched. King was pummeled more than fifty times with nightsticks, kicked, and repeatedly shocked with a stun gun. An alert citizen captured the beating on videotape, which created a national stir when shown on television. Angry citizens charged the LAPD with a continuing pattern of racist brutality against black citizens; they claimed the only difference between the King incident and hundreds of others is that the beating of King was captured on film. Police Chief Daryl Gates condemned the officers involved, but insisted King's beating was an aberration. However, statistics released by a private police monitoring group showed there had been thousands of complaints of police brutality against the LAPD in recent years. On Wednesday, April 29, 1992, the nation was shocked when the jury returned "not guilty" verdicts for four white police officers charged with beating black motorist Rodney King. Los Angeles, the "city of angels," erupted into mayhem. In the days immediately following the verdict, riots in Los Angeles destroyed nearly $1 billion worth of property and claimed the lives of fifty-three people, thus becoming the worst riot in modern U.S. history.

Incidents such as these are reported in the media with troubling regularity. Hardly a week goes by without reading about another **police scandal** somewhere in the United States. While the major cities like New York, Los Angeles, Chicago, Detroit, Philadelphia, Miami, and Dallas have their share of scandals, police misconduct is by no means confined to the larger cities; small towns and rural areas have problems as well. Police misconduct is also not limited to low ranking officers on the streets—many police leaders have been toppled either because of direct involvement in illegal activities or by condoning the illegal activities of others.

The Problem of Police Misconduct

Police misconduct should not be tolerated, regardless of whether the misconduct is only a minor transgression of department rules (e.g., sleeping on the job) or a major violation of criminal law (e.g., extorting money from a businessperson). But why does the public seem surprised when a "bad cop" is discovered? After all, police officers are only human, the pay is modest, and the enticements are many. Police officers are just as likely as anyone to succumb to temptation. And why does the public become enraged when one of their local police officers is caught driving while intoxicated, having sex on the job, or stealing from their employer? A dishwasher or construction worker caught doing any one of these activities would generate little public outcry; few townsfolk would even hear about the crime much less care about it. By way of contrast, the local media would blast away at the unscrupulous police officer with bold newspaper headlines, a barrage of radio reports, and television footage. A major police scandal can set a town abuzz with rumor, innuendo, and character aspersions as detractors and defenders of the police stake their positions.

There are a number of valid reasons why citizens should be greatly concerned with the integrity of the police. We can identify several of them here:

• Police misconduct detracts from the effectiveness of the police and their willingness to perform required tasks;

In the violent wake of the verdict exonerating four Los Angeles officers from charges of beating him, Rodney King asked a moving question: "Can't we all get along?"

- Police misconduct hurts people (financially, emotionally, and physically) without justification;
- Police misconduct helps undermine the credibility of the police, thereby diminishing needed citizen support;
- On a large scale, police misconduct invites disrespect of the entire government system;
- Police become the hypocritical enforcers of the law.

On this last point, the police are supposed to patrol the moral boundaries between right and wrong, between lawfulness and lawlessness. When the police engage in the same type of illegal behaviors they arrest others for doing, such as distributing drugs for personal profit, it is nearly impossible to sustain the level of public confidence necessary to carry out their assigned duties. Hypocritical enforcers of the law send the unpalatable message to citizens that the law applies to everyone except those who wear a badge. This is similar to the popular parental adage, "Do as I say, not as I do!"

Benefits of Police Misconduct

At first glance, it may seem absurd to speak of the "benefits" of police misconduct. What possible benefits can there be when the police lie, cheat, and steal from the very people they are sworn to protect? Yet there is some truth to this notion. As in many things in life, out of the bad comes some good. Despite the many negative consequences of police misconduct, it is equally important to note that positive change sometimes follows. The two important qualifiers here are (1) the misconduct must be made public, and (2) the misconduct must be of sufficient severity, and must affect a significant number of people, in order to shock the citizenry into demanding change. Lawrence Sherman, one of the nation's leading scholars on police misconduct and author of *Scandal and Reform* (1978), states this idea clearly in the preface to his book:

> Scandal is a mighty weapon. It can topple governments and destroy careers. It can tarnish the reputation of an entire profession. It can cause misery and suffering among the families of its subjects. Like any punishment, it may harm the innocent as well as the guilty. But it can also be an agent of change.[3]

In short, departmental reform is often preceded by departmental scandal. Corrupt officers are replaced with conscientious officers, and inept administrators are replaced with progressive, professional police leaders. Policies and procedures are rigorously scrutinized, updated, and disseminated throughout the ranks. And perhaps the most important benefit of all, a scandal often produces reform, generally rekindling public confidence and support in its police.

THE PREVALENCE OF MISCONDUCT

How bad is the problem of police misconduct? Are U.S. police officers more abusive and corrupt than officers in other nations? Is police misconduct worse today than in the past? How many officers are corrupt, and how many police departments secretly condone corruption? These are a few of the questions often raised about police misconduct. Unfortunately, raising the questions is much simpler than answering them.

Nearly everyone is concerned about the level of police misconduct, especially in their own community, and everyone seems to have an opinion about how deviant the police really are. Opinions differ because our vantage points from which we observe and hear about the police differ. This, in turn, intimately shapes our perceptions. For example, a wealthy elderly widow living in the comfort and security of an exclusive residential neighborhood would likely view police misconduct very differently than a young urban male living on the streets. Perhaps, to a lesser extent, the same applies to the views of college students versus college professors.

Among police scholars there is overwhelming consensus that misconduct has been—and continues to be—a serious problem in American policing. Sherman notes that, "Virtually every urban police department in the United States has experienced both organized corruption and a major scandal over that corruption."[4] Albert Reiss concluded from his observational study of officers in three American cities that, "during any year a substantial minority of all police officers violate the criminal law, a majority misbehave towards citizens in an encounter, and most engage in serious violations of the rules and regulations of the department."[5] And in a 1975 report by the Police Foundation, Herman Goldstein stated simply, "Corruption is endemic to policing."[6] Goldstein's assessment was based, in part, on newspaper clippings on police misconduct the Police Foundation had sent to it over a sixty-day period. Articles were received from more than half of the states with reports of police misconduct existing in all types of agencies, ranging from minor bribes to major payoffs. Clearly the police are not, and have never been, "boy scouts."

Police Misconduct: Past and Present

From a historical perspective there is nothing new about police misconduct; widespread corruption, brutality, and moral ineptitude has plagued public policing since its inception. Throughout most of the last century, police misconduct was directly tied to city politics and organized crime. The political machines that dominated local government in major urban places like Chicago, Philadelphia, and New York needed the cooperation of the police department for jobs and other favors. It was common to find police officers accepting bribes for not enforcing vice laws (mainly prostitution, gambling, and liquor violations) and other regulatory statutes (e.g., health, traffic, building codes). It was also common for prospective officers to pay a fee to join the police department. Prior to the Civil War in Kentucky, the office of sheriff was routinely auctioned off to the highest bidder with the expectation that the amount "invested" would be quickly recouped by the extensive graft money available.[7] The **Lexow Investigation** of *Tammany Hall*, the powerful and corrupt Democratic political machine that ran New York City during the latter part of the 1800s, stirred up tremendous controversy. The Lexow committee mushroomed into an enormous investigation of the corruption and incompetence of the New York City Police Department.

The twentieth century also has been witness to repeated and appalling incidents of police misconduct. In 1929 President Hoover established the National Commission on Law Observance and Enforcement to study, among other issues related to crime and justice, the problem of police misconduct.[8] Better known as the **Wickersham Committee** after its chairman, Attorney General George W. Wickersham, Report No. 11 focused on *Lawlessness in Law Enforcement*. Published in 1931, the Wickersham report found widespread use of threats, beatings, prolonged questioning, and other assorted "third degree" tactics to get information from criminal suspects. For example, the report noted that in one case a murder suspect was forced to go to the morgue and touch his victim when he refused to talk to the police, and another suspect was hung out a third-story window by the ankles.

The Wickersham report raised the public's consciousness regarding the prevalence of police misconduct, but it had little noticeable effect on its control. By the late 1930s, major scandals were rocking urban police departments across the country. During the years of WWII the problem of police misconduct seemed to quiet somewhat, but again gathered steam in the 1950s with new scandals in Pittsburgh, Philadelphia, Cleveland, New Orleans, Washington, D.C., and elsewhere.[9] The Senate Committee to Investigate Organized Crime in Interstate Commerce published its findings in 1951.[10] Better known as the **Kefauver Commission** (after its chairman, Senator Estes Kefauver of Tennessee), the report found evidence of police collusion with organized criminals in many U.S. cities. In Miami, Detroit, and New Orleans gangsters violated vice laws with complete impunity following payoffs to the police.

Although serious attempts to eliminate police misconduct have been made in recent decades, the second half of the twentieth century has not been immune to the problem. The following section describes the problem of misconduct in the nation's largest police department.

Special Case: Corruption in New York City

New York City is home to what may be the most scandal-ridden police department in the country. Former Police Commissioner Patrick V. Murphy aptly called New York City the "city of sharks."[11] Being the largest department in the country increases the chance that at least a few of the officers are dishonest or abusive. Moreover, the New York City Police Department is the proverbial "fishbowl" of policing—the high visibility and magnified media attention of the NYPD allows the entire nation to peer inside. The country hears what is good about the department, and it also hears what is bad.

A major police scandal erupts in New York at a rate of one every twenty years with nearly perfect regularity.[12] Minor scandals occur with even greater regularity. Indeed, a recurring pattern of scandal and reform dot the history of the NYPD. Yet none of the scandals in New York compare to the one that

LEXOW COMMITTEE INVESTIGATION—1894

The committee began its hearings in the New York County Courthouse in Manhattan on March 9. For five weeks Republican ballot clerks, poll watchers, and election inspectors told how the police had threatened Republican voters, ignored Democratic repeaters, tampered with ballot boxes, and committed or permitted, in the committee's words, "almost every conceivable crime against the elective franchise." Up to this point the investigation attracted modest attention. Not only was its approach flagrantly partisan, as Police Counsel Delancy Nicoll and Democratic Senator Jacob Cantor charged, but in a community where elections had often triggered sporadic violence, its revelations were common knowledge. The situation changed abruptly on May 21 when the committee resumed its hearings and widened the scope of its inquiry. Under Goff's direction it now subpoenaed not only patrolmen, detectives, captains, and inspectors but also judges, politicians, saloon keepers, policy bankers, con men, gamblers, prostitutes, peddlers, storekeepers, and scores of citizens of every class whose daily lives brought them into close touch with the police department. For a while many police officials and local politicians attempted to undermine the investigation. Some defied subpoenas; others intimidated witnesses; and at least one, the Tammany Hall leader Richard Croker, took a trip to Europe. But gradually it became clear that the Lexow Committee could not be stopped.

Coaxed, prodded, and sometimes bullied by Goff, the witnesses told a shocking story. According to them, the police secured appointments and won promotions through political influence and cash payments. In return for regular payoffs they protected gambling, prostitution, and other illicit enterprises. Officers extorted money from peddlers, storekeepers, and other legitimate businessmen who were hard pressed to abide by municipal ordinances. Detectives allowed con men, pickpockets, and thieves to go about their business in return for a share of the proceeds. Officers also assaulted ordinary citizens with impunity. As Captain Max Schmittberger, a twenty-two-year veteran whose testimony was the high point of the investigation, charged, the department was "corrupt to the core." On December 29, 1894, the committee adjourned, having issued fully 3,000 subpoenas, heard almost 700 witnesses, and taken more than 10,000 pages of testimony. Front-page news for months, the committee's hearings commanded widespread interest throughout the United States and even parts of Western Europe, an accomplishment well beyond the expectations of Senator Lexow and his fellow legislators. If not "the most important political event of the year and probably the decade," as one journal wrote, the Lexow Committee investigation was at least the most thorough probe of its kind in the nation's history.

The report, which came out on January 18, 1895, was anticlimactic. After briefly describing the origins and activities of the committee, Senator Lexow and all but one of his colleagues came up with four main conclusions. First, the police behaved at the polls not "as guardians of the public peace," trying to maintain order, but rather "as agents of Tammany Hall," seeking to influence elections. Second, far from suppressing gambling, prostitution, and the numbers racket, the officers regularly and systematically licensed vice in return for a share of the proceeds. Third, the detectives looked for stolen property only if the owner offered a reward and agreed to repay the pawnbroker the money advanced to the thieves. Fourth, the police frequently intimidated, harassed, and otherwise oppressed the defenseless and law-abiding citizens whose protection was their central duty. The committee blamed these outrageous practices not on the patrolmen, who were "true, reliable, and incorruptible," if perhaps a trifle quick with a club, but on the superior officers. It attributed the scandalous conditions in general to Tammany Hall's pervasive influence over the police department and the other parts of the criminal justice system.

Source: Robert M. Fogelson, *Big-City Police* (Cambridge, MA: Harvard University Press, 1977), pp. 2–4. Reprinted by permission.

shook the city and the nation in the spring of 1970. This particular scandal was of enormous magnitude.

The story made national headlines when, on April 25, 1970, the *New York Times* began a series of exposes following allegations by **Detective Frank Serpico** of widespread corruption and coverup within the police department. An ill-fated committee was appointed to investigate the *Times* charges, however it disintegrated because of political pressure. Mayor John V. Lindsay then appointed a second committee to look into the problem, headed by sixty-one-year-old Wall Street lawyer Whitman Knapp. The **Knapp Commission** held televised public hearings (where Serpico publicly testified against his fellow officers), questioned key players in the system, and infiltrated the police department with undercover operatives who secretly recorded private conversations with unsuspecting officers. The final report was released to Mayor Lindsay in December of 1972, bringing to an end a thirty-month investigation.

The Knapp Commission findings were absolutely staggering. Corruption had grown like a cancer throughout the entire department. Not only were officers on regular street assignment (i.e., the patrol, vice, and detectives divisions) directly implicated in corruption, ranking superior officers were also involved. In all, the Knapp Commission found that approximately *one half* of the NYPD was accepting some form of illegal payoff, or around 15,000

Detective Frank Serpico testifying before the Knapp Commission in 1971.

officers![13] The amount of dirty money received by officers varied in amount depending on assignment and rank, but normally averaged several hundred dollars per month.

Unfortunately, few police departments have completely avoided the problem of police misconduct. The sad reality is that the reputation of public police has been seriously tarnished by nearly two centuries of intermittent police scandals. It would be grossly unfair and inaccurate, however, to give the impression that most police departments are "dirty" or that the majority of officers are morally and ethically bankrupt. The truth is that proportionately few officers willfully engage in unbecoming conduct, and all evidence points to a diminished level of misconduct in recent years.

SUMMARY OF KNAPP COMMISSION FINDINGS

We found corruption to be widespread. It took various forms depending upon the activity involved, appearing at its most sophisticated among plainclothesmen assigned to enforcing gambling laws. In the five plainclothes divisions where our investigations were concentrated we found a strikingly standardized pattern of corruption. Plainclothesmen, participating in what is known in police parlance as a "pad," collected regular bi-weekly or monthly payments amounting to as much as $3,500 from each of the gambling establishments in the area under their jurisdiction, and divided the take in equal shares. The monthly share per man (called the "nut") ranged from $300 and $400 in midtown Manhattan to $1,500 in Harlem. When supervisors were involved they received a share and a half. A newly assigned plainclothesman was not entitled to his share for about two months, while he was checked out for reliability, but the earnings lost by the delay were made up to him in the form of two months' severance pay when he left the division.

Evidence before us led to the conclusion that the same pattern existed in the remaining divisions which we did not investigate in depth. This conclusion was confirmed by events occurring before and after the period of our investigation. Prior to the Commission's existence, exposures by former plainclothesman Frank Serpico had led to indictments or departmental charges against nineteen plainclothesmen in a Bronx division for involvement in a pad where the nut was $800. After our public hearings had been completed, an investigation conducted by the Kings County

District Attorney and the Department's Internal Affairs Division—which investigation neither the Commission nor its staff had even known about—resulted in indictments and charges against thirty-seven Brooklyn plainclothesmen who had participated in a pad with a nut of $1,200. The manner of operation of the pad involved in each of these situations was in every detail identical to that described at the Commission hearings, and in each almost every plainclothesman in the division, including supervisory lieutenants, was implicated.

Corruption in narcotics enforcement lacked the organization of the gambling pads, but individual payments—known as "scores"—were commonly received and could be staggering in amount. Our investigation, a concurrent probe by the State Investigation Commission and prosecutions by Federal and local authorities all revealed a pattern whereby corrupt officers customarily collected scores in substantial amounts from narcotics violators. These scores were either kept by the individual officer or shared with a partner and, perhaps, a superior officer. They ranged from minor shakedowns to payments of many thousands of dollars, the largest narcotics payoff uncovered in our investigation having been $80,000. According to information developed by the S.I.C. and in recent Federal investigations, the size of this score was by no means unique.

Corruption among detectives assigned to general investigative duties also took the form of shakedowns of individual targets of opportunity. Although these scores were not in the huge

To this point in the chapter, our use of the term "police misconduct" has been very general and inclusive. We have not pinned a specific definition to the term, nor have we established precisely what does and does not constitute misconduct. In this section, we focus on the different types of police misconduct.

The literature on police misconduct is expansive and continually growing. Books and articles abound on the subject. There is even a monthly journal called the *National Bulletin on Police Misconduct* to keep police leaders and other professional abreast of the latest developments in the field. It is not possible to provide an exhaustive listing of every type of police misconduct—

amounts found in narcotics, they not infrequently came to several thousand dollars.

Uniformed patrolmen assigned to street duties were not found to receive money on nearly so grand or organized a scale, but the large number of small payments they received present an equally serious if less dramatic problem. Uniformed patrolmen, particularly those assigned to radio patrol cars, participated in gambling pads more modest in size than those received by plainclothes units and received regular payments from construction sites, bars, grocery stores and other business establishments. These payments were usually made on a regular basis to sector car patrolmen and on a haphazard basis to others. While individual payments to uniformed men were small, mostly under $20, they were often so numerous as to add substantially to a patrolman's income. Other less regular payments to uniformed patrolmen included those made by after-hours bars, bottle clubs, tow trucks, motorists, cab drivers, parking lots, prostitutes and defendants wanting to fix their cases in court. Another practice found to be widespread was the payment of gratuities by policemen to other policemen to expedite normal police procedures or to gain favorable assignments.

Sergeants and lieutenants who were so inclined participated in the same kind of corruption as the men they supervised. In addition, some sergeants had their own pads from which patrolmen were excluded.

Although the Commission was unable to develop hard evidence establishing that officers above the rank of lieutenant received payoffs, considerable circumstantial evidence and some testimony so indicated. Most often when a superior officer is corrupt, he uses a patrolman as his "bagman" who collects for him and keeps a percentage of the take. Because the bagman may keep the money for himself, although he claims to be collecting for his superior, it is extremely difficult to determine with any accuracy when the superior actually is involved.

Of course, not all policemen are corrupt. If we are to exclude such petty infractions as free meals, an appreciable number do not engage in any corrupt activities. Yet, with extremely rare exceptions, even those who themselves engage in no corrupt activities are involved in corruption in the sense that they take no steps to prevent what they know or suspect to be going on about them.

It must be made clear that—in a little over a year with a staff having as few as two and never more than twelve field investigators—we did not examine every precinct in the Department. Our conclusion that corruption is widespread throughout the Department is based on the fact that information supplied to us by hundreds of sources within and without the Department was consistently borne out by specific observations made in areas we were able to investigate in detail.

Source: *Commission to Investigate Allegations of Police Corruption, and the City's Anti-Corruption Procedures*, The Knapp Commission Report on Police Corruption, August 3, 1972.

deviance and deceit assume an astounding number of forms. One writer assembled a partial inventory of disciplinary actions taken against police officers that have been upheld in court:

> Abuse of sick leave, failure to adequately enforce traffic laws, lying/perjury, lying about the drug use of an acquaintance, failure to investigate a possible crime while off duty, commission of a crime, threatening another officer with physical violence, unexcused absences from work, use of excessive force, unacceptable job performance, use of offensive language, co-habitation, off-duty drunkenness, excessive parking tickets, leaving duty to conduct personal business, off-duty firearms incidents, failing to complete reports, failing to obey a direct order, conduct unbecoming an officer, recommending an attorney to an accident victim, misuse of firearms, accepting gratuities, unauthorized release of police records, falsifying overtime records, failure to report misconduct of a fellow officer, failure to inventory confiscated property or evidence, sleeping on duty, cheating on a promotional exam, sexual improprieties with co-workers and/or citizens, patronizing a bar while on sick leave, and refusing to take a polygraph exam.[14]

Given the wide variety of behaviors that comprise police misconduct, it makes sense to try to categorize them in a way that parsimoniously captures the major types of deviance. We will examine two different classifications that have received substantial attention.

Geller's Five-Fold Typology

William Geller provides an important classification of police misconduct in his report for the American Bar Foundation.[15] Geller identifies five basic types of police misconduct:

- Brutality;
- Harassment;
- Corruption;
- Violation of constitutional rights;
- Failure to take required or appropriate action.

Police *brutality* refers to the excessive use of force that goes beyond the normal or proper level. *Harassment* involves police activities like repeated shakedowns of selected targets (e.g., blacks, gays, college students), verbally badgering subjects, or making "unnecessary" arrests. *Corruption* is a major type of police misconduct that takes many forms. The distinguishing characteristic of corruption is that an officer does something illegal for personal gain. *Violation of constitutional rights* is Geller's fourth type of misconduct. Illegal arrests, improper searches, and third degree tactics are examples. And *failure to take required or appropriate action* refers to actions such as refusing to prevent someone from harming another, willful delays in responding to calls for service, or sleeping on the job (called **cooping** in New York, or **holing** in Chicago). Geller notes that in a study of five cities during the 1970s, failure to take required or appropriate action was the most common reason for citizen complaints against the police.[16]

Barker and Carter's Two-Fold Typology

Thomas Barker and David Carter's classification of police misconduct is even more succinct than Geller's. According to these authors, the incredibly vast array of police misdeeds may be synthesized into one of two types: **occupational deviance** and **abuse of authority**.[17]

Occupational Deviance

Barker and Carter define occupational deviance as "deviant behavior—criminal and noncriminal—committed during the course of normal work activities or committed under the guise of the police officer's authority."[18] Occupational deviance applies directly to the misdeeds of an officer as an employee rather than to the practice of policing per se. In other words, occupational deviance occurs within the occupational environment of the officer and includes the functions and relationships that police officers have with fellow officers, superiors, offenders, and community residents. Occupational deviance is roughly equivalent to Geller's "corruption" and "failure to take appropriate action."

Many similar types of occupational deviance afflict different occupations. Falsifying time sheets, sleeping on the job, pilfering company equipment, having sex on duty with co-workers, or stealing the possessions of fellow employees are considered deviant in any occupation. However, there are certain forms of deviance that are occupationally specific. Examples include doctors who pad their bills by ordering unnecessary tests, TV service technicians who invent mysterious and costly technical illnesses, dock workers who take merchandise from damaged crates, and college professors who assign grades without reading term papers. Police officers, too, have their own specific forms of deviance unique to their jobs, such as accepting free drinks from a bar owner to ignore liquor violations, or taking $20 from a motorist in lieu of a speeding ticket. As we shall see in a later section, this type of police misconduct—known as police corruption—is a long-standing tradition in policing.

Abuse of Authority

Abuse of authority is the second type of police misconduct identified by Barker and Carter. The authors describe this type of misconduct as "any action by a police officer without regard to motive, intent, or malice that tends to injure, insult, trespass upon human dignity, manifest feelings of inferiority, and/or violate an inherent legal right of a member of the police constituency in the course of performing 'police work.' "[19] In other words, abuse of authority is when the police push their badges beyond the legal authority given to them in order to further some police task. This can happen in three different ways: (1) *physical abuse* (brutality and violence), (2) *psychological abuse* (verbal lashings, racial epithets, harassment, threats, promises to arrest, etc.), and (3) *legal abuse* (violation of constitutional rights). Abuse of authority is wide-ranging and consumes three of Geller's five types of misconduct (i.e., brutality, harassment, violation of constitutional rights).

Police **entrapment** is a special type of abuse of authority. Entrapment means the police coax someone into breaking the law when the person originally had no intention of committing a crime. The essential element to entrapment is whether the person is already *predisposed* to commit the crime. The police are not permitted to randomly "test the character" of seemingly innocent persons, such as by offering money, clothes, or concert tickets to teenagers in exchange for breaking the law. But as long as the police merely provide the "opportunity" to someone already predisposed to break the law, no entrapment has taken place. For example, a "fence operator" (i.e., someone who deals in stolen property) could not claim entrapment if he or she were arrested for buying several stolen televisions from an undercover officer. Nor could a mugger claim entrapment after being arrested by the "granny squad" (police officers dressed like frail old women). Clearly fence operators and muggers are already intent on committing crime.

Barker and Carter suggest two further distinctions between occupational deviance and abuses of authority. First, occupational deviance has an *internal focus* because it is concerned with how an officer performs as an employee of an organization (and not the method by which the officer performs his or her duties). Abuse of authority, on the other hand, has an *external focus*; physical, psychological, and legal abuses of police authority are always in relation to police clientele beyond the immediate organizational environs. Second, the driving motivation behind the two general types of police misconduct differs. Whereas the motivation for engaging in occupational deviance is one of self-interest and personal gain, the motivation for abuses of authority is to accomplish a legitimate police goal, albeit with improper means.[20] Table 9.1 depicts the key components of Barker and Carter's typology.

Seriousness of Police Misconduct

Not all types of police misconduct have a similar effect on the department or community. Rather, some forms of police misconduct are more harmful—and more shameful—than others. Minor infractions of departmental rules outside the public eye generally do little to undermine the effectiveness or credibility of the police. For example, many officers run personal errands while on duty even though most departments forbid such activity. However, such minor forms of misconduct are more of a supervisory/accountability problem than a cause of widespread public concern. In fact, many people do not seem to mind if officers "occasionally" conduct personal business while on duty. The critical concern is that calls for service are not left unanswered.

On the other hand, serious criminal violations by police officers are of grave concern to the department and the community. Bribery, extortion, theft, sexual assault, physical abuse, torture, and unjustified use of deadly force place the police in direct opposition to the welfare of the community. When

Table 9.1 Key Components of Barker and Carter's Two-Fold Classification of Police Misconduct

	Occupational Deviance	Abuses of Authority
Description	Misdeeds as police *employees*	Misdeeds as police *officers*
Examples	Accepting bribes or kickbacks Fabricating overtime records Stealing items from crime scene	Illegal search and seizure Third degree tactics Harassing minorities
Focus	Internal to department	External to department
Motivation	Self-interest/Personal gain	Enforce law/Protect honest citizens

Source: Adapted from Thomas Barker and David L. Carter, *Police Deviance* (Cincinnati, OH: Anderson Publishing Co., 1986).

this type of police deviance is limited to only one or two officers out of the entire department, we commonly refer to them as a few **rotten apples** in an otherwise clean barrel. The management strategy is fairly simple in this type of situation—come down hard and early on the rotten apples (bad officers). The benefit of coming down hard and early on bad officers is that it sends an unmistakable message to other officers: *this type of activity will not be tolerated!* It also reassures the community that the department is willing to police its own members.

Unfortunately, officers sometimes engage in serious illegal activity with the knowledge, approval, and support of fellow officers, all under a heavy blanket of secrecy and cover-up. This is police misconduct in its worse form. When police misconduct is serious, organized, and prevalent throughout a department—what we may call a **rotten barrel**—nothing less than a major scandal, followed by intense public outrage, culminating in a complete reform effort, can rectify the problem. Inevitably, the old chief must be removed to make room for a new, progressive, reform-minded chief. Such was the case in Los Angeles in the early 1950s when William Parker took over the scandal-ridden LAPD, and it was also the case in the early 1970s when Patrick V. Murphy assumed the reins of the troubled NYPD. It is important to note, however, that major departmental reform is a painful organizational process. It is often vigorously resisted by officers and administrators alike who naturally have career interests at stake.

POLICE CORRUPTION

The vast majority of research and writing on police misconduct focuses particularly on one type of misconduct—**corruption.** The literature is so dominated by the problem of corruption that for many, police misconduct *is* police corruption. As we know now, however, corruption is only one type of the general problem of police misconduct.

Given the abundant attention devoted to police corruption, a careful examination of this type of misconduct is in order.

Police corruption may be defined as the *inappropriate use of an officer's job for personal gain*. The "personal gain" may be in the form of direct *monetary* benefits to officers, like money from speeding motorists, or it may be *nonmonetary* such as free consumer goods or services. Corruption exists when an officer wrongly uses his or her position to get something he or she is not entitled to receive. This means that police corruption is a form of occupational deviance as described earlier.

Important for understanding what is police corruption is to understand what is not corruption. First, the illegal activities officers occasionally engage in when off duty normally do not constitute corruption. This is because the officer is acting as a private citizen and not in the capacity of a police officer. For example, officers who cheat on their income taxes, steal from their neighbors, or defraud their insurance companies are no different from other citizens who do the same thing. These activities are criminal violations that apply to everyone. However, if off-duty officers tried to use their occupational affiliation to commit their misdeeds, this would qualify as police corruption. And there are innumerable accounts of off-duty officers working "overtime" to supplement their regular paychecks.

Second, the abuse of police power in furtherance of the basic police task is not corruption. For example, officers who use personal threats to coerce information from suspects or who perjure themselves on the witness stand are engaging in police misconduct, but not corruption. When officers abuse their power in this way, they are presumably doing so to benefit the department and to protect society, not for their own benefit. In the real world, of course, just who does and does not benefit from abuses of police authority is not altogether clear.

When it comes to the most minor forms of impropriety by police officers, opinions differ as to what is corruption. For example, many departments have no formal restrictions on receiving "freebies" or discounts from local businesses and restaurants. Other departments strictly forbid officers from accepting anything free. Former New York Police Commissioner Patrick Murphy is noted for once saying, "Except for your paycheck, there is no such thing as a clean buck."[21]

Among the more serious acts of impropriety, there is universal agreement about what is corruption. Officers who rob hoodlums of their money, steal items at crime scenes, deal in stolen merchandise, traffic in drugs, or extort money from pimps and prostitutes are engaged in serious police corruption.

The Knapp Commission Report popularized the terms **grass eater** and **meat eater** to distinguish corrupt officers from the very corrupt. According to the Knapp report, police officers characterized as grass eaters engage in *reactive, passive* corruption. These officers limit their illegal take to whatever happens to come their way; grass eaters do not actively seek out situations to enhance their chances of scoring, they simply take advantage of situations when they occur. The term itself evokes the image of a harmless animal grazing in a pasture.

Meat eaters are a breed apart. In the world of corrupt police officers, a meat eater is one who engages in *active, aggressive* corruption. Meat eaters do not just accept money from citizens, they eagerly extort it. Unlike the image of a docile herbivore grazing in the pasture, the term "meat eater" evokes the image of a vicious carnivore devouring a weak and unprotected animal. In the words of the Knapp Commission:

> The meat-eaters are those policemen who aggressively misuse their police powers for personal gain. The grass-eaters simply accept the payoffs that the happenstances of police work throw their way. Although the meat-eaters get the huge payoffs that make the headlines, they represent a small percentage of all corrupt policemen.
>
> Grass-eaters are the heart of the problem. Their great numbers tend to make corruption "respectable." They also tend to encourage the code of silence that brands anyone who exposes corruption a traitor.[22]

Corruption Inside and Outside the Department

Police corruption may exist both inside and outside the department.[23] **Internal corruption** refers to the corrupt working relationships among fellow employees. Corrupt internal activities include *consensual arrangements* among officers who are willing participants in activities such as payoffs, drug trafficking, and bribes. Internal corruption also includes *nonconsensual arrangements* where one or more officers victimize another. Blackmailing, extortion, and stealing from co-workers all fall under this category.

Internal corruption was common in past years as officers illegally tried to improve their working conditions. For example, it was not unusual for officers to pay money to (1) join the police department; (2) be transferred to a different district, shift or supervisor; (3) get the best vacation times; or (4) be promoted. As with all forms of corruption, a strict code of silence serves to perpetuate the problem once it already exists.

External corruption refers to the corrupt relationships between officers and citizens outside the department. As with internal corruption, external corruption may be characterized as either *consensual*, where the officer and citizen both agree to the illegal arrangement (e.g., "protection money" paid by organized crime syndicate) or *nonconsensual* (e.g., where the officer steals drugs from a pusher). Since most of the police literature as well as public concern centers on external corruption, it may be helpful to describe some of the more common forms of this type of corruption.

Common Forms of External Corruption

As with police misconduct in general, police corruption assumes a variety of different forms. For our purposes, we are concerned with three different types, listed here in their general order of severity: (1) gratuities; (2) bribes, kickbacks, and extortion; and (3) theft. Figure 9.1 depicts these three forms of corruption in relation to the grass eater/meat eater distinction.

Gratuities

Police in most American cities receive small favors from local merchants and restaurant owners. These favors are called **gratuities.** Gratuities bestowed upon police officers are usually innocent enough: free coffee and donuts, cheap meals, and discounts from dry cleaners, drug stores, and the local deli. Many merchants are pleased to extend special favors to police out of a sense of civic responsibility and pride. They support the local police and like to feel as if their small contribution makes the difficult job of policing a little easier. Of course, having patrol cars parked in front of one's business throughout the day is a sure way to deter would-be robbers from targeting one's store. Moreover, merchants who are on the "good side" of the police often believe the police are more responsive when they have to call them for help. Neighboring merchants have been known to compete for police patronage by offering the best coffee, cheapest meals, friendliest service, and so on.

Quite obviously, the acceptance of a gratuity is a very minor form of corruption. In fact, one could argue that gratuities are too insignificant to be considered wrong, and they may even enhance feelings of goodwill between the police and the business community. Furthermore, the police are not the only ones to receive special discounts from merchants. Ministers, postal carriers, church groups, and senior citizens are frequently given price discounts as well.

Consider the common practice of accepting free coffee and donuts from a local restaurant. Is this the "inappropriate use of an officer's job for personal gain" as specified in our definition of corruption? Clearly the free refreshments

FIGURE 9.1
Corruption Barometer

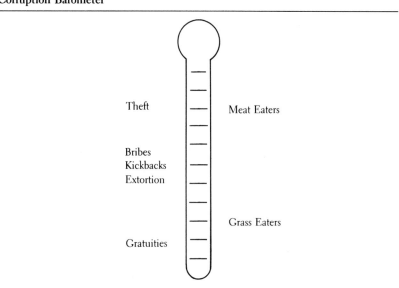

Theft — Meat Eaters

Bribes
Kickbacks
Extortion

Grass Eaters

Gratuities

satisfy the "personal gain" component of the definition. But what about the "inappropriate use of the officer's job?"

The criminal law does not prohibit officers from receiving free coffee and donuts from a willing merchant. Therefore, what determines whether it is an "inappropriate" activity is the formal policy of the department mixed with community sentiments. Some departments strictly forbid officers from accepting any discounted meals or services. Other departments forbid officers from accepting gratuities but do not enforce it. And still other departments have no rules regarding gratuities. Among departments that forbid officers from accepting gratuities, the general reason is that any gratuity "looks bad" and communicates the wrong message to the community. It also places the department in a difficult situation when the police are called to enforce some regulation against a "friendly" business. Occasionally, officers who are prohibited from receiving gratuities come across a stubborn merchant or waitress who refuses to write a bill. The police learn to either avoid the restaurant in the future or simply leave a "tip" large enough to cover the cost of the refreshments.

The system of gratuities looses its innocence when (1) officers come to expect gratuities and place pressure on merchants to provide them, and (2) merchants begin to demand special favors in return. Inciardi recites the case of a Brooklyn liquor store owner:

> Less than two weeks after I opened this place, two cops walk in and tell me they're from this sector. Then they start fingering some bottles of Scotch so I ask them if they need any help. They ask me if I give special discounts and I say no, everything is already marked down. With that they just give me a funny look and walk out of the store. I guess it made them mad, 'cause from then on I never got any cooperation from the police.
>
> Then comes Christmas time and I guess they figured they'd give me a second chance. One of the same two cops walks in and announces "I've come to say Merry Christmas." So I say Merry Christmas to him, and give him a calendar. Well that must have really ticked him, 'cause three days later they set me up for a bust. . . . So now they get their Christmas gifts, and Easter gifts, and Columbus Day gifts . . . and gifts and gifts and gifts.[24]

When officers begin to use the power of their position to demand goods and services from citizens, and when citizens expect special treatment from the police in return, we move beyond the relatively minor problem of gratuities to more serious forms of police corruption.

Bribes, Kickbacks, and Extortion

Bribes normally take the form of payments to the police to guarantee the nonenforcement of the law. Payoffs to the police sometimes come from "law-abiding" citizens such as bar owners who wish to stay open past the legal hours or contractors who find it convenient to violate local ordinances. Police officers also have been known to take money from motorists in lieu of a traffic ticket. In some jurisdictions, speeding motorists who understand how the system works attach a twenty dollar bill to their license as they hand it over to the officer; the license is returned minus the money and without a citation. Interestingly, many citizens prefer this method of "street justice" because it is cheaper and faster to bribe the patrol officer than to go to court and pay a fine.[25]

Sometimes law-abiding citizens, particularly merchants, pay bribes to police just to receive the basic police services they are already entitled to receive ("We won't come to your aid unless you've paid"). At other times, merchants pay the police for extra service. Detectives may be rewarded as an incentive to recover stolen property, or merchants may offer drastic markdowns if the police patrol their area often.

The **kickback** is similar to a bribe. Here, officers receive payment whenever they refer someone to a particular place of business. For example, an officer may have a special arrangement worked out with an automobile towing company to refer business to them. In exchange, the towing company gives the officer a kickback for every referral. Similar arrangements may exist with auto mechanics, doctors, lawyers, ambulance services, or morticians.

Officers also may demand regular payments from criminals as protection money. This is a serious form of corruption known as **extortion.** Pimps, prostitutes, pushers, and owners of illegal gambling establishments often pay the police sizable amounts so that they may continue to freely violate vice laws. The Knapp Commission discovered that corrupt New York City police officers received hundred of dollars every month from gamblers and narcotics users to ensure nonenforcement.

Theft

The opportunity for the police to steal money and other items of value is tremendous. Imagine the temptation drug enforcement officers must feel when they routinely find thousands of dollars in drug raids—who would ever find out if they peeled off a few hundred for themselves? Or what about when the police are called to the scene of a burglary? How easy it would be to put something of value in their pocket. The homeowner would believe the item was stolen by the thief, not the officer. Construction materials and tools are easily swiped by officers patrolling job sites late at night. Drugs, bicycles, weapons, and other items confiscated during regular police work may not make it to the police property room.

Corrupt police officers commit theft out of opportunity and happenstance (grass eaters), or by careful deliberation (meat eaters). Police theft reaches its worst form when groups of officers organize themselves into a burglary ring. Denver and Chicago both had major problems with police burglary in the late 1950s.

THEORIES OF POLICE MISCONDUCT

Describing the problem of police misconduct is one thing, explaining why it happens is another. As we have seen, police misconduct assumes a variety of forms, and different officers go bad for different reasons. This means that no one theory can adequately explain why officers engage in misconduct, just as no one criminological theory can completely explain why some people engage in crime.

Most theories of police misconduct incorporate two critical elements—*motivation* and *opportunity*. The explanations vary, however, in how motivation and opportunity are blended, and where the focus of the theory is directed. Given the unbalanced nature of the literature on police misconduct, most existing theories concentrate on corruption.

Among the numerous explanations of police misconduct (again mostly on corruption), we can identify three different types. Some explanations focus on the shortcomings of the police officer, others center on the deviant-producing police subculture, and still others emphasize the nature of the police task. We shall discuss each of these below.

Bad Police Officers

Most police departments try diligently to weed out unsuitable candidates before they are hired as police officers. For instance, applicants who have a history of assaults or who display signs of a violent personality are normally excluded. Also, applicants with past felony convictions, an existing drug or alcohol problem, or who have a reputation for being sexually unscrupulous are usually eliminated from the candidate pool. Unfortunately, some bad police officers invariably slip through. This was far more of a problem in years past when recruitment and screening procedures were less rigorous. It is still a problem today in departments that fail to screen recruits thoroughly.

Despite the relatively small number of so-called "rotten apples" in policing today, their presence can tarnish the reputation of an entire department, especially if the department is fairly small. Bad police officers can undermine the existing goodwill between the police and the community. The behavior of officers does not have to be uncontrollably abusive or corrupt to generate negative community sentiments—even a few "sleazy" officers can do great harm. For example, police officers sometimes use their jobs as a pretext for meeting members of the opposite sex:

> Sure! I see a good-looking chick driving around by herself or even a couple of foxes together, I pull them over and check them out. You can always claim a stoplight isn't working or something like that. Most people are so shook up when you stop them and they don't question what you tell them. You'd be surprised how many times I end up with a phone number or an invitation to stop by. I've been invited to some wild parties, too. I always write down the chick's name, address and license number and sometimes I see her again somewhere or maybe see her on the street and stop her just for a chat and that leads to some action. Lots of time it sure doesn't lead anywhere but you'd be surprised how much action I get just from stopping chicks.[26]

Most experts reject the rotten apple explanation as a general theory of police misconduct.[27] First, it fails to explain the pervasiveness of police misconduct (there simply cannot be that many bad apples in policing). Second, it does not adequately explain why many officers apparently go bad after they join a department. Third, it cannot explain why police misconduct varies so much from one department to another. And fourth, the rotten apple theory leaves us wondering why the problem of police misconduct has fluctuated so much over time. The Knapp Commission rejected the rotten apple theory as an explanation of widespread police misconduct. Patrick Murphy has also dismissed this explanation:

> The "rotten apple" theory won't work any longer. Corrupt police officers are not natural born criminals, nor morally wicked men, constitutionally different from their honest colleagues. The task of corruption control is to examine the barrel, not just the apples—the organization, not just the individuals in it, *because corrupt police are made, not born.*[28]

Deviant Police Subculture

William Westley first described the characteristics of a police subculture in his early study of the Gary Indiana Police Department. The police subculture, which exists in nearly all departments, has a distinct set of customs, rules, and morality combined with a strong feeling of loyalty among officers. What is more, the subculture of policing is encased in a strict code of silence, or what Barker and Carter refer to as the *blue curtain of secrecy.*[29] The subculture of policing has a powerful influence on police officers, and is the major frame of reference for new recruits. The police subculture often supports the basic law enforcement mission and encourages other officers to be professional, evenhanded, and caring enforcers of the law. However, when this group actively encourages and supports police misconduct, it is known as a **deviant police subculture.**

Police officers normally do not become abusive or corrupt all at once. It is a developmental process that takes place over time as officers interact with their surroundings and cultivate relationships with other officers. The attitudes and behaviors of officers are gradually influenced. In other words, "going bad" involves a series of decisions and contingencies that confront officers over time; it is not like the immediate chemical reaction that occurs when two substances are mixed together. The movement from conformity to corruption is a tentative, evolving process.

Lawrence Sherman suggests that **becoming bent** (i.e., deviant) is usually a long, drawn-out process, often taking place over a period of years rather than weeks or months.[30] Sherman maintains there are two major steps involved in becoming corrupt: (1) becoming a police officer, and (2) becoming bent.

Becoming a Police Officer. It is more than obvious that a person must become a police officer before they can become a "bent" officer. But Sherman says there is more to this step than the obvious. Being a police officer greatly shapes one's frame of reference. New recruits quickly learn the "real" duties of police work from fellow officers. And since fresh recruits are anxious to do well and to be accepted by their colleagues, they often take these early street lessons seriously. It does not take long for the police culture to radically change the frame of reference of recruits. If new recruits are introduced to police misconduct and do not want any part of it, they had better keep their mouth shut "or else." Frank Serpico's public allegations of widespread corruption in New York City and the ensuing resentment by many fellow officers is testimony to the dangers of breaking the code of silence. Serpico was shunned, scorned, threatened, and rebuked by fellow officers. There is even speculation that Edgar "Mambo" Echevaria, the twenty-four-year-old drug dealer who shot Serpico in the face in February of 1971, was hired by Serpico's enemies to quiet him for good.

Becoming Bent. While all police officers satisfy the first of Sherman's stages, most officers do not reach the second. The great majority of police officers in the United States are not abusive or corrupt. It appears that the "key contingency" for an officer to become bent is *whether brutality or corruption already exists in the department or immediate work group to which a new officer is assigned.* When brutality and corruption are already firmly embedded in the department and thoroughly enmeshed in the officers' working lives, it is very enticing for a new member to become bent as well. In fact, when a deviant police subculture already exists, it is extremely difficult for new recruits to resist. This is true not only because of the extra money that can be made but also because of the pressure to do so by other officers. Consider the case of Max Schmittberger as told by Sherman:

> Max Schmittberger was a tall, handsome, but naive baker's apprentice in the 1880s when some Tammany (political) leaders offered to get this fine specimen on the police force—free! Without understanding, Max joined up and was soon directing traffic on Broadway. Since he pleased his superiors, he was transferred to the "fat" Tenderloin precinct, the major vice market of New York.
>
> One night a brothel owner pressed ten dollars in his hand. Confused, he presented it to his captain. Angered by Max's honesty, the captain explained graft to him and began to assign him to posts more and more crucial to the graft system. He moved from liaison with the hack thieves to regulation of the brothels, finally to be promoted to the job of "bagman"—collecting twenty thousand dollars a month for the captain.
>
> When the Lexow investigation began (1884), he was jarred back to honesty. As the star witness, he told the commission of all the details of the graft system. Though punished by his peers for years after, the forces of reform eventually had him appointed chief of police.[31]

As noted in the section above, some officers are rotten apples before they join the force. For most officers, however, the transformation from good cop to bad cop, from dedication to decadence, occurs subtly, almost imperceptibly at first. Officers may start off accepting minor perks that seem to go with the job, such as a free cup of coffee. Later, officers may not think it too bad to accept a few dollars or a free drink to allow a bar to stay open after legal hours—after all, the customers want to drink and the bar owner is making money, so what is the harm? Certain regulatory crimes are easily ignored as long as nobody is hurt. A few officers even graduate up to accepting money from organized gamblers, prostitutes, or narcotics dealers for not arresting them.

Note that as officers move from the so-called minor perks to taking money from pimps and pushers, not only is their corruption involving more serious crimes but also their self-images are changing. "Grass eating" officers commonly rationalize their misdeeds by reasoning, "I may stretch the rules, but I am not that bad." Once corrupt officers establish a consistent pattern of "meat eating," their self-images adjust to match. The deviant police subculture helps encourage and support the new self-identity of officers.

The Nature of the Police Task

The third explanation of police misconduct focuses on the nature of the police task. The enforcement of vice laws like gambling, narcotics, and prostitution is particularly conducive to corruption. The Knapp Commission Report found corruption to be at its worst form among vice officers. There are several reasons why. Vice officers usually work undercover, live amongst crime and criminals, wield enormous discretionary authority, and come into contact with large sums of money. As such, vice officers are placed under tremendous temptation to "score" on their own—in the form of money, drugs, jewelry, sex, and so on. In addition, the low visibility of their activities (from police supervisors and the general public) gives them ample opportunity to violate the law.

In contrast to undercover vice officers, patrol officers on regular assignment have less opportunity to engage in misconduct. Patrol officers do not normally develop intimate relationships with the criminal underworld, are more closely monitored by headquarters and, because of the uniform and marked squad car, are constantly in the public eye. As we have seen, however, this does not preclude them from engaging in various forms of police misconduct.

CONCLUSION

Police misconduct assumes a variety of different forms, from very minor infractions of department regulations to serious criminal conduct. There is no way of knowing how many officers engage in some type of police misconduct. It is hard to imagine any officer completing a career without doing something for which he or she could be disciplined, just as it is difficult to imagine anyone completing any type of career without violating some agency rule.

But minor violations of agency rules has not been the focus of this chapter. We have been concerned with serious acts of police misconduct such as corruption, theft and brutality. Again there is really no way to know precisely how many officers engage in serious acts of police misconduct. However, an educated guess would place the number at a small percentage of all officers.

Fortunately, most law enforcement personnel are professional, morally righteous, and dedicated to serving the people. Unfortunately, however, some officers are thoroughly unprofessional, morally bankrupt, and self-serving. These are the officers who lie, steal and are occasionally abusive.

At the end of this chapter, the reader is likely to have reached two important conclusions. First, by all indications the problem of police misconduct is far less prevalent today than in years past. This may be attributed to a number of different factors. Most important among these are the improved recruitment, training, and education of new police officers, heightened vigilance by the media and citizen watch groups, elevated expectations of police performance by the general public, improved police administration and leadership, and the continuing drive toward police professionalism.

Second, the reader no doubt also realizes that police misconduct is still endemic to policing, *and will probably always be.* MacNamara offers this thoughtful observation on the subject:

> Although the decades from August Vollmer through J. Edgar Hoover and O. W. Wilson to Pat Murphy, Ed Davis, Frank Rizzo, and Tony Bouza have produced reams of rhetoric on police professionalism, codes of police ethics, tens of thousands of college-educated law enforcement officers, judicial and legislative limitations on the police abuses of the past, and an alert and intelligent public appreciation of the need for a controlled and disciplined police, the reality is that the battle is far from won.[32]

Police officers are only human, subject to the same weaknesses and basic drives as all humans. Furthermore, and what often amounts to the proverbial "final straw" on the camel's back, police officers are subjected to incredible temptation to deviate. Not only are the opportunities for easy money, drugs, and sex seemingly endless, but the added encouragement from fellow officers to deviate makes misconduct nearly irresistible. In short, society must continue to aggressively control wayward police.

KEY TERMS

police scandal
Lexow Investigation
Wickersham Committee
Kefauver Commission
Detective Frank Serpico
Knapp Commission
cooping and holing
occupational deviance
abuse of authority
entrapment
rotten apples
rotten barrel

corruption
grass eater
meat eater
internal corruption
external corruption
gratuities
bribes
kickback
extortion
deviant police subculture
becoming bent

DISCUSSION QUESTIONS

1. Identify and discuss the reasons why the integrity of the police is an important issue.
2. Do you think police officers are any more abusive and corrupt than average citizens? Do you think the police in your community are any more abusive and corrupt than average police officers?

3. Should officers be allowed to accept free coffee and doughnuts? What are the arguments for and against police accepting minor gratuities? If you were police chief, what would be your policy on gratuities?

4. Discuss the major theories of police misconduct. Which theory do you believe best explains police misconduct. Why?

PART IV

Police Administration

The three chapters in this section cover the basic issues in police administration. Chapter 10 discusses in considerable detail the complicated and complex area of police recruitment, screening, and training. As we shall see, the realm of police personnel is a crucial concern to modern-day administrators. Chapter 11 discusses the organizational nature of police departments and examines the most basic of police operations—patrol work. Chapter 12 continues our view of policing from an administrative perspective. Here, we look at police management with a keen eye on what it is managers do and how they do it. This chapter also discusses performance evaluation of officers and the influence of labor unions on American policing.

CHAPTER TEN

POLICE RECRUITMENT, SCREENING, AND TRAINING

It has yet to be recognized that the work of the modern policeman requires professional training comparable to that for the most skilled profession.
—*August Vollmer*

All organizations rely on workers to achieve their basic missions. Whether the organization is a police department, a hospital, a trucking company, or a professional baseball team, the job only gets done as well as the employees do it. Organizations with the most qualified, motivated, and well-trained work force invariably perform the best; organizations with an incompetent staff generally perform incompetently. Imagine what would happen if a professional baseball team did not adequately scout top-notch high school and college players or did not build a first-rate farm system—the team would be unable to compete with other ball clubs that carefully develop young players. As the number of wins decreased so too would team morale, fan support, and revenues. In the absence of high caliber players, the ball club would be a loser.

In many ways a police department is not much different from a baseball team (or a hospital or trucking company) in that the effectiveness of the organization depends on the quality of individual workers. Unfortunately, we have not always hired the best and the brightest people as police officers.

This chapter examines the process of selecting and training police officers. The topics flow in a "developmental sequence" covering the time from hiring to the day of retiring. Normally it takes about a year and a half before the neophyte police recruit becomes a genuine police officer.[1] Although many officers leave police work early to pursue other careers, a police officer may work twenty to thirty years or more before retiring. With the proper mix of talent, training, and motivation, a police officer can be a valuable asset to the department and to the community.

HUMAN RESOURCE MANAGEMENT

Police leaders have come to realize the importance of carefully selecting and training police officers. The current management philosophy is known as **human resource management.** Human resource management stresses the worth of individual human beings. It assumes that employees are more than just workers—employees are a valuable commodity and a significant investment for the organization.

This view applies particularly to police work. Policing is a labor-intensive service industry. A typical agency spends anywhere from 80 to 90 percent of its budget on personnel costs.[2] New equipment and facilities or the latest computer technology may be important to modern law enforcement, but alone they are insufficient to assure high quality police work. Even more money is not the answer, although it would help in attracting top applicants to the job. Hence, any serious attempt to upgrade policing needs to concentrate on ways to improve the quality of police personnel.

Prior to the 1970s, little attention was devoted to the recruitment and screening of prospective police officers. Eligibility standards were kept low yet many jobs went unfilled. In recent years, police work has attracted a large number of good candidates. There are several reasons for the improved quality of the applicant pool: (1) the nation's economy and labor market have changed, thus making law enforcement a more viable career alternative; (2) salaries of police officers have improved; (3) the growth of criminal justice programs at colleges and universities has stimulated interest in policing as a career; (4) the entertainment industry's fascination with police shows has influenced countless viewers; and (5) the highly visible "war on crime" provides young people with a legitimate and morally righteous cause to identify with as a career. Because of the increasing popularity of police work, police administrators can now be more selective in whom they hire.

241

CHAPTER 10:
Police
Recruitment,
Screening, and
Training

What are the qualities or characteristics most desired in a police officer? A study funded by LEAA at Indiana University identified 12 characteristics deemed important for a police officer to have:

- Reliability
- Leadership
- Judgment
- Persuasiveness
- Communication skills
- Accuracy
- Initiative
- Integrity
- Honesty
- Ego control
- Intelligence
- Sensitivity[3]

Clearly we cannot expect all police officers to be equally strong in every one of these areas. For instance, some officers may be natural leaders while others may be more sensitive and intelligent. However, a few of the characteristics listed above are crucial for every police officer to have: all police officers must be persons of *honesty*, *integrity*, and sound *judgment*. Qualities like accuracy, persuasiveness, and leadership are also important but less crucial. Notice that the study did not identify physical strength, weapons expertise, or fearlessness as crucial qualities.

POLICE RECRUITMENT

Hiring is an interactive process. It brings together men and women interested in police work with a police agency that is searching for new officers. In years past, there were generally more jobs than job applicants which resulted in the practice of **negative selection.** This meant that only those applicants clearly not suited for police work were eliminated from the applicant pool. Today, with an excess of good applicants seeking police work, recruiters are able to practice **positive selection,** where only the best among the qualified are hired. As long as policing continues to be an attractive career for many young people, the hiring process may remain more selective.[4]

Many police agencies recruit officers by restricting their job search to an ad in the local newspaper. Local searches may work reasonably well for small departments, and in fact may be all that a small department can afford. For most medium and large departments, however, recruitment efforts extend beyond the local area. Departments that are geographically removed from a college or university also find it necessary to expand recruitment efforts outside the local areas to attract college graduates. Some of the largest and most progressive police departments are known to recruit nationwide. These departments generally target colleges and universities.

As American policing strives to upgrade the quality of its personnel, it is in fierce competition for the same human resources as corporate America. Policing needs bright, ambitious, and educated employees just as business and industry does. Unfortunately for policing, the corporate world is able to attract a large proportion of the brightest and most ambitious young people because of better job enticements (more money, greater prestige, company car, better working conditions, less danger, etc.). The desire to professionalize American policing, coupled with the competition for quality employees, makes it doubly important for police agencies to become more aggressive recruiters.

Job Enticements

Why would someone want to become a police officer? The pay is not great, job prestige is minimal, the hours are long and erratic, it is dangerous, arrested criminals return quickly to the streets, and the public screams for more service and better protection. So what are the job enticements?

For starters, policing is exciting work. Every day serves up a rich variety of challenges and experiences for the officer. Indeed, the lack of a nine-to-five routine is one of the major reasons why many young people seek out policing as a career.

Another benefit of joining a police agency is job security. Most law enforcement positions are covered by *civil service* protection. This means that an officer cannot be fired, demoted, or otherwise discriminated against unfairly. Job security has been an important considerations for minorities who have not fared well in the American labor market. Nicholas Alex's book *Black in Blue* reports the result of a study he conducted in the late 1960s on black police officers.[5] Alex found that many blacks became police officers because it was one type of civil service work available at the time. Civil service jobs for blacks, especially in the 1960s but still true today, offer the twin advantages of (1) job security, and (2) a limited path to upward social mobility that does not normally require advanced education. The same benefits, of course, also hold true for whites.

The pay for police officers, while traditionally modest, has been steadily improving. The improvement in police salaries is due largely to the influence of police labor unions, along with increased competition for quality applicants. In 1990, the average starting salary for police officers nationwide was $18,910, while salaries for new officers in some larger departments approached $30,000.[6] Salaries for senior patrol officers and ranking officers are substantially higher.

A final job enticement mentioned here is the retirement plan. Police recruiters often stress the retirement plan to prospective applicants. Many departments offer full retirement benefits after twenty or twenty-five years of service. This means that someone hired at the age of twenty-five is normally eligible for retirement at the age of forty-five or fifty. Using Dallas as an example, police officers are eligible for full retirement benefits after twenty years of service or on their fiftieth birthday. The retirement plan pays 50 percent of the average salary of officers during their five highest years of pay.

The federal government is known for its generous retirement plan. Most federal law enforcement agents are regulated by Public Law 93-350. This law states that criminal investigators may retire at age fifty if they have twenty years of service in the federal government. The *mandatory* retirement age for criminal investigators is fifty-seven, meaning that all criminal investigators must be hired before their thirty-seventh birthday to serve their twenty years. War veterans received additional retirement pay. There are a number of federal law enforcement agencies not under PL 93-350 (e.g., United States Park Police, Federal Aviation Administration Police) that have a different retirement system.[7]

243

CHAPTER 10:
Police
Recruitment,
Screening, and
Training

The traditional reason given for retiring officers so early is because the job of police work is physically, mentally, and emotionally demanding. It therefore requires a younger officer to perform it well (a similar reason is given for early military retirement). The argument is highly debatable and overlooks the many positive contributions that older officers have to offer the department (wisdom, maturity, technical expertise, leadership, role models, etc.). It also neglects the issue that "twenty years and out" retirement plans are extremely expensive to maintain. Nonetheless, generous retirement plans are one of the benefits of a career in law enforcement that job applicants often seriously consider.

SCREENING RECRUITS

Application forms provide hiring authorities with an initial profile of job candidates. The following pieces of information are commonly derived from the application: marital status, family background, education, military service, foreign travel, employment and unemployment history, financial history, juvenile and criminal record, driving record, acquaintances, references, and willingness to take a lie detector test.[8]

Hiring authorities are barred from asking applicants questions that have no bearing on an individual's ability to perform the job. This rule applies to questions appearing on the application form or asked in personal interviews. For example, information regarding political party alliance, religious affiliation or sexual preference is considered irrelevant to the job of policing and may not be legally asked.

Police agencies have a number of general requirements that all applicants must satisfy before their candidacy is considered further. General requirements differ slightly from agency to agency. Applicants must be of a certain age, be in excellent physical condition, have good eyesight and adequate hearing, be a high school graduate (or more), U.S. citizen, resident of jurisdiction (or willingness to relocate), have no felony convictions, and have a clean driving record. Failing to satisfy one or more of these conditions can be grounds for rejection.

Selecting Applicants

If an individual satisfies the general requirements for employment, there is no assurance the agency will hire the applicant. The training to be a police officer is a lengthy and expensive process. Therefore, it makes sense for the department to carefully weed out applicants who are mentally, emotionally, or physically unfit before embarking on a training program.

Police departments use a variety of tests for screening police applicants. Standard screening procedures include the written exam, physical fitness exam, medical exam, psychological exam, oral exam, and background investigation. Some agencies use all of these screening methods and occasionally a few additional ones (e.g., polygraph test); other agencies may perform little more than a cursory background check of each applicant.

Police administrators disagree on which screening methods work best. The professional literature on police selection also lacks a unitary voice on the matter. As a general rule, a multiple testing strategy is preferred over any single test because it provides the hiring authority with more than one reference point on which to judge the applicant.

The sequential examination process is identified by Stone and DeLuca as the **multiple-hurdle approach.** They describe the process this way:

> The tests used vary from one agency to the next, and the order in which the tests are applied also varies. However, a typical sequence might begin with a

---

NORTH CAROLINA STATE TROOPERS:
GENERAL REQUIREMENTS FOR EMPLOYMENT, 1992

- *Age:* Minimum—21 years as of date of application. Maximum—Cannot have reached your 33rd birthday prior to the 1st day of Patrol School.
- *Height:* Maximum 6'5" (without shoes).
- *Weight:* Maximum—240 pounds. (Weight must be commensurate with height and body frame.)
- *Physical Condition:* Must be in excellent physical condition, with no obvious condition that will impair performance of Patrol duties.
- *Education:* As a minimum, an applicant must have graduated from an accredited high school or hold an approved General Education Development Certificate; college or university level education desired.
- *Citizenship:* Must be a citizen of the United States, and must have resided in North Carolina for 12 months immediately preceding date of application. Military service in North Carolina qualifies.
- *Criminal History:* Must not have pled guilty to, entered a plea of no contest to, or have been convicted of any crime other than a minor misdemeanor; must not, during the three years preceding the date of his/her application, have been convicted of a traffic offense that required suspension or revocation of driving privileges; must not have accumulated more than eight points against his/her driving record during the preceding three years. An applicant must meet the minimum standards for law enforcement officers established by the North Carolina Criminal Justice Training and Standards Division.
- *Acceptance of Conditions and Benefits:* Must be willing to live and work in any section of the State and to be transferred at the discretion of the Patrol Commander.
- *Vision Requirements:* Must have 20/20 vision in each eye; uncorrected vision of no more than 20/50 in each eye is acceptable if corrected with lens; must not be color blind or affected by night blindness; must pass depth perception test.

Source: North Carolina State Troopers brochure, 1992

written test that the applicant must pass with a specific minimum score. Those who fail the written test are immediately dismissed. Those who pass the written test are then given a thorough physical examination; those who pass it are required to complete a physical agility test. After that, some agencies either use a written psychological test or applicants are interviewed by a clinical psychologist or psychiatrist. Each test or "hurdle" produces a clear pass-or-fail decision; those who fail any one test are not allowed to continue.[9]

245

CHAPTER 10:
Police
Recruitment,
Screening, and
Training

Because of the importance of screening tests in determining the suitability of police applicants, we shall take a closer look at the major screening procedures used.

Written Exam

One of the most common screening devices for selecting police officers is the written examination. The written exam is usually a multiple choice or true/false test that is easily administered to a large group of police applicants at one time. There are many different versions of the written exam; however, most are constructed to test an applicant's general knowledge, reading comprehension, and basic reasoning skills. Because the written examination is inexpensive to administer relative to other screening procedures (e.g., complete medical exams or oral interviews), police departments tend to give the written exam early in the screening process to reduce the size of the applicant pool.

In order not to discriminate against any minority group, departments must be careful that the exam is written in a clear, unambiguous style and that it is not culturally biased. The written test is useful for eliminating a certain portion of police applicants who fail to pass the exam. However, the written test has a more important purpose than simply "weeding out" the weaker applicants. A properly constructed and administered written test provides the hiring agency with specific information regarding the likelihood that the applicant would perform satisfactorily as a police officer.[10] A good test is a reasonably accurate predictor of future job performance. The ability of a screening device to adequately predict future job performance is a critical issue in police selection today. This applies to all screening procedures and not just to the written test. Federal guidelines established by the Equal Employment Opportunity Commission (discussed later) stipulate that all screening devices must be specifically related to the job for which they are designed. It is not known whether a factor is directly linked to an individual's ability to perform their job, the hiring agency is prohibited from using that factor to screen recruits.

Physical Fitness Exam

Because of the nature of police work, it is especially important for officers to be physically fit. Unpredictable situations develop quickly that require unusual expenditures of energy. A police officer should be sufficiently conditioned to handle the physical demands of the job.

Yet most routine police work is of a sedentary nature requiring little physical exertion. The irregular working hours, the long periods of inactivity, and the typical police diet consisting of fast foods, coffee, cigarettes, and donuts makes it difficult for officers to stay in top physical condition.

Not all police jobs demand the same level of physical conditioning as that of the patrol officer. A police administrator, for instance, need not run with blazing speed to be a good administrator, but he or she should be in sufficient condition to deal with the grueling pace of their work without succumbing to frequent illnesses. The same is true for dispatchers, supervisors, and officers assigned to desk duty. Police recruits, however, seldom begin their law enforcement careers in these positions. Moreover, the public's confidence in the police would quickly diminish if the typical police officer was far less fit than the typical criminal.

As a screening mechanism, fitness exams measure whether a police applicant can satisfactorily perform the common physical demands of police work. Muscle strength and physical agility are related to police work, but only to a degree; officers of superior strength are not necessarily better officers than those with only average strength. In other words, it is illegal to design fitness

---

DALLAS POLICE DEPARTMENT SELECTION PROCEDURE

The selection process involves a series of tests and interviews, which, if you qualify, lead to your appointment to the Dallas Police Academy. If you do not meet the minimum requirements in any phase of the selection process, you can be disqualified.

These are the tests that comprise the selection process:

- *Preliminary Interview*—matches your credentials to the department's minimum requirements as detailed on the requirement insert of this brochure. You will be asked about your driving history, and any criminal record or illegal drug use.
- *Physical Fitness Exam*—requires pull-ups, a 25-meter sprint, a grip-strength test, and a run on a treadmill machine. You should wear clothing that allows EKG electrodes to be attached easily to your torso during the treadmill test. You will need gym shoes, shorts, a tee-shirt and socks.
- *Civil Service Exam*—tests your reading comprehension and critical thinking skills.
- *Psychological Tests*—includes a three-hour written exam and an interview by a psychologist.

- *Polygraph Test*—determines the validity of the answers given on previous questionnaires and interviews.
- *Medical Exam*—includes a physical examination and a urinalysis.
- *Applicant Interview Board*—a three-member panel conducts a structured in-depth interview on a variety of police and non-police related topics.
- *Background Investigation*—checks your work record, the opinions and statements of references, and your background. A final review completes the selection process and consists of a thorough check of your test results to date. If you have passed, your composite test and interview scores will be ranked with those of other applicants. The higher your score, the quicker you will be assigned to the academy.

In addition to the tests, these documents are required: birth certificate, official high school and college transcripts stamped with your school's official seal, and if applicable, marriage license, divorce decree, military DD214 and naturalization papers. You also must complete a personal history statement provided by the police department.

Source: Dallas Police Department Recruitment brochure, City of Dallas 86/87-30.

exams that are excessively rigorous. For example, requiring police applicants to bench press two hundred pounds would be excessive because such strength is not a requirement for normal police work. Moreover, it would likely eliminate most people (male and female) from the applicant pool.

247

CHAPTER 10:
Police
Recruitment,
Screening, and
Training

Medical Exam

The medical examination of the police applicant complements the physical fitness exam. The purpose of the medical exam is to ensure the employment of police personnel who are free of physical disabilities, neurological defects, and pathological conditions that would detract from their ability to be effective police officers.[11] The medical exam, which is performed by a licensed physician, generally assesses the condition of the following:

- Abdominal organs
- Blood test
- Blood pressure
- Ears, nose, and throat
- Urinary tract
- Heart
- Lungs
- Joints
- Spine
- Vision
- Hearing
- Height and weight
- Venereal disease

Comprehensive medical examinations are a high-cost screening procedure. Therefore, they make a tempting area to cut when trying to hold the line on expenses. But to do so is unwise. Mistakenly hiring unhealthy recruits often costs a department far more in the long run because of increased illnesses, missed days, sick leave, and early disability retirement.

Psychological Exam

A major purpose of the psychological exam is to detect the presence of any psychological disturbance in the applicant that could negatively affect future police performance. If the job candidate displays a serious personality disorder or mental disfunction, the individual is *screened out* from the applicant pool. The initial push for psychological assessments of police recruits came during the 1960s by progressive police administrators and the International Association of Chiefs of Police (IACP) as a way to promote police professionalism through rigorous police selection. In recent years, the growing number of civil liability suits against police departments has given police administrators an additional reason to insist on psychological assessments of all recruits.

The identification of police applicants who are mentally or emotionally unfit for police work is a major function of the psychological exam. Yet many believe there is a second function. An effective psychological exam is able to identify police applicants possessing desirable personality traits who would likely make effective police officers. This is known as the *select-in* procedure (see figure 10.1).

The problem with the select-in procedure is that it assumes a degree of precision and accuracy to psychological tests that just does not exist.[12] On the one hand, not a great deal is known about how valid these pre-service police tests are at selecting-in recruits. Although numerous tests are currently in use to screen candidates, there are too many unanswered questions about how well they predict future police performance.[13]

On the other hand, even if we could demonstrate the technical validity of a psychological exam, selecting-in good police officers through psychological screening encounters difficulties because we have been unable to agree on what constitutes a "good" police officer. As Alan Benner suggests:

> . . . the situation is analogous to building something before deciding exactly what that "something" is supposed to do. In terms of "building" better police officers, the problem is that it is difficult to obtain consensus on what it (the police officer) should and should not do or should and should not be.[14]

It is estimated that over 50 percent of the nation's police departments use some type of psychological test to screen recruits.[15] The Minnesota Multiphasic Personality Inventory (MMPI) and the California Psychological Inventory

FIGURE 10.1
"Select-In" or "Screen-Out"

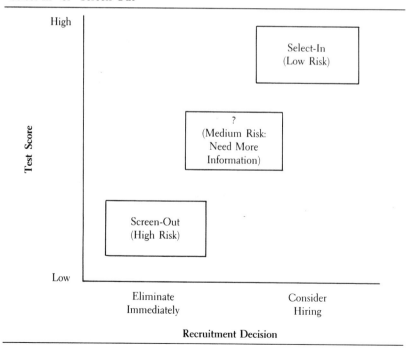

(CPI) are two of the best known and most commonly used tests to screen recruits. Research on the MMPI reports significant relationships between MMPI scales and automobile accidents, career length, academy performance and retention, problems on the job, supervisors' ratings, and promotions.[16] Less is known about the predictive validity of the CPI, yet studies show significant relationships between CPI scales and academy performance and supervisors' ratings.[17]

It is important that psychological tests be administered and interpreted by a qualified psychologist or psychiatrist. Ultimately, however, it is up to the police administrator (or other hiring authority) to decide whether to follow or ignore the advice of the experts.

Oral Exam

The oral exam is basically a high-pressure job interview. Candidates are asked a series of difficult questions by a panel of reviewers. The reviewers evaluate how well interviewees (1) answer the questions, (2) communicate their thoughts, and (3) handle their stress. Each reviewer scores the interviewee based on an agreed upon rating system.

Knowing that the applicant being interviewed is not a trained officer and probably unfamiliar with standard procedures, the review panel is not looking for textbook responses. They are looking for whether the applicant is able to maintain composure and speak with confidence, as would be expected of an officer on the street. The applicant who gets excessively flustered or whose answers are entirely inappropriate would receive a low score. Whether or not the applicant would be eliminated at this point would depend on the weight given to the oral exam and how well other candidates performed.

Background Investigation

The background investigation is often the final "hurdle" in the screening process. The background investigation attempts to verify the accuracy of information supplied by the job candidate on the application form and to discover additional information relevant to the hiring process. Practically all police departments conduct background investigations of potential officers, yet not all of the background investigations are conducted with equal thoroughness. An extensive background investigation involves collecting information on the applicant's past work record, education, military service, financial history, and criminal convictions including driving offenses. A critical part of the background investigation is to interview people who know the candidate. When possible, the background investigator contacts references, past employers, teachers, and neighbors about the general character of the applicant.

LEGAL GUIDELINES IN SCREENING RECRUITS

Police selection and screening procedures have been closely scrutinized by legislative, judicial, and administrative authorities. Hiring authorities must ensure that: (1) the recruitment process does not adversely discriminate against women and minority candidates; (2) testing procedures are valid and predictive

249

CHAPTER 10:
Police
Recruitment,
Screening, and
Training

of on-the-job performance; and (3) "bad apples" are screened out to avoid expensive liability suits. For example, a police department and the city may be held liable if a careless background investigation failed to screen out a police recruit who had several DWI convictions and, subsequently, injured someone by driving under the influence of alcohol while on duty. Yet civil suits such as these are a part of the legal landscape in the 1990s.

Civil Service

We discussed previously the powerful influence that local political machines had in many U.S. cities in the post-Civil War era. This was known as the *spoils system,* so named after Andrew Jackson's well-known phrase, "To the victor belongs the spoils."[18] It was not uncommon for new "victors" to entirely clean house in police departments (and other public sector jobs) when assuming power, which meant that hiring, promotion, and dismissal decisions were being made without regard to merit or job performance. The reform movement that caught fire in the latter part of the 1800s sought to end the political spoils system and the corruption and bribery that went with it.

It was in 1883 that a reform-minded Congress passed the famous **Pendleton Act.** The Pendleton Act called for a competitive examination procedure to select qualified individuals for certain federal positions based on experience and ability, and instituted guidelines that forbid the indiscriminate dismissal of federal employees on grounds other than gross incompetency or dishonesty. The *U.S. Civil Service Commission* was created with the Pendleton Act of 1883 to ensure compliance with the new federal law.

Although Pendleton-style laws soon passed in several states as well, the civil service system was unable to completely tame the then-powerful political machines. Eventually, however, as civil service laws and later the drive for police professionalism fought back, the political spoils system in most departments across the country was rendered defunct, but certainly not in all departments. As recently as 1973, for instance, a national study of police departments found that 16 percent of all municipal police departments, 22 percent of all county departments, and 36 percent of state-level agencies were not under civil service.[19] While the absence of civil service does not mean the presence of political spoils, it is clear that political influences are more prone to affect hiring, promotion, and dismissal decisions in non-civil service departments.

The civil service system has benefitted American policing. It was instrumental in dismantling the political spoils system of the past and helped to ensure long-term job security for competent employees. But to many critics, the drawbacks of civil service outweigh its advantages. Well-intentioned, professional police administrators are often frustrated in their attempts to maintain high quality police personnel; lazy, inept, and abrasive employees are difficult to fire under civil service guidelines, and many bright, ambitious young people face bureaucratic delays in the hiring process because of civil service regulations. The U.S. Civil Service Commission mushroomed into such a rigid and massive federal bureaucracy by the 1970s that President Jimmy Carter replaced the Civil Service Commission with the *Office of*

251

CHAPTER 10:
Police
Recruitment,
Screening, and
Training

Personnel Management (OPM). To a large extent, OPM has significantly streamlined the federal hiring process.[20] A number of states have followed a similar path.

Recent Legislation

The Civil Rights Act of 1964 contained a number of provisions directed at ending discriminatory personnel practices by private employers, labor organizations, and employment agencies that have twenty-five or more workers.[21] The specific language relating personnel practices is found in **Title VII** of the Civil Rights Act:

> It shall be unlawful employment practice for an employer (1) to fail or refuse to hire or to discharge any individual or otherwise to discriminate against any individual with respect to his compensation, terms, conditions, or privileges of employment, because of such individual's race, color, religion, sex, or national origin; or (2) to limit, segregate, or classify his employees or applicants for employment in any way which would deprive or tend to deprive any individual of employment opportunity or otherwise adversely affect his status as a employee, because of such individual's race, color, religion, sex, or national origin.[22]

Congress amended the 1964 Civil Rights Act in 1972 by extending its provisions to private employers with as few as fifteen workers. The 1972 amendment also created the **Equal Employment Opportunity Commission** (EEOC) as the regulatory agency charged with ensuring compliance with Title VII. But what is most important for American policing is that the 1972 amendment cast its equal employment provisions to all *public employers* with fifteen or more workers. Originally, EEOC concentrated on entry-level requirements and testing procedures because of the longstanding practice of not hiring certain minorities. In more recent years, EEOC has expended its vigilance to promotion practices and other police personnel decisions.[23]

The initial duty of EEOC was to prohibit employment discrimination in the public and private realm based on race, color, religion, sex, or national origin. Since then, *age* has been added to the list. In 1979, EEOC took over responsibility for enforcing the *Age Discrimination in Employment Act of 1967* (amended in 1978) from the Department of Labor. The Age Discrimination Act is a federal law that protects individuals between the ages of forty to seventy from unfair employment practices relating to hiring, promotion and retirement.

Bona Fide Occupational Qualification

Federal law allows employers to "discriminate" against workers under certain conditions. For example, if the employer can establish that males are incapable of properly performing a particular job because of their gender, then the employer has a right to hire only females for the job. This is referred to in Title VII as a **bona fide occupational qualification** (BFOQ). While most occupations cannot claim gender as a BFOQ, there are a few jobs (e.g., modeling female clothes) that can. Gender is not a BFOQ for police work and neither are race, religion, color, or national origin. However, there are times when gender (or race or color, etc.) naturally excludes an individual from certain police assignments, such as barring women from going undercover as a male stripper in a seedy nightclub.

The courts have held that *age* is a BFOQ in most types of police work. This has given the legal OK to police departments to have mandatory retirement programs beginning at age fifty or fifty-five. In the 1976 *Murgia* case, the U.S. Supreme Court held that the Massachusetts law requiring mandatory retirement at age fifty was reasonable for police officers.[24] The court found no violation of the equal protection laws because, in its view, there is a logical relationship between advancing age and declining physical ability to effectively perform police work. However, if the mandatory retirement policy is challenged in court, the burden of proving that age is a BFOQ rests on the department. The American Association of Retired Persons (AARP), a powerful political voice for mature Americans, supports a policy abolishing mandatory retirement for police officers.[25] At the present time, the mandatory retirement issue is far from settled and is bound to receive additional legislative and judicial attention.

In an important New York case, the court ruled that the maximum cutoff age of twenty-nine for becoming a police officer was too restrictive and therefore illegal.[26] The normal age range for accepting police applicants is twenty-one to thirty-five, although some departments are hiring officers as young as age eighteen.[27] Moreover, a number of departments eagerly recruit officers in their forties and even fifties.

In addition to age, the courts also have considered whether *height* and *weight* requirements are acceptable BFOQs for police work. The traditional height requirement for police officers ranged from a minimum of 5′7″ to 5′11″ to a maximum of around 6′6″. The belief was that an officer had to be a certain minimum height in order to handle the physical aspects of the job and evoke citizen respect. On the other hand, officers who were exceptionally tall were thought to summon ridicule from citizens (especially children), look too menacing, be uncomfortable in a patrol car, and have a greater tendency to develop health problems as they grew older.[28] Traditional arguments for not hiring overweight police recruits were based on the presumed inability to perform the physical aspects of the job and the added long-term expense of hiring unhealthy officers.

Although there is some inconsistency, the courts have held that stringent height and weight requirements are not a necessary component of police performance. Therefore they do not qualify as a BFOQ. In *Smith v. the City of East Cleveland* (1973),[29] for instance, an Ohio court ruled that a 5′8″, 150 lbs. minimum height and weight requirement was not sufficiently job related.[30] The court expressed concern that such restrictive minimum height and weight requirements are not demonstratively related to police work, and that they serve to unfairly discriminate against women and certain minority group males. The effect of this and similar court rulings is that most departments have expanded the acceptable height and weight limits. The key concern now is whether a recruit's weight is roughly in proportion to his or her height.

Discrimination in Employment Decisions

253

CHAPTER 10:
Police
Recruitment,
Screening, and
Training

Discrimination in employment practices exists when employment decisions work to the disadvantage of any individual or group. A pre-entrance examination that is not job related yet disproportionately excludes members of a certain race, religion, sex, or national origin is discriminatory. Such an examination would be considered to have an **adverse impact** on the affected group. This is true even if the employer had no desire to discriminate. In *Griggs v. Duke Power Company* (1971), the U.S. Supreme Court ruled that testing procedures used by the Duke Power Company were discriminatory against blacks, not because they excluded more blacks than whites from desired job assignments, which they did, but because the tests were not relevant to the job.[31] The court

Courts have held that stringent height and weight requirements do not qualify as a BFOQ. As testament to this loosening of restrictions, sheriff's deputy Anette Zella of the Syracuse, New York, police force, stands 4 feet, 9 inches high, and weighs 85 pounds.

found that the IQ tests used by the company had an adverse impact on blacks (who failed more often than whites) because they had insufficient bearing on job performance. The *Griggs* case has become the guide for employers in constructing written tests for employment decisions.

Not all tests that *discriminate* against certain groups are legally considered *discriminatory*. A test that eliminates a large proportion of a certain group may not be discriminatory if the test is a valid predictor of job performance. For example, the fitness test used to screen police applicants may "discriminate" against the millions of handicapped people in America, but physical ability is important to police work. Therefore, the physical fitness exam given to police applicants does not adversely impact handicapped people. But again, it is up to the employer to prove that tests used for employment decisions accurately predict job performance.[32]

Affirmative Action

If we recognize that employers have discriminated against women and minorities in years past, what are the legal obligations today to "make up" for past unfair labor practices? Is aggressive minority recruitment sufficient? If a minority and a majority candidate are equally qualified, should the minority candidate be hired? If the majority candidate is better qualified but the minority candidate meets the minimum job requirements, should the minority be hired over the majority candidate? These questions are the source of considerable controversy and heated debate. They also directly affect police recruitment.

Lawmakers and the courts seem to be sending conflicting signals on what needs to be done. The 1972 Equal Employment Opportunity Act prohibits preferential treatment to any individual or group even if past employment practices systematically worked to their disadvantage. This specifically implies that **affirmative action** employment policies—where minority candidates are given preferential employment consideration—is illegal. The courts, however, have been willing to allow preferential treatment in the workplace to make up for past discrimination. In other words, the courts have given their legal stamp of approval to affirmative hiring practices. And it is the will of the courts that currently guides employment decisions.

Even today the percentage of minorities and women employed by police departments is far less than their statistical representation in the population.[33] However, the proportion of minority group members hired by police departments has increased in recent years.[34] Table 10.1 demonstrates that blacks have the largest minority group representation in local police departments, comprising 10.5 percent of all sworn officers. Hispanic officers represent 5.2 percent of all officers, and other minorities such as American Indians and Asians represent 1.3 percent. Minority group representation tends to increase in the larger departments.

Females continue to be the most underrepresented group in U.S. policing—females comprise over 50 percent of the population, but only around 8 percent of all sworn officers. While it cannot be gleaned from table 10.1, the

Table 10.1   Characteristics of Full-Time Sworn Personnel in Local Police Departments, by Size of Population Served, 1990

		\<- Percent of Full-time Sworn Employees							
		White		Black		Hispanic		Other	
Population Served	Total	Male	Female	Male	Female	Male	Female	Male	Female
All Sizes	100%	77.5%	5.5%	8.5%	2.0%	4.7%	.5%	1.2%	.1%
1,000,000 or more	100%	65.4%	7.0%	12.4%	4.2%	8.4%	1.5%	.9%	.1%
500,000–999,999	100	62.9	5.7	15.6	4.4	5.6	.5	5.0	.4
250,000–499,999	100	68.0	6.8	13.0	3.2	7.2	.7	1.0	.1
100,000–249,999	100	76.7	6.0	9.1	1.8	4.1	.4	1.9	.1
50,000–99,999	100	84.2	4.9	5.7	.8	3.4	.2	.7	—
25,000–49,999	100	85.8	4.4	5.6	.5	2.9	.1	.6	—
10,000–24,999	100	89.4	4.3	3.5	.3	2.1	.2	.3	.1
2,500–9,999	100	88.2	4.6	3.6	.4	2.6	—	.5	.1
Under 2,500	100	87.6	3.8	4.5	.2	2.4	.3	1.2	0

NOTE: "Other" category includes American Indians, Alaskan Natives, Asians, and Pacific Islanders. Detail may not add to total because of rounding.

—Less than 0.05%.

Source: U.S. Department of Justice, Bureau of Justice Statistics Bulletin, *State and Local Police Departments, 1990* (Washington, DC: U.S. Government Printing Office, 1992), p. 5, table 11.

statistical representation of minorities and women in advanced police ranks is even lower.

The courts have established *hiring quotas* for some police departments to rectify the problem of past discrimination in employment practices. A hiring quota means the department is legally obligated to hire (or promote) a fixed number of members from the group that the department discriminated against in the past. Hiring quotas remain in effect for the duration of the court order. An employer who falls behind the quota is subject to legal sanction.[35] In practice, hiring quotas mean that police departments have to set aside a certain number of positions for women, blacks, and Hispanics because these groups have traditionally suffered the greatest amount of discrimination in police employment decisions.

Affirmative Action: Pros and Cons

Affirmative action is in a swirl of controversy. Supporters of affirmative action argue strongly that minority groups deserve *preferential* treatment in the workplace to rectify the effects of past discrimination. A history of racist and sexist practices in American society has forced a "second class citizenship" on a large portion of our population. The problem still exists today. Although the policy of *equal* treatment in the workplace is a long-term goal of affirmative action enthusiasts, their view is that even equal treatment would be unfair until minorities achieve sufficient representation in the occupational sector. Affirmative action is one mechanism for balancing the scales of justice to achieve true equality in the workplace.

Many do not share the same view of affirmative action. A strong argument also can be made that preferential treatment to any group is not fair— it was not fair in the past when members of minority groups were discriminated against, and it is not fair today when we discriminate against majority members. The practice of hiring minority job seekers first, even if they are no more qualified (and sometimes even less qualified) than majority job seekers, is referred to as **reverse discrimination.** White male police officers are usually the most vocal critics of reverse discrimination in policing because they are the ones most likely to be overlooked in hiring and promotional decisions when affirmative action policies apply.

A second argument against affirmative action is that "dipping" down into the applicant pool bypasses the best police applicants; the further down departments have to "dip" to achieve hiring quotas, the more likely they are to come up with unsatisfactory recruits. There are many horror stories floating around police locker rooms—some true, many embellished—about the dangers posed by new recruits who slip through the normal screening procedures on an affirmative action pass. The prospect of not being able to hire the best possible recruits also places some departments in a double bind. On the one hand, the courts have ordered a number of departments to achieved fixed hiring quotas that tend to reduce the quality of police recruits; and on the other hand, departments are increasingly being sued in court because of officer mistakes. It is little wonder that police administrators frequently criticize the courts for excessive meddling in department affairs.

The debate over affirmative action continues. On balance, however, affirmative action has played an important and much needed role in American policing. If it were not for the federal laws, civil suits, and court orders, most police departments would still be adhering to blatant discriminatory hiring and promotional practices. The fact that discriminatory employment practices still exist—albeit in more subtle forms—is sufficient evidence of the continued need for affirmative action protection.

257

CHAPTER 10:
Police
Recruitment,
Screening, and
Training

POLICE TRAINING

Police training is another issue at the forefront of American policing. Teaching recruits the knowledge, techniques, and skills required for effective police work is essential given the complex nature of police work and the growing number of suits filed against police departments. The current logic is "the better the training, the better the officer." Such logic is difficult to refute.

Police administrators have not always concerned themselves with training issues. Historically, a few weeks of *on-the-job training* (OJT) was all the training new recruits received. Under this strategy, an experienced officer would take a new officer "under his wing" for a short while to "show him the ropes." By passing the collective pearls of police wisdom from one generation to another, it helped to maintain a degree of stability in the department. This traditional OJT worked reasonably well in the past when police work was less complex. Today, however, nearly all departments augment OJT with formal police training.

We can distinguish between two types of police training: *pre-service* and *in-service* training. Both of these share an important place in an overall training program.

Pre-Service Training

Formal police training began in the early 1900s. August Vollmer established one of the first police training academies in Berkeley, California, in 1908. A few of the larger departments in the country started formal training programs for new officers at about this time. By 1930, over a dozen police academies were in operation.[36]

Despite the early growth of police training programs found in a few progressive departments, the nation's police departments as a whole lagged far behind. Former Police Chief Herbert Jenkins describes the training program he was placed on when he first became an officer:

> When I joined the Atlanta Police Department in the early thirties I was issued a badge, a revolver, blackjack and Sam Browne belt, and sent out on patrol with a senior police officer. After one week of "training" I was a full fledged policeman on my own.[37]

The 1967 President's Commission on Law Enforcement and Administration of Justice expressed dismay at the inadequacy of police training programs nationwide. The commission recommended that all training programs establish a minimum of four hundred hours of pre-service training for recruits. The 1973 National Advisory Commission on Criminal Justice Standards and Goals echoed a similar plea when it said that all states should establish mandatory minimums for police training. Virtually every state today has established minimum training standards to qualify as a sworn police officer.

But the fact that states now require minimum training standards for police officers overlooks several important issues. First, there is great variation in minimum standards from state to state. As shown in table 10.2, in 1985 the total number of training hours required for police officers ranged from a high of 954 hours in Hawaii to a low of 120 hours in Missouri. The national average is approximately four hundred hours of pre-service training. This typically translates into a ten- to twelve-week training program of forty hours per week.

Second, the number of training hours required within each competency area varies tremendously. As table 10.2 shows, classroom instruction in the "Criminal Justice System" ranged from zero hours in seven states to thirty-six hours in West Virginia. The greatest variation appears in the realm of "Patrol and Criminal Investigations" where the state of Rhode Island required 480 hours of instruction while Missouri demanded only fifty-five hours.

Third, many police training programs lack appropriate balance. One scholar estimates that 90 percent of recruit training pertains to knowledge and skills that comprise no more than 10 percent of the officer's job.[38] For example, recruit training programs tend to underemphasize "human relations" and "interpersonal communication" even though police work relies most heavily on these skills. Gary Post asks the question, "If police officers spend 80–90 percent of their time communicating, why is only 5 percent of recruit training spent teaching them to communicate?"[39] Post suggests that this is an area police trainers should cover more completely.

Fourth, police training programs are frequently taught by seasoned police officers who have little formal education in the art and science of teaching. Classroom lectures are frequently uninspiring and the curriculum undemanding. The educational philosophy, if there is one, emphasizes rote memorization of specific police policies, procedures, and techniques over larger issues such as the role and duty of police in modern society. Even the area of "police ethics" is seldom discussed other than to note the penalties for violating department rules.

A fifth issue regarding training programs is the weak relationship between measures of *performance in training* and *performance on the job*. The research literature on police officer selection indicates that the performance record of recruits in the training academy is seldom a significant predictor of how well recruits perform as police officers.[40]

As a way to improve the relevancy of police training programs, a few departments have conducted *job task analyses*. A job task analysis attempts to identify all of the tasks that accompany a job so that the training of new workers can target these important areas. **Project STAR** was one of the first major job task analyses performed on police work.[41] The researchers of Project STAR

259

CHAPTER 10:
Police
Recruitment,
Screening, and
Training

identified thirty-three unique tasks required of police officers that ideally should be covered in a comprehensive training curriculum. Other departments have undertaken less ambitious job task analyses than Project STAR with promising results.

There are several drawbacks to job task analyses. They are difficult to conduct, time consuming, and expensive. Just as the job of policing defies easy definition, developing job-related tasks defies a simple solution.[42] Moreover, the recommendations from a job task analysis may not be readily translated into the existing training program.

Police training programs are operated by state agencies, city departments, and local colleges and universities. Training programs fulfill a dual purpose: first, they teach the skills and techniques necessary for effective police work; and second, they *indoctrinate* new recruits to policing.[43] Some training academies require recruits to live on-base for the duration of the training program (sometimes up to six months), similar to military boot camp. "Live-on" police academies typically are more intense and more demanding of recruits than "live-off" police schools. While the live-off recruit may put in eight hours of instruction and then leave for the day, the live-on recruit is immersed in the "police world" twenty-four hours a day. Although live-on and live-off training programs may be equally effective in teaching the skills and techniques of policing, the live-on academy style of police training is better at indoctrinating new recruits to policing.

The federal government has two well-known training academies for federal law enforcement agents. One is in Georgia and the other is in Virginia.[44] The Federal Law Enforcement Training Center (FLETC) in Glynco, Georgia, was established in 1975 under the authority of the Department of Treasury. All federal law enforcement agencies in the Department of Treasury (Secret Service; Internal Revenue Service; Bureau of Alcohol, Tobacco, and Firearms; and Custom Service) use FLETC facilities as do many other federal agencies. One of the primary courses offered by FLETC is the eight-week, three hundred-hour criminal investigator course that is the basic training for new federal investigators. All totalled, FLETC provides over a dozen different law enforcement training programs for a wide variety of federal agencies.

The FBI Academy in Quantico, Virginia, is the second major training facility operated by the federal government. Established in 1935, new FBI agents are sent to Quantico for an intensive fifteen-week, six hundred-hour training regimen that includes classroom instruction, firearms qualification, and self-defense. The FBI Academy provides training to other federal agencies and to many state and local police departments as well.

In-Service Training

Once recruits pass the pre-service police training, they are not yet ready to patrol alone. Regardless of how comprehensive the initial training program is, new recruits still lack sufficient experience, knowledge, and self-confidence to make them good officers. Most departments require an additional *probationary* period of anywhere from several weeks to one year. During the probationary

Table 10.2   Requirements for Police Entry-Level Training Programs (in hours)

State	Total Number of Hours Required	Human Relations	Force and Weaponry	Communications	Legal	Patrol and Criminal Investigations	Criminal Justice Systems	Administration
Hawaii	954	17	153	65	133	444	29	113
Rhode Island	661	42	65	0	48	480	0	26
Vermont	553	4	80	30	74	330	3	32
Maine	504	27	62	17	73	277	21	27
West Virginia	495	14	98	20	120	195	36	12
Pennsylvania	480	76	88	10	94	196	16	0
Maryland	471	0	0	0	73	366	0	32
Massachusetts	460	35	132	28	90	167	8	0
Utah	450	19	73	27	49	247	15	20
Connecticut	443	23	48	8	64	284	11	5
Indiana	440	21	73	4	83	192	32	35
Michigan	440	9	105	8	48	244	0	26
Washington	440	34	152	24	85	145	0	0
New Hampshire	426	20	75	8	60	205	8	50
New Mexico	421	30	69.5	18	56	238.5	9	0
Arizona	400	24	110	16	78	135	12	25
California	400	15	80	15	60	185	10	35
Iowa	400	33	75	12	44	175	13	48
Kentucky	400	6.5	84.5	3.5	75.5	182.5	6	41.5
South Carolina	382	18	77	12	72	178	2	23
Texas	381	14	48	18	68	233	0	0

State							
North Carolina	369	28	64	20	72	170	0	15
Delaware	362	12	64	17	87	174	6	2
Montana	346	22	77.5	14	19.5	183.5	15	14.5
Nebraska	341	36	58	10	62	158	2	15
Colorado	334	19	55	22	79	141	18	0
Florida	320	24	39	18	54	158	9	18
Kansas	320	34	42	20	45	170	1	8
Mississippi	320	8	70	20	50	153	7	12
Wyoming	320	10	71	14	53	119	33	20
North Dakota	313	10	23	20	84	139	16	21
Idaho	310	0	47	9	51	169	16	18
New Jersey	310	26	40	13	49	116	17	49
Arkansas	304	14	60	6	19	190	0	15
New York	285	9	38	7	44	169	10	8
Alabama	280	14	49	8	48	138	3	20
Ohio	280	16	42	10	76	111	20	5
Oregon	280	14	64	12	62	104	8	16
Alaska	276	1	20	7	74	139	13	22
Georgia	240	18	45	5	47	110	2	13
Louisiana	240	16	57	8	36	78	5	40
Tennessee	240	2	50	7	31	136	8	6
Wisconsin	240	18	30	9	16	121	10	36
Nevada	200	8	28	11	46	96	2	9
South Dakota	200	17	32	8	22	109	6	6
Missouri	120	3	23	10	28	55	1	0

Source: Robert J. Meadows, "An Assessment of Police Entry Level Training in the United States: Conformity or Conflict with the Police Role?" Reprinted in *Sourcebook of Criminal Justice Statistics—1987* (U.S. Department of Justice, Bureau of Justice Statistics, Washington, DC: U.S. Government Printing Office, 1988), table 1.30, p. 43.

period new officers gradually gain knowledge and skills through real experiences on the streets. Normally a senior officer is assigned as the new officer's mentor. The supervising officer closely evaluates the young officer's performance on a regular basis and offers valuable feedback. For departments under civil service, the probationary period is the only time when officers may be terminated for almost any reason (laziness, poor attitude, insubordination, too timid, etc.) without the protection of civil service.

There is a conceptual difference between *in-service training* and *on-the-job experience*, though in practice the two are often blurred. In-service training is formalized, structured training with specific objectives and anticipated learning outcomes; on-the-job experience is informal, generalized, and diffuse learning. While there is little debate that on-the-job experience is a valuable teacher of new recruits, departments are now realizing that on-the-job experiences alone are too diffuse and unstructured to teach the proper foundation of police work.

In 1972, the San Jose Police Department initiated one of the earliest and most widely emulated **field training programs** in the nation. The San Jose Field Training Project started because of a 1970 traffic accident involving a

A rigorous physical training course at the FBI Academy in Quantico, Virginia.

263

CHAPTER 10:
Police
Recruitment,
Screening, and
Training

new police officer and another vehicle. The officer was cited for operating his patrol car negligently, which resulted in the death of a passenger in the second vehicle. Although the young officer was fired for his actions, a subsequent investigation revealed major deficiencies in the way the police department recruited and trained new officers. These findings, which became public information, provided the motivation to develop a better training program for recruits.[45]

Field training programs are designed to assist new officers by providing them with tutelage and support from experienced officers. The heart of a police field training program is the *Field Training Officer* (FTO). The FTO serves as the new officer's mentor and supervisor during the probationary period. Typically, FTOs are seasoned patrol officers who receive specific classroom instruction before assuming their role as a training officer. New officers work alongside an FTO and gradually start to handle calls on their own.

Formal field training programs offer several important benefits to police departments. First, field training programs are an effective way to train new officers. Second, field training programs "standardize" the training process, thus ensuring that all recruits are trained in a similar manner. Third, FTOs can quickly spot officers who show promise but need a little extra help or encouragement to get them through the difficult probationary stage. And fourth, field training programs provide effective documentation of officer performance. Such documentation can help young officers gain insight into their strengths and weaknesses. It also aids the department in decisions regarding recruit retention.[46]

Many police administrators agree that periodic in-service training is vital for all officers throughout their policing careers (some states even mandate in-service training). Changing laws, court decisions, investigative techniques, patrol strategies, and administrative philosophies make it necessary for all officers to keep abreast of the many developments in police work. In recent years the administrator's task of keeping officers current on important developments has been made easier by the incredible growth of seminars and workshops held at the local, regional, and national levels.

CAREER MOVES

Individuals are attracted to police work for a variety of reasons. As mentioned earlier, some officers find police work enticing because of the excitement and lack of routine; others see police work as a "calling," as a way of serving humanity; still others are attracted to police work because of the job security (especially civil service departments) and because policing normally does not require extensive higher education.

James Leo Walsh identified three distinctive *career styles* in his study of police officers in London, England.[47] *Street cops* consist of officers attracted to police work by the secure work environment. Most street cops value their family and home life, and few aspire to career advancement beyond the patrol division. *Action seekers* find police work satisfying for other reasons. Most action seekers have "knocked about a bit" in other jobs, often the military, and find police work highly stimulating. Action seeks are less concerned with job security and fewer of them are involved in a serious relationship. *Middle-class mobiles* view police work as offering a ladder to social achievement that does not require the arduous entry criteria of many occupations. Middle-class mobiles are eager for promotion to higher and higher ranks within the police structure. Walsh contends that career motivations change as officers' life situations change and as the normal challenges and frustrations of police work take their toll. Middle-class mobiles are often forced to lower their career aspirations due to limited opportunities for advancement through the ranks. For instance, most departments set a minimum of three to five years experience before a patrol officer is eligible to take the sergeant's exam, and the average length of time sergeants serve at the officer level is over twelve years.[48]

SAN JOSE POLICE TRAINING PROGRAM

The San Jose Police Department's field training program has become a model for law enforcement agencies across the country. The San Jose program is highly structured and goes far beyond the usual field training process.

Control is the one word that best describes San Jose's program. The department controls the entire 14-week process very tightly by using standardized lesson plans, training guides, and departmental policies. Every effort is made to ensure that all recruits receive the same opportunity to succeed.

The Patrol Division administers the field training program; six-officer teams consisting entirely of FTO's and their sergeants conduct the training. These teams work only in specific sections of the city that have been identified as areas that provide the best opportunity to introduce the recruits to a cross section of police work. The recruit normally spends 4 weeks with three different FTO's. As in other field training programs, the FTO's must train recruits in addition to performing their normal patrol duties.

Recruits receive a combination of classroom and practical skills instruction in addition to on-the-job training with the FTO. FTO's evaluate recruits daily; sergeants evaluate them weekly. In the final 2 weeks of training, an FTO rides in plain clothes with the recruit and if performance is satisfactory, the recruit is then allowed to work a beat in a solo capacity. If not, the recruit is given remedial training in weak areas and reevaluated at a later date. Exhibit 1 shows the San Jose training process.

Exhibit 1: San Jose Field Training Process

Phase I
Weeks 1–16: Academy and in-house training.

Phase II
Weeks 17–18: Assigned to primary FTO. No evaluations.

Weeks 19–28: Daily observation reports by FTO's with weekly evaluation reports by supervisors.

Weeks 29–30: Daily and weekly reports continue, but primary FTO rides in plain clothes with recruit.

Phase III
Weeks 31–36: Recruit works a solo beat outside the Training District. Supervisors evaluate biweekly.

Weeks 37–40: Recruit continues solo beat. Supervisors evaluate monthly.

Weeks 41–44: Recruit continues solo beat. Ten Month Review Board meets to recommend retention, remedial training, or dismissal.

Weeks 45–52: Reserved for remedial training if needed. Special board meets to review the performance of recruits with deficiencies.

Source: Michael S. McCampbell, "Field Training for Police Officers: State of the Art," *National Institute of Justice, Research in Brief* (U.S. Department of Justice, Washington, DC: U.S. Government Printing Office, November 1986), pp. 3–4.

For officers who desire advancement in their work, several career paths are available. As depicted by the three models in figure 10.2, officers may choose to *move-up*, *move-out*, or *move-on*. The "move-up" model signifies advancement through the ranks within a single police organization. Patrol officers may advance to specialty units (e.g., detective, crime scene investigator, juvenile division, public relations unit), or they may advance directly to lower supervisory positions, then to middle management and finally to upper police administration. Each advance carries additional responsibility, status, and pay. The "move-out" model refers to advancing to larger departments where the pay is usually higher and where there exists a greater opportunity for job specialization. Finally, the "move-on" model describes officers who wish to someday leave local law enforcement and move on to state or federal investigatory positions. It is common for officers who are unable to directly enter state or federal law enforcement to "temporarily" accept a position in a local department. After a few years they hope to use their local experience as a stepping-stone to state or federal employment.

265

CHAPTER 10:
Police
Recruitment,
Screening, and
Training

Lateral Entry

With all the attention devoted to attracting the best available recruits to policing, it is ironic that most agencies do not permit the **lateral entry** of

FIGURE 10.2
Common Career Moves of Police Officers

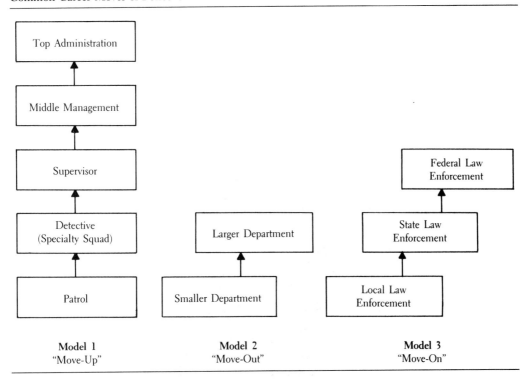

officers from one police department to another. Lateral entry occurs when an employee is hired by a different agency while keeping the same relative salary, position, and benefits. Most professions view lateral entry as a way of hiring competent and experienced people to positions above entry level. Unfortunately, policing has shown an unwillingness to follow the professional model. The only police employees who have lateral movement options are officers at the very bottom (who have nothing to lose) and police leaders at the very top (police chiefs are frequently hired from outside agencies). Officers who wish to "move-out" or "move-on" normally must sacrifice any career advances they have already obtained (seniority, rank, prestige, pay) and start at the bottom in the new agency. Hence, the longer an officer stays in one agency the more he or she becomes "locked" into his or her position because the sacrifices of moving become too great.

There are several reasons why police departments do not allow lateral entry. One reason is because the localized nature of police pension systems prevents officers from transferring their pension to other jurisdictions. There is talk of developing a national pension system for officers that would transfer anywhere in the country, but such a system is unlikely to take shape in the near future. A second reason is because training standards, department policies, and policing problems vary considerably from state to state and from department to department. Laws and municipal ordinances also are not the same. An experienced officer in one police department may not have sufficient knowledge and training to perform effectively in a different department. Although one might reason that an experienced officer should be able to start above the entry level after only a little extra training, this normally is not permitted. Experienced yet newly hired officers are required to start at the bottom with the rest of the recruits.

A third reason why lateral entry is virtually nonexistent in police work is because the few positions that become available above the entry level are fiercely protected. Policing is noted for its bottom-up, closed promotional system.[49] Police officers vigorously oppose the idea of outsiders snatching away promotions that "belong to one of us." Moreover, making rank to the level of sergeant and above is a major motivator. Officers who desire promotion are encouraged to work hard and perform well. A system of lateral entry may unintentionally lower officer satisfaction and morale in its very efforts to improve the quality of police personnel.

Leaving Police Work

There are perhaps as many reasons why officers leave police work as why they enter it. Aside from the obvious reasons of death, retirement, and forced dismissal, a sizable number of officers voluntarily resign each year. The rate of voluntary resignations is generally higher in smaller departments than in larger ones.[50] Overall, however, little is known about why officers decide to leave police work, what type of officers are likely to leave, or what new careers they tend to pursue. Research in this area would have important implications for police work because of the tremendous expense of recruiting, screening, and training police recruits.

267

CHAPTER 10:
Police
Recruitment,
Screening, and
Training

CONCLUSION

Hiring top quality police officers is a time-consuming and expensive endeavor. The entire process of recruiting, screening, and training new recruits often takes a couple of years and cost thousands of dollars per officer. Litigation and literature on police personnel issues is expanding very quickly. Police administrators face a constant challenge staying abreast of current developments.

Is there something about police work that attracts a certain type of person? Is a police officer a common, everyday type of person, or is he or she different? Looking at some of the early research, one gets the impression that maybe police officers are of a certain type. For instance, some suggest that police recruits are more authoritarian, more likely to be from the working class, and more politically conservative than the average person. Regarding this last issue, the renowned political scientist Seymour Martin Lipset wrote an article in 1969 titled "Why Cops Hate Liberals and Vice Versa" where he discussed the liberal/conservative rift in police work.[51]

The problem with the majority of research on personality types, social class, and political orientation of police officers is that it is seriously dated. Much has changed in the past quarter century in policing. So what kinds of people are police officers today? Overall, they are not out of the ordinary—most are mainstream, middle class, and support middle-of-the-road politics.[52] And, because of the effects of federal laws and court orders, present-day recruits are more reflective of the racial, ethnic, and gender composition of our communities than in the past. Nonetheless, we still have a long way to go before minorities and women achieve full and equal representation in American policing.

KEY TERMS

human resource management
negative and positive selection
multiple-hurdle approach
Pendleton Act
Title VII
Equal Employment Opportunity
    Commission

bona fide occupation qualification
adverse impact
affirmative action
reverse discrimination
Project STAR
field training programs
lateral entry

DISCUSSION QUESTIONS

1. Rank the five most important personal qualities that you think an officer should have. List at least five personal characteristics that officers should not have. Now, if you were put in charge of hiring new recruits, how would you *select-in* and *screen-out* applicants based on your criteria?

2. Do you think a recruit who admits to having smoked marijuana a few times in the past on a polygraph test should be rejected because of past drug usage or hired because he or she is honest? Which is more important in policing—"honesty" or "purity"?

3. What are your thoughts on affirmative action? What about reverse discrimination? As of this writing, 98 percent of the U.S. Senate are white males and the other 2 percent are white females; there are no blacks. Is this discrimination? Should the same affirmative action law passed by the Senate (along with the House of Representatives) apply to this highest elected deliberative body in the country?

4. Discuss the pros and cons of lateral entry in policing. Do you think lateral entry is in the best interests of American policing?

CHAPTER ELEVEN
POLICE ORGANIZATION AND OPERATIONS

The act of organizing is indispensable to proper management, and without some form of organizational structure, most police operations could not be carried out.

—*O. W. Wilson*

Contemporary American society is organizationally complex. Organizations, namely "human collectivities designed to achieve some goal,"[1] are virtually everywhere. Organizations dominate our lives and channel social interaction. Schools, churches, grocery stores, car dealerships, cable companies, professional sports, amateur sports, banks, pizza parlors, and old age homes are organizations. The list is nearly endless.

Police organizations exist because they are needed to combat crime and maintain public order. As we have learned earlier in our study, an unorganized mass of individuals is incapable of rendering adequate police service in contemporary society. Police organizations not only affect the social environment in which they operate but also are affected by that same environment in return. Police departments never operate in a vacuum.

ORGANIZATIONAL FEATURES OF POLICE DEPARTMENTS

Police departments in the United States have not strayed far from the original British style of policing. More than a century and a half after Robert Peel fashioned the first public police agency, there is little variation today in the organizational structure of police departments. Practically all police departments have certain organizational features in common. While not all police departments are organized exactly alike, the similarities in organizational design are overwhelming. We shall examine three important organizational features of police departments below: (1) bureaucracy, (2) semi-military model, and (3) police organizational environment.

Police Departments as Bureaucracies

In everyday language the term **bureaucracy** conjures up images of inefficiency, waste, and red tape. This negative view of bureaucracy is no doubt partly due to our own frustrating experiences in dealing with large organizations, not to mention the horror stories told by others who have had to confront the "bureaucratic monster." But according to Max Weber (1864–1920), the German sociologist who developed the modern theory of bureaucracy around the turn of the twentieth century, the *pure* bureaucratic structure was suppose to be the most efficient organizational design:

> Experience tends universally to show that the purely bureaucratic type of administrative organization—that is, the monocratic variety of the bureaucracy—is, from a purely technical point of view, capable of attaining the highest degree of efficiency and is in this sense formally the most rational known means of carrying out imperative control over human beings.[2]

Eventually, Weber recognized that few large bureaucracies approached the pure or ideal type. Although Weber believed bureaucracy was inevitable, he thought it might crush the spirit of capitalism by strangling human initiative. Other scholars have voiced a similar concern. One writer was able to catalog over one hundred problems with bureaucratic organizations. Among these problems are: (1) bosses are often less competent than their underlings, (2) rules are arbitrary and zany, (3) workers experience conflict over spheres of authority, (4) subordinates are cruelly treated, (5) systems become stalled and hopelessly outdated, and (6) personalities are modified to reflect the needs of the organization (i.e., dull, gray, and conditioned).[3]

The bureaucratic complexity of police departments varies according to the size of the organization. Small departments frequently avoid the bureaucratic maze that large departments find inescapable. However, police departments large and small have been described as being inflexible and uncreative, especially in times of rapid social change when flexibility and creativity is most needed. Moreover, the bureaucratic organization of police departments is believed to underutilize the talents and energy of its personnel, thereby stifling the personal growth of employees. Thus, the modern police manager faces a difficult dilemma in attempting to achieve the full potential of the department while satisfying the needs of employees.

Semi-Military Model

Another basic feature of police departments is their reliance on the military style of organization. We use the phrase **semi-military model** because police departments are modeled loosely after the military. The police follow similar organizational principles, but they are not part of the armed forces.

There are a number of reasons why the original police were organized along military lines. First, Sir Robert Peel wanted the tight control over his men that the model offered. Second, no other viable organizational model was available during Peel's time. Third, the police were taking over some of the domestic protection duties then provided by the military. Fourth, the first commissioner of the new police was a former military commander. And fifth, most of the original officers were also from the military. The new police officers knew and understood the military structure.[4]

What is meant by the semi-military model? The more typical characteristics may be listed:

- Centralized command structure with a rigid chain of command (orders flow from top to bottom);
- Strong demarcation between ranks with rank designations similar to military terminology (officers, sergeants, lieutenants, captains);
- Clearly marked lines of communication and authority;
- Control over workers exercised by general commands and orders;
- Rules and regulations enforced through strong discipline;
- Authoritarian leadership motivating workers by threats and coercion;
- Emphasis on the status quo.[5]

Another striking similarity between the police and the military concerns the structural arrangement of units. Different working units within a police department are classified as one of three types: **line, staff** or **auxiliary** units.

Table 11.1   Common Types of Line, Staff, and Auxiliary Services

Line	Staff	Auxiliary
Uniform Patrol	Training	Records
Traffic	Personnel	Communications
Detective	Planning and Research	Data Processing
Youth Bureau	Community Relations	Crime Lab
Vice and Narcotics	Crime Prevention	Jail Unit
Tactical Unit	Budget and Procurement	

These terms are borrowed from the military. Line services refer to units directly involved in performing the basic mission of the organization. In the army, for example, the infantry is a primary line service; in police work, the patrol division is a primary line service. But not all military personnel can be soldiers and not all police officers can work patrol. The organization requires an internal support structure to arrange schedules, hire and train new personnel, procure supplies, etc. This is the responsibility of staff services. Community relations, planning and research, and training units are common types of staff services in police departments.

Auxiliary services are slightly different from regular staff services in that they offer more direct and immediate help to the line units. Examples of police auxiliary services are records and communications, crime lab, and data processing. Table 11.1 highlights the line, staff, and auxiliary services generally found in urban police departments. As noted in chapter 3, many of these support tasks are performed by "civilians," which is another term borrowed from the military.

The police and the military have more in common than just the organizational model—in several ways their tasks are similar as well. For instance, both deal with critical life-and-death situations.[6] The police and the military also share the element of danger. This is best exemplified by the issuance of weapons, a requirement for few occupations. Many observers claim the element of danger is what bonds soldiers together in the trenches and officers on the streets.[7]

Police Organizational Environment

Because of the very nature of the police task, police departments are more of an **open system** than a **closed system**. A "closed" system refers to an organization that is independent of external influences. In theory, a closed organization is able to maximize rationality because it can concentrate on organizational goals and objectives unhindered by outside pressures. Conversely, an "open" system refers to an organization where there is continual interplay between environmental influences and the internal operation of the agency. These environmental influences impinge upon the internal dynamics of the organization, sometimes momentarily and sometimes permanently.

Environmental influences often affect police departments abruptly and unpredictably.[8] They may upset the equilibrium of the organization and displace the original goals of the department.[9] This means the police management strategy must be flexible enough to allow the agency to adapt quickly to unplanned environmental change. Experienced police administrators know very well how quickly the environmental winds may shift, and how devastating the impact may be on the department.

As depicted in figure 11.1, four environmental influences stand out as most important. These are (1) community sentiments, (2) the media, (3) politics, and (4) technology. We shall look briefly at each of these outside influences.

Community Sentiments

Our attention has returned repeatedly in this text to the important role of the community in police policy matters and police practice. As public servants, the police are in continual dialogue with various segments of the community. This is particularly true for the typical city police or county sheriff department that has frequent contact with a wide array of community residents (specialized state and federal investigative agencies have less contact).

Community pressures come to bear on departments in many ways. Historically, the police have been criticized for being more responsive to the wealthy and politically connected than to the poor. While there is much truth to this claim, it must be realized that the poorest community sectors are a major source of external pressure on the police. The poorest neighborhoods usually need the services of the police the most because crime and disorder are concentrated there. Ironically, the poorest neighborhoods also lodge the greatest number of formal complaints against the police (i.e., brutality, harassment, nonenforcement). In short, community sentiments are a potent environmental influence on police in wealthy and poor neighborhoods alike.

FIGURE 11.1
Police Organizational Environment

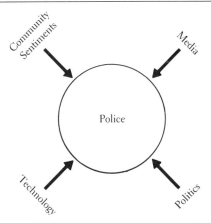

The Media

The power of the press is significant. It is sometimes said the press can either make or break a department. Although this may be a slight overstatement, it is no doubt true the media is an important environmental influence on the police.

The ideal arrangement would be for the police and the media to have a positive working relationship based on mutual trust and respect. This would aid the department in maintaining a good public relations program because the news media would be willing to report the good news about the department as well as the bad. A positive working relationship would also help the local media in their quest to gain information from the police so they may report newsworthy stories to the public.

This ideal is seldom achieved. In fact, the relationship between the police and the media is often tense. The problem lies in the competing interests at stake. On the one hand, the police frequently avoid full disclosure of information in order not to jeopardize their case. Police organizations are often "tight lipped" with the media, especially with information regarding ongoing criminal investigations. A common statement by police officials is, "I'm sorry, but I am not able to divulge that information at this time." On the other hand, the media has the responsibility of reporting the news accurately and completely to the public—and members of the news media have been known to go to great lengths to get a news story.

But there is more to freedom of the press than meets the eye. Most media sources are business organizations with a need to sell their "product" in order to make a profit. The more people who watch the news or read the paper, the more the news agency can charge for advertising space. Stories of serious crime are of premium value to the media because the public loves to hear about crime. It is not unheard of to have more reporters converge on a major crime scene than police officers. As one officer was heard by the author at one of these media events, "reporters are like fleas on a dog's tail—try as you might, you can't shake them off."

Because of the persistent pressure of the media over the past several decades, police organizations have become more open and accessible to news reporters. Many medium-sized departments and practically all large departments have a separate *public information unit* whose job is to communicate with the media on a regular basis. Department spokespersons are also common.

Politics and Police

There has been a continual plea to rid the internal operations of police departments of the effects of politics. If we take this to mean the police should be removed from *partisan* political practices—such as the political spoils system or political campaigning while on duty—then we find general agreement. Most police departments have stringent rules against partisan political activities of on duty officers.

Aside from the issue of partisan politics, however, it is important to understand that as a public agency the police are unavoidably drawn into politics. The police must compete in the political arena with other agencies for scarce public resources. As a general rule, a growing agency is better able to compete for scarce funds than an agency experiencing zero growth or even retrenchment. The period of considerable growth in police departments during the 1970s is over, at least for the near future. Thus, we have seen serious efforts in recent years to increase the efficiency of departments without adding more officers to the payroll.

Technology

A fourth environmental influence on police organizations is technology. The astounding pace of technological development during this century has revolutionized modern police work. For instance, technological developments have altered *transportation* (from foot and horseback to cars, motorcycles, boats, planes, and helicopters); *weapons* (from fists and clubs to sophisticated guns and exotic electronic weapons); *protection* (bulletproof vests, gas masks, armored cars); *criminalistics* (breathalyzer, DNA profiling, automated fingerprint systems); and *communications* (telephones, two-way radios, centralized dispatch). Computer-aided information linkages such as the state-level PIN systems (police information network), NCIC (National Crime Information Center), and INTERPOL (International Police Organization) provide an invaluable service to law enforcement agencies. Virtually no aspect of police work has been left unaffected by technology.

One of the most fascinating areas of criminological study is the competitive development of technology between the police and the crooks. We usually find that as soon as the police develop a device to prevent crime or identify criminals, the criminals turn around and find some way to protect themselves, such as using gloves to avoid fingerprints or purchasing a police scanner to listen in on calls. In a classic criminology text, Sutherland and Cressey describe the history of the safe as an example of the competitive development of technology:

> Seventy-five years ago, the safe was locked with a key. Full-time safe-burglars learned how to pick these locks, and then the combination lock was invented. The criminals rigged a lever by means of which the whole spindle of the combination could be pulled out of the safe. When correction was made to prevent this, the burglars drilled holes in the safe and inserted gunpowder or dynamite. Then the manufacturers made the safe drill-proof, and the burglars secured harder drills with more powerful leverage. When the manufacturers used harder materials for the safe the clever burglars turned to nitroglycerine, which could be inserted in minute crevices around the door where powder and dynamite would not enter. Then safe-makers developed doors that fitted so perfectly that even nitroglycerine could not be inserted in the cracks. The burglars then adopted the oxyacetylene torch and turned it against the safe, and the manufacturers devised a compound which was proof against the torch.
>
> Somewhere in this process, the burglars began to kidnap bankers and compel them to open the safe, regarding this as easier than mechanical methods of opening safes. To prevent this, the timelock was invented, so that the businessmen could not open their own safes until an appointed hour.[10]

An officer of the Des Plaines, Illinois, police department using the Area-wide Law Enforcement Radio Terminal System (ALERTS), which links him to a centralized data base.

Recent technological advances in financial services have once again placed law enforcement on the defensive. A new breed of sophisticated computer criminals are now causing problems.

POLICE ORGANIZATION ACCORDING TO O. W. WILSON

No person has had a greater impact on police organization than **O. W. Wilson** (1900–1972). The brilliant career of Orlando Winfield Wilson spanned nearly five decades. Wilson held a number of positions in the criminal justice field, such as police officer, police chief, police superintendent, college professor, and dean.[11] Wilson also authored a number of influential books and articles. His most famous book, *Police Administration*, achieved international acclaim. Originally published in 1950, *Police Administration* became the organizational "bible" for a generation of police leaders.

Wilson firmly believed that police professionalism and efficiency was possible to achieve, but only through the application of sound principles of organization. According to Wilson, public, commercial, military, and industrial organizations apply similar principles that can be considered fundamental. Wilson identified these organizational principles as follows:

1. *Grouping Similar Tasks*—Tasks related in purpose, process, method, or clientele should be grouped together in one or more units (e.g., vice division, patrol division, traffic division, detective division). Grouping of similar tasks should be logical and consistent and should avoid overlapping realms of authority.

2. *Specialized versus Generalized Units*—Specialized units should be created only when they significantly enhance department capability. Specialized units use qualified personnel to perform particular tasks. This promotes a strong *esprit de corps* among co-workers. Specialization is a natural by-product of increasing size and complexity of a department.

3. *Lines of Authority*—Responsibilities should be clearly drawn by precisely defining the duties of each unit. All members should know the lines of authority so responsibility may be exactly placed. This avoids duplication and neglect of assignments.

4. *Chain of Command*—Communications should normally go up and down through established channels in the hierarchy. Diverting orders, directives, or reports around the appropriate level of command may have disastrous effects on the efficiency of the organization.

5. *Unity of Command*—Each individual, unit, and situation should be under the immediate control of one, and only one, person. The principle of unity of command minimizes the friction and confusion resulting from duplication of supervision.

6. *Span of Control*—The span of control should be large enough to provide economical supervision, but the number of units or persons placed under a person should not be more than the person is capable of managing. There is no standard for determining the optimum span of control for all occasions.

7. *Delegation of Authority*—Each task should be made the unmistakable duty of someone. The responsibility for planning, execution, and control needs to be placed on designated persons. A person cannot be held accountable for failing to complete an assigned task unless they have been delegated sufficient authority for its accomplishment. [12]

According to Wilson, these principles of organization are intended to improve the operational efficiency of the department, not hamper it. [13] Police administrators should use common sense in applying the organizational principles in practice—the principles should not be applied in careless routine.

Consider, for example, whether or not a department should create a separate juvenile division. Police administrators must determine if the juvenile crime problem is sufficient to justify the permanent assignment of officers to specialized juvenile duty. Aside from the issue of the juvenile crime problem, there are also the important issues of space allocation, funding, and personnel. The decision to transfer the major responsibility for juvenile cases from regular patrol to a designated youth division is one that most often has to be made in small police departments. (The great number of juvenile cases that must be handled by a large department makes a specialized youth division a necessity.) The police administrator has to decide how best to specialize, the extent of specialization necessary, the responsibilities of the juvenile officers, and the organizational arrangement of the unit.

In theory, as highly trained specialists, juvenile officers would be much more knowledgeable than regular patrol officers about the problems of youth. A separate juvenile unit would concentrate the understanding and control of delinquency in a cadre of concerned professionals. A separate juvenile unit may also eliminate the detrimental influences of the criminal justice system by protecting dependent, neglected, and mistreated youth who come into contact with the police.

In practice, there are potential dangers to implementing a separate youth division that may cause unintended organizational problems for the police administrator. One danger is that regular patrol officers may ignore youth matters because they no longer see it as their job ("save it for the diaper dicks"). Another danger is that separate divisions have a tendency to move further away

---

COMMON POLICE ORGANIZATIONAL TERMINOLOGY

FUNCTIONAL TERMINOLOGY

- *Bureau*—The largest unit within a department (e.g., uniform bureau, criminal investigation bureau, technical services bureau). In larger departments, the bureau is usually headed by a major or deputy chief. Each bureau consists of different divisions.
- *Division*—A subdivision of a bureau, usually commanded by a high-ranking officer such as a major, captain, or lieutenant.
- *Section*—A functional unit within a division (e.g., a homicide section, burglary section or auto theft section in the detective division). Sections are normally only found in large departments where an intricate division of labor is necessary.
- *Unit*—Technically a subdivision of a section. A unit refers to a small organizational component; however, police organizational terminology is not always used precisely. The term "unit" is also used generically to refer to any functional unit below the level of a bureau.

TERRITORIAL TERMINOLOGY

- *Area*—A geographic section of a large city comprised of designated districts.
- *District*—A territorial subdivision of a city used for assigning patrol. In some large cities, each patrol district has its own station commanded by a captain.
- *Sector*—An area containing two or more beats or posts.
- *Beat*—A consolidated area normally used for assigning individual officers to foot or motorized patrol. Sergeants often serve as immediate supervisors for beat officers.
- *Post*—A fixed point (e.g., corner) to which an officer is assigned to duty.

OTHER TERMINOLOGY

- *Shift or Watch*—A division of time for assigning officer work schedules. Shifts normally run in eight to twelve-hour periods (also called "tour of duty").
- *Platoon*—The entire patrol squad assigned to the same shift. Several overlapping platoons are required to provide police services twenty-four hours a day while accommodating peak service loads.

Source: Adapted from O. W. Wilson and Roy Clinton McLaren, *Police Administration*, 4th ed. (New York: McGraw-Hill, 1977), pp. 71–72.

from each other as their responsibilities become more narrow and defined. This has the potential to create conflict in the department as separate units begin struggling for recognition and resources.

Finally, enhanced specialization often creates morale problems for the regular patrol division. Members chosen for specialized work (e.g., detective, vice, narcotics, SWAT, K-9) are usually the more experienced patrol officers and/or the "cream of the crop." Selecting the best and the brightest patrol officers for special duty not only depletes the regular patrol division of quality personnel, it often has a negative psychological effect on the entire patrol division—that is, officers regard patrol work as a necessary but low-status stepping stone to advancement. With regard to establishing a separate juvenile division, this final danger of specialization has not been a serious problem (it has for other specialty units). Indeed, many police officers shun assignment to the juvenile division because they do not see it as "real police work."[14] The unpopular image of the youth division has been reinforced over the years by the disproportionate assignment of women to juvenile work.

POLICE OPERATIONS: PATROL

In the second half of this chapter, we turn our attention away from the organizational structure of police departments to a discussion of basic police operations. The focus here is on two major line services: *police patrol* and *criminal investigations*. We begin with police patrol.

O. W. Wilson described the *patrol* division as the "backbone" of the police department.[15] Police patrol is the primary task of the local police department. It therefore requires the largest share of personnel, resources, and money. Officers generally begin their policing careers at the patrol level. The obvious exception to this rule is found in specialized law enforcement agencies that normally do not handle routine police patrol.

Police administrators are faced with many important decisions when it comes to patrol services. The central challenge is how to use available personnel and equipment in the most effective way. We shall examine several important issues in patrol administration.

Car Patrol

Since the 1920s when it was first introduced, car patrol has become the dominant method of mobilizing officers on the street. A survey for the Police Foundation found that over 90 percent of all beats in the United States are covered by automobiles, with most of the remaining 10 percent of the beats covered on foot.[16] The patrol car cruising city streets is a familiar image to Americans, who have come to accept vehicular patrol as an essential part of policing. Indeed, many of us have difficulty visualizing the police without images of the patrol car creeping in our thoughts.

Conspicuous versus Inconspicuous Patrol

Most patrol cars are clearly distinguishable by a department's insignia, color scheme, emergency telephone number (usually 911) and red or blue emergency lights. This is known as **conspicuous patrol.** Patrol cars exist in a variety of shapes, sizes, colors, and equipment. However, there is enough uniformity in marked patrol cars that we are able to distinguish them from taxi cabs and pizza delivery cars, even when we are in unfamiliar jurisdictions.

One argument in favor of conspicuous patrol is that it serves as a deterrent to crime. A person contemplating committing a crime is likely to be thwarted when they spot the patrol car coming down the street. On a large scale, the hundreds of thousands of marked patrol cars on the roads every day prevent an immeasurable amount of crime. Additionally, the presence of a clearly marked patrol car in one's neighborhood may put residents at ease, thereby lessening their fear of crime.

However, many people argue that the easily spotted patrol car deters crime only momentarily until the police are out of sight. Similarly, to many residents a police car in their neighborhood is a sign of trouble rather than relief—it may elevate citizens' fear as much as it reduces it. In actuality, the research on deterrence and on fear of crime is not clear on either of these important issues.

Yet we do know that (1) conspicuous patrol is not always a deterrent to crime, and (2) potential law breakers have the advantage when they know where the police are located. Thus, many departments augment the use of conspicuous patrol with **inconspicuous patrol** (unmarked patrol cars) as a way to capitalize on the element of surprise. Inconspicuous patrol is the dominant mode of mobilizing plainclothes detectives. It also works well in the realm of traffic enforcement.

One-Officer versus Two-Officer Patrol

Our views on how many officers should be assigned to a single patrol car has changed over time. In the past, two-officer patrol was most common. The logic of two-officer patrol was that the second officer in the car could spot trouble more easily because he was relieved of driving responsibility. Also, the second officer served as immediate backup whenever a serious situation arose. Starting in the 1950s, however, departments began switching to one-officer patrol. Today, the one-officer patrol car is commonly used in the United States.

There were many early criticisms of one-officer patrols. It was argued that a single officer in a patrol car was less safe, deprived of emotional support, and more likely to have his credibility challenged without the corroborating testimony of a partner. But O. W. Wilson endorsed the one-officer concept. Wilson believed the criticisms against one-officer patrol were unfounded. Research appears to have vindicated Wilson. Studies from Wichita, Kansas City, San Diego, and other cities have demonstrated that one-officer patrol is just as effective and safe as the traditional two-officer patrol.[17] In addition, one-officer patrol is arguably more efficient, results in fewer discipline problems, and simplifies performance evaluation of each officer.[18]

Switching from two-officer to one-officer patrol involves more than simply removing one of the officers from the car. Patrol districts need to be made smaller, policies and procedures need to be revised, and officers need additional training to perform routine tasks without a partner (e.g., conducting traffic stops or breaking up a fight).

Car Patrol: Pros and Cons

There are many advantages of patrolling by car, and these account for its widespread use. Here is a summary of some of these advantages.

1. Cars can patrol large areas with speed. Given our sprawling urban centers and vast rural areas, cars are indispensable.
2. Patrol cars allow the police to keep pace with criminals who also have cars.
3. Patrol cars are self-contained information centers. Radios, maps, report forms, laptop computers, telephone numbers, and other necessary items are easily stored in a car.
4. Patrol cars can carry various types of equipment, such as first aid, emergency gear, and weapons.
5. Patrol cars can be used for transporting prisoners.
6. Patrol cars protect officers from rocks, insults, and the weather.

The many advantages of vehicular patrol make the automobile an indispensable police tool. But the automobile is no panacea. One drawback is the large cost associated with keeping a reliable fleet of patrol cars on the road. Patrol cars need to be replaced every three to four years because of their constant use. The original purchase price of a new patrol car averaged around $15,000 in 1990. (Police departments traditionally rely on large "muscle" cars for patrol work. Special performance features and equipment added at the factory make police cars more expensive than standard cars.) On top of the original purchase price is the additional cost of operating, maintaining, and insuring the cars. Many departments suffering from fiscal cutbacks have had to stretch the usable life of worn-out patrol cars.

A second drawback of car patrol is also its largest. By placing officers in a car and assigning them to large beats, we in fact remove them from everyday contact with average citizens. The patrol car has done more to strain police-community relations in the past half century than any other single factor. The officer in a patrol car may be *in* the neighborhood, but he or she is not *a part* of the neighborhood. Inside the metal and glass confines of the patrol car, the officer cannot hear or see or even smell the neighborhood, at least not very well. The police stare out their windows at community residents, and community residents stare back at the police—no meaningful human interaction takes place. The only names and faces the police come to learn are those of troublemakers. The regular citizens remain anonymous.

Foot Patrol

Foot patrol, the second major type of patrol, is undergoing renewed interest. We have begun to recognize that while car patrol is an indispensable part of modern-day policing, it also has created a significant void in police-community relations. We are realizing that rapid response to serious crimes is not the only thing that we want out of the police. Professional crime fighters are fine, but we also want service providers and maintainers of the social order. In fact, we are finding that it is not necessarily the serious violent crimes that bother most of the people most of the time—it is the disorderly panhandlers, rowdy youth, and marginal vagabond types that destroy the sense of community.[19]

In a growing number of cities, police officers are being reassigned from car patrol to permanent foot patrol. Modified approaches such as the "park and walk" strategy are also common. *Community policing* (see chapter 5) is an extension of this idea. Developed in Flint, Michigan, community policing is more of a shift in police philosophy than just another foot patrol program. Community policing attempts to bring back the "human element" of policing. In our efforts to be professional crime fighters, we have ignored this necessary dimension of police work for too long.

In short, an important advantage of foot patrol over car patrol is the improvement in police-community relations. A secondary advantage is the increased exchange of crime-related information between citizens and the police. However, foot patrol has its drawbacks too. Generally speaking, the benefits of car patrol noted above are limitations to the foot patrol officer; a foot patrol officer can cover only a small geographical area; a foot patrol officer is not able to carry the wide assortment of weapons and equipment stored easily in a car; foot patrol is hard work and leaves the officer unprotected from the elements. It is not difficult to understand why foot patrol is seldom a high status assignment among officers.

Alternative Types of Patrol

While car and foot patrol are the two dominant forms of patrol in the United States, there are other methods of mobilizing officers. Horses, bicycles, motorcycles, snowmobiles, boats, and aircraft are occasionally used by police departments. Each of these methods of patrol offer certain advantages depending upon the geographical terrain, climate, and enforcement problem at hand. For instance, boats are necessary for departments responsible for patrolling waterways and harbors. Snowmobiles are indispensable for patrol and rescue in snowy mountainous areas. And bicycles are an extremely useful—although highly underrated—method of patrol in many places, but particularly urban centers. Bicycles are quiet, quick, easy to maneuver, and inexpensive. Horses, too, are of tremendous value in urban areas. Horse patrol is highly visible, mobile, inexpensive, and excellent for crowd control. A mounted division is also a boost for police-community relations as citizens stop to talk with the officer and pet the horse.

Supplementing Patrol Strength

An important consideration in patrol administration is whether to supplement the patrol strength. The greatest expenditure of typical police budget goes to the patrol division. One way to meet citizen demand for quality police service when faced with the dual problems of extensive crime and monetary shortages is to utilize alternative sources of personnel. For the police administrator interested in supplementing patrol strength, there are several strategies available.

Police Reserves

Police reserves function much like the military reserves. Several days a month, ordinary men and women who hold a variety of nonenforcement positions in the community serve as reserve police officers. Reserve officers normally must go through the same screening and background checks as regular police officers, and they are required to undergo rookie training. The amount of training reserve officers receive varies from one jurisdiction to the next, but is seldom as extensive as regular officers receive.

There is substantial variation in how departments equip and utilize police reserves. Some departments uniform reservists similar to regular officers with the only difference being the badge. However, most departments outfit reserve officers with distinctive uniforms so citizens may properly identify them. Reserves are frequently teamed with a regular patrol officer, but occa-

Seattle's squad of twenty bike officers gets around town on special, heavy duty, 18-speed mountain bikes.

sionally they are assigned to patrol alone. Police reserves are especially valuable during emergency situations or special events when personnel supplies are stretched to the limit. Reserves are generally permitted to carry a firearm while on duty and to aid in the arrest of a criminal.

Police Cadets and Explorers

Police cadets are another option for supplementing the patrol strength. Young men and women (usually age eighteen to twenty-three) who are interested in police work as a career may be employed as police cadets. Cadets handle many of the nonenforcement duties around the station house. In so doing, cadets free sworn personnel from desk duty. Cadets occasionally accompany officers on regular patrol. Unlike police reserves, however, police cadets are not sworn officers of the law. Therefore, cadets are not permitted to carry firearms or to make arrests.

The police cadet system offers several important benefits. First, it is a good way to screen potential recruits before they become regular officers. Second, when cadets do eventually become fully sworn officers, they will have a wide range of experience within the department. Third, cadets normally discharge their nonenforcement tasks with enthusiasm and excitement. The presence of young, motivated cadets frequently boosts the morale of the station house work group.

The **law enforcement explorers** program, sponsored by the Boy Scouts of America, offers similar training and experience as the police cadet program. Law Enforcement Explorers are young people between the ages of fourteen and twenty who also are interested in learning about police work. Explorers participate in traffic and crowd control, crime prevention, crime lab, records, and communications. The success of the explorers program is evident in its dramatic growth; between 1979 and 1989 the number of explorers increased from 32,000 to 46,000.[20] Currently, there are over 2,200 explorer posts nationwide.[21]

In short, supplementing the regular patrol division with police reserves, cadets, and explorers can save the department money by increasing the available personnel for patrol assignment. While not all departments have experienced success with their programs, most have found these strategies for supplementing the regular patrol division highly beneficial.

Preventive Patrol

The conventional wisdom prior to the 1960s held that the police were nearly always engaged in some law enforcement action, such as investigating a crime, making an arrest, questioning a suspect, or staking out a crime scene. The occasional "service" call was only a momentary interruption in an otherwise busy crime-fighting day. But startling research conducted in the 1960s and 1970s documented that the great majority of the patrol officer's day involved simply moving around the beat; looking, listening, and waiting for something—anything—to happen.

Police administrators countered the research by claiming this "looking, listening, and waiting" was **preventive patrol.** In other words, what appears to be wasted patrol time is actually preventing crime. By driving or walking in random fashion around the neighborhood, an officer gives residents the impression of continual police protection. As the argument goes, preventive patrol reduces crime by (1) increasing the chances of catching criminals in the act, and (2) deterring would-be criminals from committing a crime in the first place. In the process, preventive patrol also reduces the level of fear among citizens.

But what is the evidence on preventive patrol? Does preventive patrol

SPECIAL SUPPLEMENTARY UNIT: K-9

There is an alternative to supplementing the patrol strength that does not involve additional personnel as in the use of reserves and cadets. It involves the use of canines (i.e., dogs), hence the term K-9 patrol. There is nothing new or silly about trained dogs working police patrol. Police dogs have been used in Belgium and Holland since 1900, and have been adopted by other European countries as well. A few departments in the United States began experimenting with police dogs as early as the 1920s. Today, hundreds of law enforcement agencies across the United States have established their own K-9 patrols. Most small agencies that use K-9 patrol have only one police dog and one officer as its handler. Larger departments may have an entire K-9 unit with fifty or more police dogs.

The bigger, more powerful breeds such as German shepherds, Doberman pinschers, Rottweilers, and Labrador retrievers are popular choices for police dogs. These dogs are large, powerful, highly intelligent, and easy to train. An important consideration in choosing a police dog is to select an even-tempered dog that responds well to adults and children in public. A vicious "killer dog" is of no use to a department for routine patrol—such a dog would jeopardize police-community relations and invite a major lawsuit if an innocent person were ever bitten. Another important consideration is the K-9 handler. To a very large degree, the police dog is only as good as its handler. Dog handlers should be carefully selected and extensively trained before they are qualified to work K-9 patrol. Refresher courses for both the dog and the handler are periodically required.

The benefits of K-9 patrol are well-recognized within law enforcement circles. Dogs are available twenty-four hours a day, never complain, never become corrupt, and never demand more for their labor than food and companionship. The initial cost of training a dog may run into several thousands of dollars, yet over the usable "street life" of a police dog (normally five to eight years) the cost is minimal. Police dogs can run faster and jump higher than any two-legged officer. In a fight, even the largest criminals are no match for a police dog. The tenacious bite of a Rottweiler, for instance, can tear flesh and crush bone. Police dogs are taught to bite a suspect's arm or leg (not the head or neck) and to hold on tightly until the suspect either stops resisting or the K-9 handler gives the command (usually in a foreign language) to release. If a dog is killed in the line of duty, it is regrettable but far better than losing an officer.

More impressive than a police dog's speed, power, and fighting ability is its capacity to literally sniff out crime. The olfactory sense of dogs is far superior to that of humans. When properly trained, dogs are a tremendous enforcement tool. Police dogs are noted for being able to smell minute traces of drugs hidden in luggage, cars, pockets, desks, walls, ceilings, shipping crates, and just about anywhere else that drugs are concealed. Trained detector dogs in narcotics cases have scored thousands of arrests that would not have been possible without them.

In addition to sniffing drugs, police dogs are useful for tracking suspects, sometimes several hours after the trail is "cold." Police dogs are invaluable on burglary calls because they can quickly locate a suspect inside a building. Fire investigators have used dogs to seek out accelerants in arson detection. And state wildlife officers have found dogs useful for smelling illegal deer meat or shell casings. Dogs also have been used to find hunters lost in the woods.

prevent crime? Does it reduce citizens' fear of crime? Two classic studies in police patrol provide some clues.

Operation 25

Operation 25 was a patrol experiment conducted in New York City's Twenty-fifth Precinct (hence the name). The patrol experiment started September 1, 1954 and ended December 31, 1954. The purpose of Operation 25 was to determine whether greatly increased patrol coverage prevents crime.

New York City's Twenty-fifth Precinct was located in the upper east side of Manhattan. The precinct's population in 1954 was approximately 120,000 (30 percent black, 33 percent Hispanic and 37 percent white) and was ordinarily patrolled by 188 officers.[22] In September of 1954, the patrol strength was increased by an additional 276 men, most of whom just graduated from the police academy. This **saturation patrol** enabled commanders to reduce the average walking beat from ten blocks to just four. The four blocks were arranged in a straight line to enable officers to see their entire beat at all times. As added motivation, each officer was made answerable to the captain when a crime was committed on his beat. A few days before the experiment began, officers received twenty hours of special training to prepare them for their new assignment. This included lessons in conversational Spanish, slide presentations of the area, and mug shots of known criminals.

Statistics were collected and compared to the same four-month period from the previous year. The results were impressive. Felonies decreased by 55 percent in the Twenty-fifth Precinct. Misdemeanors fell by an equal amount. Street muggings dropped by 90 percent and burglaries by 78 percent (when entry was made from the front of the building). The only crime that did not drop was murder (all eight murders were committed inside, but were quickly solved). The clearance rate climbed from 20 percent to 65 percent. Moreover, morale among officers and supervisors ran high throughout the entire experiment. Ratings of citizen satisfaction with the study and its effect on fear of crime were not made.

The results of Operation 25 suggest that saturation patrol clearly decreases crime and improves the apprehension rate by police. Although the expense of saturation patrol makes it impractical as a large-scale patrol strategy, the implication to be drawn from Operation 25 is that preventive patrol, if done properly, can prevent crime. Unfortunately, Operation 25 was not designed as a true experiment. There was no control for other possible causes of the reduction in crime, only police statistics were used to evaluate the program, and the study did not address the potential problem of *crime displacement*—i.e., did the criminals go somewhere else?

We should note a similar study was conducted in New York's Twentieth Precinct by the Rand Institute in 1966. The Twentieth Precinct was saturated with a 40 percent increase in patrol officers. This study made efforts to control for the problem of crime displacement that had left the results of Operation 25 in doubt. The Rand researchers reported a 33 percent reduction in street robberies and a 50 percent reduction in car thefts with no significant increase in crime in neighboring precincts.

Kansas City Patrol Experiment

287

CHAPTER 11:
Police
Organization and
Operations

The **Kansas City patrol experiment** is the most widely cited and methodologically sophisticated study of preventive patrol to date.[23] Beginning on October 1, 1972 and ending September 31, 1973, the Kansas City Police Department, along with the help of the Police Foundation, conducted a study to determine if conspicuously marked police patrol had an appreciable effect on (1) the rate of crime, and (2) citizens' fear of crime.

The South Patrol Division of the Kansas City Police Department was chosen for the study. This division was responsible for thirty-two square miles and 148,000 residents. Fifteen beats were subdivided into five different groups, each containing three beats. A computer analysis was used to match each beat on the basis of reported crime, number of calls for service, ethnic and racial composition, and median income. Matching was done to assure that any differences found at the conclusion of the study were attributable to the experiment itself and not the idiosyncratic characteristics of a particular beat. The study's expansive geographical area and the large number of beats helped minimize the problem of crime displacement.

Three different patrol strategies were used. In *reactive* areas, patrol cars entered the beat only when there was a call for service. The rest of the uncommitted time was spent on the boundaries of the beat in the proactive areas. *Proactive* areas intensified the degree of preventive patrol by two to three times the normal amount. In beats considered *control* areas, the Kansas City police patrolled as usual. Figure 11.2 should aid in visualizing the geographic design of the study.

Data to evaluate the study were collected from a variety of sources.

FIGURE 11.2
Diagram of the Kansas City Patrol Experiment

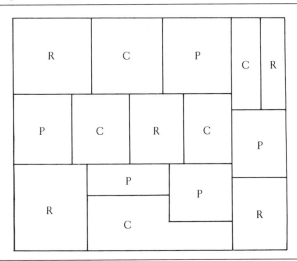

P = Proactive,
C = Control,
R = Reactive

Source: From George L. Kelling et al., *The Kansas City Patrol Experiment* (Washington, DC: Police Foundation, 1974), p. 9.

Community surveys; trained observers; in-depth interviews of officers, supervisors, and citizens; and department records were used. To measure the rate of crime, victimization data were obtained.

Contrary to the optimistic findings of previous patrol studies like Operation 25, the results of the Kansas City study were quite sobering. The comparison of the three different patrol beats revealed the following results:

1. There was no significant difference in the rate of victimization.
2. There was no significant difference in the number of arrests.
3. There was no significant difference in the level of fear of crime among citizens.
4. There was no significant difference in citizens' attitudes toward the police.
5. There was no significant difference in amount of time it took police to respond to calls.[24]

Critics claim the findings of the Kansas City study warrant careful analysis because of certain unanticipated flaws in the research design. For example, the extent of police activity in the reactive areas was far greater than originally planned.[25] These and other problems notwithstanding, the overall conclusion of the Kansas City study cannot be dismissed: *routine preventive patrol does not necessarily prevent crime, nor does it automatically allay citizens' feelings of fear.* It is worth noting that a replication study in Albuquerque, New Mexico, reached a similar conclusion.[26] And another group of researchers found no evidence that police employment practices reduces violent crime or property crime. As the authors of this later study point out:

> Although cities and suburbs responded to violent crime by increasing the size of their police forces between 1960 and 1970, this response was ineffective. In neither cities nor suburbs did a marginal increase in police strength reduce reported violent crime or property crime.[27]

Current Trends in Police Patrol

The impact of the Kansas City study and others on our thinking about police patrol has been substantial. We realize that simply assigning more officers to the streets will not automatically result in direct payoffs in terms of crime control. And we should not forget to mention the expense of continually increasing the number of patrol officers whenever there is an increase in crime. Instead, we are exploring other avenues to improve the effectiveness of patrol.

Problem-Oriented Policing

Problem-oriented policing is a general approach to patrol work designed to help the police work *smarter*, not *harder*. Formally conceived by Herman Goldstein in 1979,[28] problem-oriented policing views many types of crime as having a history and a future; they are not just isolated events. For example, a robbery of a convenience store might only be a single event. But it also may be related to a rash of recent robberies, all tied together by a serious drug problem that has made its way into a certain section of the inner city. Problem-oriented policing takes us beyond the traditional "pin-map" approach to crime to a thorough and comprehensive analysis of the problem.

Problem-oriented policing tries to alleviate the underlying problems that give rise to crime. Officers work closely with businesses and private citizens to develop practical solutions to the problems, and then evaluate their responses to determine if they are working.[29] The success of problem-oriented policing is evident by improvements in the quality of community life, not just by the absence of crime. Police officers generally rate this approach highly since it allows them to use their knowledge and problem-solving skills to help their communities.

Crackdowns

Another patrol strategy that is attracting growing attention is the police **crackdown**. Crackdowns are related to problem-oriented policing in that they identify a specific problem and then target patrol resources to it. The difference is in the transitory, more fleeting nature of police crackdowns—the police hit hard, they hit fast, and then they move on.

Police crackdowns have been used widely in the past decade. The police frequently target drunk drivers, drug corners, crack houses, and streetwalking prostitutes for crackdowns.[30] Because police crackdowns substantially increase the probability of arrest, they are extremely useful for deterring specific forms of misconduct.

Differential Police Response

Differential police response (DPR) provides an alternative method of assigning radio patrol cars to calls for service than the traditional approach. DPR is based on the following premise: "it is not always necessary to rush a patrol car out in response to a call. A delayed response is often just as effective—and just as satisfactory to the caller as long as he or she knows what to expect."[31]

Alternatives to rapid response by a radio patrol car are often feasible, especially if the crime scene is already "cold" or if the crime is of a minor nature. For example, instead of sending a patrol unit, the crime report may be given over the phone. The use of non-sworn crime technicians to go to the crime scene to take the report is another alternative to consider. In the three-city experimental test of DPR, police administrators were impressed with how well the system worked. In Toledo, Ohio, for example, patrol units would have had to handle 6,325 more calls during the study period if the DPR project had not been in operation. Toledo's Chief John Mason said his department "picked up thousands of hours we can apply towards better investigations, preventive patrol, and enforcement."[32]

POLICE OPERATIONS: CRIMINAL INVESTIGATION

Criminal investigators—better known as *detectives*—typically operate as a separate division from patrol and report to their own commander. Small

It's a hot, summer night and a woman is going to the refrigerator for a refreshing bowl of ice-cream, only to discover that the freezer is "on the blink." Fearing the worst, she calls a refrigerator repair service advertised in a phone directory. Several hours later, she is presented with a bill in excess of $100 and told that the defrost timer was defective and had to be replaced. As she writes the check to the smiling repair man, she is overwhelmed by a feeling of helplessness and mistrust. Although she does not know it, she has just become a victim of crime, because the repairman intentionally sold her a part she did not need.

Every customer has known the feeling of being at the mercy of someone in the repair industry. What many consumers don't know is that the above scenario is played out thousands of times each day, and that their worst fears are often justified. In fact, dishonest repairmen steal millions of dollars annually.

The average homeowner, who knows very little about how appliances operate, presents an easy target for con-men in the appliance repair industry. In most states, this industry is vastly unregulated and little more is needed than an occasional license and a tool box to enter the appliance repair business.

In an effort to curb appliance repair fraud, the State Attorney's Office in Jacksonville, FL., designed and implemented an undercover operation entitled "Operation Freezer Burn." Investigators were shocked at the results. Almost half of the 28 repair companies called charged for parts they never used or for work they never performed. In fact, 12 repairmen were charged with various criminal offenses, and an almost equal number were labeled as incompetent by refrigeration experts acting as consultants to the investigation.

THE INVESTIGATION PROCESS

The method of investigation was simple, yet precise. And, because these transactions would be the subject of criminal court proceedings, all evidentiary and investigative guidelines were followed to ensure the integrity of the case.

The first step in the operation was to secure the services of two refrigeration experts whose integrity and ability were unquestionable and who would maintain secrecy about the investigation. One expert was chosen from the teaching profession; the other owned his own repair business. Their testimony would be essential should any case go to trial.

Next, a vacant house in an average neighborhood, donated for use during the investigation, was set up for the operation. A used refrigerator was also placed in the house, and its essential parts were carefully marked for future identification with a red, indelible marking pen. Then, the refrigerator's temperature and on/off cycles were graphed using a standard temperature cycle machine. The graph would later prove that the refrigerator was in proper working order. Then, the refrigerator was disabled in a variety of ways. The evaporator fan motor wire was disconnected, the temperature dials were turned to the wrong setting, and the refrigerator was unplugged from the wall receptacle.

An initial call to a repair company dispatcher was made and recorded. The investigators were instructed to avoid being specific and to simply state that the refrigerator was not cooling properly. Thus, the repairman could not later offer the defense that he was only performing a repair which the customer requested.

To assure that the repairman arrived at a certain time, the investigator presented himself as a real estate agent and explained that the refrigerator was in a vacant house, the sale of which was contingent upon all the appliances working. In order to not waste time waiting for the repairmen to arrive, appointments were set up for the "real estate agent" to meet the repairmen at the vacant house.

As each repairman arrived at the appointed time, he was greeted by an undercover officer who was wearing a body transmitter. Another investigator in a surveillance position outside the house also photographed each suspect's vehicle upon arrival and recorded its vehicle identification number and license information because the repair trucks could be the subject of civil forfeiture. This also helped to later identify the workmen who, in every instance, gave their real names in the initial introduction. When directed to the refrigerator, the repairman was told that it was not cooling properly. Officers in an adjoining room videotaped the repairman's actions. The undercover officer then informed the repairman that he had to check something outside and excused himself to allow the repairman to work privately.

Returning a few minutes later, the investigator would inquire as to the exact problem and what repairs were performed to correct it. After getting as detailed an explanation as possible and assurances that the repairs were necessary, the investigator asked for the old parts to show the prospective buyers of the property that the repairs were performed. Many of the repairmen, who had not actually replaced a part or who had replaced a perfectly good part with another, had a particularly hard time at this point. They were observed going back to the refrigerator and, out of sight of the investigator, but on camera, taking new parts out of their tool boxes, breaking terminals off and presenting the broken parts to the investigators. In addition, some repairmen also returned parts that did not bear the red markings; checking revealed that the original part was still in the refrigerator after the repairman charged to replace it.

The video tape also revealed many other indiscretions. In one instance, a repairman was revealed tapping a screwdriver against the side of the refrigerator to simulate repair noise after he had already found the loose wire and connected it minutes before. In this particular case, parts were paid for that were never replaced. In addition, some workmen even billed for allegedly performed service checks on parts of the refrigerator which are accessible only from the rear of the unit. In these instances, the video tape clearly showed that the refrigerator had never been pulled away from the wall. It also revealed that some repairmen even looked into other areas of the house when they thought they were alone.

"CLOSING IN"

At the conclusion of the investigation, the cases were reviewed by an Assistant State's Attorney and arrest warrants were obtained. However, in order to catch all of the suspects before word of the operation spread through the tight-knit industry, everyone had to be arrested simultaneously. Using a different location, appointments were made with the repairmen who allegedly committed the fraud, giving the excuse that they had been recommended by a friend. At 10 minute intervals, the suspects arrived at the new location and were arrested as they entered the house. Their vehicles were taken to impoundment lots, and items used in the commission of the crime, such as pagers and portable telephones, were seized, all of which were subject to civil forfeiture.

CONCLUSION

From the beginning of the operation, heightened public awareness was the major goal. In fact, the newspaper and television coverage of the investigation and arrests exceeded expectations, and public response was overwhelming. Letters of encouragement from the public were printed for weeks afterward on editorial pages, and phone calls poured in to consumer groups reporting similar problems and requesting information prior to calling a repair company. In addition, legitimate appliance repairmen called for legislation to regulate their own industry. From all indicators, the project had been a tremendous success.

The conviction rate for those arrested was 100%, with no cases going to trial. And the total cost of the investigation, excluding investigators' salaries, was approximately $2,000 which was for parts purchased and repair bills paid to the 28 companies, making this project well within reach of most law enforcement agencies. After the fines and forfeitures to police investigative funds were tabulated, the cost of the investigation was actually recovered several times over.

However, in order to make a truly lasting impact on the repair industry, there must be assurances that future investigations of a similar nature will occur. Even so, this chilling effect of Operation Freezer Burn proved invaluable in curbing fraud in the repair industry. As one repairman aptly said, "Guys in this town are so busy looking for hidden cameras they don't have time to rip off customers any more."

Source: P. R. Beseler, "Operation Freezer Burn," *FBI Law Enforcement Bulletin* (Washington, DC: U.S. Government Printing Office, September 1989), pp. 14–17.

departments do not have the personnel or the need to create a separate investigation division, and so they normally assign patrol officers to investigate crimes. Police chiefs in small towns often take charge of serious investigations.

The word "detective" was first used in the 1840s, although detective-type activities were employed to investigate crimes as far back as the 1500s.[33] When the London Metropolitan Police Act was passed in 1829, there was no provision for a detectives division; the new concept of public police was still too fragile to rely on citizen support. By 1842, however, the London police established a small detectives unit. The detectives worked exclusively on the serious cases like murder, robbery, and rape, presumably because they were assured of public support.[34] This started the tradition of having detectives work on the most difficult and complicated cases.[35]

Today, detective work is one of the most sought-after jobs in policing. Uniformed patrol officers often set their career sights on making detective. The role of detective is well-defined and highly specialized. Unlike patrol officers who perform a wide variety of tasks, detectives are primarily "crime fighters." They investigate crimes, question witnesses, follow leads, hold stake-outs, and apprehend offenders. The popular image is that detectives do the "real" police work. Moreover, detectives dress in civilian clothes, work at their own pace, are relatively free from direct supervision, use their own ingenuity to solve cases, and are normally paid more than patrol officers. All these aspects combine to make detective work both desirable and rewarding.

How Good Are Detectives?

For a long time, the perception has been that detectives are highly effective at solving crimes. Through years of street experience, coupled with specialized criminological training, the wise and cunning detective could piece together the facts of a crime when men and women of ordinary intelligence could not. It was almost as if detectives were able to understand the minds of criminals and anticipate their next move. This notion was further enhanced by popular TV shows like *Kojak* and *Columbo*, which glorified the investigative skill of detectives, not to mention the glamorous and exciting lifestyle.

But are detectives master sleuths of extraordinary ability? Research in the late 1970s began to question the effectiveness of detectives in solving crimes. The first detailed analysis of detective work was a 1975 study by the Rand Corporation.[36] The Rand Corporation received a grant from the National Institute of Justice to conduct a mail survey of over 150 metropolitan police departments nationwide. They also interviewed police officials in twenty-nine departments. The purpose of the Rand study was to examine how criminal investigations were organized and managed in police departments, and to assess the overall contribution of detectives to police work.

The findings of the Rand researchers were both stunning and controversial. Detective work was found to be largely superficial and nonproductive. Less than one in three residential burglaries assigned to criminal investigations received any attention by detectives, and less than one in five larcenies were investigated. It appeared that most of the crimes that were solved nearly "solved themselves" (i.e., eyewitness, victim's testimony, physical evidence at crime scene). The work of the detective frequently entailed "behind the scenes" paper shuffling and case processing. In other words, the Rand study raised the notion that detectives contribute little above and beyond the cursory initial investigation of the responding patrol officer. The study recommended that patrol officers be given a larger role in preliminary investigations in order to minimize errors and redundancies by detectives.

Other police scholars have also shattered the idealized image of detectives. Harold Pepinsky, writing at the same time the Rand study came out, noted that "Most detectives spend the bulk of their time at their desks, going through papers and using the telephone."[37] Carl Klockars is equally unimpressed with the work of detectives:

> All but about 5% of serious crimes that are solved by detectives are solved because a patrol officer has caught the perpetrator at the scene, because a witness tells the detective whodunit, or by thoroughly routine clerical procedures. In a very small percentage of cases, perhaps 3%, extraordinary efforts by detectives may contribute to a case solution, but this is a far cry from the image the classical detectives promoted with their cases.[38]

Solving Crimes: New Evidence

A study conducted by the Police Executive Research Forum (PERF) shows that detectives are more effective in solving crimes than earlier research suggested. The PERF study documented the entire criminal investigation process, from the time the first officer arrived at the crime scene until the case was completed by detectives (arrest made or case dropped).[39] The study collected information on 3,360 burglaries and 320 robberies in three police agencies (DeKalb County, Georgia; St. Petersburg, Florida; Wichita, Kansas). Several different data sources were used to evaluate the results.

Similar to the previous studies, the PERF study found that **case screening** results in rapid attrition of different cases. Nearly 50 percent of the burglary cases were never assigned to a detective because of too little evidence. Among the burglaries that were assigned, three out of four were dropped after the first day. Moreover, while all robberies were initially assigned to detectives, 75 percent of these cases were abandoned after one day. The study further reported that the majority of burglary and robbery cases were investigated no more than four hours.[40]

However, among those cases that were assigned and investigated, the detectives' efforts *did* make a difference. Cases were solved and arrests made that would not have happened without the follow-up investigation of detectives. Thus, while earlier studies touted the value of patrol officers in solving crimes while minimizing the worth of detectives, the PERF study demonstrates that both patrol officers and detectives make important contributions.

CONCLUSION

This chapter focused on the central organizational and operational characteristics of police departments. All police departments are organizations, meaning they are comprised of human beings who are assembled in some fashion for a particular purpose. The major organizational principles of police departments identified here were its bureaucratic structure, reliance on a semi-military model, and the police organizational environment. We noted that four environmental influences affect police organizations (community sentiments, media, politics, and technology). These influences are often abrupt and unpredictable. The police management strategy must be flexible enough to allow the department to survive unplanned environmental shifts without completely displacing the original goals of the department. The important contributions of the late O. W. Wilson to police organizational principles were also noted. Wilson's long career and many written works influenced an entire generation of police administrators.

The discussion of police operations concentrated mainly on patrol—the "backbone" of policing. Car patrol and foot patrol, the two main types of police patrol, were carefully examined. We discussed several ways of supplementing the patrol strength such as police reserves, police cadets, and law enforcement explorers. Each of these strategies offer certain advantages to the police administrator, especially when expansion funds for additional police officers are limited.

The most important study of preventive patrol to date, namely the Kansas City study, showed that conspicuous random patrol does not necessarily prevent crime, nor does it reduce citizens' fear. New patrol strategies such as problem-oriented policing, crackdowns, and differential police response were described as ways to help the police work *smarter*, not *harder*.

We concluded the chapter by looking at the myth and reality of detective work. Although detective work may not be as glamorous as portrayed on TV, and while most detectives are not as ingenious as *Kojak* or *Columbo*, recent research suggests that criminal investigators do contribute importantly to solving crimes.

KEY TERMS

bureaucracy	law enforcement explorers
semi-military model	preventive patrol
line, staff, and auxiliary units	Operation 25
open versus closed system	saturation patrol
O. W. Wilson	Kansas City patrol experiment
conspicuous patrol	problem-oriented policing
inconspicuous patrol	crackdown
police reserves	differential police response
police cadets	case screening

DISCUSSION QUESTIONS

1. Identify and discuss the central organizational features of police departments. Can you think of a better way to organize police? What about removing rank designations and operating in a more democratic and collegial fashion?

2. Why do the interests of the police and the media often clash? Whose interests should prevail? Why?

3. What are your thoughts on using animals in police work? If you believe, as many do, that dogs and horses can substantially improve the effectiveness of the police, what about the argument that animals detract from the professional image of police? How do you think the police and citizens would react if we started using monkeys on patrol? Should we draw the line somewhere?

4. Discuss the research on preventive patrol. Even if studies cannot confirm the preventive effect of preventive patrol, should we eliminate this basic patrol strategy? Why or why not?

5. Why is detective work thought to be more important and glamorous than ordinary patrol work? What personal characteristics do you think distinguish a *good* detective from a *great* detective?

CHAPTER TWELVE

POLICE MANAGEMENT

The efficiency with which the police or any other organization can operate will depend to a considerable measure on how effectively the personnel can be managed and utilized.

—Calvin Swank and James Conser

Police personnel management can no longer be taken for granted in police organizations. Times have changed. Police managers are forced to grapple with many troublesome contemporary issues confronting American law enforcement. Police unions, collective bargaining, lawsuits, civil service, equal employment legislation, affirmative action, disciplinary measures, fiscal restraints, AIDS, and numerous other critical issues demand the attention of police managers.

Every generation of police managers have their share of problems. This is why "police" management and "problem" management are often one and the same. But managing police organizations today is highly complex. The growing number of seminars, workshops, training sessions, and college-level courses devoted specifically to police management is a reflection of its complexity. The professional literature on police management is also growing, so much so that professional police leaders and police scholars have difficulty staying abreast of this expanding field. This chapter will cover the major issues in contemporary police management.

THE TASK OF MANAGEMENT

Modern management theory was born in the early part of the twentieth century with the time-and-motion studies of Frederick Taylor.[1] Taylor attempted to prove that running an organization—*any* type of organization—was more of a science than an art.[2] In the decades since Taylor's pioneering work, management theory has evolved into a sophisticated field of professional study. Modern management theory has progressed from the simplistic "stopwatch" efficiency studies of yesterday to a holistic, *human relations approach* to personnel management today. Unfortunately, too many police managers are not well-schooled in modern management techniques, leaving them a step or two behind the more successful management strategies found in business and industry.

The basic task of management is not at all mysterious. The following description should suit our general purpose: *Management involves bringing together people and resources to accomplish some end or objective. Managers make plans and decisions about what is to be accomplished. Managers also motivate people to carry out the work.*

Personnel management is not new. People have been managing other people since the beginning of time. Even during prehistoric days, tribal chiefs had management responsibilities assigned to them—securing food, clothing, warmth, and protection for members of the tribe involved all the tasks specified in our definition above. We marvel at some of the colossal management feats in human history, such as the building of the Great Wall of China or the interstate highway system in the United States. But we should not overlook the more mundane management feats, like organizing a neighborhood baseball game or managing a classroom.

It may be useful to identify the broad parameters of the management task. Luther Gulick, an early leader in formulating general management principles, published an influential paper in 1937 called "Notes on the Theory of Organization."³ Gulick argued that the task of management entailed seven fundamental activities, represented by the acronym **POSDCORB**:

- Planning—deciding what needs to be done and the best methods for doing it;
- Organizing—establishing a formal structure of authority through which work subdivisions are arranged, defined, and coordinated for the defined objective;
- Staffing—hiring and training employees and maintaining favorable conditions of work;
- Directing—making decisions, embodying them in specific and general orders and instructions, and serving as the leader of the enterprise;
- Coordinating—interrelating the various parts of the organization;
- Reporting—keeping superiors and subordinates informed as to what is going on, which includes record keeping, research, and inspection;
- Budgeting—planning, accounting, and controlling the organization's budget.⁴

The POSDCORB activities apply to police managers. Running a police organization involves planning, organizing, staffing, directing, coordinating, reporting, and budgeting. Successful police management requires a proper mix of leadership ability, intellect, integrity, technical expertise, and the ability to motivate people. Few individuals who enter police work possess all the desired qualities of a top-notch police manager. This is why a competent, progressive, and professional police manager is of tremendous value to a police organization.

Who Are Police Managers?

When we speak of "police managers" or members of the "management team," to whom are we referring? As a general rule, police managers are medium- to high-ranking officers in a police agency with administrative responsibilities (police managers are also called police administrators). For example, the ranks of chief, deputy chief, captain, lieutenant, and sergeant all have management responsibilities assigned to them. The ranks of deputy chief and chief are considered *upper* management while captains and lieutenants are part of *middle* management; sergeants are technically part of the management team but are normally classified separately as *supervisors*. Police supervisors are the direct link between the line services (patrol, traffic, vice, etc.) and administrative ranks (see figure 12.1).

The number of police managers in an agency depends largely on the size of the department—the bigger the agency, the greater the number of managers. The nature of administrative responsibilities assigned to police managers also depends on the size of the department. In a small department, the police chief may do all of the POSDCORB activities for the entire department. The small-town police chief may occasionally perform basic line duties as well. In a large department, by comparison, the chief is kept busy with key executive responsibilities such as approving unit reports, establishing department policy, overseeing officer disciplinary procedures, and planning a budget. This means the big-city police chief has to delegate many of the daily management tasks (assigning work schedules, procuring supplies, reviewing arrest reports, handling routine complaints from the community, etc.) to other administrators.

In many other countries, individuals with extensive college study can immediately enter police work at the level of management. Police managers in the United States, however, almost always start at the level of patrol regardless of prior education. Because *lateral entry* is seldom permitted in the United States (see chapter 10), promotion "through the ranks" normally occurs within the same department. The one notable exception to this rule is for police chiefs. Police chiefs often move from the top position in one agency to another.

There are a number of reasons why an officer would want to become a police administrator. For starters, the pay is better than line officers receive and the hours are usually less grueling (at least for upper managers who do not have to do shift work). Ranking officers enjoy greater prestige, are given the opportunity to lead others, and are able to share their knowledge and experience with younger officers. Many ranking officers enjoy the challenge of administrative work and feel they are able to make significant contributions to the department.

FIGURE 12.1
The Ranks of Management

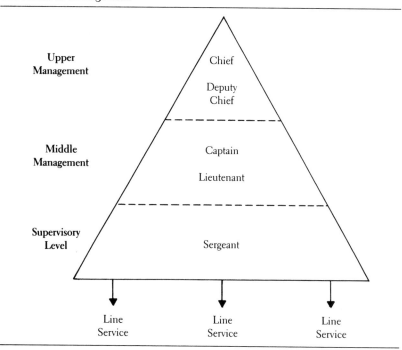

Lawrence "Lonnie" Hurlbut left his position as chief of security at the Ford Motor Company near Cleveland in 1982 to become police chief in San Juan Bautista, California, a town of 1,300. He credits a drop in the crime rate to his frontier-marshal style of policing the streets.

On the negative side of police managerial work, no job is perfect. The euphoria of "making rank" quickly abates as the realities of the job become apparent. For instance, a patrol officer who seeks promotion to get away from the hassles of patrol work will find being a sergeant has its own share of headaches. Similarly, promotion from the ranks of middle to upper management brings with it a whole new set of job pressures and problems. And finally, promotion through the ranks entails more than just job changes—with each advancement the police manager drifts further away from the camaraderie and close friendship of patrol officers. New alliances are established as ranking officers find themselves associating more frequently with departmental "equals." Ranking officers must learn early in their managerial career that regular officers view them differently now; they are no longer one of the guys or gals. The lesson is typically driven home the first time a police supervisor must reprimand a police officer for some mistake.

Leaders and Leadership

The *organizational health* of a police department depends in large measure on the success or failure of its leadership.[5] Successful leaders have the ability to organize personnel and resources to be most effective. They also have the ability to "win the confidence, inspire the loyalty, and maintain the enthusiastic interest of subordinates."[6] Whatever other ailments an unhealthy police organization may have, it is sure to have an ineffective leader at the helm.

Successful leadership entails the proper mix of a number of desirable qualities, some of which are learned and others which seem inherent in the personality of the person. Research has been unable to identify the right combination of qualities that make a leader successful in all situations. For example, Lee Iacocca might have been able to transfer his winning leadership style from Ford Motor Company to Chrysler, but it is unlikely he would be able to lead the Chicago Cubs to a major league championship. Likewise, police chiefs who periodically move from the top position of one department to another typically experience varying levels of success at each stop.

SPOTLIGHT ON A POLICE CHIEF: CHARLESTON, SOUTH CAROLINA

When Reuben Greenberg became Charleston, South Carolina's first black chief of police in 1982 he inherited a city besieged by high crime rates. Charleston was known as the nation's rape capital, and its homicide, burglary and robbery rates were on the rise. Compared with the size of its population, Charleston's crime rate was unacceptably high.

After eight years of Chief Greenberg's common sense, proactive approach to crime reduction, Charleston now boasts its lowest auto, burglary and armed robbery rates in many years. Since 1982, criminal arrests in Charleston have tripled. Greenberg has succeeded in reducing not only the crime rate, but also citizens' fear of crime. In Charleston, the crime rate is decreasing, while elsewhere in South Carolina and in many U.S. cities it is increasing steadily.

Greenberg believes two factors are important to decreasing crime: (1) preventing crime before it happens, and (2) reducing the incidence of victimization. His programs have significantly improved Charleston's crime reduction efforts. The city's police department is South Carolina's largest with 250 sworn officers and 110 civilians. It is split into two sections, one of which operates like a traditional law enforcement agency. The other section, the Bureau of Special Operations, specializes in aggressive crime prevention tactics.

REDUCING INMATE RECIDIVISM

One of Greenberg's most successful programs works to keep inmates in prison as long as possible. Greenberg recognized that the high-repeat offenders—traditionally those who commit sexual assaults, armed robberies and burglaries—were likely to return to Charleston after parole, and would commit more crimes there. Although he could not keep these offenders out of Charleston indefinitely, Greenberg saw he could keep them out longer by opposing their paroles.

Greenberg appointed a Victim Witness Services officer who visits the Parole Board in Columbia every time a high-repeat offender from the Charleston area comes up for parole. Whenever possible, the crime victims, or their survivors, and the officer who investigated the case accompany the Victim Witness Services Officer.

Since Greenberg began his parole program in 1985, he has been 85 percent successful at opposing the release of high-risk repeat offenders. Greenberg contends that the program is such a cost-efficient method of reducing crime, he would still run it if it was only 15 or 20 percent effective. The program has decreased Charleston's crime rate because many potential re-offenders are kept inside. Another positive result is that officers have fewer crimes to investigate, so their workloads decrease.

Greenberg said his Victim Witness Services Officer is "more effective than all the detectives in the detective bureau, because they're investigating *after* somebody has been raped, *after* somebody's been assaulted, *after* somebody has been burglarized." Instead, the Victim Witness Services Officer works to prevent the crime from happening in the first place. "We already know

In the police organizational structure, the chief (also sheriff, commissioner, or other administrative head) is the *top cop* of the department. Typically, police chiefs come up through the administrative ranks by way of consecutive promotions. This means that chiefs are often in the latter stages of their careers before they assume the top executive position. It also means that chiefs have extensive experience in law enforcement. But this is not always the case. During the early part of the 1900s, for instance, the mayor of Indianapolis selected the police chief on the basis that he "would be a good chief because he has been my tailor for 20 years" and "knows how to make

that 80 percent of the crimes are committed by 20 percent of the criminals," Greenberg said. "We try to zero in on the 20 percent high-repeat offenders."

SURVEILLANCE

In another of Greenberg's programs, officers confront people they know to be former felons, on the streets of Charleston, and question them about their activities. The officer may ask questions like "where are you going?" or "what are you carrying in that bag?" The person does not have to answer, or if he does, he may lie, but the answer is not that important. What is important is that the felon knows the police are watching him. He knows that if a crime is committed in that neighborhood that day he will be a suspect. "What we find that we've done essentially is immunized, for that day, that neighborhood against that particular criminal, without us actually watching him," Greenberg said.

Often the person may take off running when the officer approaches him, Greenberg said. The officer may not even know if a crime has been committed, but he pursues the person anyway. Greenberg's officers are selected for these patrols based on their ability to run and fight.

The Charleston Police Department has a number of foot patrol beats; small beats covering three block areas. "We felt it was much more

effective to have a high concentration in a small area where the response time for the officer on foot would be the same or faster than that of an officer in a car," Greenberg said. He picks young officers who can run well and, instead of the traditional boots, gives them running shoes to make them more equally matched with the people they are trying to catch.

PUBLIC HOUSING

When Greenberg came to office, Charleston's public housing communities were suffering from a high rate of violent crime. Initially, the department saturated these areas with foot patrol officers, which was somewhat successful but expensive. Greenberg assigned one officer to deal with public housing full-time. The officer works with the landlord and conducts background investigations on prospective tenants to determine if they are likely to do something criminal. If a current resident commits a crime, the housing officer immediately starts working on an eviction.

"We have an obligation to provide safe housing for people in public housing," Greenberg said. People who cannot afford to live anywhere else except public housing deserve protection and should not have to be subjected to crime and drugs, he said. By making it difficult for criminals to get into or stay in Charleston's public housing, Greenberg has reduced the crime rate there.

Source: North Carolina Department of Crime Prevention and Public Safety, *Crime Prevention Journal*, Vol. 1 (Summer 1990), pp. 12–14.

good clothes; he ought to be a good chief."[7] Moreover, sheriffs are generally elected directly by citizens, meaning that individuals with limited or no police experience are sometimes voted into office. However, most sheriffs are career police officers with extensive experience.

As a group, police chiefs in our country enjoy little job security. The average length of tenure for our nation's police chiefs is less than five years. For municipal agencies, the average tenure for police chiefs is only two to three years.[8] Some of these chiefs retire, others are demoted or fired (chiefs are not covered by civil service protection), and still others are hired to head a different police agency. The end result is a high level of career mobility among our nation's top police executives.

Selecting a police chief is a critical process that deserves very careful consideration. The search may be limited to qualified officers within the department or it may extend beyond the department.

The most common procedure for selecting a police chief is **inside promotion.** According to one study of the career paths of over one-hundred police chiefs, 68 percent rose to the top within a single agency.[9] To many people, inside promotion is the preferred method of selecting chiefs. The reason is because the new chief is already familiar with established departmental policies, its personnel, and the internal and external factors that affect the department. Promotion from within also helps build morale among department personnel who believe they have a better chance for upward mobility.

Yet inside promotion has its drawbacks. Departmental "inbreeding" typically spawns police chiefs who lack broad vision and experience. This fosters conformity to the old ways of doing things rather than innovation. Insider chiefs may also have strong allegiances to certain personnel or political figures that may limit their ability to make necessary changes. Finally, the "cream" does not always rise to the top. Promoting from within when there exists only mediocre talents results in mediocre leadership.

A substantial portion of police departments select their chiefs through **outside promotion.** There currently exists a sizable number of professional, marketable, highly mobile police chiefs who frequently move from one top administrative post to another. This is similar to the proven model of leadership acquisition long used in the private sector. Outside promotion encourages the infusion of new ideas by someone unshackled by existing personnel cliques or political struggles. What is more, outside promotion is a valuable method of fostering department reform when corruption, brutality, or inefficiency exists.

There are several reasons why most departments still do not go outside to recruit their top administrative leaders. First, promotion from within creates new openings in the management hierarchy through the *ratcheting effect*— "as people move up, openings move down."[10] The rank-and-file frequently resent hiring an outsider because it limits their promotional opportunities. Second, department regulations typically prohibit lateral entry of police chiefs. In a survey by the Police Executive Research Forum of departments serving over 250,000 residents, 88 percent stipulated that chiefs shall be hired from within the department.[11] And third, lateral entry of police chiefs is sometimes unworkable because pension funds do not transfer from one agency to another.

Many police chiefs who move laterally must be willing to sacrifice their pension benefits.[12] For a department that wishes to hire a highly qualified chief from across the country, the department must be willing to offer a high salary as well as other inducements to attract the candidate.

Tenure for Chiefs

The issue of **tenure** for police chiefs, meaning guaranteed job security, has surfaced numerous times over the years. As it is practiced today, most police chiefs have little or no job security and can be released at any time. For example, municipal chiefs can be fired by the city council, city manager, or the mayor, depending who has the authority; bureau chiefs and agency heads at the state and federal levels also can be let go at just about any time (sheriffs are the most difficult to remove since they are "hired and fired" by the voters). The lack of guaranteed tenure in large part explains the limited time most chiefs hold their positions.

Few people would deny the benefit of being able to quickly remove an ineffective leader. However, a strong argument also may be made in favor of guaranteed tenure for police chiefs. It takes time to implement reform and bring about positive change to a department. If chiefs are "looking over their shoulders" all the time to see who is being offended by their leadership, they are not acting from a position of strength. As Herman Goldstein notes, "the chief's strength is heavily influenced by the degree of job security he enjoys."[13] And Edward Davis, in his acceptance speech for the presidency of the International Association of Chiefs of Police, spoke in favor of some type of job security for police chiefs:

> As I review the state of our profession throughout this nation, I have grown increasingly concerned about the plight of many police chiefs. In the vast majority of police departments, the agency's chief serves at the pleasure of a mayor or city manager. Because a great deal of politics can both be implied and involved where the chief does not have some type of procedural due process, there is a very high turnover rate for police chiefs in America. . . . Probably the best method of insuring impartiality in policing and preventing improper political interference is some kind of security for police chiefs.[14]

Davis goes on to argue that police chiefs should only be removed for some act of impropriety or malfeasance. In such a situation, the chief should be given a formal administrative hearing before an impartial tribunal. The chief also should be given every opportunity to defend himself or herself against the charges being made.

ADMINISTRATIVE RULE MAKING

Establishing policies and procedures for department personnel is an upper management responsibility. Most police leaders find writing clear and accurate department standards a most difficult task. But establishing useful policies and procedures is a necessary administrative responsibility since these rules are the vital link between police authority and police practice. In other words, while the law gives the police authority to act in various situations, the law does not instruct officers *how and when* to act. This is the function of department policies and procedures.

The traditional rule-making model has been for the police chief to issue the rules and regulations for department personnel to follow. New orders may be only temporary and set to terminate on a specific date, or the orders may be permanently entered into the duty manual.[15] The chief will usually consult with high-ranking officers in the department and sometimes with the town attorney before finalizing any new policy. Officers then receive word of new rules through oral and written communication. Most departments evaluate their *standard operating procedures* (SOPs) on an annual basis to be sure existing policies are both accurate and up to date.[16]

A common criticism of the traditional rule-making model in police departments is that its "top-down," unilateral nature completely ignores the insights of many knowledgeable people, such as rank-and-file officers or key citizens. Instead, new policies are decreed by the police leadership and imposed on the entire department. The traditional rule-making model increases the likelihood that officers will resist the new rules since they do not have a hand in developing them.[17] It also increases the risk of running into unanticipated consequences that could have been prevented with greater input. For example, the new chief of a tourist town might direct patrol officers to rigorously monitor parking meters for violators. However, such a policy could meet with heavy resistance from merchants who rely on the tourist trade for business. Before implementing an aggressive parking meter enforcement policy the chief would be wise to consult with the patrol commander, the Chamber of Commerce, individual store owners, and perhaps even with members of the town council. The chief may learn that what is really needed to control the parking problem is more parking spaces, not more tickets.

An alternative design to the traditional rule-making model is a process called **administrative rule making.**[18] Administrative rule making is an open process which solicits the opinions of employees and interested citizens before a new policy goes into effect. All federal agencies and many state agencies practice administrative rule making.[19] Administrative rule making is thought to be closer to the professional model of management where the opinions of employees are solicited before policy changes are made. This minimizes the degree of resistance and alienation among workers to new rules. Additionally, the feedback from different vantage points to a proposed policy allows administrators to better anticipate the multiple ramifications of a policy. Administrators may be able to "fine tune" the new policy to diminish opposition.

Administrative rule making has not had much of an impact on policing. A few agencies have adopted the basic principles of "notice and comment" prior to implementing new policies, yet most departments continue to rely on the traditional "top-down" rule-making process. Some observers argue that the special nature of police work is not well-suited for the administrative rule-making model, but others disagree. Given the available evidence, it appears that the major stumbling block to administrative rule making is not the unusual nature of police work; rather, it is the resistance of the entrenched leadership to open up the policy-making process. The rise in citizen "consumerism" of police services in recent years, coupled with the growing influence of police labor unions, is forcing police managers to listen to other voices when it comes to establishing police policy.

STRATEGIES OF POLICE MANAGEMENT

The preceding section concentrated on the policy-making responsibility of police managers. This no doubt is an important management task. But police managers are responsible for much more than simply establishing the policies and procedures of the department—they also must organize department resources and personnel in such a way to provide police protection to the community in the most productive way. It is here that the true management skills of police executives are put to the test.

The literature contains many different management strategies designed to get the most out of available resources and personnel. The vast majority of these management strategies originated out of efforts to improve operational production in the manufacturing and business sector. A number of these strategies have been adopted by public police agencies—either in whole or in part—with varying degrees of success. In the following sections, we shall examine two police management strategies that have attracted attention in recent years: (1) management by objectives, and (2) neighborhood team policing.

Management by Objectives

A widely acclaimed strategy of management first developed in the mid-1950s is **management by objectives** (MBO).[20] Management by objectives is a *results-oriented* management philosophy.[21] George Odiorne, one of the early formulators of this approach, describes MBO as:

> . . . a process whereby the superior and subordinate managers of an organization jointly identify its common goals, define each individual's major areas of responsibility in terms of the results expected of him, and use these measures as guides for operating the unit and assessing the contribution of each of its members.[22]

In condensed form, MBO involves setting objectives for the organization or sub-unit, establishing a plan for achieving those objectives, and evaluating the results. As one observer noted, "the better a manager understands what he hopes to accomplish (the better he knows his objectives), the greater will be his chances for success."[23] An effective MBO program is similar to an organizational "road map;" it gives a sense of where the organization is today, forces the organization to set goals of where it wants to be tomorrow (or next week, month, year, etc.), and lays out the direction to get there.

Simple as it sounds, establishing a MBO program in an agency is a complicated process involving a number of intricate steps.[24] Implementing an MBO program requires significant organizational change. Unfortunately, many police managers are not fully committed to MBO.[25] It is estimated that "a fully developed and properly implemented MBO system may require two to five years of sustained effort in large organizations before it takes hold."[26] This is one reason why not all police managers have been sold on the approach—MBO takes a great deal of time and energy to establish properly. As one textbook suggests, "it cannot simply be dropped into the police department like a set of spark plugs into a car."[27] Despite these obstacles, MBO is a proven management technique that has benefitted many departments.

Neighborhood Team Policing

There is a sociological concept called the *iron law of oligarchy*.[28] This means that as organizations expand, they have a natural tendency to centralize power among a small group of leaders, or oligarchy. Police departments are like any other large bureaucratic organization in that the center of power and authority tends to become increasingly concentrated at the top. **Neighborhood team policing** may be viewed as a management strategy designed to counteract the iron law of oligarchy by decentralizing the command structure.[29]

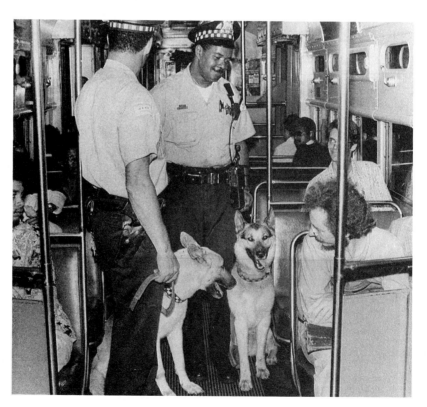

Police canine units patrol rapid transit trains in Chicago. They are assigned to high-crime routes.

The concept of team policing originated in Aberdeen, Scotland, just after World War II.[30] Two decades later, in the backdrop of urban unrest and police-community tension, team policing eventually aroused the attention of Americans. Progressive police leaders were searching for alternative management strategies to make their departments more responsive to community needs,[31] and team policing seemed to hold the answer. The Syracuse Police Department established the first team policing program in 1968. This apparently started a national trend. Within five years, as many as sixty U.S. police departments had initiated their own team policing programs.[32]

Several different models of team policing have been identified, some of which entail more extensive reorganization of the department than others.[33] The most complete model of team policing is the *full-service team*, or neighborhood team policing.

Under neighborhood team policing, a semi-autonomous team of twenty to forty officers and a commander are assigned to an identifiable geographical area (neighborhood) containing anywhere from 10,000 to 40,000 residents. The entire team is responsible for controlling crime in the area, providing police services twenty-four hours a day, and improving relations with the community. The highest ranking officer of the team is the commander, who is a middle-level police manager. The team commander is responsible for motivating team members, defining and allocating resources, and acting as the liaison between the team and the rest of the department.[34] The team carefully monitors the area to become familiar with neighborhood resources and the needs of residents. The team is encouraged to be creative in planning specific programs for the area. Individual officers find their views and experience eagerly sought. The result is a much more flexible and responsive approach to policing than the traditional management design.

Key Features of Neighborhood Team Policing

The major components of neighborhood team policing are compared to the traditional method of policing in table 12.1. We shall identify a few of the more important components.

1. *Decentralization*—This is the primary organizational strategy behind neighborhood team policing.
2. *Semi-autonomous*—The team is responsible for planning, organizing, and delivering police services to the area with minimal interference from central headquarters.
3. *Permanent assignment*—Team officers are assigned to an area on a permanent (or long term) basis. This allows officers to become familiar with community needs and residents.
4. *Job enlargement*—Team members are expected to become generalists in the performance of police services. This includes basic patrol work as well as traffic, juvenile, vice, narcotics, tactical responses, and criminal investigations.
5. *Participatory management*—Individual officers play an important role in setting team priorities and establishing a plan of action. This places

more authority *and* responsibility on the line personnel for the delivery of police services.

There are several stated advantages of neighborhood team policing: (1) it enhances police-community relations, (2) it improves the quality of police services, (3) it elevates the morale and self-image of team members, and (4) it more fully utilizes the potential of individual officers. However, few experiments in neighborhood team policing have realized all these benefits. The best known and most thoroughly evaluated team policing experiment was Cincinnati's **Community Sector Team Policing** (COMSEC) program. The results of the COMSEC program, which ran from 1973 to 1977, were not impressive. Some of the initial results of the experiment showed some improve-

Table 12.1   Comparison of Traditional and Neighborhood Team Policing

Traditional	Neighborhood Team Policing
1. Smallest patrol unit (precinct or division) has 100–250 officers.	1. Team has 20–30 officers.
2. Supervision is quasi-military.	2. Supervision is professional, with consultation, setting of objectives, and in-service training program, encouraging suggestions, permitting the exercise of responsibility within necessary limits.
3. Shift responsibility includes eight-hour tours, with only unit commanders—captains or inspectors—responsible for around-the-clock operations.	3. Team commander is responsible for all aspects of police service on an around-the-clock basis.
4. Assignment is on the basis of the first available car to call for police service—with priority for emergency calls.	4. Team provides all police service for its neighborhood. Team members are sent out of the neighborhood only in emergencies. Nonteam members take calls in the neighborhood only in emergencies.
5. Officers are rotated to new divisions or assignments.	5. Officers are given extended assignments to a neighborhood.
6. Special police units (tactical, detective, etc.) operate in local neighborhoods without informing local patrol officials.	6. Special police units inform themselves of team goals and, whenever possible, consult in advance with the local team commander.
7. Community relations is seen as "image building" (special units for community relations plus speaking engagements for officials).	7. Community relations is seen as an essential patrol function, planned by the team commander and the team, and consists of good police service, friendly street contacts, and attendance at meetings of various community groups.
8. Reactive policing (responding to calls) or aggressive policing (stop and frisk and street interrogations) are prevalent.	8. Decentralized planning (crime analysis, use of plainclothes or special tactics, investigations, preventive programs, referral programs, service activities).
9. Planning is centralized (innovation through orders from the chief or other important officials).	9. Planning is decentralized (innovation by team commanders, subject to review by their superiors).

Source: Peter Block and David Specht, *Neighborhood Team Policing* (Washington, DC: U.S. Government Printing Office, 1973), p. 2.

ment (better community relations, drop in crime), but by the end of the project the initial improvements leveled off as did officer enthusiasm.[35] Other team policing experiments have also failed to live up to expectations, largely because of ineffective planning.[36]

One of the biggest challenges to the successful implementation of team policing is the major redistribution (decentralization) of authority. Team policing alters the traditional command structure of the organization.[37] Police managers often perceive this change as threatening. In the Police Foundation study of seven different team policing experiments, it was discovered that managers sometimes resisted and occasionally sabotaged the team policing projects.[38]

In short, while the concept of neighborhood team policing still holds promise as an effective management strategy, it is no longer a driving force in policing. However, team policing bears close resemblance to the broader police philosophy of "community policing" (discussed fully in chapter 5), which currently is having a major impact in American policing.

MANAGEMENT STYLES

Anyone who has worked in various job settings knows firsthand that bosses do not all manage the same way, nor are they equally effective at motivating people or accomplishing job assignments. Some bosses are highly task-oriented while others are more people-oriented; some bosses are strict while others are easygoing; some bosses are bright, attentive, and organized while others seem to hold on to their jobs only by "muddling through."[39]

Bosses, or in our case police managers, have varying **management styles.** The management style adopted by a police leader is a combination of his or her personality characteristics, past experiences, the task at hand, and the quality of subordinates. We noted earlier that no single factor or combination of factors guarantees an individual will be a successful police manager. However, there are a number of personal qualities that successful police managers should possess. Among these qualities are *patience, wisdom, virtue, empathy, kindness, trust, knowledge* and *self-control.*[40] The extent to which a police manager possesses these qualities and utilizes them on a day-to-day basis influences the likelihood the manager will be able to garner the support of employees and to meet department objectives.

Management styles have been classified in a number of different ways.

Table 12.2   Comparison of Theory X and Theory Y Management Styles

Theory X	Theory Y
1. Employees are by nature lazy.	1. Employees find work as natural as play.
2. Employees are unimaginative and uncreative.	2. Employees have imagination and creativity just waiting to be tapped.
3. Employees have to be closely supervised.	3. Employees are goal oriented and need minimal guidance.
4. Employees cannot be trusted.	4. Employees deserve trust and respect.

FIGURE 12.2
Comparison of Management Styles

McGregor

Theory X   Theory Y

Tannenbaum and Schmidt

Tell	Sell	Consult	Join

Authoritarian   Democratic
(Task-Oriented)   (People-Oriented)

Perhaps the most general classification to date is Douglas McGregor's well-known **Theory X** and **Theory Y**.[41] In essence, Theory X managers are strict, authoritarian, and task-oriented; Theory Y managers are also task-oriented but are more concerned with developing trusting relations with employees. Table 12.2 summarizes the views commonly held by Theory X and Theory Y managers.

The traditional management style of police leaders leaned more toward Theory X. This, however, is slowly changing. The rising level of education among police officers plus the growing influence of police unions is pressuring departments to adopt the more democratic Theory Y management style. Recently, a *Theory* Z management style has been proposed.[42] Theory Z emulates the Japanese management philosophy of group work culture, consensus building, and the use of high technology. While it is unlikely the Japanese management style will have much impact on American police departments, at this time it is still too early to tell.[43]

Another useful classification of management styles has been advanced by Robert Tannenbaum and Warren Schmidt.[44] According to these writers, there are four management styles: *tell, sell, consult,* and *join.* The "tell" type leader makes the decisions and simply announces them to employees. The "sell" type leader also makes the important decisions but then attempts to persuade employees to accept the decisions. Managers who use the "consult" style of leadership make important decisions after talking with employees and soliciting their advice. Finally, the "join" type leader delegates most of the decision-making authority to subordinates. Clearly "tell" and "sell" are closer to the authoritarian, Theory X management style whereas "consult" and "join" are closer to the democratic, Theory Y management style. This can be seen in figure 12.2.

Is there a best style for police managers, one that works well in all situations and for all types of employees? The answer is obviously no, there is no *one* management style for all occasions. According to Lynch, the best police managers are those who are reasonably *balanced* and *flexible.*[45] Police managers must be able to balance the two primary concerns of the job—the concern for production and the concern for people. Police managers who lean too strongly toward production or toward people limit their range of effectiveness. They also must be flexible enough to adapt to changing situations and work settings. For example, an authoritarian "tell" management style would be appropriate in a short-term crisis situation, and a democratic "consult" or "join" management style would be more appropriate in neighborhood team policing. In the end, however, as Lynch warns, the "police manager must always realize that he, as a leader, is only as effective as his subordinates will allow him to be, and in most group situations the entire group is really responsible for the success or failure of the stated objectives."[46]

PERFORMANCE EVALUATION

Recent years have seen an increasing concern over measuring the performance of the police to determine not only *if* the police are doing what they are suppose to be doing, but also *how well* they are doing it. The objective is to hold the police more accountable to the public by having them justify their expense.

Performance evaluation of the police is a slippery process. On the one hand, all police personnel should be evaluated at least once a year. This includes assessing officers from the lowest to highest ranks. Performance evaluations (also called appraisals or ratings) provide feedback on the effectiveness of personnel. Police managers find performance evaluations necessary when making decisions regarding assignment, salary, promotion, and discipline. Performance evaluations of the entire agency are equally useful for policymakers (who set the budget) and the public.

On the other hand, evaluating the performance of the police is not an easy thing to do. Multiple measures of police performance have been used over the years, not all of which are equally valid. For instance, promotional decisions are all too often based on informal impressions of police managers (Who do they like the most?) rather than accurate and objective indicators of job performance. Moreover, even when carefully developed performance rankings are used for personal decisions, there is no guarantee that police supervisors will interpret them properly or put the results to good use. And, as always, evaluating the performance of an employee can create animosity between the superior and subordinate when they disagree on the rating.

Traditional Performance Measures

Over the years a number of measures have been used to evaluate the performance level of the police. Most citizens are familiar with these measures as they are frequently reported in the news media. We shall identify the measures used to evaluate the performance of individual officers and the entire department.

Evaluating Officers

The job of police patrol is a complex "bundle of tasks"[47] including law enforcement, social service provision, and order maintenance. Most of the traditional indicators of job performance, however, are geared only toward assessing the law enforcement aspect; the quality of social services rendered or effectiveness in maintaining social order receive less attention.

Conventional indicators of officer performance normally involve counting *positive* law enforcement activities. The following indicators are typical:

- The number of field reports written;
- The number of tickets handed out;
- The number of referrals to other agencies;
- The number of arrests made;
- The number of felony arrests made.

Evaluations of police officers can also include counting *negative* indicators of job performance. For example,

- The number of citizen complaints;
- The number of days absent;
- The number of dismissed cases because of officer error;
- The number of formal reprimands or disciplinary actions.

The problem with evaluating police performance by simply "counting" the activity level of officers is that it only provides an indication of the *quantity* of police behavior, but not the *quality* of that behavior. Imagine you are a police manager who has to choose one of three patrol officers to promote to sergeant. Assume that all three officers have about the same experience on the force and all have scored equally well on the sergeant's exam. By knowing which officer wrote the most tickets, made the most arrests, or was generally more active in the previous year in no way assures that you will make the best promotion decision. It is quite likely the three officers were assigned to different districts and shifts, which could account for the different levels of enforcement activity. Moreover, and more importantly, an active patrol officer may not necessarily make a good sergeant. As a police manager you would want to know as much information as possible about each of the candidates for sergeant before you made your decision.

Progressive police managers recognize the need to have highly accurate and reliable measures of performance. Several different advanced methods of performance evaluation exist, such as the *performance domain rating scale* (PDRS) and the *behaviorally anchored rating scale* (BARS).[48] Advance performance methods like the PDRS and BARS are tied directly to the specific work assignment that the officer is suppose to be doing, which is determined by a thorough *job analysis*. These advanced methods avoid the pitfalls of other evaluation methods that tend to measure more global (less specific) aspects of job performance.[49] Police managers who utilize these advanced methods of evaluating officers have accurate and reliable performance information at their disposal.

Evaluating Departments

In addition to measuring the performance of police officers, we also need to know how the police department as a whole is performing. Once again, the issue often boils down to counting law enforcement activities; social service and order maintenance activities are usually overlooked. The following are conventional indicators of police department performance:

- The number of crimes known to police;
- The number of arrests made by all officers;
- The number of major "busts";
- The number of major convictions;
- The clearance rate.

The **clearance rate** is an established measure of police department performance. While there are several problems with its exclusive use, the clearance rate is still arguably the best summary measure of how well the department is doing.

A crime is "cleared" whenever it is solved. Normally, the suspect is either arrested or charges are filed. Occasionally, a crime is cleared without any subsequent police action. For example, the suspect to a crime may already be dead, or a criminal may confess to a string of previously unsolved burglaries under the guarantee that no additional charges will be filed.

As a rule of thumb, the police in the United States clear approximately 20 percent of the Part I Index Offenses of the UCRs. Murder has the highest rate of clearance of the Part I Index Offenses (approximately 70 percent) while burglary and motor vehicle theft have the lowest (approximately 15 percent). Another way to look at this 20 percent clearance rate is to say that the police are unable to solve 80 percent of the serious crimes reported to them. (By

CALCULATING THE CLEARANCE RATE

The clearance rate is the standard measure of police performance reported in both the professional police literature and in the general media. As such, it is readily recognized by the police and citizens alike. The clearance rate may refer to the proportion of all crimes solved, such as the Part I Index offenses, or the proportion of one type of crime solved by the police. It is important to note that not all crimes cleared result in an arrest, and many do not end in conviction. The following example demonstrates how simple the clearance rate is to calculate:

$$\text{Clearance Rate} = \frac{\text{Crimes cleared}}{\text{Crimes known to police}} \times 100$$

Problem: Calculate the 1990 clearance rate for theft in Pilfer City, United States.

Necessary Statistical Information
—50 thefts reported to the Pilfer City police in 1990
—25 cases solved

$$\text{Theft Clearance Rate} = \frac{25 \text{ thefts cleared}}{50 \text{ thefts known to police}} \times 100$$

Theft Clearance Rate = 50 percent

comparison, the Japanese police boast of a clearance rate for felony offenses of over 80 percent.[50])

The large percentage of unsolved crimes in the United States is actually worse than it first appears. This is because the denominator of the clearance rate (crimes known to police) seriously underestimates the true extent of crime; only one-fourth to one-third of the index offenses ever becomes known to the police. When proper adjustments are made in the denominator to compensate for the problem of *hidden crime*, the clearance rate for the Part I Index Offenses drops to less than 10 percent. In reporting the department's annual clearance rate to the public, however, few police leaders mention this statistical problem associated with its calculation. Also left unstated is fact that "crimes cleared" frequently do not result in a criminal conviction.

Effectiveness versus Efficiency

The terms **effectiveness** and **efficiency** are routinely used interchangeably in discussions of performance evaluation, yet the two terms are quite different. Effectiveness refers to the extent to which an organization (or person) achieves its objectives; efficiency refers to the amount of energy, resources, time, money, etc., expended. Usually, an effective organization is an efficient organization, and vice versa. But clearly you can have one without the other. For example, an "efficient" police department may not waste much, but it may not accomplish much either. Conversely, a department may be "effective" in achieving its objectives, yet it may expend far more resources than need be. It is the direct responsibility of management to maximize the effectiveness and efficiency of the police department. The great many improvements made in policing in recent years (computerization, selection and training, management techniques, criminalistics, differential police response, etc.) have vastly improved both the effectiveness and efficiency of the police.

The Complexity of Evaluating the Police

Needless to say, evaluating police agencies and police officers is not a simple, straightforward process. It is not the same—and not as easy—as evaluating the performance of a business. For instance, if a basket company does not produce enough baskets (effectiveness), or does not produce them at a low enough cost (efficiency), the company will not show a profit. Similarly, if individual basket workers do not keep adequate pace, supervisors can easily determine this.

In policing, the product is not so easily quantifiable. This is a common problem to all human service agencies. But since counting human activities is so much easier than properly evaluating programs, we often find that performance measures in human service agencies boil down to counting the number of forms filed, number of clients seen, number of referrals made, and so on. In police work, the tendency has been to count the number of tickets handed out, arrests made, crimes committed, and crimes solved because it is easy to do. These numbers may or may not tell us what we want to know.

Standardized units of work measurement are not well established in policing. How many cases should a juvenile officer handle in a month? How many tickets should a traffic officer hand out? How many field reports should a patrol officer write? How many prostitutes should the vice squad arrest? The important point here is that it all depends—it depends on how serious the crime problem is to begin with, the wishes of the community, the department's resources, and the department's mission.

Certainly one should not attempt to evaluate a police department by its buildings, uniforms, patrol cars, or press notices, just as one should not judge a book by its cover. And one should not judge the quality of a police agency only by the level of crime in the community. Some communities are so crime free that an entire platoon of bumbling officers would look good. However, some communities are so crime infested that the best and brightest officers would be unable to contain it. In other words, *the level of crime is not necessarily a reflection of the performance of officers or the department: it may be a reflection of the community*. Efforts to evaluate the performance of the police, especially if they are linked to local crime rates, need to take the community factor into account.

POLICE LABOR ORGANIZATIONS

It is difficult to overstate the profound impact that police labor organizations have had in the past several decades. Walker describes police unionism as the *hidden revolution* in modern-day American policing.[51] Swanson and his associates go even further:

> No single force in the past half-century has had as much impact on the administration of police agencies as collective bargaining by officers. Police unions represent a major force that must be reckoned with by police managers.[52]

Private sector collective bargaining rights by employees were recognized as early as 1935 when the *National Labor Relations Act*, better known as the **Wagner Act,** was passed.[53] The Wagner Act gave employees in the private sector the right to form labor unions and to collectively negotiate the terms of their working conditions with their employers. Collective bargaining vastly improved the salary, fringe benefits, and grievance procedures of private sector employees, particularly workers in the manufacturing industries. Yet it was not until the 1960s that similar legislation was passed that permitted *public sector* collective bargaining. Until this time, employees in the public sector (e.g., teachers, sanitation workers, fire fighters, and police officers) were often prohibited by state law from forming labor unions. While police unionism has grown dramatically in recent years, several states still prohibit police officers from organizing a labor union.

The Boston Police Strike of 1919

Prior to the 1960s, there were several serious attempts to bring labor unions to policing. Almost without exception, these early attempts to unionize the police were quickly crushed—police administrators and city officials simply refused to recognize the collective bargaining rights of unions, and they had public opinion and the courts on their side.

The **Boston police strike of 1919** offers a valuable historical lesson in the police labor movement. The officers in Boston were not the first to try to unionize their department, nor were they the first to strike. Officers in the Ithaca, New York, Police Department walked off the job in 1889 when their wages were cut from $12 a week to $9. In 1897, officers in the Cleveland Police Department sought a charter from the American Federation of Labor (AFL) to organize a union. And, in 1918, there was a major strike by officers in Cincinnati and in London.[54]

The plight of Boston police officers during the early part of the twentieth century was symbolic of the plight of nearly all U.S. police officers.[55] Working conditions had deteriorated so badly over the years that the police officers in Boston would no longer tolerate it. Most patrol officers were working seventy-five to one-hundred hours per week for a little over $20. And because they were expected to work odd shifts with only a few hours off duty between assignments, officers frequently had to sleep at the station. Competitive exams for promotions were given, but the results were ignored. The police administra-

Police leaving Boston's city hall in the 1919 police strike.

tion hired and promoted whomever they wanted; lucky officers were usually political cronies being rewarded for their allegiance rather than their competence. To alleviate the terrible working conditions, the informal social club of the rank-and-file officers—the Boston Social Club—attempted to become a charter member of the AFL. On August 15, 1919, the AFL granted the request.

Now the trouble began. Three main players emerged as the drama unfolded over the next few weeks: Boston Police Commissioner Edwin Curtis, Boston Mayor Andrew Peters, and Massachusetts Governor Calvin Coolidge.[56] Police Commissioner Curtis did not want to bend at all to the demands of the officers, and he absolutely prohibited any of his men from organizing a union. As a result of Commissioner Curtis' stubbornness, the police threatened to strike. Mayor Peters had to act at this time to avert a crisis. Mayor Peters established a thirty-four-member investigating committee to look into the matter. Governor Calvin Coolidge conveniently stayed out of the picture. Mayor Peters and the investigating committee requested that Coolidge step in and arbitrate the situation, but Coolidge was hesitant to act.

Tensions continued to mount. On September 8, Commissioner Curtis suspended nineteen leaders of the unionization movement for violating his orders. Thinking this was the final straw, the officers agreed to go on strike the following morning, which they did—1,134 of them! With the exception of only a few volunteers, the city of Boston was without a police force.

A nervous standoff developed, not only between the police officers and the police administration but also between Mayor Peters and Governor Coolidge. Neither Mayor Peters nor Governor Coolidge wanted to make the first move out of fear that a wrong decision would be politically disastrous. The police strike was too volatile an issue to predict how the public would react to any political leadership.

But a crisis situation existed and *something* had to be done. Mayor Peters gave in first and took personal charge of the situation. Peters called in the National Guard to restore order in the city of Boston, and he fired Police Commissioner Curtis. Peters had to act forcefully, knowing full well that he would either emerge as the hero or the villain. The city streets initially erupted into mayhem. There was looting, extensive damage to property, and riots which ended the lives of seven persons. But the crisis soon subsided as the National Guard was able to restore order. It appeared that Mayor Peters was the champion.

The political story of the Boston police strike does not end here. Coolidge's absence from the entire ordeal was conspicuous and his political situation was beginning to look bleak. Mayor Peters was able to keep the city together through the crisis, yet the city was in need of a hero to champion, someone to rally behind. Mayor Peters did not fit the image, but Governor Coolidge did. Coolidge entered the scene in flamboyant fashion. This apparently was what the public wanted. Coolidge proclaimed that he was the "commander-in-chief," and asked the citizens of Boston to "aid me in the maintenance of law and order." Then Coolidge gave Commissioner Curtis his job back with the stipulation that he obey only the orders of the Governor.

It was obvious by this time that public sentiment was against the striking policemen, who were being portrayed as Benedict Arnolds. Coolidge used this discontentment to his advantage. The striking police officers voted unanimously to return to work, yet Coolidge refused. All striking police officers were permanently fired! Although Coolidge was sympathetic to the plight of the police officers, as a wise politician he could not go against the strong public opinion. It was then that Coolidge issued his most famous statement: *"There is no right to strike against the public safety by anybody anywhere, anytime."*[57]

In short, Coolidge became the hero of the Boston police strike through clever politics. Coolidge won another term as governor of Massachusetts and later went on to the White House. The Boston police strike helped stir up the idea of police unions. But its lack of success created an effective management strategy for police leaders to follow for the next forty years when faced with a unionization movement—that is, *crush it!*

Unionization in the 1960s

The growth of police unions in the 1960s was perhaps less "revolutionary" than "evolutionary." The idea of unionizing the police never entirely drowned in the wake of the Boston police strike; unionization has been an on again/off again issue in policing. What largely accounted for the success of the police union movement when earlier attempts failed was the changing social and legal landscape of the 1960s. One major factor was the changing state laws that permitted public sector collective bargaining. Wisconsin became the first state to pass such a law in 1959, and many other states soon followed. Another important factor was the continuing dissatisfaction with the salary, fringe benefits, and working conditions of police work. The police felt the working conditions were unfair and that they were not adequately compensated for their difficult job.

Police Labor Organizations Today

It is not easy to get exact figures on the number of police officers who are members of a labor organization. First, many officers belong to more than one association, which complicates the counting process. And second, some police associations are labor-oriented while others are merely social clubs. Nonetheless, the percentage of officers who belong to some type of labor organization is estimated to be somewhere between 50 to 75 percent.[58]

There are many different types of police labor organizations in the United States. Some labor organizations are backed by a large national industrial union, some are independent government employee organizations, and some are independent police organizations.[59] The following list identifies several of the more common labor organizations for police officers:

• AFSCME—The American Federation of State, County, and Municipal Employees (affiliated with the AFL-CIO);

- *AFGE*—The American Federation of Government Employees (also affiliated with the AFL-CIO);
- *IBT*—The International Brotherhood of Teamsters, Chauffeurs, Warehousemen, and Helpers of America (better known as the Teamsters);
- *IBPO*—International Brotherhood of Police Officers;
- *ICPA*—International Conference of Police Associations;
- *IUPA*—International Union of Police Associations;
- *FOP*—Fraternal Order of Police.

Collective Bargaining

At the heart of all labor organizations is the process of **collective bargaining.** As the name implies, collective bargaining represents a unified and powerful voice in negotiating the conditions of workers' employment. It replaces the practice of individual employees dealing directly with management for the terms of employment, such as salary, fringe benefits, grievance procedures, etc. Currently, several states still do not recognize the right of collective bargaining by police associations. Most of these states are in the southern region of the country, which traditionally has been "anti-union." Even in states that permit public sector collective bargaining, there is substantial variation in how it is conducted.

In private sector collective bargaining, the negotiations are *bilateral.* Bilateral refers to the fact that only two sides are involved in the bargaining process—the union and the employer. However, in the public sector the process of collective bargaining is *multilateral*, meaning that more than just the police union and police management are involved in the contract talks. For example, in a municipal police department the mayor's office and city council also may be involved in the negotiation. The county manager and commissioners may be involved in contact negotiations with a sheriff's department, and representatives from the governor's office and state legislature may be involved in negotiations with state-level police agencies. Over the years, the role of the police chief in direct contract negotiations has diminished. As a general rule, the mayor has the authority to agree to a new police contract but it is up to the city council to pay for it. This may require increasing taxes.

The collective bargaining process sometimes comes to a halt when the negotiators cannot agree on a final contract. This is called an **impasse.** Several different approaches exist to try to work through the impasse. *Mediation* is a voluntary procedure where a neutral third party comes in and tries to settle the problem. The recommendations of a mediator are nonbinding. *Fact-finding* is similar to mediation in that the suggestions offered are nonbinding. A neutral third party gathers information relevant to the impasse and then offers a recommendation, which either or both sides may reject. Finally, *arbitration* uses an outside party to make a binding decision. Arbitration may be voluntary or compulsory. In voluntary arbitration, the sides agree to let an outside person or agency arbitrate the problem, and they also agree beforehand to accept the decision. When arbitration is compulsory, the government steps in and appoints an outside arbitrator to make a binding decision regardless of whether the disputing sides want to go to arbitration.[60]

Occasionally, police officers take it upon themselves to alter their work habits as a way to express their dissatisfaction. This is known as a **job action.** Police officers can be highly creative when dissatisfied, resulting in a wide variety of job actions. For example, the mysterious "blue flu" has struck hundreds of police departments in recent years. *Work slowdowns* are a common type of job action, as are *work speedups* (e.g., writing many tickets to anger the public). And while most state laws forbid police officers from engaging in the ultimate job action of striking (because of the essential nature of police services), this has not stopped officers in a number of departments from walking off the job. Interestingly, at least one study has found that police strikes have no significant impact on rates of reported crime.[61] Erdwin Pfuhl examined FBI data of police strikes in eleven U.S. cities and found no appreciable increase in reported rates of burglary, robbery, larceny, or auto theft.

POLICE UNIONS: STRATEGIES FOR SUCCESSFUL COLLECTIVE BARGAINING*

1. *Balance the power*
   The police union must establish a strong sense of solidarity among the officers ("one for all and all for one"). A cunning management strategy is to break up the solidarity. Firing union leaders used to be common, but this is no longer legal. Police management may try to co-opt the union leaders by promoting them to management, or they may try to transfer the union leaders around the department to diminish their effectiveness.

2. *Lock the union in so it cannot bargain*
   A part of successful bargaining is not to bargain. Police unions should elevate the expectations of their members so even reasonable offers by the other side will be rejected. (Watch out! The city may lock its side in by saying there is no additional money in the budget.) Locking your side in is very much like the game of "chicken." The rational bargaining strategy here is to be irrational.

3. *Bargain away what is not wanted*
   Doing so gives the appearance that the union is bargaining in good faith. This may encourage the other side to start giving real concessions. The union has the option of categorizing each clause in the contract as *expendable* (meaning they may drop the request as a show of good faith), *trade-off* (union will drop the demand if management offers something in return), *negotiable* (union will not drop this one without a fight), or *non-negotiable.* Mark every clause in the contract "non-negotiable."

4. *Strike*
   Police unions must convince the other side they are foolish enough to go out on strike if their demands are not met. (Watch out again! Management may be foolish enough to let you strike.) An occasional strike is beneficial because it maintains the credibility of the union.

5. *Don't strike for long*
   Strikes are disastrous. Solidarity quickly diminishes, the public gets mad at the union, and striking officers are not paid. If the strike lasts more than a few days, the strikers may never make up in lost wages what they eventually win at the bargaining table.

*Note: These strategies are *not* guaranteed to work.

Job actions engaged in by a large share of the police force are a particularly difficult problem for police management to handle properly. Obviously the best management strategy is to try to avoid them, but this is not always possible. If the job action appears to be minor and only temporary, the best approach may be to ignore it and plan to rectify the problem that led to the action. On the other hand, if the job action blatantly undermines the ability of the department to serve the public, swift and decisive administrative action is in order.

CONCLUSION

Police management is a highly complex and multifaceted endeavor. This is especially true today as many troublesome issues confront American law enforcement. The contents of this chapter touched on only some of the more pressing issues relating to modern-day, professional police management. The task of management was described as the bringing together of people and resources to accomplish some end or objective. Managers are also responsible for motivating people to carry out the work of the organization. Among the specific tasks of management are the classic POSDCORB activities: *p*lanning, *o*rganizing, *s*taffing, *d*irecting, *co*ordinating, *r*eporting, and *b*udgeting.

The organizational health of a police department is contingent in large part on the success or failure of its top leadership. Not all police leaders are equally effective. Top-notch police leaders possess a number of desirable qualities, such as intelligence, integrity, technical expertise, vision, and the ability to motivate people. The majority of "top cops" rise through the administrative ranks by way of consecutive promotions. This is known as *inside promotion*. However, a sizable minority of departments select their chiefs through *outside promotion*. As noted in the chapter, both recruitment methods for police chiefs offer advantages and disadvantages. Regardless of how police leaders are selected, they generally enjoy very little job security (police chiefs hold their positions, on average, only around three to five years). Several prestigious professional organizations for police managers (e.g., the International Association of Chiefs of Police) have advocated some type of guaranteed job tenure for police chiefs.

Labor organizations have had a profound impact on American policing in the last three decades. Although the earliest attempts to unionize the police failed, as exemplified by the Boston police strike of 1919, the 1960s were a boon for police labor organizations. While not all police labor organizations are as potent or powerful as others, they do share something in common—through collective bargaining, they attempt to represent the interests of all rank-and-file officers. Police labor organizations have won important victories for police officers in the United States in terms of improved salaries and fringe benefits, better working conditions, fairer grievance procedures, and greater influence in administrative decision making. Overall, labor organizations have made many positive contributions to policing. However, not all activities of labor unions have served the immediate needs of citizens (e.g., work slowdowns, strikes, "blue flu"), and many believe that police unionism is antithetical to police professionalism. Whether or not police labor organizations will promote or detract from police professionalism in the future, only time will tell.

KEY TERMS

POSDCORB
inside promotion
outside promotion
tenure
administrative rule making
management by objectives
neighborhood team policing
Community Sector Team Policing
management styles
Theory X and Theory Y

performance evaluation
clearance rate
effectiveness
efficiency
Wagner Act
Boston police strike of 1919
collective bargaining
impasse
job action

DISCUSSION QUESTIONS

1. Why is the task of police management becoming more difficult with time?
2. Discuss the pros and cons associated with inside and outside selection of police chiefs. Which do you believe is better, and why?
3. Discuss the different styles of management identified in the chapter. In what ways have police management styles been changing in recent decades? What type of police manager do you think you would be?
4. Suppose you were given the job of developing new measures of performance evaluation for police officers. Suppose further that your method of evaluation was to be the model of the twenty-first century. What would you come up with? (Remember, the police do more than just enforce the law.)

The two remaining chapters of this book examine important contemporary concerns and future challenges in American policing. Chapter 13 assesses some of the most critical issues in modern-day police work. Crucial topics such as the effectiveness of women patrol officers, deadly force, controlling police misconduct, and AIDS receive our serious attention. The final chapter of the book presents a general synthesis and conclusion. Here we identify ten of the more important lessons to be learned from our study of American police. We also provide a profile of the emerging role of the police. The last section in chapter 14 ends our study of American police with a brief discussion of *good* policing.

Contemporary Concerns and Future Challenges

CHAPTER THIRTEEN

CRITICAL ISSUES IN AMERICAN POLICING

The struggle to maintain a proper balance between effective law enforcement and fairness to individuals pervades the entire criminal justice system.

—President's Commission on Law Enforcement and Administration of Justice, 1967

328

PART V:
CONTEMPORARY
CONCERNS AND
FUTURE
CHALLENGES

There are a great number of critical issues in American policing today. Many of these issues have been discussed in previous chapters, some only in passing and others in depth. This chapter takes a closer look at a few of these more pressing issues.

It must be noted that the topics covered here have been selected somewhat arbitrarily—other critical issues also deserving of our attention could have been selected just as easily. We shall begin with the issue of women doing police patrol work.

WOMEN ON PATROL

Police work is a male-dominated occupation. This was true hundreds of years ago when early laws required all able-bodied "men" to serve their communities as citizen police, and it is still true today although to a lesser extent. Over the past several decades, women have struggled to enter occupations traditionally the domain of men. With the clear exception of professional sports, it is difficult to identify an occupation that is strictly segregated on the basis of gender. Although we are far from achieving true equality in the workplace, women continue to make significant strides.

It is important to realize that women have been working as police officers for over one hundred years. Policewomen in the last decades of the nineteenth century and the first years of the twentieth century were usually appointed to serve as police matrons for women and children in custody.[1] Most of these early policewomen had a background in social work and, for all practical purposes, were social workers rather than police officers. Over the years, female officers performed other duties as well, such as clerical work, records, communications, and parking enforcement. It was not until 1968 in Indianapolis, Indiana, that the first two female officers began working as regular patrol officers.[2] Washington, D.C., was the first U.S. city to send women out on patrol in large numbers in 1972, and New York City did the same the following year. By comparison, both Britain and Germany have utilized females in regular patrol work since the early years of this century.[3]

Lola Baldwin was the first woman police officer of distinction in the United States. In 1905, the town fathers of Portland, Oregon, appointed Baldwin to handle the growing number of spirited young women soliciting the lumberjacks, miners, and vacationers in the area. Baldwin was instrumental in creating the Department of Public Safety for the Protection of Young Girls and Women to deal with the problem.[4]

Alice Wells became the first sworn policewoman with the power of arrest in 1910 in Los Angeles.[5] Wells convinced the police department and the city council that she could be far more effective protecting women and children if she had arrest powers. Other cities were soon requesting the aid of Wells to set up similar programs for female officers in their cities. Wells is also credited with organizing the first association for female officers in 1915, known as the *International Association of Policewomen*. This organization sought to encourage professionalism among female officers by raising work standards and by promoting the concept of protective services in police departments.[6]

Today it is common to see female officers working the streets, not simply as meter maids or juvenile officers as was the case in years past, but as fully functioning patrol officers. However, many female patrol officers have not been fully accepted by male officers. Making inroads into the male-dominated world of policing has been difficult, to put it mildly. Although women comprise approximately one-half of the total population, they still comprise less than 10 percent of all sworn police officers in this country. The representation of women police officers in managerial ranks is even lower. Optimistic projections to the end of the twentieth century estimate there will be 50,000 women in U.S. law enforcement. This will still only represent about 20 percent of all sworn officers.[7]

Arguments Against Women Patrol Officers

Among detractors, there is no shortage of reasons why women should not be patrol officers:

- Women are too weak physically;
- Women are too delicate emotionally;
- Women tend to fall apart in crisis situations;
- Women do not see policing as a long-term career;
- Women are not able to command the respect of citizens;
- Women undermine citizen confidence in police;
- Women patrol partners destroy marriages.

Female officers and administrators are becoming more prevalent. Here, Elizabeth A. Watson is sworn in as police chief of Houston in 1990.

330

PART V:
CONTEMPORARY
CONCERNS AND
FUTURE
CHALLENGES

"Physical fragility" seems to be the most persistent reason given why women—at least ordinary women—should not become patrol officers. As the argument goes, since women are genetically smaller and weaker than males, they do not have the physical size and strength, particularly upper-body and forearm strength, to properly perform the job. As a result, even minor scuffles exceed the limited physical capacity of female officers. The inability of the typical female officer to handle such disturbances on her own forces the strapping male officers to protect the female officer. Police leaders mindful of their dual responsibility of protecting citizens *and* protecting their officers are forced to either "spread out" female officers among the regular platoons, or assign them to the "easy" beats.

The arguments against female officers comes close to Susan Martin's description of **police*women*.**[8] Police*women* adopt the more traditional feminine role as they struggle to maintain their "ladylike" self-image both on and off the job. Police*women* believe they truly are at a disadvantage on the streets due to their physical limitations, and they often feel like they do not fit in with the other officers. Police*women* are noticeably uncomfortable interacting with citizens and tend to be passive in demeanor. Generally, police*women* do not think about policing as a long-term career commitment and are not interested in promotion.

Martin contrasts police*women* with ***police*women.** *Police*women share the predominant police norms and strive hard to be as good as male officers. *Police*women are law-enforcement oriented, enjoy the challenges of the job, and interact confidently with citizens. And just like many male officers, *police*women also view police*women* with disdain:

> I know I'm a woman and have different plumbing from the men I work with. . . . Some other women think what they sit on is worth a million dollars and fail to see themselves as human beings. . . . They think all the men want to get into their pants. This is an immature and egotistical attitude. If you act with self-confidence, people treat you as a human being and you can carry yourself accordingly. . . . The men would rather be protected by a policewoman on duty than screw her afterwards. . . . What they care about is that you do your job.[9]

Debunking the Arguments

To begin with, it must be made clear that the arguments listed above against female officers have never been substantiated by empirical evidence. In other words, (1) female officers are not *too* weak or *too* emotional for the job, (2) females are just as committed as males to law enforcement as a career, (3) citizens have not lost faith in the police because of female officers, and (4) there is absolutely no credence to the argument that female patrol partners destroy marriages. While an occasional adulterous affair does happen in policing, as it will in any occupation, clearly no party is innocent. In addition, as we shall discover momentarily, extensive research on female patrol officers shows them to be just as effective on the streets as male officers. Nonetheless, the skeptics are hard to convince and generally do not want to hear what the research has to say.

Let us take another look at the persistent theme that females as a group are not strong enough for the rigors of police work. Surely the average female officer is physically weaker than the average male officer—genetics assures us of this basic fact. But to argue that females make unsatisfactory police officers because they are physically weaker than males is to make an error in logic on two counts. First, the argument assumes that effective police work *requires* above-average strength, which it does not. What police work does require is intelligence, composure, quick thinking, and exceptional verbal skills. These traits may be found in both sexes. While it is true that female officers sometimes have to rely on pure physical strength to perform their duty (as do other traditional female jobs such as nursing, teaching, and cleaning), gladiator-style confrontations are a statistical rarity. Yet when street battles occur, a female officer wielding a nightstick can be just as effective as a male officer with a nightstick.

The second error of logic is the assumption that all male officers are physically endowed for the job. Many, in fact, are not. Too many hefty male officers are incapable of sustained physical exertion like that required in chasing a mugging suspect on foot. And there is a fair number of slight male officers who posses only minimum upper body strength. These male officers would be at a grave disadvantage if paired off against a large, angry man if they were not properly trained in self-defense tactics or nightstick use. The point here is that "massive muscles" and the eagerness to use them is not—and should not be—a necessary requirement for the modern-day, professional police officer.

We may even speculate that female officers are likely to reduce the need for aggression. Unlike large male officers whose physical presence and intimidating body language is usually perceived as threatening by suspects, the smaller physical presence of female (and slight male) officers is more disarming than menacing; if a suspect expects less trouble, they are likely to give less trouble. The reason why police departments across the country have eliminated minimum height requirements of 5'9" and above is because physical size (and exceptional strength) has never been demonstrated to be an occupational qualification for police work.

Arguments in Favor of Women Patrol Officers

Linn and Price identify several reasons why women should be employed in all facets of law enforcement:

- It is illegal to discriminate against women in employment decisions;
- Women officers are often good at getting useful information from crime victims and witnesses;
- Women officers signal the message that the police department is committed to serving the interests of the entire community;
- Law enforcement policy needs diverse views, especially from women and minorities;
- Women officers serve as useful role models. [10]

332

**PART V:
CONTEMPORARY
CONCERNS AND
FUTURE
CHALLENGES**

An additional argument in favor of women police officers may be made—American policing might benefit from being *de-machoed*. Recall from chapter 2 our comparison of the stereotypical "gentleman bobbie" of Britain and the rough, tough, predominately male, and decidedly macho U.S. cop. To paraphrase an anonymous policewoman, it used to be that all you had to do was to put on the blue uniform and you became a man with "all the symbols of manhood hanging from your belt." Bringing women onto the force as patrol officers takes away this automatic symbolic source of manhood, thereby serving to emasculate the profession.

The entry of large numbers of women into police work offers the opportunity to radically redefine this common negative stereotype from the "macho cop" to the "compassionate professional," an image much more in step with the modern ideal of police professionalism. This will only happen as long as women do not try to emulate the exaggerated masculine image of a police officer.

Evaluating Women Patrol Officers

Female police officers have been patrolling American streets for over two decades. This is a sufficient period of time to assess their performance. The first and best study to date was the 1974 Police Foundation study of women patrol officers in Washington, D.C.[11] For an entire year, eighty-six rookie female patrol officers and a matched control group of eighty-six newly hired male officers were thoroughly evaluated by supervisors, trained field observers, and citizens. Given the extensiveness of comparisons, one would expect some differences between male and female officers, which there were. Specifically, the study found that women tended to make fewer arrests and to issue fewer traffic tickets than males, but the conviction rates between the two groups were nearly identical. Also, though women did not take more sick days than men, they were more likely to be assigned to light duty as a result of job-related injuries. One of the most striking differences was that males officers were more likely to be charged with conduct unbecoming an officer.

Despite the few differences between rookie male and female officers, the similarity in style and performance was remarkable. The final report summarizes the investigators' findings:

> The men and women studied for this report performed patrol work in a generally similar manner. They responded to similar types of calls for police service while on patrol and encountered similar proportions of citizens who were dangerous, angry, upset, drunk, or violent. Both men and women officers were observed to obtain similar results in handling angry or violent citizens. There were no reported incidents which cast any serious doubt on the ability of women to perform patrol work satisfactorily.[12]

A similar study of the first wave of female officers in New York City from October 1973 to March 1974 came to the same overall conclusion as the Washington, D.C. study—that is, no meaningful statistical differences were found between male and female officers.[13] The overwhelming weight of more recent evaluations also confirm these earlier findings.

To summarize our discussion, it is clear that women patrol officers have proven themselves quite capable of doing the job, even though not all citizens nor all male police officers fully agree with this conclusion. Nonetheless, women police officers are here to stay, and policing will never again be the same. As was previously suggested, the large-scale entry of women into policing has the potential to radically redefine and improve the image of police work.

DEADLY FORCE

One of the most volatile issues in American law enforcement is the use of **deadly force**. Drawing, aiming, and firing a weapon at another human being is the ultimate street-level discretionary decision a police officer can ever make. When an officer uses deadly force, he or she is literally making a life-and-death decision. Tremendously complicating the decision to use deadly force is the necessity for clear, levelheaded thinking in a split second when "all hell is busting loose." Concerned citizens, the media, and the courts have the luxury of time to review a deadly force decision. All the facts pertinent to the case can be carefully assessed, safely removed from the time and place of the shooting. The police officer has no such luxury—the decision to use deadly force is thrust upon the officer, and a spontaneous decision must be made.

Accurate statistics are not readily available on the number of firearm discharges by police officers in the line of duty. It is difficult just to get a complete count of the number of criminal suspects killed every year in the United States by police officers; getting an accurate count on the number of non-lethal firearm discharges is even more difficult. A national system of recording line-of-duty firearm discharges does not exist, and police departments are seldom eager to publicize their figures. Also unavailable are data revealing the number of times officers are able to avoid the use of deadly force in apprehending a suspect when they would have had legal justification to fire their weapon.

William Geller of the American Bar Foundation conservatively estimates that every year the police kill approximately six hundred criminal suspects, wound another 1,200 suspects, and shoot at but miss around 1,800 suspects.[14] This totals around 3,600 deadly force decisions (attempted and completed) by public police officers every year. While at first glance the figures appear to be rather high, the number of deadly force decisions must be considered relative to the millions of potentially dangerous situations the approximately 750,000 public police officers confront yearly.

Most firearm discharges by the police happen at night, take place in the larger cities, occur in public areas, and involve uniform patrol officers. Criminal suspects shot by the police are more likely wanted for armed robbery than any other offense category.[15]

The Question of Unequal Deadly Force

A major reason why shootings by police officers are highly contentious is because certain segments of the population are more likely to be killed by the police. By overwhelming odds, blacks, males, and young adults between the ages of eighteen and thirty are the most frequent targets of police shootings. For example, data from Chicago, New York, and Los Angeles reveal that approximately 70 percent of the people wounded or killed by police bullets are black, 20 percent are Hispanic, and 10 percent are white.[16] Over 90 percent of criminal suspects shot by the police are males, most of whom are in their young adult years. The shooting pattern by police appears to have remarkable consistency from one place to another and over time, fluctuating only in response to the different sociodemographic composition of local communities.

The unequal distribution of deadly force provides critics of the police with powerful ammunition. Police shootings have the appearance of being prejudicial and discriminatory. While few critics charge the police with *ageism* or *sexism* for their disproportionate shootings of "young" "males," charges of *racism* abound. One outraged scholar contends that "police have one trigger finger for whites and another for blacks."[17] Adding credibility to the charges of racism are three additional factors. First, far too often and for too long throughout our history some police officers have been racists. Second, an

---

14 FATAL SHOOTINGS BY NYC POLICE TRIGGER REVIEW OF DEADLY-FORCE RULES

New York City Police Commissioner Lee P. Brown, whose tenure has been scarred by a rash of police shootings that have resulted in 14 civilian fatalities so far this year, is not ready to say there are problems with the department's shooting policy, but neither is he about to take any chances. On March 21, he named a five-member committee of law enforcement experts to review existing guidelines on the use of deadly force.

"We see an unprecedented level of violence in the city—violence of citizen against citizen, unprovoked attacks against police officers, and indeed we are concerned about the number of shootings that members of the department have been involved in," said Brown in announcing the formation of the Firearms Policy Committee.

Brown said his appointment of the committee does not imply that current regulations on the use of firearms are a failure, but said the policy may need revision because the nature of crime in

the city "has undergone a dramatic transformation" due to the epidemic of crack use since the mid-1980's. The guidelines, drafted in 1972 during the administration of Commissioner Patrick V. Murphy, are similar to those of the FBI and numerous other police agencies, permitting the use of deadly force when a life is in jeopardy.

The committee will review firearms guidelines and training procedures and examine the way shootings by police are reported. It will have three months to study the problem before making its final recommendations.

Five of the shooting deaths were of teenagers, and the incidents have angered city residents and sparked protests. The latest fatal shooting occurred on March 2, when a knife-wielding Brooklyn man who had threatened to kill himself lunged at police, who were responding to a 911 call made by the 20-year-old man's father.

Source: *Law Enforcement News* (John Jay College of Criminal Justice, New York, 1990) XVI (No. 311): p. 3.

undeniable yet undocumentable proportion of shootings by police officers today are racially motivated. And third, activist organizations such as the NAACP (National Association for the Advancement of Colored People) and the ACLU (American Civil Liberties Union) mount effective media campaigns in the aftermath of police shootings that appear to be racially motivated.

In defense of seemingly racist (also ageist and sexist) deadly force decisions, police leaders are quick to point out that nearly all shootings are determined to be justified, not only by internal department inquiry but also by prosecutorial investigation and through impartial judicial hearings. In most police shootings, officers fire their weapons in self-defense or in defense of another person. Yet findings of "justified deadly force" do not always make citizens feel better or make the department look good. Such was the case in Arlington, Texas a few years ago when a police officer fatally shot three suspects in a six-month period and was later cleared of any wrongdoing. The police chief fired the officer in early 1989 after notches were found etched into his 9mm pistol, apparently as death tallies.

The fact that police shootings disproportionately affect certain groups is easily explained. That is, while the police shoot a greater proportion of young black males compared to their representation in the general population, the number shot is *not* out of proportion to their representation in serious violent crime, nor their residence in high-crime neighborhoods. The same rationale is used to explain why most police shootings happen at night, in public places, and in larger cities—this is the time and place of the most serious crime and the most danger to police officers. Assignment to more dangerous districts is also the main reason why black police officers are more likely to shoot—and be shot at—than white police officers.

Controlling Deadly Force

Deadly force decisions by police officers have come under increased scrutiny in recent years. The rash of civil and criminal litigation has pressured police leaders to tighten their control over deadly force decisions of street officers. Most departments have had to rethink their existing deadly force policies, and many departments have had to entirely revise vague polices to limit the extent of police officer discretion. Stricter guidelines on the use of deadly force are both a necessary and positive development in modern policing. The restrained, closely controlled use of deadly force is consistent with police professionalism.

The courts have been instrumental in controlling excessive use of deadly force. Several important decisions have found fault with certain deadly force practices. The 1985 *Garner* case is the most sweeping decision.[18] In *Tennessee v. Garner* the U.S. Supreme Court banned the use of deadly force to stop unarmed, fleeing felony suspects, a police practice with roots dating back to the Middle Ages. The court limited police to use deadly force *only as a last resort* to prevent a felony escape *if and only if* the fleeing suspect is believed to pose a grave danger to the officer or to others. The police are strictly forbidden to use their revolver to halt a fleeing misdemeanor suspect.

Disarming the Police

We mentioned in a previous chapter that the British police do not carry guns while on routine patrol. While this practice may seem foolhardy to many Americans, most Britons (and probably most British police officers as well) would not want their police to be armed. The major reason is because Britain does not have a serious gun problem, at least not compared to the United States. For example, since the beginning of this century fewer than one hundred British police officers have been feloniously killed in the line of duty. Yet during the decade of the 1980s alone, 801 U.S. police officers were killed, mostly by handguns.[19] But another reason is that being unarmed provides a crucial benefit to British police-community relations—that is, the police might risk losing public support if they were to start carrying guns. Moreover, being armed may attract the "wrong" type of police recruit.

Nearly all U.S. police departments require officers to carry a firearm while on duty, and many departments (especially the larger ones) require off-duty officers to be armed when in public. On more than one occasion, armed

---

TENNESSEE V. GARNER (1985)

FACTS OF CASE

On the evening of October 3, 1974, at approximately 10:45 P.M., Officers Elton Hymon and Leslie Wright of the Memphis Police Department responded to a call about a prowler inside a house. Arriving at the scene, the officers saw a woman on her porch motioning the police toward the adjacent house. She said she heard glass breaking and believed an intruder was trying to enter the house. Officer Wright radioed that they were at the scene while Officer Hymon went to the back of the house, where he heard a door slam and saw someone run away. The suspect, a fifteen-year-old eighth grader named Edward Garner, was stopped by a six-foot high chain link fence at the edge of the yard. The officer had his flashlight trained on Garner so he could plainly see the suspect's face and hands; no weapon was observed. Officer Hymon yelled "Police! Halt!" as he approached Garner. Garner proceeded to climb the fence. The officer felt sure that if the suspect made it over the fence, he would escape completely. At that point Officer Hymon aimed his revolver at Garner and pulled the trigger. The bullet hit Garner in the back of the head—he died on the operating table later that evening. Police recovered from Garner ten dollars and a purse taken from the house. No gun was found.

Subsequent investigation found the shooting by Officer Hymon in compliance with the Tennessee statute that authorized the use of deadly force to stop unarmed fleeing felons. Cleamtee Garner, the victim's father, brought suit claiming that the Tennessee statute was unconstitutional. The Tennessee courts upheld the constitutionality of the fleeing felon statute. The case was appealed to the Supreme Court of the United States.

COURT DECISION

The High Court ruled in favor of Cleamtee Garner. The Tennessee fleeing felon statute was declared unconstitutional.

IMPACT OF CASE

The Garner case established new guidelines for the use of deadly force to stop fleeing felons. Police are no longer able to use deadly force to stop *all* fleeing felons as this is now considered constitutionally impermissible. The Supreme Court held that the use of deadly force against a fleeing felon is permissible only when there is no other way to prevent escape *and* the suspect poses a real threat of death or serious injury to the officer or someone else.

off-duty officers (as well as armed, on-duty undercover detectives) have been mistaken as a criminal suspect and shot by uniformed officers. By one count, police bullets wounded 38 percent of the 187 Chicago police officers shot from 1974 to 1978. So frequently do police bullets strike police officers that the *armed robber* and the *armed officer* are jokingly referred to as the deadliest threats to police.[20]

Consider the following facts: (1) many shootings by law enforcement officers represent less than meritorious police work; (2) a substantial percentage of police officers who are shot are struck by their own bullets (accident, suicide, or suspect wrestles gun from officer) or the bullets from another officer's gun (accident or mistaken identity); and (3) the average U.S. police officer never fires his or her weapon in a deadly force situation during an entire career. Given these facts, does it follow that police sidearms are too deadly for society? Is it feasible to disarm U.S. police officers? *Can we emulate the British model of "no guns"?*

Perhaps the only rational answer to the question is "No!" We cannot disarm U.S. police officers, *at least not now.* To do so would prove disastrous for police officers and law-abiding citizens alike. But why?

First, unlike in Britain, the gun is truly part of the American heritage, history, and culture. Gun ownership is considered by many Americans a basic constitutional right and a symbol of individual liberty. A strict ban on gun ownership for any law-abiding segment of the population would be defined as *un-American.* Second, criminals are often better armed than the police and hardly likely to voluntarily disarm themselves if the police disarm. Criminals are also more erratic shooters than the police as they lack comparable firearms expertise. Third, unarmed police officers would face tremendous personal risk in dangerous situations. Fourth, disarming the police would weaken deterrence, thereby increasing crime and social disorder. And fifth, in the wake of increasing crime and elevated citizen fear, vigilantism would likely increase. Citizens would feel the need to protect themselves and take the law into their own hands.

There is no denying that the United States has a different gun problem than the British. To exaggerate, "everyone and their brother has a gun." Handguns are a major problem in the United States; they are readily available, require no special training or physical skill to use, and are easily concealed.

Opponents of handgun control claim the following: "Handguns don't kill, people do." In only the most technical sense is this statement true— people are the ones who aim and pull the trigger. Yet handguns are extremely effective in destroying human tissue and organs. The only trick is to hit the target:

> The fury of a victim can exceed his skill at handling a weapon defensively. A Kansas City couple, Thomas Hill, 76, and his wife Lillian, 72, were surprised by an intruder in their home. Thomas picked up a pistol off a table and fired. The intruder grabbed the gun. Thomas pulled a second pistol out of his pocket and tried six shots. The robber seized that gun too. Lillian emerged from the kitchen and squeezed off three more shots. Not one bullet hit the invader, who

338

PART V:
CONTEMPORARY
CONCERNS AND
FUTURE
CHALLENGES

escaped with all three guns. As he fled, he avoided three more rifle shots from a neighbor.[21]

The important point is that using one's fists, a club, or a cutting instrument requires close proximity and some physical ability to be dangerous. However, even the weak and timid can fire a handgun

Disarming Off-Duty Police

If disarming police officers who are on duty is not feasible, what about off-duty police? Should officers who are off duty and out of uniform carry a firearm?

It is estimated there are between 250,000 and 500,000 armed off-duty police in the United States at any one time. Some departments *permit* officers to carry a firearm while off duty, and other departments *require* officers to be armed. Conventional wisdom offers three rationales for allowing off-duty officers to carry guns: (1) police work is a twenty-four-hour-a-day job, meaning that police officers are expected to actively intervene in crime situations at all times; (2) armed off-duty officers provide an important crime control function; and (3) police officers need protection at all times from vindictive criminals.[22] As laudable as these rationales seem, a high percentage of firearm discharges by off-duty officers are of dubious integrity.

James Fyfe examined firearm discharges by off-duty New York City police officers.[23] Off-duty New York City police officers are required to be armed when inside city limits and are permitted to carry a firearm when outside the city. Between 1971 and 1975, Fyfe documented 681 firearm discharges by off-duty officers excluding target practice. The shootings took place under a variety of circumstances.

Fyfe discovered the vast majority of off-duty shootings were justified. Approximately seven in ten shootings were either for defense purposes (self-defense or defense of others) or to stop a crime in progress. If the destruction of dangerous or seriously injured animals is included, roughly 75 percent of firearm discharges by off-duty officers appear valid. However, this means 173 of the 681 bullets (25 percent) discharged by off-duty officers were not valid. Over half of these "bad" shootings (eighty-six) were accidental, another twenty-six were suicidal, and sixty-one were not ascertainable.[24]

Fyfe's study is two decades old and predates the 1985 *Garner* decision. But if New York City of the 1970s was at all typical of police departments today, and we cannot be sure until more research is conducted, the most immediate policy question is whether departments should stop requiring off-duty officers to carry a gun. First, it is not altogether clear if the harm caused by armed off-duty officers (to themselves and others) is outweighed by the public good. And second, it may not be fair to the officer or the officer's family. An off-duty officer is likely to be (1) less alert than when on duty, perhaps even under the influence of alcohol; (2) in regular clothes, which may cause responding patrol officers to mistake the officer for the suspect; (3)

out of communication with headquarters; and (4) without adequate backup.

339

CHAPTER 13:
Critical Issues in
American Policing

Whether or not we should disarm off-duty officers is a serious policy question with no clear answer at this point in time. However, it is a necessary decision that police leaders and law makers need to carefully consider.

CONTROLLING POLICE MISCONDUCT

American policing has established two general mechanisms to control police misconduct—**internal** and **external control** (not to be confused with internal and external *corruption* as discussed in chapter 9). Both internal and external control are useful strategies for holding the police accountable to the public. They may be used simultaneously or independently of one another. Broadly speaking, internal control relies on managerial and administrative efforts to control police misconduct while external control utilizes the monitoring capacity of groups outside the police agency. In short, internal review means the police are policing their own; external review means others are assigned this important task.

Internal Control Mechanisms

One hallmark of a profession is the capacity to discipline its own members whenever an ethical or legal violation occurs. For example, the *American Bar Association* performs this "internal review" function for the legal profession, and the *American Medical Association* does the same for the medical profession. Even elected representatives of the state and federal government have the authority to investigate and censor wayward colleagues; a House or Senate ethics committee examines all pertinent evidence against the member in question and makes a disciplinary decision. In serious cases of misconduct, the elected representative may be removed from office. Similarly, a crooked lawyer or an incompetent doctor may have his or her license revoked through internal review. By comparison, American policing has not attained this level of professional control, nor does the *professional prototype* of internal control appear likely to materialize in the near future.

Nonetheless, law enforcement has available other strategies of internal control that can be highly effective in controlling police misconduct. Three internal control strategies are most common: (1) enhanced supervisory control, (2) strong leadership, and (3) internal affairs divisions.

Enhanced Supervisory Control

One useful technique to improve the internal monitoring of personnel is enhanced supervisory control. Enhanced supervisory control is often accomplished by tightening existing department regulations, reformulating ambiguous policies and procedures, or by establishing closer field contact between officers and supervisors. Requiring officers to "check in" regularly with dispatch

340

PART V:
CONTEMPORARY
CONCERNS AND
FUTURE
CHALLENGES

or to keep daily logs of their patrol activities are other useful supervisory strategies.

Strong Leadership

Strong police leadership is another internal control mechanism. The top administrators in a police agency set the tone for the entire department. Progressive, reform-minded leaders with effective administrative skills can do more to control misconduct among the rank and file than perhaps any other factor.

Strong police leaders make department policy *explicit* regarding what is not permissible police conduct. The policies range from serious acts of theft, corruption, and brutality to where the department stands on the acceptance of simple gratuities. Goldstein calls this "drawing the line."[25] For instance, Patrick Murphy drew the line when he warned 180 commanders of the NYPD: "I hold each of you personally responsible for any misconduct within the ranks at any level of command."[26] By following through with disciplinary actions whenever a violation occurs, the leadership sends the message to all department personnel that corruption and brutality will not be tolerated.

Internal Affairs Division

Most large and medium-sized departments delegate the responsibility of investigating complaints against police officers to a specialized unit, normally referred to as the **internal affairs division** (IAD). The IAD is normally kept independent from the regular operating divisions as a way to minimize the pressure on IAD officers to cover up any wrongdoing of fellow officers. Hence, the head of the IAD generally reports directly to the chief.

In many police circles, IAD officers are held in contempt by fellow officers as "snoops" or "turncoats." The IAD officer's job is perceived as "trying to catch officers screwing up, and then reporting them." It is not uncommon to find IAD officers isolated from the daily precinct banter or off-duty social cliques. For this reason, IAD work is not very appealing to many officers.

During the height of Patrick Murphy's reform efforts as NYPD's commissioner, the number of IAD officers was greatly increased—from less than one in five hundred line officers before the Knapp investigation to approximately one in sixty for a period of time after Knapp. The New York police department was literally saturated by the IAD. In certain divisions, the number of the undercover "spies" was roughly one in ten.[27]

One controversial method IAD officers sometimes use to determine whether a police officer is honest is to conduct an **integrity test**. An undercover IAD agent might offer the officer a bribe or may hand a "lost" wallet to the officer to see if the wallet (and the money) is returned to the property room. Although most officers do not resent IAD officers for investigating formal charges made by citizens—most IAD investigations clear the officer of wrongdoing—many officers do resent the proactive integrity tests. Ironically, the integrity tests used by IAD officers generally employ the same investigatory techniques that undercover officers use when enforcing vice laws against unsuspecting offenders.

There are three types of external control mechanisms also deserving of our attention: (1) the courts, (2) citizen involvement, and (3) special investigative units. We will explore each of these below.

The Courts

Since the middle of the twentieth century, the courts have emerged as a major mechanism of police accountability and control.[28] As an external control mechanism, the courts play both a *watchdog* and *punitive* role. The court serves in its "watchdog" capacity on a daily basis. It does so by ruling on the admissibility of evidence gathered by police, accepting or denying applications for arrest and search warrants, dismissing criminal charges due to major procedural errors in the police investigation, acquitting innocent suspects arrested by the police, and so on.

In its "punitive" capacity, the courts may convict brutal or corrupt police officers on criminal charges or award damages to citizens in civil suits. Someone who has been harmed by the actions of a police officer may bring civil suit under state or federal law. Civil suits against the police are of enormous variety. The police have been sued for wrongful death, excessive force, false imprisonment, malicious prosecution, libel, slander, invasion of privacy, brutal treatment of prisoners, reckless vehicle operation, failure to administer first aid, failure to arrest, and intentional infliction of emotional distress, just to name a few. If the suit is successful, the victim is normally entitled to financial compensation. The monetary award may range from several hundred dollars to tens of thousands of dollars or more.

Citizen Involvement

A second external mechanism of police control is citizen involvement. As consumers of police services, citizens have a vested interest in the performance of their police. Of course, not all citizens want the same from their police. The pluralistic support structure of the police is evident when we look at the different types of citizen groups that make demands on the police—for example, churches, chambers of commerce, service groups, occupational groups, neighborhood associations, merchants, youth clubs, and college campuses. Additionally, the NAACP and the ACLU are often outspoken critics of the police, especially in the wake of civil rights violations of minorities. As is often the case, a particular police action draws applause from one community sector and bitter rebuke from another.

A **civilian review board** is the formal organization of selected citizens who serve as outside monitors of the police department. The members of the review board are ordinary citizens from the community who serve voluntarily. Since they owe no particular allegiance to the department, many believe their decisions are less likely to conceal acts of wrongdoing from the public. Several major cities adopted civilian review boards in the past to handle charges of police misconduct; however, the police typically resented the existence of these outside boards. The most famous of all civilian review boards, New York

342

PART V:
CONTEMPORARY
CONCERNS AND
FUTURE
CHALLENGES

City's *Civilian Complaint Review Board*, was eventually abandoned because of the persistent efforts of the Patrolmen's Benevolent Association. Yet recent years have seen a renewed interest in civilian review boards. According to one source, thirty of the nation's fifty largest cities have created some type of citizen review of the police.[29]

Special Investigative Units

When police misconduct reaches dangerous levels within a department, or when citizens have little confidence in the department to police its own, it may be necessary to form a *special investigative unit* to deal with the problem. The Lexow Investigation Committee of late last century was one of the first external groups to inquire into police misconduct. The more recent Knapp Commission is the best known special investigative body.

Advantages and Disadvantages of Control Mechanisms

Internal and external mechanisms of controlling police misconduct help to ensure that the police are held accountable to the public. However, they share different advantages and disadvantages. Continuous internal control is an effective way to monitor police misconduct when it is not already a serious problem in the department. Internal control provides a proactive, early warning system if problems occur, has greater access to internal records, and, as in the case of IAD inquiries, uses trained investigators to conduct the review. On the negative side, citizens may not believe the department's findings and

Mayor John Lindsay announcing his civilian appointments to New York City's Civilian Complaint Review Board in 1966.

Table 13.1 Comparison of Internal and External Mechanisms of Controlling Police Misconduct

	Internal Control	External Control
Description	Police monitor themselves	Outsiders monitor police
Major Types	1. Improved supervision 2. Administrative leadership 3. Internal affairs unit	1. Courts 2. Citizen involvement 3. Special investigation
Advantages	—Experienced investigators conducting review (can't be "snowed") —Greater access to internal records —Proactive, early warning system	—Independent; not likely to whitewash problem —Citizens feel sense of control over police —Necessary when police misconduct is pervasive
Disadvantages	—Risk of cover-up —Often creates tension within department —Citizens may lack faith in findings	—Reactive, post-hoc system —Limited access to records —Difficult to break "blue curtain" of silence

suspect a cover-up. Moreover, rigorous IAD investigations frequently create tension, bitterness, and morale problems within the department.

External control is often necessary when police misconduct is pervasive in a department. An important advantage of external control is that it is independent of the department and therefore not likely to result in a "whitewash" of the problem. External review also gives citizens a sense of control over the police that they do not have with internal review. However, external control is normally limited to post-hoc reviews of police problems once they have already surfaced. In addition, outside groups attempting to collect needed information have greater difficulty gaining access to internal records or winning the confidence of officers (see the summary in table 13.1).

Suffice it to say that both internal and external mechanisms of control have their proper place. Police officers and police unions generally prefer to have most charges of misconduct investigated internally. This is no doubt an effective approach when alleged incidents of misconduct are infrequent and minor. However, when brutality and corruption are rampant, and when citizens no longer have confidence in the police, some mechanism or mechanisms of external control become necessary before the department can begin to rebuild the public's faith.

CONSOLIDATING POLICE ORGANIZATIONS

The issue of **police consolidation** is another source of continuing debate in American law enforcement.[30] During the late 1960s and early 1970s, a number of prestigious study commissions sang a chorus of criticism over the highly fragmented system of U.S. law enforcement (e.g., President's Commission on Law Enforcement, 1967; Advisory Commission on Intergovernmental Relations, 1971; Committee for Economic Development, 1972; National

344

**PART V:
CONTEMPORARY
CONCERNS AND
FUTURE
CHALLENGES**

Advisory Commission on Criminal Justice Standards and Goals, 1973). The criticisms centered on the lack of standards and coordination among departments, the inefficiency of police operations, and the inability of small departments to provide the full array of police services. As the 1967 President's Commission charged, "A fundamental problem confronting law enforcement today is that of fragmented crime repression efforts resulting from the large number of uncoordinated local governments and law enforcement agencies."[31]

As a way to combat what many view as the "problem" of fragmentation, numerous experts have recommended that neighboring police agencies should consolidate *key units* or *entire agencies* in order to enhance the quality and efficiency of police services. In the words of the President's Commission, "each metropolitan area and each county should take action directed towards the pooling, or consolidation, of services through the particular techniques that will provide the most satisfactory law enforcement service and protection at the lowest cost."[32] According to the proponents, consolidation will increase coordination among departments, limit unnecessary duplication, and reduce the per capita expense of policing.

Strategies of Police Consolidation

Two different strategies of police consolidation exist: *total* and *partial* consolidation. We shall look at each of these strategies below.

Total Consolidation

Under this plan, two or more adjacent police departments are merged together, thus creating a single larger department. One way to create a consolidated department is from the equal blending of the original departments. What generally happens, however, is that one or more smaller agencies are "absorbed" into a larger agency. Total police consolidation entails drastic organizational reshuffling. Not surprisingly, most officers are apprehensive about police consolidation—while some officers may enjoy substantial benefits from the reorganization, others may be demoted (in rank, salary, or seniority), reassigned, or released.

The complete merging of police departments usually occurs as a result of the consolidation of local units of government, such as a city merging with the surrounding country. The two most notable city-county consolidation efforts in this country are Nashville/Davidson County, Tennessee, and Miami/Dade County, Florida. Scores of other city-county consolidation proposals have been generated across the country, but most have been defeated by the voters.[33] Residents of smaller communities are seldom convinced that "bigger government is better government" and are generally unwilling to relinquish local control over important services such as the police, fire protection, and the schools.

A different type of "total" consolidation is to merge the local police and fire departments into a single *public safety department*. A number of small towns in the United States use this arrangement. The major advantage to police-fire consolidation is the immediate increase in public safety officers who are available for fighting crime or fighting fires. Public safety officers cross-train so they are able to do both duties. If there are no fires to control, which is most of the time, public safety officers concentrate on police work; when a major fire breaks out, public safety officers double as fire fighters.

As with city-county consolidation, talk of creating a single public safety department normally brews resentment among police officers and fire fighters. The quality of protection and overall cost are other important considerations.

CONSOLIDATION GETS POLITE THUMBS-DOWN IN FARGO

After months of study, Fargo, N.D., officials decided late last month not to pursue a plan to cross-train and consolidate the city's police and fire departments because of the prohibitive costs involved and concerns over whether such a move would enhance the level of services currently provided by the two agencies.

City Commissioner Steven Sydness, who heads the commission's public safety planning committee, said that while the three-month study found that a cross-training program would have provided some long-term economic benefits, the start-up costs could not be justified at present.

"From an economic perspective, while the consolidated departments would have been less costly, it would have taken us many years to recover the start-up costs associated with consolidation, and it was the consensus of the majority of the commission that the level of savings weren't sufficient to warrant the disruption and all of the potential aggravation that might have gone along with the consolidation," Sydness told LEN.

The plan was formulated in an effort to "provide a higher level of service to the community . . . for the same amount of money or, if possible, a lesser amount of money," he added.

Start-up costs were estimated at nearly $1.6 million, a figure that included $860,000 in equipment expenses and an additional $726,000 in training costs. The biggest single cost involved a new communications systems that would put fire and police personnel on the same frequencies, Sydness said. "We would have had to totally retrofit our communications systems and that

would have been about a half-million-dollar operation," he noted.

Sydness said the city's fire and police officials "did not embrace the [cross-training] concept enthusiastically and were rather reluctant" to put the plan in motion—a feeling that Police Chief Ron Raftevold did not deny.

"I personally feel that you lose quality by having the same people do the same two jobs," Raftevold told LEN. He also noted that the amount of training required by the plan would have an impact on officers' duties. "You'd have to double the amount of training for each individual," he noted.

"Naturally, the rank-and-file were opposed to it—both police and fire," Raftevold said. Questions arose over whether members of both agencies could be adequately trained to provide quality service in both areas without affecting their primary duties, he added.

Sydness said the city is considering other means to improve public safety services and may make changes in the current policy of first response by the Fire Department to medical emergencies, who arrive at those scenes before ambulances do.

"We're looking at whether there is a better way of providing first-responder service rather than having a four-person fire crew with a quarter-of-a-million-dollar piece of apparatus run to a scene," he said. "We recognize the need and we'll continue to provide first-responder services to the citizens, so the question is not whether we will discontinue that, but rather is there a better way to do it?"

Source: *Law Enforcement News* (New York: John Jay College of Criminal Justice), December 31, 1990.

Partial Consolidation

An increasing trend among smaller departments is to combine key *auxiliary* services (e.g., records, communication, jail services, crime lab) with other police agencies in the area without merging entire departments. Partial consolidation offers many of the benefits of consolidation without the political hassle. And some agencies have merged important *line* services. This is done by combining officers from several departments (e.g., city-county vice and narcotics units). Cross-jurisdictional crime units are especially effective in combating crime that is cross-jurisdictional in nature.

There is an alternative strategy to consolidation in small towns that do not have, do not want, or cannot afford their own police force. **Contract law enforcement** is an arrangement where a township enters into a formal contract with a nearby police department to provide police protection *for a fee*. For example, a newly incorporated town may have the desire or the expertise to establish a police department on its own, so the town contracts with an adjacent department for police protection. The fee for contracted police services varies from place to place and is usually not cheap, but it is often less expensive than what the town would have to spend to start up and operate their own police force. This makes contract law enforcement a popular choice in small towns with limited treasuries. On the negative side, residents sometimes feel like the contracted police agency is less accessible and not wholly responsive to their particular needs.

Consolidation: Implications for Police

Police consolidation, particularly total consolidation, can create enormous political problems (e.g., What agency will lead the new department? Who shall be in charge? Will taxes rise? Will all residents pay equally? How will the new agency be organized? Who will report to whom? Will the department be civil service or non-civil service?). Consolidation also creates a number of practical problems (e.g., purchasing new uniforms, repainting squad cars, re-housing, re-training, standardizing policy manuals, equalizing salaries and benefits). Consolidation often results in morale problems among officers, difficult and confusing transition periods, cost overruns, and citizen disillusionment.

What is more, research fails to support the argument that "bigger" police departments are "better" police departments. To the contrary, there is evidence that the quality of police service in small and medium-sized departments is sometimes superior to the quality of service in large departments.[34] While it is true that smaller departments may not be able to deliver the full array of police services, they can usually rely on neighboring departments to share their resources and expertise. According to one group of scholars who researched the subject, smaller departments have "a much richer network of interrelationships among agencies, and a much higher use of auxiliary services in general than we would have expected."[35] Other researchers found that total government spending actually increased following city-county consolidation in Miami-Dade County[36] and Jacksonville-Dual County.[37]

For most small towns interested in consolidation, partial police consolidation of key services is a more realistic alternative. Merging key police services offers many of the advantages of consolidation without the significant political instability caused by complete reorganization. Many communities have found partial consolidation to be very successful.

AIDS AND THE POLICE

AIDS (acquired immune deficiency syndrome) is one of the most emotionally charged issues in policing today. AIDS is caused by the HIV virus (human immunodeficiency virus), which attacks healthy white blood cells. The virus limits the body's ability to fight off disease. Individuals infected with HIV die not from AIDS but from diseases like pneumonia and cancer that invade the body. A person may be infected with the virus for years without knowing it because visible symptoms do not appear. Once end-stage AIDS is developed, few people live more than two years. Presently, there is no cure for AIDS.

The AIDS virus is transmitted by bodily fluids. Contact with contaminated blood, semen, and vaginal secretions are the usual mode of transmittal. Police officers worry about contracting AIDS for two reasons. First, they have frequent contact with high-risk individuals like intravenous drug users, prostitutes, and homosexuals. Second, the very nature of police work increases the risk of being exposed to the deadly virus. While AIDS is not transmitted by casual contact, an infected suspect who bites or scratches an officer increases the chance of exposure. Officers are also at risk when handling infected hypodermic needles.

The problem of AIDS raises vexing legal and policy issues for law enforcement. Theodore Hammett has identified six pressing concerns:

- What are the department's responsibilities to report incidents in which the AIDS virus may have been transmitted?
- What department policies should be established regarding HIV testing in such cases?
- What would be the department's liability if an officer contracted the AIDS virus in the line of duty?
- What legal or labor relations issues are involved when an officer refuses to perform duties out of fear of AIDS?
- What are the department's responsibilities for protecting the public from infection when dealing with potential carriers of the virus?
- What are the department's responsibilities to prevent AIDS virus transmission in a police lockup?[38]

Answers to these and other questions are not readily available. The AIDS issue is an evolving one and its future impact on law enforcement is not fully known. At this point in time, however, it is understood that police officers have an obligation to perform their sworn duties even at the risk of AIDS exposure. For example, an officer who refused to arrest an assaultive intravenous drug user out of fear of contracting AIDS could be subject to departmental reprimand or dismissal. The reason why an officer cannot refuse is because the officer accepts a certain amount or risk as part of his or her job responsibility (e.g., risk of being shot, beaten, or hurt during a natural disaster). An officer who contracts AIDS while on duty normally would be unable to hold the department liable. However, the department could be held liable if it was negligent in training officers in the proper way to handle suspected AIDS carriers.[39]

All police officers must stay abreast of recent developments in AIDS-related research. This advice applies as much to police administrators in their offices as to patrol officers on the street. New information about AIDS must be quickly and effectively communicated to officers. Just as important, police departments must clearly specify to officers the policies it adheres to and the procedures it recommends for handling suspected AIDS carriers.

AIDS AND THE LAW ENFORCEMENT OFFICER

Issue/Concern	*Educational and Action Messages*
Human bites	Person who bites usually receives the victim's blood; viral transmission through saliva is highly unlikely. If bitten by anyone, milk wound to make it bleed, wash the area thoroughly, and seek medical attention.
Spitting	Viral transmission through saliva is highly unlikely.
Urine/feces	Virus isolated in only very low concentrations in urine; not at all in feces; no cases of AIDS or AIDS virus infection associated with either urine or feces.
Cuts/Puncture wounds	Use caution in handling sharp objects and searching areas hidden from view; needle stick studies show risk of infection is very low.
CPR/First aid	To eliminate the already minimal risk associated with CPR, use masks/airways; avoid blood-to-blood contact by keeping open wounds covered and wearing gloves when in contact with bleeding wounds.
Body removal	Observe crime scene rule: Do not touch anything. Those who must come into contact with blood or other body fluids should wear gloves.
Casual contact	No cases of AIDS or AIDS virus infection attributed to casual contact.
Any contact with blood or body fluids	Wear gloves if contact with blood or body fluids is considered likely. If contact occurs, wash thoroughly with soap and water; clean up spills with one part water to nine parts household bleach.
Contact with dried blood	No cases of infection have been traced to exposure to dried blood. The drying process itself appears to inactivate the virus. Despite low risk, however, caution dictates wearing gloves, a mask, and protective shoe coverings if exposure to dried blood particles is likely (e.g., crime scene investigation).

Source: Theodore M. Hammett, "AIDS and the Law Enforcement Officer," *National Institute of Justice—Research in Action* (Washington, DC: U.S. Department of Justice, November/December 1987), p. 6.

The AIDS problem is most definitely a critical issue affecting policing in the 1990s. Yet through proper education and training of officers, the effect of AIDS can be minimized.

POLICING: A PROFESSION?

Is policing a *profession*? The answer depends on who you ask. Most police officers argue vehemently that they are professionals who make critical life and death decisions affecting the lives of many people. Others argue just as vehemently that policing is not a profession and that police officers will never be professionals in the strict sense of the word.

Sam Walker identifies three elements that normally determine whether an occupation is a profession: *extensive knowledge, autonomy and independence,* and a *service ideal.*[40] Using medical doctors as a best-case model, it is clear that the medical "profession" has all three. Medical doctors must take years of advanced study beyond the four-year bachelor degree just to learn the basics. Doctors also have considerable autonomy and independence. Through the AMA and state regulatory boards, doctors control the entry, licensing, and discipline of their own members. Finally, medical doctors subscribe to an ideal of service. They promise to use their knowledge and skills to help their patients as signified in the age-old Hippocratic Oath.

It is safe to say that policing falls short of the *true* professional model. First and perhaps foremost, the entry-level educational requirement for most police departments is only a high school degree or GED. This is more true of local police departments than state or federal law enforcement agencies, which usually require at least some college education for new recruits. As shown in table 13.2, the minimum educational requirement for 90 percent of local police departments in 1990 was completion of high school, only 6 percent of local departments required education beyond high school, and the remaining 4 percent had no formal educational requirement for new officers.

There are other important ways that policing falls short of a true profession: pre-service training is usually limited to a few hundred hours of questionable instruction; police unions are labor-oriented and often subvert department goals to press their demands; far too many police officers are complacent and their leaders inept; and the job of policing is perceived by many as being dirty and undesirable work.

Noted authority James Q. Wilson takes a strong stand on the issue of police professionalism. He contends that the police are closer to being "subprofessionals" than true professionals:

> The police are not . . . professionals. They acquire most of their knowledge and skill on the job, not in separate academies; they are emphatically subject to the authority of their superiors; they have no serious professional society, only a union-like bargaining agent; and they do not produce, in systematic written form, new knowledge about their craft.[41]

But there are others who take a more flexible view of what makes an occupation a "profession." Although policing may not fit the professional mold

Table 13.2 Minimum Educational Requirements for New Officer Recruits in Local Police Departments, by Size of Population Served, 1990

| | | | | Percent of Departments | | | |
| | | | | | Requiring a Minimum of: | | |
Population Served	Total	Without Requirement	All with Requirement	High School Diploma	Some College*	2-year College Degree	4-year College Degree
All sizes	100%	4%	96%	90%	2%	4%	—
1,000,000 or more	100%	7%	93%	71%	21%	0%	0%
500,000–999,999	100	0	100	82	7	11	0
250,000–499,999	100	2	98	78	12	5	2
100,000–249,999	100	0	100	91	4	5	1
50,000–99,999	100	1	99	81	13	6	0
25,000–49,999	100	0	100	83	4	13	0
10,000–24,999	100	1	99	90	3	5	0
2,500–9,999	100	1	99	93	2	4	—
Under 2,500	100	7	93	89	1	2	0

Note: Detail may not add to total because of rounding.

—Less than 0.5%.

*No degree requirement.

Source: U.S. Department of Justice, Bureau of Justice Statistics Bulletin, *State and Local Police Departments, 1990* (Washington, DC: U.S. Government Printing Office, 1992), p. 6, table 12.

as well as the medical profession, it approximates the professional model, which may be good enough. Educational requirements are slowly increasing, there is a growing body of knowledge that police officers must acquire, police associations are amplifying the voice of officers in administrative decisions, and police officers generally share the service ideal. Police officers even have their own *Law Enforcement Code of Ethics.*

In the nation today, numerous police departments are striving to professionalize. The road to professionalism is paved by college education, rigorous recruitment standards, clear and current departmental policies and procedures, continual in-service training, dedicated and compassionate police officers and progressive police leaders. Unfortunately, far too many departments have shown little commitment or desire to professionalize. This indeed is one of the most disheartening aspects of American policing today.

CONCLUSION

This chapter examined a number of critical issues in contemporary police work. As noted at the chapter's outset, the particular topics included for discussion were selected somewhat arbitrarily as there are a great many important issues in American policing today. Depending on who one asks, a different set of critical issues may surface.

Let us return briefly to the issue of deadly force. Deadly force decisions occur with surprising infrequency. In fact, the average police officer never fires a gun at a suspect during the course of an entire career. It is estimated that the police kill around six hundred suspects per year, while between sixty-five and seventy-five officers are murdered in the line of duty each year. This

⌐ LAW ENFORCEMENT CODE OF ETHICS ─────

As a Law Enforcement Officer, my fundamental duty is to serve mankind; to safeguard lives and property; to protect the innocent against deception, the weak against oppression or intimidation, and the peaceful against violence or disorder; and to respect the Constitutional rights of all men to liberty, equality and justice.

I will keep my private life unsullied as an example to all; maintain courageous calm in the face of danger, scorn, or ridicule; develop self-restraint; and be constantly mindful of the welfare of others. Honest in thought and deed in both my personal and official life, I will be exemplary in obeying the laws of the land and the regulations of my department. Whatever I see or hear of a confidential nature or that is confided to me in my official capacity will be kept ever secret unless revelation is necessary in the performance of my duty.

I will never act officiously or permit personal feelings, prejudices, animosities or friendships to influence my decisions. With no compromise for crime and with relentless prosecution of criminals, I will enforce the law courteously and appropriately without fear or favor, malice or ill will, never employing unnecessary force or violence and never accepting gratuities.

I recognize the badge of my office as a symbol of public faith, and I accept it as a public trust to be held so long as I am true to the ethics of the police service. I will constantly strive to achieve these objectives and ideals, dedicating myself before God to my chosen profession . . . law enforcement.

352

PART V:
CONTEMPORARY
CONCERNS AND
FUTURE
CHALLENGES

establishes an approximate ratio of one police officer feloniously killed by criminal suspects for every 8.5 suspects killed by the police.

Technological advances could drastically alter police use of deadly force in the future. For example, hand-held, battery-operated stun guns are used in many prisons and jails to control unruly inmates. Officers in some departments have also started using stun guns when on patrol. Stun guns are inexpensive, lightweight, and easy to use. The electric shock produced by the gun causes a suspect's muscles to involuntarily relax for a minute or so. The suspect is likely to drop whatever weapon he or she might be holding, and the officer can safely complete the arrest. Stun guns are an intermediate use of force, falling somewhere between yelling at the suspect and hitting them with a nightstick. As refinements in the stun gun are made, and as other technological innovations make their way into policing, the traditional line of "Stop or I'll shoot!" may give way to "Stop or I'll zap!"

KEY TERMS

Lola Baldwin
Alice Wells
police*women*
*police*women
deadly force
Garner case
internal control

external control
internal affairs division
integrity test
civilian review board
police consolidation
contract law enforcement
AIDS

DISCUSSION QUESTIONS

1. Discuss the pros and cons of women patrol officers. What are your personal views about women in law enforcement?
2. The police are taught that when they fire their guns they should "shoot to kill" (i.e., aim toward body mass–vital organ area). Should the policy of "shoot to kill" be changed to "shoot to maim or incapacitate"? Why not shoot for the knee caps or the arm? Wouldn't that do the trick?
3. Do all patrol officers need to carry guns while on duty? Andy Taylor, the sheriff of TV's Mayberry, North Carolina, does not carry a gun, and he makes Deputy Barney Fife carry the one bullet for his gun in his shirt pocket. There are many "Mayberrys" in the United States. It is one thing to argue that patrol officers in the South Bronx of New York City need to be armed, but it is another to argue that all officers need to be. What do you think?
4. Discuss the relative advantages and disadvantages to *internal* and *external* mechanisms of controlling police misconduct. Which method do you thinks works best?
5. Is policing a profession? Why or why not?

CHAPTER FOURTEEN

SYNTHESIS AND CONCLUSION

Police departments should place less emphasis on educating the recruited and more emphasis on recruiting the educated.

—*The Sherman Report*

354

**PART V:
CONTEMPORARY
CONCERNS AND
FUTURE
CHALLENGES**

Our study of the police has taken us on a long and fascinating journey. We have traveled across time and space, from the earliest types of kin police in ancient society, through the various forms of amateur citizen police in the Middle Ages, to the paid, full-time public police of modern society. At the main stops along the way, we took note of the social and economic conditions of society, how those conditions affected the level of crime, and the manner in which society responded to the crime problem. Occasionally we caught glimpses of police forms that seemed to work reasonably well, but mostly we saw police forms that were grossly inadequate.

Of course, the central interest inspiring our journey has been American policing. We carefully documented the very serious (and seemingly ever growing) crime problem in the United States, and how the police have responded to crime over the years. From our study we know that American police have improved dramatically in the past two centuries, and continue to make significant improvements in police efficiency and effectiveness. Yet despite the many notable improvements in American policing, brutality, corruption, and inefficiency continue to exist. We have much work to do before American policing is elevated to the level of other respected professions.

In this final chapter, we will begin by identifying some of the important lessons to be drawn from our study of American police. So many topics and so much material has been covered in this textbook that it would be foolish to try to mention all the lessons here. Although it is difficult to whittle the expansive list of potential lessons down to a manageable number, we shall highlight ten *major* lessons that every student of American policing should know. Once this groundwork is laid, the second section of the chapter will identify some of the many factors that are currently shaping the emerging role of the police. Finally, we shall conclude our study with a call for good policing.

WHAT LESSONS HAVE WE LEARNED?

In this section we attempt to identify the major lessons from our study of American police. Given the many important lessons we have gleaned, the ten lessons that follow are highly selective. However, these lessons do capture the central themes of our investigation.

1. *The police cannot cure the crime problem in the U.S.—they can only help to control it.*

Of all the things we ask the police in modern society to do, perhaps the most critical thing we ask of them is the very thing they cannot do, or at least not do very well. The police are asked to cure the crime problem by attacking its root causes. We see this public mentality surface again and again. In recent years, for example, public sentiment has forced the police to wage an all-out "war" on drugs in an effort to search and destroy its root causes.

In reality, the police are unable to attack the root causes of society's ills. There are two reasons why. First, we are not sure what the root causes of most social problems are or how to ameliorate them. When it comes to crime, experts point to many different underlying causes, thus leaving a highly tangled mess of roots to attend to. Second, the police operate only on the *surface* of society. Even if we agreed on the root causes of crime and deviance, the police are not in the position to attack these roots. For example, if we agreed as many do that the ultimate cause of inner-city drug use is the *culture of poverty* (slums, unemployment, high-density housing, personal despair, bleak futures, dysfunctional families, lack of mental stimulation, poor nutrition, etc.), what if anything could the police do to fix the problem? The police may aggressively patrol these communities to control the illegal use of drugs, but this will not eliminate the causes. The roots will still flourish.

In short, students of the police must have a realistic understanding of what the police can and cannot do when it comes to fighting crime. Generally speaking, society expects too much from the police. The police cannot make greedy people less greedy, and they cannot change the social and historical factors that shape people's lives. The police may be able to *control* the crime problem through effective patrol strategies, but on their own they are unable to *eliminate* it.

2. *The police can often contribute more to the maintenance of an orderly society by the underenforcement of the law than by its full enforcement.*

It is impossible for the police to enforce all of the criminal laws on the books; it is equally impossible for the police to enforce any single law all of the time. The U.S. legal system has a tendency to "overreach" its current boundaries by continually establishing new laws and setting new penalties. Behaviors considered only mildly mad or bad are often made illegal through legislative action, and are thus brought under the enforcement responsibility of the police. With literally thousands of criminal laws on the books and millions of opportunistic criminals walking the streets of our society, the odds are overwhelmingly against the full enforcement of the law.

Yet even if the police had the ability to fully enforce all of the laws all of the time, would this be beneficial to society? The answer is a resounding no! Not all laws are as important as others (e.g., laws prohibiting murder versus laws banning panhandling), and some laws are of questionable merit (off-track betting?). More important than this, however, is the fact that circumstances have a way of altering the wisdom of fully enforcing the law. For example, the ends of justice would not be served well if every speeder received a ticket or if all loud party participants were arrested. In other words, there are numerous occasions when the police can better serve society by enforcing the law in its *spirit* rather than to its *letter*.

3. *As society modernizes and becomes increasingly complex, the simplistic forms of kin policing and citizen policing eventually fail to provide adequate protection. In the end, some type of organized public police system must prevail.*

We have seen this sequence of events unfold several times in our study of the police. Modernization, combined with a fast-growing population,

356

PART V:
CONTEMPORARY
CONCERNS AND
FUTURE
CHALLENGES

creates a highly diverse, mobile, and anonymous people less bound to the traditional way of life. Greed-driven appetites are whetted by the accumulation of wealth and the abundance of material possessions. Informal networks of social control begin to weaken, especially in the urban centers. Citizens are no longer able to protect themselves or their property as they were in the past. The problem of crime escalates to such momentous proportions that its control becomes a full-time, twenty-four-hour-a-day job. Eventually, the formal responsibility for protecting society is passed on to an organized police force. Thus, we find that public policing is a necessary agent of formal social control in modern society.

4. *The establishment of a public police system in no way diminishes the need for average citizens to help control crime.*

While citizens in modern society desperately depend on the help of the police, it is equally true that the police desperately depend on the help of citizens. The reason is because the police are not the only ones who police. Citizens also police by our natural tendency to look out for ourselves, our family, neighbors, and friends. Multiplied by the millions, our watchful collective eyes monitor the environment for signs of trouble. As Sir Robert Peel once said, "The police are the public and the public are the police." In short, while the police may be the premier agency of social control in modern society, they will always need the help of citizens. We are still the "eyes and ears" of the police; indeed, we are still the police.

5. *The police in America have three fundamental responsibilities: order maintenance, social service, and law enforcement. The police should recognize that their roles as keepers of the peace and social servants are as important to the public as their role as crime fighters.*

Police work entails a wide assortment of job-related activities, nearly all of which may be classified into one of the above three types. An important lesson from our study of American policing is that departments should not make law enforcement their *one and only* priority; keeping community order and rendering social services to the public are equally important. Too many departments continue to downplay the significance of their non-enforcement duties, but research demonstrates convincingly that this is a mistake. The public expects the police to be more than crime fighters; the police must learn to accept this fact and eagerly embrace their expansive responsibilities to the public.

6. *Policing is by nature a conservative task.*

The police strive to preserve the existing order of society by enforcing the dominant rules. The police protect social institutions, uphold contemporary morality, and maintain domestic peace. As employees of the government, the police must work to preserve the established order. Over the long haul, the police tend to enforce the will of the powerful over the powerless, or at least the will of the more powerful over the less powerful. In this capacity, the police are rarely vanguards of social change. The police serve a conservative role by maintaining the existing power structure of society.

7. *The police are human beings, not angels or saints. The temptations of the job are real and their state-backed authority is immense. The problems of corruption and brutality will likely always exist.*

No other aspect of modern day policing evokes more negative feelings toward the police than bad and brutal cops. Police misconduct tears at the delicate fabric of trust between the police and the community. Even one bad officer in a department is too many, as the pernicious effects of the officer's actions reverberate throughout the department; when the problem is widespread, police misconduct can entirely destroy the faith citizens place in their police.

Police misconduct is a reality. While most officers are professional, morally righteous, and dedicated to serving the people, a small minority of officers regularly lie, steal, and abuse their authority. Even though the problem of police misconduct is not nearly as bad as it once was, it is unfortunately true that police misconduct is still endemic to policing, and probably always will be. This is why police departments and entire communities must continually control wayward police.

8. *The police are only as good as their leaders.*

This axiom is true of all organizations, not just for police departments. Effective leadership is crucial for an organization to realize its full potential. The organizational health of a police department is largely determined by the success or failure of its top administrator. An unhealthy organization is sure to have an ineffective leader at the helm.

9. *By almost any standard one applies, American police are doing a better job today than at any time in the past.*

The police in American society have made commendable strides in the twentieth century. The reform effort to wrangle partisan politics out of policing has been successful on most fronts, police recruits today are better qualified and better trained than recruits of yesteryear, and the police appear sincerely committed to improving their relations with the public. One reason why so many criticisms of the police are still heard is because the public has come to expect so much more from the police than in the past. Yet this increased reliance on the police is another indication of the progress the police have made during this century.

Progress is a continuing process, not an end state. While it is rewarding to stand back and applaud the many improvements made in American policing, so much more needs to be done. The police in America still have tremendous room for improvement.

EMERGING ROLE OF THE POLICE

To speak of the emerging role of the police implies that it is changing or evolving into something different than it was in the past. It is true that the police officer of today is a cut above the typical police officer of fifty or one hundred years ago; a "strong back and weak mind" is no longer sufficient to be a good officer. It is also true that the job of policing is different. Policing today is difficult; it requires officers to be more knowledgeable and less sloppy in their enforcement efforts. American policing is certainly changing, but why?

There are a great many factors shaping the emerging role of the police, some of which are more important than others. The following sections summarize the effects of five primary factors: (1) the shifting profile of police officers, (2) the research revolution, (3) technological advances, (4) increased accountability, and (5) police professionalism. Careful readers will recognize each of these factors as they have been discussed at various points throughout the text. Here, at the end of our study, we bring together these diverse factors under one umbrella.

The Shifting Profile of Police Officers

One major factor shaping the emerging role of the police is the shifting profile of police officers. Police work used to be an occupation dominated by white males, but that is changing. Active minority recruiting is encouraging women and minorities to enter police work in substantial numbers. Minorities and especially women are still underrepresented in most police departments, yet the impact of the progressive recruitment efforts is already evident.

The active recruitment of women and minorities has come about in two ways: (1) by the voluntary and progressive efforts of police leaders who recognize the value of diversity within their department; and (2) by the involuntary dictates of equal employment statutes, affirmative action requirements and court-ordered quotas. While some "old guard" police officers may resent the infusion of women and minorities into police work, their numbers are rapidly diminishing as is their credibility. We now know that the quality of police work is not contingent on one's race or ethnic group, nor is it dependent on one's gender. Individuals who continue to argue that police work is best left to one particular social group are clearly out of touch with the research evidence. They are also out of step with the times.

The Research Revolution

Another factor to affect the emerging role of the police is the research revolution. Since the late 1960s, police researchers have produced an explosion of new knowledge and ideas. Formally christened by the 1967 President's Commission on Law Enforcement and Administration of Justice, researchers began in earnest to fill the very large void in our understanding about the police. The now defunct *Law Enforcement Assistance Administration* (LEAA) was instrumental in giving the research revolution its initial momentum. LEAA grew out of the earlier *Office of Law Enforcement Assistance* (OLEA), created in 1965, to make federal funds available to states and localities to improve the criminal justice system, particularly the police. The *Police Foundation*, the *Police Executive Research Forum* and the *National Institute of Justice* also have been major promoters of police research over the years.

The research revolution is far from over. There are still so many things we are only beginning to understand. However, the long-term effect of the revolution is already clear. Many of the once-entrenched "truisms" of policing have been called into question. As our knowledge of policing continues to develop, the role of the police will continue to evolve.

Technological Advances

Another primary factor to influence the emerging role of the police has been the astounding pace of technological development. Technology has altered nearly every aspect of modern police work, from transportation, weapons, and protection devices to criminal forensics and advanced communication systems. Technology is virtually revolutionizing police work.

Not only are the police far better equipped because of technological developments but so are the criminals. Sophisticated thieves of today no longer stalk the streets for innocent victims, and they no longer use clubs, knives, or guns to steal—they use computers and other advanced forms of scientific wizardry. And who is to say what crime or crime control will be like in the next fifty or one hundred years due to continuing technological developments. Nonetheless, of two things we can be certain: (1) technological discoveries will continue to be made, and (2) mischievous minds will always find ways to misuse technology for personal gain. Therefore, it is imperative for the police to stay abreast of technological advances in order to remain effective enforcers of the law.

Increased Accountability

In years past, little was expected of the police other than to keep a minimal level of order in society. This is no longer true. American police are currently held to a higher level of accountability than at any time in past. Citizens have come to expect premium quality services from the police, and they are not shy about making their demands known. After all, citizens pay dearly for police protection by way of taxes. Naturally, they expect a fair return on their

360

PART V:
CONTEMPORARY
CONCERNS AND
FUTURE
CHALLENGES

investment. The call for police accountability is further fueled by our nation's serious and persistent crime problem ("Why aren't the police doing what we pay them to do?"). The *community policing movement* so prominent today is a direct offshoot of the increased accountability of the police to the community.

A major mechanism of police accountability to surface in recent years is the system of courts. The courts not only serve as a watchdog in criminal cases to assure that police procedure is legal, but also the police are held accountable in civil cases. With troubling regularity the police are being taken to court. Disgruntled citizens, with the aid of enterprising lawyers, are suing the police for a variety of reasons. So frequently are the police being sued that departments nationwide are forced to practice *defensive policing* (similar to defensive medicine). As just one example of defensive policing, it is increasingly common for the police to have motorists sign a waiver of liability before the police attempt to unlock a car door when the keys are inside (some departments refuse to unlock car doors anymore—motorists must call a locksmith). The reason for this precaution is because the new electronic locks are easily damaged. Apparently, a number of police departments have been sued for destroying private property.

As a result of the increased accountability, the police are forced to justify *what* they are doing and *how well* they are doing it. For the most part, the increased accountability is a positive development. The police should be held to a high level of accountability to the public. Increased accountability promotes increased professionalism, which leads us to our final factor shaping the emerging role of the police.

Police Professionalism

A driving force in contemporary American policing is the serious push toward professionalism. So much of the progress police have made in recent years is directly tied to professionalism. Police departments across the country are striving to elevate their level of performance in order to serve their communities better. The push toward professionalism is a long-overdue and much needed development in American policing.

One important indicator of police professionalism is the many successful attempts to upgrade recruitment standards and to improve the overall level of training officers receive. Some departments now require over 1,000 hours of rigorous training before a recruit can be certified as an officer. Once the rookie hits the streets, he or she may be placed under the guidance of a qualified field training officer for a period of six months to a year for additional on-the-job training. To further enhance the training of officers, some departments are subscribing to special cable television programs like the *Law Enforcement Television Network* (LETN), which provides current news, information, and training tips to help officers sharpen their skills.

An even better indicator of police professionalism is the growing number of departments that now require a four-year college degree. Police departments generally prefer a college degree in criminal justice or some related social science discipline (sociology, psychology, or political science); however, degrees from other disciplines are usually acceptable. It is worth noting that a college degree is no assurance that a rookie officer will become a good officer—too many other factors come into play (e.g., motivation, personality, physical ability). However, requiring a college degree is sure to improve the overall quality of young recruits entering police work.

Perhaps the best indicator of the push toward professionalism is the growing number of progressive, well-educated, and highly dedicated police leaders. This is one of the most encouraging developments in modern-day policing—police professionalism is impossible without professional leaders. Several progressive associations exist for the benefit of police leaders, such as the *International Association of Chiefs of Police* (IACP), the *National Sheriffs Association* (NSA), and the *National Organization of Black Law Enforcement Executives* (NOBLE). Each of these associations, along with the *Police Executive Research Forum* (PERF), has actively promoted the concept of law enforcement *accreditation*. The *Commission on Accreditation of Law Enforcement Agencies* was created in 1983 to oversee the accreditation process. This purely voluntary process entails meeting hundreds of standards covering all facets of the police department. Accreditation is an expensive and difficult process. It may take several years before a department is fully accredited.

POLICING AMERICAN SOCIETY: EPILOGUE

The central focus of our concluding chapter (and one of the underlying themes of the entire book) is *good* policing. The emerging role of the police is one that actively supports good policing. Good policing is a two-pronged approach, with one prong focusing on individual officers and the second focusing on police departments.

First, *good police officers* perform their assigned duties with morality, perspective, and intelligence. Good police officers have an immense passion for their work, and reap immeasurable satisfaction by helping others. Good police officers, although kind and understanding, are never weak. Good police officers know they do not have to be ruthless to be effective, but are not afraid to assert their authority when the situation warrants it.

Second, *good police departments* hire the best possible recruits, train them to the highest caliber, and subsequently reward meritorious police work. Good police departments assemble a competent management team headed by professional leaders. Good police departments are always open, honest, and accessible to the public. And finally, but no less important, good police departments strive to protect and serve their communities well.

Our ending plea for good policing is more than overzealous idealism—it is a realistic possibility. Good policing is becoming a reality in many departments across the country, although most departments still lag far behind. A major challenge facing the next generation of police leaders is to transform American policing into good policing. In our continuing efforts to improve the police in American society, the benefits are well worth the effort.

NOTES

Chapter 1. Crime and Crime Control

1. U.S. Department of Justice, Bureau of Justice Statistics Bulletin, *Criminal Victimization in the United States, 1990* (Washington, DC: U.S. Government Printing Office, 1992), p. 102.
2. U.S. Department of Justice, *Uniform Crime Reports for the United States, 1990* (Washington, DC: U.S. Government Printing Office, 1991).
3. U.S. Department of Justice, *Criminal Victimization in the United States, 1990*, p. iii.
4. Ibid., p. 22.
5. U.S. Department of Justice, Bureau of Justice Statistics Technical Report, *Lifetime Likelihood of Victimization* (Washington, DC: U.S. Government Printing Office, 1987), p. 1.
6. Ibid.
7. U.S. Department of Justice, Bureau of Justice Statistics Special Report, *International Crime Rates* (Washington, DC: U.S. Government Printing Office, 1988).
8. U.S. Department of Justice, *International Crime Rates*, p. 3.
9. Émile Durkheim, *The Division of Labor in Society*, trans. George Simpson (Glencoe, IL: Free Press, 1960), p. 102.
10. Extrapolated figure from U.S. Department of Justice, Bureau of Justice Statistics Bulletin, *Justice Expenditures and Employment, 1988* (Washington, DC: U.S. Government Printing Office, July 1990).
11. Lillian B. Rubin, *Quiet Rage: Bernie Goetz in a Time of Madness* (New York: Farrar, Straus, and Giroux, 1986).
12. U.S. Department of Justice, National Institute of Justice Research in Brief, *The Growing Role of Private Security* (Washington, DC: U.S. Government Printing Office, October, 1984).
13. *Webster's New Collegiate Dictionary* (Springfield, MA: G. & C. Merriam Company, 1980).
14. Matthew Lippman, "Iran: A Question of Justice" *C. J. International* 3 (Nov.–Dec. 1987): 6.
15. A.C. Germann, Frank D. Day, and Robert R. J. Gallati, *Introduction to Law Enforcement and Criminal Justice* (Springfield, IL: Charles C. Thomas, Publisher, 1973), p. 23.
16. Ibid., p. 9.
17. From Reinhard Bendix, *Max Weber: An Intellectual Portrait* (Garden City, NY: Doubleday and Company, 1962), p. 290.

18. Germann et al., *Introduction to Law Enforcement and Criminal Justice*, p. 15.

Chapter 2. Development of Public Policing

1. Joseph Reither, *World History at a Glance* (New York: Barnes and Noble, 1958), p. 3.
2. A. C. Germann, Frank D. Day, and Robert R. J. Gallati, *Introduction to Law Enforcement and Criminal Justice* (Springfield, IL: Charles C. Thomas, Publisher, 1973), p. 43.
3. Ibid.
4. Edward Eldefonso, Alan Coffey, and Richard C. Grace, *Principles of Law Enforcement*, 2nd ed. (New York: John Wiley and Sons, 1974), p. 59.
5. Reither, *World History at a Glance*, p. 6.
6. Ibid., p. 7.
7. Ibid.
8. Ibid.
9. Ibid., p. 18.
10. Ibid.
11. Larry J. Siegel, *Criminology* (New York: West, 1983), p. 31.
12. G. E. Berkley, M. W. Giles, J. F. Hackett, and N. C. Kassoff, *Introduction to Criminal Justice: Police, Courts, Corrections* (Boston: Holbrook Press, Inc., 1976), p. 46.
13. Germann et al., *Introduction to Law Enforcement and Criminal Justice*, p. 44.
14. Eldefonso et al., *Principles of Law Enforcement*, p. 60.
15. Germann et al., *Introduction to Law Enforcement and Criminal Justice*, p. 44.
16. Eldefonso et al., *Introduction to Law Enforcement*, p. 60.
17. Germann et al., *Introduction to Law Enforcement and Criminal Justice*, p. 45.
18. Ibid., p. 50.
19. Ibid.
20. Ibid., p. 48.
21. The Norman invasion transformed the localized type of tithing police into the centralized frankpledge system. Because the frankpledge was simply a variation of the tithing system, we will continue to call it by its original name to avoid confusion.
22. Carl Klockars, *The Idea of the Police* (Beverly Hills, CA: Sage Publications, 1985), p. 24.
23. Ibid., p. 23.
24. Ibid., p. 25.
25. Ibid., p. 26.
26. Germann et al., *Introduction to Law Enforcement and Criminal Justice*, p. 55.
27. Allan Silver, "The Demand for Order in Civil Society: A Review of Some Themes in the History of Urban Crime, Police, and Riot," in David J. Bordua, ed., *The Police: Six Sociological Essays*, (New York: John Wiley and Sons, Inc., 1967), p. 1.
28. Ibid., p. 3.
29. Klockars, *The Idea of Police*, p. 28; emphasis added.
30. Germann et al., *Introduction to Law Enforcement and Criminal Justice*, p. 60.
31. Klockars, *The Idea of Police*, p. 29.
32. Ibid., p. 34.
33. Philip John Stead, "The New Police," in David H. Bayley, ed., *Police and Society*, (Beverly Hills, CA: Sage Publications, 1977), p. 73.
34. Silver, "The Demand for Order in Civil Society," p. 15.
35. Ibid., p. 74.
36. W. Clinton Terry, ed., *Policing Society: An Occupational View*, (New York: John Wiley and Sons, 1985), p. 38.
37. Quote cited in Germann et al., *Introduction to Law Enforcement and Criminal Justice*, p. 61.
38. Robert Pursley, *Introduction to Criminal Justice* (New York: Macmillan Publishing Co., 1984), p. 140.
39. Klockars, *The Idea of Police*, p. 41.
40. Stead, "The New Police," p. 81.
41. M. Lee, *A History of Police in England* (Montclair, NJ: Patterson Smith, 1971), p. 240.
42. This statement is by Sir Robert Mark as quoted in Ben Whitaker's *The Police In Society* (London: Eyre Methuen, 1979), p. 49.
43. Stead, "The New Police," p. 83.
44. Ibid.
45. Throughout the text we use the terms "America" and "United States" interchangeably, although technically America refers to all of North America (including Canada), Central America, and South America. "Britain" and "England" are used interchangeably as well.

However, since Great Britain formally includes England, Wales, Scotland, and Northern Ireland, when the word Britain is used we are referring *only* to England and Wales. This is a common practice because the criminal justice systems in Scotland and Northern Ireland depart substantially from the English style.

46. Germann et al., *Introduction to Law Enforcement and Criminal Justice*, p. 65.

47. Pursley, *Introduction to Criminal Justice*, p. 143–44.

48. Ibid., p. 141.

49. Roger Lane, *Policing the City, Boston 1822–1885*, (Cambridge, MA: Harvard University Press, 1967), p. 10.

50. Ronald Tannehill, "The History of American Law Enforcement," in Dae H. Chang and James A. Fagin, eds., *Introduction to Criminal Justice: Theory and Application* (Geneva, IL: Paladin House, 1985), p. 161.

51. Samuel Walker, *The Police in America: An Introduction* (New York: McGraw-Hill Book Company, 1983), p. 6.

52. Wilbur R. Miller, *Cops and Bobbies: Police Authority in New York and London, 1830–1870* (Chicago: University of Chicago Press, 1977).

53. Quoted in Walker, *The Police in America*, p. 6.

54. Tannehill, "The History of American Law Enforcement," p. 161.

55. Germann et al., *Introduction to Law Enforcement and Criminal Justice*, p. 66.

56. Eric H. Monkkonen, *Police in Urban America, 1860–1920* (Cambridge: Cambridge University Press, 1981).

57. Randy L. LaGrange, "The Future of Police Consolidation," *Journal of Contemporary Criminal Justice* 3 (February 1987): 6–16; Richard J. Terrill, *World Criminal Justice Systems* (Cincinnati, OH: Anderson Publishing Co., 1984).

58. Klockars, *The Idea of Police*, p. 41.

59. This idea is pointed out by Klockars (Ibid., p. 61) in reference to Geoffry Gorer's work, *Exploring English Character* (London: Cresset, 1955).

60. Miller, *Cops and Bobbies in the Mid-Nineteenth Century*, p. 51–52.

61. Quoted in Stead, "The New Police," p. 76.

62. Germann et al., *Introduction to Law Enforcement and Criminal Justice*, p. 63.

63. "The Police of London," *London Quarterly Review* (July 1870): 48, as quoted in Silver, "The Demand for Order in Civil Society," p. 14.

64. Silver, "The Demand for Order in Civil Society," p. 12.

65. Louis A. Radelet, *The Police and the Community* (New York: Macmillan Publishing Co., 1980), p. 4.

Chapter 3. Contemporary Police Systems in American Society

1. U.S. Department of Justice, Bureau of Justice Statistics Bulletin, *Justice Expenditure and Employment, 1988* (Washington, DC: U.S. Government Printing Office, July 1990).

2. Ibid.

3. Ibid.

4. U.S. Department of Justice, Bureau of Justice Statistics, *BJS Data Report, 1988* (Washington, DC: U.S. Government Printing Office, April 1989), p. 36.

5. Katherine M. Jamieson and Timothy J. Flanagan, eds., *Sourcebook of Criminal Justice Statistics—1989.* U.S. Department of Justice, Bureau of Justice Statistics (Washington, DC: U.S. Government Printing Office, 1990), Table 1.5, p. 5.

6. U.S. Department of Justice, Bureau of Justice Statistics Special Report, *Police Employment and Expenditure Trends* (Washington, DC: U.S. Government Printing Office, 1986).

7. Ibid.

8. Ibid.

9. U.S. Department of Justice, *Justice Expenditure and Employment, 1988.*

10. Samuel Walker, *The Police in America: An Introduction* (New York: McGraw-Hill Book Company, 1983), p. 32.

11. U.S. Department of Justice, *Uniform Crime Reports for the United States, 1990* (Washington, DC: U.S. Government Printing Office, August 1991), p. 237.

12. Jeffrey Slovak, *Styles of Urban Policing* (New York: New York University Press, 1986), p. 50.

13. U.S. Department of Justice, *Uniform Crime Reports for the United States, 1990*, p. 237.

14. Ibid., p. 64.

15. David Jacobs, "Inequality and Police Strength," *American Sociological Review* 44 (1979): 913–24.

16. Slovak, *Styles of Urban Policing*, p. 59.

17. U.S. Department of Justice, Bureau of Justice Statistics Bulletin, *State and Local Police Departments, 1990* (Washington, DC: U.S. Government Printing Office, 1992).

18. U.S. Department of Justice, *Uniform Crime Reports for the United States, 1990*, p. 64.

19. U.S. Department of Justice, Bureau of Justice Statistics Bulletin, *State and Local Police Departments, 1990* (Washington, DC: U.S. Government Printing Office, 1992).

20. U.S. Department of Justice, *Uniform Crime Reports for the United States, 1990*, p. 90.

21. Walker, *The Police in America*, p. 37.

22. U.S. Department of Justice, Bureau of Justice Statistics Bulletin, *Sheriffs' Departments 1990*, (Washington, DC: U.S. Government Printing Office, 1992), p. 2.

23. Donald A. Torres, *Handbook of State Police, Highway Patrols, and Investigative Agencies* (New York: Greenwood Press, 1987), p. 2.

24. U.S. Department of Justice, *Sheriffs' Departments 1990*, p. 2.

25. Ibid.

26. Ibid.

27. Ibid.

28. U.S. Department of Justice, *Report to the Nation on Crime and Justice, 1988*, (Washington, DC: U.S. Government Printing Office, March 1988), p. 106.

29. Lee P. Brown, "The Role of the Sheriff," in Alvin W. Cohn, ed., *The Future of Policing*, (Beverly Hills, CA: Sage Books, 1978), pp. 227–47.

30. Ibid., p. 240.

31. Ibid., p. 233.

32. Ibid., p. 245.

33. Randy L. LaGrange, "The Future of Police Consolidation," *Journal of Contemporary Criminal Justice* 3 (February 1987): pp. 6–16.

34. Walker, *The Police in America*, p. 40.

35. Ibid., p. 41.

36. U.S. Department of Justice, *Uniform Crime Reports for the United States, 1990*, pp. 304–308.

37. Diane C. Bordner and David M. Peterson, *Campus Policing: The Nature of University Police Work* (New York: University Press of America, 1983), p. xii.

38. Gordon Dillow, "The Lone Ranger,"

39. Torres, *Handbook of State Police, Highway Patrols, and Investigative Agencies*, p. 289.

40. Ibid., p. 6.

41. Katherine Mayo, *Justice to All: The Story of the Pennsylvania State Police* (New York: Putnam, 1917), pp. 5–6.

42. Torres, *Handbook of State Police, Highway Patrols, and Investigative Agencies*, p. 15.

43. U.S. Department of Justice, *Profile of State and Local Law Enforcement Agencies, 1987*, p. 7.

44. U.S. Department of Justice, *Uniform Crime Reports for the United States, 1990*, p. 243.

45. Ibid.

46. Frank M. Sorrentino, *Ideological Warfare: The FBI's Path Toward Power* (New York: Associated Faculty Press, Inc., 1985), p. 109.

47. Ibid., p. 126.

48. Donald A. Torres, *Handbook of Federal Police and Investigative Agencies* (New York: Greenwood Press, 1985).

Chapter 4. The Police Charge

1. Robert K. Merton, "Social Structure and Anomie," *American Sociological Review* 3 (October 1938): 672–82.

2. This definition is a hybrid of sorts that combines the ideas from two sources: Harry C. Bredemeier and Richard M. Stephenson, *The Analysis of Social Systems* (New York: Holt, Rinehart and Winston, Inc., 1962), ch. 6.; and Jackson Toby, "The Socialization and Control of Deviant Motivation," in D. Glaser, ed., *Handbook of Criminology*, (Chicago: Rand McNally, 1974), pp. 85–100.

3. The following on achieving social control is based on the loose adaptation of the work of Bredemeier and Stephenson, *The Analysis of Social Systems*, pp. 146–76.

4. Toby, "The Socialization and Control of Deviant Motivation," p. 86.

5. Walter C. Reckless, *The Crime Problem*, 3rd. ed (New York: Appleton-Century-Crofts, 1961).

6. Mark H. Moore and George L. Kelling, " 'To Serve and Protect': Learning From

Philip Morris Magazine (July–August 1989): 10.

Police History," in Abraham S. Blumberg and Elaine Niederhoffer, eds., *The Ambivalent Force*, (New York: Holt, Rinehart and Winston, 1985), p. 37.

7. Mark H. Moore, Robert C. Trojanowicz, and George L. Kelling, "Crime and Policing," *Perspectives on Policing*. U.S. Department of Justice, National Institute of Justice (Washington, DC: U.S. Government Printing Office, June 1988).

8. Everett C. Hughes, *Men and Their Work* (Glencoe, IL: Free Press, 1958).

9. James Q. Wilson, *Varieties of Police Behavior* (New York: Atheneum, 1972).

10. Eric J. Scott, *Calls for Service: Citizen Demand and Initial Police Response* (Washington, DC: U.S. Government Printing Office, 1981).

11. Joel Samaha, *Criminal Justice* (New York: West Publishing Co., 1988), p. 178.

12. Richard J. Lundman, "Police Patrol Work: A Comparative Perspective," in Richard J. Lundman, ed., *Police Behavior: A Sociological Perspective* (New York: Oxford University Press, 1980), pp. 52–65.

13. Ibid., p. 55.

14. James Q. Wilson, *Thinking About Crime*, revised ed. (New York: Vintage Books, 1985), pp. 111–12.

15. Egon Bittner, *The Functions of the Police in Modern Society* (Washington, DC: National Institute of Mental Health, 1970), pp. 36–47.

16. Samuel Walker, *The Police in America: An Introduction* (New York: McGraw-Hill, 1983), p. 217.

17. John F. Galliher, "Explanations of Police Behavior: A Critical Review and Analysis," in *The Ambivalent Force*, p. 60.

18. Moore and Kelling, " 'To Serve and Protect': Learning from Police History," in *The Ambivalent Force*, pp. 39–40.

19. Ibid., p. 40.

20. Ibid.

21. Ibid.

22. George L. Kelling and Mark H. Moore, "The Evolving Strategy of Policing," *Perspectives on Policing*, U.S. Department of Justice, National Institute of Justice (Washington, DC: U.S. Government Printing Office, November 1988).

23. Robert Trojanowicz and David Carter, *The Philosophy and Role of Community Policing*, Community Policing Series No. 13 (National Neighborhood Foot Patrol Center, Michigan State University, 1988).

24. Carl Klockars, *The Idea of Police* (Beverly Hills, CA: Sage Publications, 1985), p. 12.

Chapter 5. Police and the Public

1. Mary Jeanette Hageman, *Police-Community Relations* (Beverly Hills, CA: Sage Publication, 1985), p. 18.

2. *Brown v. Board of Education*, 347 U.S. 483, 98 LEd 873, 74 SCt 686 (1954).

3. *Plessy v. Ferguson*, 163 U.S. 537, 41 LEd 256, 16 SCt 1138 (1896).

4. Mark Schaver, *Wilmington Morning Star*, Wilmington, NC, February 2, 1990.

5. John C. Klotter and Jaqueline R. Kanovitz, *Constitutional Law for Police*, 2nd ed. (Cincinnati: The W. H. Anderson Co., 1973), p. 384.

6. Ibid.

7. *Detroit Times*, July 17, 1943.

8. Robert Trojanowicz, *Preventing Civil Disturbances: A Community Policing Approach*, Community Policing Series No. 18 (National Center for Community Policing, Michigan State University, 1989), p. 6.

9. Ibid., pp. 5–6.

10. U.S. National Advisory Commission on Civil Disorders, *Report of the National Advisory Commission on Civil Disorders* (Kerner Report) (Washington, DC: U.S. Government Printing Office, 1968), p. 5.

11. Paul M. Whisenand and Fred Ferguson, *The Managing of Police Organizations* (Englewood Cliffs, NJ: Prentice Hall, 1989), p. 266.

12. Jack R. Greene, "Police and Community Relations: Where Have We Been and Where Are We Going?" in Roger B. Dunham and Geoffrey P. Alpert, eds., *Critical Issues in Policing* (Prospect Heights, IL: Waveland Press, 1989), p. 355.

13. Pamela D. Mayhall and David Patrick Geary, *Community Relations and the Administration of Justice* (New York: John Wiley and Sons, 1979), p. 24.

14. Green, "Police and Community Relations," p. 350.

15. Mayhall and Geary, *Community Relations and the Administration of Justice*, p. 24.

16. Ibid., p. 33.

17. Whisenand and Ferguson, *The Managing of Police Organizations*, p. 268.

18. Ibid.

19. Louis A. Radelet, *The Police and the Community* (New York: Macmillan Publishing Co., 1980), p. 21.

20. Mayhall and Geary, *Community Relations and the Administration of Justice*, pp. 38–40.

21. Jerome H. Skolnick and David H. Bailey, *The New Blue Line: Police Innovation in Six American Cities* (New York: The Free Press, 1986), p. 73.

22. Ibid.

23. James Q. Wilson, *Thinking About Crime* (New York: Vintage Books, 1985), p. 95.

24. Peter H. Rossi et al., "Between Black and White: The Faces of American Institutions in the Ghetto," in *Supplemental Studies for the National Advisory Commission on Civil Disorders* (Washington, DC: U.S. Government Printing Office, 1968), p. 104.

25. Ibid., p. 106.

26. Everett C. Hughes, "Dilemmas and Contradictions of Status," *American Journal of Sociology*, 50 (March 1945): 353–59.

27. Wilson, *Thinking About Crime*, p. 96.

28. Arthur Niederhoffer, *Behind the Shield* (Garden City, NY: Doubleday and Company, 1967), p. 1.

29. August Vollmer, *The Police and Modern Society* (Berkeley, CA: University of California Press, 1936), p. 222.

30. Mervin F. White and Ben A. Menke, "A Critical Analysis of Surveys on Public Opinions Toward Police Agencies," *Journal of Police Science and Administration* 6 (June 1978): 204–5.

31. Raymond M. Momboise, *Community Relations and Riot Prevention* (Springfield, IL: C.C. Thomas, 1967), p. 91.

32. Cited in Katherine M. Jamieson and Timothy J. Flanagan, eds., *Sourcebook of Criminal Justice Statistics—1988*. U.S. Department of Justice, Bureau of Justice Statistics (Washington, DC: U.S.

Government Printing Office, 1989), Table 2.26, p. 207.

33. Ibid., p. 200.

34. Louis Harris, *The Harris Survey* (New York: The Chicago Tribune—New York News Syndicate, February 26, 1981), p. 3.

35. George Gallup, Jr. *The Gallup Poll* (Princeton, NJ: The Gallup Poll, March 20, 1991), p. 2.

36. George L. Kelling and Mark H. Moore, "The Evolving Strategy of Policing," *Perspectives on Policing*. U.S. Department of Justice, National Institute of Justice (Washington, DC: U.S. Government Printing Office, November 1988).

37. Robert Trojanowicz and Bonnie Bucqueroux, *Toward Development of Meaningful and Effective Performance Evaluations*, Community Policing Series No. 22 (National Center for Community Policing, Michigan State University, 1992), p. 4.

38. Kelling and Moore, "The Evolving Strategy of Policing," in *Perspectives on Policing*.

39. James Q. Wilson and George L. Kelling, "Broken Windows: The Police and Neighborhood Safety," in Abraham S. Blumberg and Elaine Niederhoffer, eds., *The Ambivalent Force* (New York: Holt, Rinehart and Winston, 1985), pp. 220–28.

40. Ibid., p. 222.

41. Stephen D. Mastrofski, "Community Policing as Reform: A Cautionary Tale," in Jack R. Greene and Stephen D. Mastrofski, eds., *Community Policing: Rhetoric or Reality* (New York: Praeger, 1988), p. 53.

42. Peter K. Manning, "Community Policing as a Drama of Control," in Greene and Mastrofski, eds., *Community Policing*, p. 38.

43. Jack R. Greene and Ralph B. Taylor, "Community-Based Policing and Foot Patrol: Issues of Theory and Evaluation," in Greene and Mastrofski, eds., *Community Policing*, pp. 195–223.

44. Robert Trojanowicz and David C. Carter, *The Philosophy and Role of Community Policing*, Community Policing Series No. 13 (National Center for Community Policing, Michigan State University, 1988).

45. Terry C. Cox and Mervin F. White, "Traffic Citations and Student Attitudes Toward the Police: An Examination of Selected Interaction Dynamics," *Journal of Police Science and Administration* 16 (June 1988): 120.

Chapter 6. Working the Streets

1. Bernard Phillips, *Sociology: From Concepts to Practice* (New York: McGraw Hill, 1979), p. 12.
2. Richard J. Lundman, ed., *Police Behavior: A Sociological Perspective* (New York: Oxford University Press, 1980).
3. Ibid., p. 14.
4. Terry C. Cox and Mervin F. White, "Traffic Citations and Student Attitudes Toward the Police: An Examination of Selected Interaction Dynamics," *Journal of Police Science and Administration* 16 (1988): 119–20.
5. Jonathan Rubenstein, "Controlling People," in Robert B. Culbertson and Mark R. Tezak, eds., *"Order Under Law"* (Prospect Heights, IL: Waveland Press, 1981), pp. 84–85.
6. Mary Glenn Wiley and Terry L. Hudik, "Police-Citizen Encounters: A Field Test of Exchange Theory," *Social Problems* 22 (1974): 119–27.
7. Ibid., p. 124.
8. Richard E. Sykes and John P. Clark, "Deference Exchange in Police-Civilian Encounters," in Richard J. Lundman, ed., *Police Behavior* (New York: Oxford University Press, 1980), pp. 91–105.
9. Ibid., p. 96.
10. William Ker Muir, Jr., *Police: Streetcorner Politicians* (Chicago: University of Chicago Press, 1977), p. 227.
11. Walter B. Miller, "Lower Class Culture as a Generating Milieu of Gang Delinquency," *Journal of Social Issues* 14 (1958): 10.
12. Jerome H. Skolnick and David H. Bailey, *The New Blue Line: Police Innovation in Six American Cities* (New York: The Free Press, 1986, p. 91.
13. Quote of a veteran patrolman, in John Van Maanen and Peter K. Manning, eds., *Policing: A View from the Street* (New York: Random House, 1978), p. 221.
14. James Q. Wilson, *Varieties of Police Behavior* (New York: Atheneum, 1972).
15. Ibid., p. 13.
16. Donald Black, "The Social Organization of Arrest," *Stanford Law Review* 23 (1972): 1104–10.
17. Ibid., p. 1105.
18. Jerome H. Skolnick, *Justice Without Trial: Law Enforcement in a Democratic Society* (New York: John Wiley and Sons, 1966).
19. John J. Broderick, *Police in a Time of Change* (Prospect Heights, IL: Waveland Press, 1987).
20. Paul B. Horton and Chester L. Hunt, *Sociology* (New York: McGraw-Hill, 1976), p. 88.
21. Phillips, *Sociology: From Concepts to Practice*, p. 66.
22. Skolnick, *Justice Without Trial*.
23. Julie Baumgold, "Cop Couples: Till Death Do Them Part," *New York* (June 19, 1972): 33.
24. Morris Janowitz, *The Professional Soldier: A Social and Political Portrait* (New York: The Free Press, 1964).
25. William A. Westley, "Violence and the Police," *American Journal of Sociology* 49 (1953): 34–41.
26. For example, E. R. Stoddard, "The Informal 'Code' of Police Deviancy: A Group Approach to 'Blue-Coat Crime,'" *Journal of Criminal Law, Criminology and Police Science* 59 (1968): 201–13; L. Savitz, "The Dimensions of Police Loyalty," *American Behavioral Scientist* (May–June 1970): 693–704.
27. Van Maanen and Manning, *Policing: A View from the Street*.
28. Stephen Mastrofski and Roger B. Parks, "Improving Observational Studies of Police," *Criminology* 28 (1990): 484.
29. Thomas F. Adams, "Field Interrogation," *Police* (March–April 1963): 28.
30. Jerome H. Skolnick, "A Sketch of the Policeman's Working Personality," in Abraham S. Blumberg and Elaine Niederhoffer, eds., *The Ambivalent Force* (New York: Holt, Rinehart and Winston, 1985), p. 82.
31. Abraham S. Blumberg, "The Police and the Social System: Reflections and Prospects," in Blumberg and Niederhoffer, eds., *The Ambivalent Force*, p. 16.

32. Arthur Niederhoffer, *Behind the Shield* (Garden City, NY: Doubleday and Company, 1967).

33. James Hernandez, Jr., *The Custer Syndrome* (Salem, WI: Sheffield Publishing Company, 1989), p. 2.

34. Niederhoffer, *Behind the Shield*, p. 95.

35. William Parker, quoted in Niederhoffer, *Behind the Shield*, p. 94.

36. David M. Rafky, Thomas Lawley, and Robert Ingram, "Are Police Recruits Cynical?" *Journal of Police Science and Administration* 4 (1976): 360.

37. Robert M. Regoli, Eric D. Poole, and John D. Hewitt, "Exploring the Empirical Relationship Between Police Cynicism and Work Alienation," *Journal of Police Science and Administration* 7 (1979): 336–39.

38. William G. Doerner, "I'm Not the Man I Used to Be: Reflections on the Transition from Prof to Cop," in Blumberg and Niederhoffer, eds., *The Ambivalent Force*, p. 394.

39. George L. Kirkham, "A Professor's 'Street Lessons,'" in Culbertson and Tezak, eds., *"Order Under Law"*, pp. 71–83.

40. U.S. Department of Justice, National Institute of Justice, Research in Brief, *Police Response to Special Populations* (Washington, DC: U.S. Government Printing Office, January 1988).

41. Linda S. Teplin, *Keeping the Peace: The Parameters of Police Discretion in Relation to the Mentally Disordered* (Washington, DC: National Institute of Justice, 1986).

42. U.S. Department of Justice, *Police Response to Special Populations*, p. 1.

43. Richard J. Lundman, "Domestic Police-Citizen Encounters," *Journal of Police Science and Administration* 2 (March 1974): 25.

44. Lawrence Sherman, *Crime File—Domestic Violence* (Washington, DC: National Institute of Justice, n.d.).

45. Ibid.

46. Lawrence W. Sherman and Richard A. Berk, *The Minneapolis Domestic Violence Experiment* (Washington, DC: The Police Foundation, 1984).

47. Ibid.

48. Franklyn W. Dunford, David Huizinga, and Delbert S. Elliott, "The Role of Arrest in Domestic Assault: The Omaha Police Experiment," *Criminology* 28 (May 1990): 183–206.

49. U.S. Department of Justice, National Institute of Justice, Research in Brief, *Danger to Police in Domestic Disturbances—A New Look* (Washington, DC: U.S. Government Printing Office, November 1986).

50. U.S. Department of Justice, National Institute of Justice, Research in Action, *Deaths in the Line of Duty* (Washington, DC: U.S. Government Printing Office, January 1985), p. 8.

51. Victoria L. Major, "Law Enforcement Officers Killed, 1980–1989," *FBI Law Enforcement Bulletin* (Washington, DC: U.S. Government Printing Office, May 1991), pp. 2–5.

52. Ibid., p. 5.

53. U.S. Department of Justice, *Danger to Police in Domestic Disturbances—A New Look*, p. 2.

54. William H. Kroes, Bruce L. Margolis, and Joseph J. Hurrell, Jr., "Job Stress in Policemen," *Journal of Police Science and Administration* 2 (June 1974): 145–55.

55. Gail A. Goolkasian, Ronald W. Geddes, and William DeJong, "Coping With Police Stress," in Roger G. Dunham and Geoffrey P. Albert, eds., *Critical Issues in Policing* (Prospect Heights, IL: Waveland Press, 1989), pp. 499–500.

56. Ibid., p. 501.

57. Several of these studies are cited in Goolkasian et al., "Coping With Police Stress," pp. 503–504.

58. Edward A. Thibault, Lawrence M. Lynch and R. Bruce McBride, *Proactive Police Management* (Englewood Cliffs, NJ: Prentice-Hall, 1990), p. 426.

59. J.T. Skip Duncan, Robert N. Brenner, and Marjorie Kravitz, *Police Stress: A Selected Bibliography* (Washington, DC: National Institute of Law Enforcement and Criminal Justice, 1979).

Chapter 7. Police Discretion

1. Herman Goldstein, *Policing a Free Society* (Cambridge, MA: Ballinger Publishing Company, 1977), p. 93.

2. Laure Weber Brooks, "Police Discretionary Behavior: A Study of Style," in Roger B. Dunham and Geoffrey P. Albert, eds., *Critical Issues in Policing*

(Prospect Heights, IL: Waveland Press, 1989), p. 121.

3. James Q. Wilson, *Varieties of Police Behavior* (New York: Atheneum, 1972), p. 7.

4. Ibid.

5. Ibid., ch. 4.

6. Goldstein, *Policing a Free Society*, pp. 94ff.

7. A.O. Archuleta, "Police Discretion v. Plea Bargaining," *Police Chief* (April 1974): 78.

8. Carl B. Klockars, *The Idea of Police* (Beverly Hills, CA: Sage Publications, 1985), p. 94.

9. Samuel Walker, *The Police in America* (New York: McGraw-Hill, 1983), p. 159.

10. Cecil L. Willis and Richard H. Wells, "The Police and Child Abuse: An Analysis of Police Decisions to Report Illegal Behavior," *Criminology* 26 (November 1988): 710.

11. Walker, *The Police in America*, pp. 157–58.

12. Wayne R. LaFave, *Arrest: The Decision to Take a Suspect Into Custody* (Boston: Little, Brown, 1965), p. 63.

13. Walker, *The Police in America*, p. 157.

14. Ibid.

15. Klockars, *The Idea of Police*, p. 97.

16. Kenneth C. Davis, *Police Discretion* (St. Paul, MN: West Publishing, 1975), p. 62.

17. Brooks, "Police Discretionary Behavior," pp. 126–34.

18. Ibid., p. 126.

19. Jerome H. Skolnick, *Justice Without Trial: Law Enforcement in a Democratic Society* (New York: John Wiley and Sons, 1966), p. 11.

20. Douglas A. Smith and J. Klein, "Police Control of Interpersonal Disputes," *Social Problems* 31 (1984): 468–81.

21. Michael Banton, *The Policeman in the Community* (New York: Basic Books, 1964), p. 11.

22. Stephen Mastrofski, "Policing the Beat: The Impact of Organizational Scale on Patrol Officer Behavior in Urban Residential Neighborhoods," *Journal of Criminal Justice* 9 (1981): 343–58.

23. Ibid., p. 344.

24. T.N. Ferdinand, "Police Attitudes and Police Organization: Some Interdepartmental and Cross-Cultural Comparisons." *Police Studies* 3 (1980): 46–60.

25. B. Cohen and J.M. Chaiken, *Police Background Characteristics and Performance: Summary* (New York: Rand Institute, 1972).

26. Geoffrey P. Alpert, "Police Use of Deadly Force: The Miami Experience," in Roger G. Dunham and Geoffrey P. Alpert, eds., *Critical Issues in Policing* (Prospect Heights, IL: Waveland Press, 1989), pp. 480–95.

27. C.D. Hale and W.R. Wilson, *Personal Characteristics of Assaulted and Non-Assaulted Officers* (Norman, OK: Bureau of Government Research, University of Oklahoma, 1974), p. 8.

28. Lawrence W. Sherman, "Causes of Police Behavior: The Current State of Quantitative Research," *Journal of Research in Crime and Delinquency* 17 (1980): 71.

29. R.J. Friedrich, *The Impact of Organizational, Individual, and Situational Factors on Police Behavior* (Ph.D. Dissertation, Department of Political Science, University of Michigan), pp. 278–84.

30. Sherman, "Causes of Police Behavior," p. 73.

31. Peter B. Bloch and Deborah Anderson, *Police-women on Patrol: Final Report* (Washington, DC: Police Foundation, 1974).

32. Sherman, "Causes of Police Behavior," p. 76.

33. Ibid., p. 75.

34. Cohen and Chaiken, *Police Background Characteristics and Performance*.

35. Wayne F. Cascio, "Formal Education and Police Officer Performance," *Journal of Police Science and Administration* 5 (1977): 89–96.

36. Friedrich, *The Impact of Organizational, Individual, and Situational Factors on Police Behavior*.

37. Banton, *The Police in the Community*, p. 74.

38. Albert J. Reiss, "Police Brutality," in Leon Radzinowicz and Marvin E. Wolfgang, eds., *Crime and Justice* Vol. 2 (New York: Basic Books, 1972), p. 303.

39. James J. Fyfe, *Shots Fired: An Examination of New York City Police Firearms Discharge* (Ph.D. Dissertation. School of Criminal Justice: State University of New York at Albany, 1978).

40. Sherman, "Causes of Police Behavior," pp. 77, 79.

41. Reiss, *The Police and the Public*, p. 51.

42. Richard J. Lundman, "Routine Police Arrest Practices: A Commonweal Perspective," *Social Problems* 22 (1974): 127–41.

43. Brooks, "Police Discretionary Behavior," p. 137.

44. Ibid.

45. Ibid., pp. 135–36.

46. Ibid., p. 135.

47. Donald Black, *The Manners and Customs of the Police* (New York: Academic Press, 1980), p. 187.

48. Marvin D. Krohn, James P. Curry, and Shirley Nelson-Kilger, "Is Chivalry Dead?" *Criminology* 21 (1983): 417–37.

49. Ibid.

50. Donald Black, "Production of Crime Rates," *American Sociological Review* 35 (1970): 733–48.

51. Irving Piliavin and Scott Briar, "Police Encounters with Juveniles," *American Journal of Sociology* 70 (1964): 206–14.

52. Richard J. Lundman, Richard E. Sykes, and John P. Clark, "Police Control of Juveniles: A. Replication," *Journal of Research in Crime and Delinquency* 15 (1978): 74–91.

53. For example, Michael K. Brown, *Working the Street: Police Discretion and the Dilemmas of Reform* (New York: Russell Sage Foundation, 1981); also, Stephen Mastrofski and Roger B. Parks, "Improving Observational Studies of Police," *Criminology* 28 (August 1990): 475–96.

54. Goldstein, *Policing a Free Society*, p. 110.

55. Klockars, *The Idea of Police*, p. 107.

56. Goldstein, *Policing a Free Society*, p. 111.

Chapter 8. Citizen Rights and Due Process of Law

1. *Marbury v. Madison*, 5 US (1 Cranch) 137, 2 LEd 60 (1803).

2. Leo Pfeffer, "Liberty and Justice: Fair Play and Fair Trial," in Abraham S. Blumberg and Elaine Niederhoffer, eds., *The Ambivalent Force* (New York: Holt, Rinehart and Winston, 1985), p. 251.

3. John C. Klotter and Jacqueline R. Kanovitz, *Constitutional Law For Police* (Cincinnati, OH: The Anderson Publishing Co., 1973), p. 17.

4. *Adamson v. California*, 332 US 46, 91 LEd 1903, 67 SCt 1672 (1947).

5. Richard J. Terrill, *World Criminal Justice Systems* (Cincinnati, OH: Anderson Publishing Co., 1984), p. 44.

6. *Kuruma v. Regina*, 2 WLR 223 (1955).

7. *Ghani v. Jones* (1970), cited in Terrill, *World Criminal Justice Systems*, p. 44.

8. *Weeks v. United States*, 232 US 383, 58 LEd 652, 34 SCt 341 (1914).

9. *Silverthorn Lumber Co. v. United States*, 251 US 385, 64 LEd 319, 40 SCt 182 (1920).

10. *Wolf v. Colorado*, 338 US 25, 93 LEd 1782, 69 SCt 1359 (1949).

11. *Mapp v. Ohio*, 367 US 643, 6 LEd (2d) 1081, 81 SCt 1684 (1961).

12. *United States v. Leon*, 468 US ———, 35 CrL 3273, 104 SCt 3405 (1984).

13. *Massachusetts v. Sheppard*, 35 CrL 3296, SCt (1984).

14. *Brewer v. Williams*, 430 US 387 (1977).

15. *Rochin v. California*, 342 US 165, 96 LEd 183, 72 SCt 205 (1952).

16. A. Louis DiPietro, "Anticipatory Search Warrants," *Law Enforcement Bulletin* (U.S. Department of Justice, Washington, DC: U.S. Government Printing Office, July 1990), pp. 27–32.

17. *Dumbra v. United States*, 268 US 435, 69 LEd 1032, 45 SCt 546 (1925).

18. Klotter and Kanovitz, *Constitutional Law for Police*, p. 149.

19. Ibid., p. 154.

20. *United States v. McDaniel*, 154 FSupp 1 (DC Cir 1957).

21. Kimberly A. Kingston, "Look But Don't Touch: The Plain View Doctrine," *Law Enforcement Bulletin* (U.S. Department of Justice, Washington, DC: U.S. Government Printing Office, December 1987), pp. 17–24.

22. Charles Moylan, "The Plain View Doctrine: Unexpected Child of the Great 'Search Incident' Geography Battle," *Mercer Law Review* 26 (1975): 1096.

23. *California v. Greenwood*, 108 SCt 1625 (1988).

24. *On Lee v. United States*, 343 US 747, 96 LEd 1273, 72 SCt 967 (1952).

25. *Ciraolo v. California*, 476 US 207 (1986).

26. *Carroll v. United States*, 267 US 132, 45 SCt 280 (1925).

27. *United States v. Ross*, 456 US 798 (1982). Emphasis added.

28. *California v. Acevedo*, 49 Crim. L. Rep. 2210, (1991).

29. *Chimel v. California*, 395 US 752, 23 LEd (2d) 685, 89 SCt 2034 (1969).

30. *Terry v. Ohio*, 392 US 1, 20 LEd (2d) 1889, 88 SCt 1868 (1968).

31. *Bivens v. Six Unknown Agents*, 403 US 388 (1971).

32. U.S. Department of Justice, *The Effects of the Exclusionary Rule: A Study of California* (Washington, DC: U.S. Government Printing Office, 1982).

33. James J. Fyfe, "The NIJ Study of the Exclusionary Rule," *Criminal Law Bulletin* 19 (May–June 1983): 253–60.

34. *United States v. Wade*, 388 US 218, 18 LEd (2d) 1149, 87 SCt 1926 (1967).

35. *Foster v. California*, 394 US 440 (1969).

36. *Martin v. Commonwealth*, 173 SE (2d) 794 (Va 1970).

37. *Brown v. Mississippi*, 297 US 278, 80 LEd 682 (1936).

38. *Malloy v. Hogan*, 378 US 1, 12 LEd (2d) 653, 84 SCt 1489 (1964).

39. *Twining v. New Jersey*, 211 US 78 (1908).

40. *Escobedo v. Illinois*, 378 US 478, 12 LEd (2d) 977, 84 SCt 1758 (1964).

41. *Miranda v. Arizona*, 384 US 436, 16 LEd (2d) 694, 86 SCt 1602 (1966).

42. *Brewer v. Williams*, 430 US 387 (1977).

43. *New York v. Quarles*, 104 SCt 2626 (1984).

44. *Moran v. Burbine*, 106 SCt 1135 (1986).

Chapter 9. Police Misconduct

1. James A. Inciardi, *Criminal Justice* (San Diego, CA: Harcourt Brace Jovanovich Publishers, 1990), pp. 292–93.

2. *Law Enforcement News*, John Jay College of Criminal Justice, New York, December 15, 1990.

3. Lawrence W. Sherman, *Scandal and Reform* (Berkeley, CA: University of California Press, 1978), p. xv.

4. Ibid., p. xxiii.

5. Albert J. Reiss, Jr., *The Police and The Public* (New Haven: Yale University Press, 1971), p. 169.

6. Herman Goldstein, *Police Corruption: A Perspective on Its Nature and Control* (Washington, DC: Police Foundation, 1975), p. 52.

7. Samuel Walker, *The Police in America* (New York: McGraw-Hill, 1983), p. 174.

8. U.S. National Commission on Law Observance and Enforcement (Washington, DC: U.S. Government Printing Office, 1931).

9. Robert M. Fogelson, *Big-City Police* (Cambridge, MA: Harvard University Press, 1977), p. 148.

10. U.S. Senate Special Committee to Investigate Organized Crime in Interstate Commerce, *Third Interim Report* (Washington, DC: U.S. Government Printing Office, 1951).

11. Quoted in Maurice Punch, *Conduct Unbecoming* (London: Tavistock Publications, 1985), p. 26.

12. Samuel Walker, *Popular Justice* (New York: Oxford University Press, 1980), p. 19.

13. Commission to Investigate Allegations of Police Corruption, and the City's Anti-Corruption Procedures, *The Knapp Commission Report on Police Corruption*, August 3, 1972.

14. E. Plitt, "Police Discipline Decisions." *Police Chief* (March 1983): 95–98. Quoted in Thomas Barker and David L. Carter, *Police Deviance* (Cincinnati, OH: Anderson Publishing Co., 1986), p. 2.

15. William A. Geller, "Police Misconduct: Scope of the Problems and Remedies," *ACJS Today* (February 1984): 6–8.

16. Ibid., p. 6.

17. Barker and Carter, *Police Deviance*, p. 4.

18. Ibid.

19. Ibid., p. 5.

20. Ibid., p. 6–7.

21. "Police Aides Told to Rid Commands of All Dishonesty," *New York Times*, October 29, 1970.

22. Commission to Investigate Allegations of Police Corruption, *Knapp Commission Report*, 1972.

23. Herbert Beigel, "The Investigation and Prosecution of Police Corruption." *Journal of Criminal Law and Criminology* 65 (1974): 135–56.

24. James A. Inciardi, *Criminal Justice* (New York: Harcourt Brace Jovanovich Publishers, 1990), pp. 290–91.

25. William Geller, "Police Misconduct: Scope of the Problems and Remedies," p. 6.

26. Allen D. Sapp, "Sexual Misconduct and Sexual Harassment by Police Officers," in Thomas Barker and David L. Carter, eds., *Police Deviance* (Cincinnati, OH: Anderson Publishing Co., 1986), p. 85.

27. Walker, *The Police in America*, p. 180.

28. Patrick V. Murphy, "Police Corruption," *Police Chief* (December 1972): 72; emphasis added.

29. Barker and Carter, *Police Deviance*, preface.

30. Lawrence W. Sherman, "Becoming Bent: Moral Careers of Corrupt Policemen," in Robert G. Culbertson and Mark R. Tezak, eds., *"Order Under Law"* (Prospect Heights, IL: Waveland Press, Inc., 1981), pp. 96–109.

31. Ibid., p. 101.

32. Donal E. J. MacNamara, "Discipline in American Policing," in Abraham S. Blumberg and Elaine Niederhoffer, eds., *The Ambivalent Force* (New York: Holt, Rinehart and Winston, 1985), p. 139.

Chapter 10. Police Recruitment, Screening, and Training

1. Edward A. Thibault, Lawrence M. Lynch, and R. Bruce McBride, *Proactive Police Management* 2nd ed. (Englewood Cliffs, NJ: Prentice Hall, 1990), p. 278.

2. Geoffrey P. Alpert and Roger G. Dunham, *Policing Urban America* (Prospect Heights, IL: Waveland Press, 1988), p. 35.

3. Reported in Henry M. Wrobleski and Karen M. Hess, *Introduction to Law Enforcement and Criminal Justice* (New York: West Publishing Company, 1990), p. 137.

4. Leonard Territo, C. R. Swanson, Jr., and Neil C. Chamelin, *The Police Personnel Selection Process* (Indianapolis, IN: Bobbs-Merrill Education Publishing, 1977), p. 8.

5. Nicholas Alex, *Black in Blue* (Englewood Cliffs, NJ: Prentice-Hall, 1969).

6. U.S. Department of Justice, Bureau of Justice Statistics Bulletin, *State and Local Police Departments, 1990* (Washington, DC: U.S. Government Printing Office, 1992).

7. Donald A. Torres, *Handbook of Federal Police and Investigative Agencies* (New York: Greenwood Press, 1985), p. 6.

8. Territo et al., *The Police Personnel Selection Process*, pp. 12–13.

9. Alfred Stone and Stuart DeLuca, *Police Administration* (New York: Wiley, 1985), p. 296.

10. Territo et al., *The Police Personnel Selection Process*, p. 39.

11. Ibid., p. 53.

12. Charles R. Swanson, Leonard Territo, and Robert W. Taylor, *Police Administration: Structure, Processes, and Behavior* (New York: Macmillan Publishers, 1988), p. 205.

13. Charles D. Spielberger, *Police Selection and Evaluation* (Washington, DC: Hemisphere Publishing Corporation, 1979), p. xi.

14. Alan W. Benner, "Psychological Screening of Police Applicants," in Roger G. Dunham and Geoffrey P. Alpert, eds., *Critical Issues in Policing* (Prospect Heights, IL: Waveland Press, 1989), p. 74.

15. Ibid., p. 79.

16. George E. Hargrave and Deirdee Hiatt, "Law Enforcement Selection with the Interview, MMPI and CPI: A Study of Reliability and Validity," *Journal of Police Science and Administration* 15 (1987, No. 2): 110.

17. Ibid.

18. Calvin J. Swank and James A. Conser, *The Police Personnel System* (New York: John Wiley and Sons, 1983), p. 47.

19. T. Eisenberg, D. Kent, and C. Wall, *Police Personnel Practices in State and Local Governments* (Washington, DC: Police Foundation, 1973).

20. Swank and Conser, *The Police Personnel System*, p. 50.

21. Ibid., p. 54.

22. Public Law 92-261, Section 703(a).

23. Swanson et al., *Police Administration*, p. 190.

24. *Massachusetts Board of Retirement v. Murgia*, 427 U.S. 307 (1976).

25. William R. Nelson and Robert N. Roberts, "Mandatory Retirement and Police Employment," *Journal of Police Science and Administration* 14 (1986, No. 1): 10.

26. *Hahn v. City of Buffalo*, 770 F.2d 12 (2d Cir. 1985).

27. Thibault et al., *Proactive Police Management*, p. 287.

28. Swank and Conser, *The Police Personnel System*, p. 134.
29. *Smith v. the City of East Cleveland*, 363 F. Supp. 1131 N.D. (Ohio, 1973).
30. Swank and Conser, *The Police Personnel System*, p. 134.
31. *Griggs v. Duke Power Company*, 401 U.S. 424 (1971).
32. Swank and Conser, *The Police Personnel System*, p. 79.
33. U.S. Department of Justice, Bureau of Justice Statistics, *Police Departments in Large Cities, 1987* (Washington, DC: U.S. Government Printing Office, August 1989), p. 6, table 16.
34. U.S. Department of Justice, *State and Local Police Departments, 1990*, p. 5.
35. Ibid., p. 64.
36. Robert M. Fogleson, *Big-City Police* (Cambridge, MA: Harvard University Press, 1977), p. 83.
37. Herbert Jenkins, *Keeping the Peace: A Police Chief Looks at His Job* (New York: Harper and Row, 1970), p. 1.
38. Robert J. Meadows, "Beliefs of Law Enforcement Administrators and Criminal Justice Educators Toward the Needed Skill Competencies in Entry-Level Police Training Curriculum," *Journal of Police Science and Administration* 15 (1987, No. 1): 1.
39. Gary M. Post, "Police Recruits: Training Tomorrow's Work-Force," *FBI Law Enforcement Bulletin* 16 (1992, March): 22.
40. Lawrence S. Kleiman and Michael E. Gordon, "An Examination of the Relationship Between Police Training Academy Performance and Job Performance," *Journal of Police Science and Administration* 14 (1986, No. 4): 293.
41. Charles P. Smith, Donald E. Pehlke, and Charles D. Weller, *Project STAR: Police Officer Role Training Program* (Cincinnati, OH: Anderson, 1976).
42. Vance McLaughlin and Robert L. Bing III, "Law Enforcement Personnel Selection: A Commentary," *Journal of Police Science and Administration* 15 (1987, No. 4): 273.
43. Swank and Conser, *The Police Personnel System*, p. 206.
44. Torres, *Handbook of Federal Police and Investigative Agencies*, appendix A.
45. Michael S. McCampbell, "Field Training for Police Officers: State of the Art,"

National Institute of Justice, Research in Brief (U.S. Department of Justice, Washington, DC: U.S. Government Printing Office, November 1986).
46. Ibid., p. 3.
47. James Leo Walsh, "Career Styles and Police Behavior," in David H. Bayley, ed., *Police and Society* (Beverly Hills, CA: Sage Publication, 1977), pp. 149–67.
48. John Van Maanen, "Making Rank: Becoming an American Police Sergeant," in Roger G. Dunham and Geoffrey P. Alpert, eds., *Critical Issues in Policing* (Prospect Heights, IL: Waveland Press, 1989), pp. 146–61.
49. Ibid., p. 146.
50. U.S. Department of Justice, *The National Manpower Survey of the Criminal Justice System: Law Enforcement*, Vol. 2 (Washington, DC: U.S. Government Printing Office, 1978), p. 2.
51. Seymour Martin Lipset, "Why Cops Hate Liberals and Vice Versa," *The Atlantic* 223 (1969): 76–83.
52. John G. Stratton, *Police Passages* (Manhattan Beach, CA: Glennon Publishing Company, 1984), pp. 28–29.

Chapter 11. Police Organization and Operations

1. Richard H. Hall, *Organizations: Structure and Process* (Englewood Cliffs, NJ: Prentice-Hall, 1977), p. 4.
2. Max Weber, *The Theory of Social and Economic Organization*, trans. A.M. Henderson and Talcott Parsons (New York: Free Press, 1947), p. 337.
3. Warren Bennis, "Beyond Bureaucracy," in Amitai Etzioni, ed., *Readings on Modern Organizations* (Englewood Cliffs, NJ: Prentice-Hall, 1969), p. 2.
4. James H. Auten, "The Paramilitary Model of Police and Police Professionalism," in Abraham S. Blumberg and Elaine Niederhoffer, eds., *The Ambivalent Force*, 3rd edition (New York: Holt, Rinehart and Winston, 1985), pp. 122–23.
5. Ibid., p. 123.
6. Morris Janowitz, *The Professional Soldier* (Glencoe, IL: The Free Press, 1960), p. 175.
7. John J. Broderick, *Police in a Time of*

Change, 2nd edition (Prospect Heights, IL: Waveland Press, 1987), p. 83.

8. Jack Kuykendall and Roy R. Roberg, "Mapping Police Organizational Change," *Criminology* 20 (August 1982): 241–56.

9. Hall, *Organizations*, p. 56.

10. Edwin H. Sutherland and Donald R. Cressey, *Criminology* (New York: J. B. Lippincott Co., 1974), p. 259.

11. Edward Eldefonso, Alan Coffey, and Richard C. Grace, *Principles of Law Enforcement* (New York: John Wiley and Sons, 1974), pp. 79–84.

12. O. W. Wilson and Roy Clinton McLaren, *Police Administration*, 4th ed. (New York: McGraw-Hill, 1977), pp. 73–86.

13. Ibid., p. 85.

14. William E. Thornton, Jr., Lydia Voigt, and William G. Doerner, *Delinquency and Justice*, 2nd ed., (New York: Random House, 1987), p. 296.

15. Wilson and McLaren, *Police Administration*, p. 105.

16. John Heapy, ed., *Police Practices: The General Administrative Survey* (Washington, DC: Police Foundation, 1978), p. 11.

17. G. Douglas Gourley, *Patrol Administration* (Charles C. Thomas, Publisher, 1974), p. 4.

18. Ibid., pp. 14–15.

19. James Q. Wilson and George L. Kelling, "Broken Windows: The Police and Neighborhood Safety," in Blumberg and Niederhoffer, eds., *The Ambivalent Force*, pp. 220–28.

20. Steve Farish, "Law Enforcement Exploring," *FBI Law Enforcement Bulletin* (Washington, DC: U.S. Government Printing Office, May 1990), p. 21.

21. Ordway P. Burden, "Scouting Police Recruits? These Know the Ropes," *Law Enforcement News* (New York: John Jay College of Criminal Justice, February 28, 1991), p. 7.

22. Gourley, *Patrol Administration*, p. 65.

23. George L. Kelling et al., *The Kansas City Preventive Patrol Experiment: Final Report* (New York: Police Foundation, 1974).

24. Ibid.

25. Richard C. Larson, "What Happened to Patrol Operations in Kansas City? A Review of the Kansas City Preventive Patrol Experiment," *Journal of Criminal Justice* 3 (1975, No. 4): 273.

26. *Criminal Justice Newsletter*, August 27, 1979, p. 4.

27. David F. Greenberg, Ronald C. Kessler, and Colin Loftin, "The Effect of Police Employment on Crime," *Criminology* 21 (1983, No. 3): 385–86.

28. Herman Goldstein, "Improving Policing: A Problem-Oriented Approach," *Crime and Delinquency* 25 (1979): 236–58.

29. U.S. Department of Justice, National Institute of Justice Reports, *Problem-Oriented Policing* (Washington, DC: U.S. Government Printing Office, January 1987).

30. U.S. Department of Justice, National Institute of Justice Reports, *Police Crackdowns* (Washington, DC: U.S. Government Printing Office, March/April 1990), p. 2.

31. U.S. Department of Justice, National Institute of Justice Reports, *Handling Calls for Service: Alternatives to Traditional Policing* (Washington, DC: U.S. Government Printing Office, September 1984), p. 4.

32. Ibid., p. 7.

33. Jack Kuykendall, "The Municipal Police Detective: An Historical Analysis," *Criminology* 24 (1986, No. 1): 175.

34. Ibid., p. 176.

35. Carl B. Klockars, *The Idea of Police* (Beverly Hills, CA: Sage Publications, 1985).

36. Peter W. Greenwood et al., *The Criminal Investigation Process, vol. 1, Summary and Police Implications* (Santa Monica, CA: Rand Corporation, 1975).

37. Harold E. Pepinsky, "Police Decision-Making," in Don Gottfredson, ed., *Decision-Making in the Criminal Justice System: Reviews and Essays* (Washington, DC: National Institute of Mental Health, 1975), p. 27.

38. Klockars, *The Idea of Police*, p. 86.

39. U.S. Department of Justice, National Institute of Justice Reports, *Solving Crimes* (Washington, DC: U.S. Government Printing Office, March 1984).

40. Ibid., p. 6.

Chapter 12. Police Management

1. Frederick W. Taylor, *Principles of Scientific Management* (New York: Harper and Row, 1911).

2. Paul M. Whisenand and Fred Ferguson, *The Managing of Police Organizations* (Englewood Cliffs, NJ: Prentice Hall, 1989), p. 4.

3. Luther Gulick, "Notes on the Theory of Organization," in Luther Gulick and Lyndall Urwick, eds., *Papers on the Science of Administration* (New York: Institute of Public Administration, 1937).

4. Ibid., pp. 1–45.

5. Whisenand and Ferguson, *The Managing of Police Organizations*, p. 72.

6. O.W. Wilson and Roy Clinton McLaren, *Police Administration*, 4th ed. (New York: McGraw-Hill, 1977), p. 120.

7. U.S. National Commission on Law Observance and Enforcement, *Report on Police* (Washington, DC: U.S. Government Printing Office, 1931), pp. 20–21.

8. *Law Enforcement Bulletin* (New York: John Jay College of Criminal Justice, January 15/31, 1991), p. 9.

9. Jack E. Enter, "The Rise to the Top: An Analysis of Police Chief Career Patterns," *Journal of Police Science and Administration*, 14 (1986, No. 4): 335.

10. John Van Maanen, "Making Rank: Becoming an American Police Sergeant," in Roger G. Dunham and Geoffrey P. Alpert, eds., *Critical Issues in Policing* (Prospect Heights, IL: Waveland Press, 1989), p. 146.

11. Police Executive Research Forum, *Survey of Police Operational and Administrative Practices* (Washington, DC: PERF, 1978).

12. W.H. Hewitt, *New Directions in Police Personnel Administration* (Lexington, MA: D.C. Health and Company, 1975), p. 3.

13. Herman Goldstein, *Policing a Free Society* (Cambridge, MA: Ballinger Publishing Co., 1977), p. 209.

14. Edward M. Davis, "Tenure and Due Process for Police Chiefs," *Police Chief* 44 (1977, No. 1): 8.

15. Edward A. Tribault, Lawrence M. Lynch, and R. Bruce McBride, *Proactive Police Management* 2nd ed. (Englewood Cliffs, NJ: Prentice Hall, 1990), pp. 125–26.

16. Ibid., p. 125.

17. Samuel Walker, *The Police in America* (New York: McGraw-Hill, 1983), p. 170.

18. Kenneth C. Davis, *Discretionary Justice* (Urbana: University of Illinois, 1971).

19. Walker, *The Police in America*, p. 166.

20. Peter Drucker, *The Practice of Management* (New York: Harper and Bros., 1954).

21. Charles R. Swanson, Leonard Territo, and Robert W. Taylor, *Police Administration* 2nd ed. (New York: Macmillan Publishing Co., 1988), p. 511.

22. George Odiorne, *Management by Objectives* (New York: Pitman Publishing Co., 1965), p. 26.

23. Charles D. Hale, *Fundamentals of Police Administration* (Boston, MA: Holbrook Press, 1973), p. 333.

24. John M. Ivancevich, Andrew D. Szilagyi, Jr., and Marc J. Wallace, Jr., *Organizational Behavior and Performance* (Santa Monica, CA: Goodyear Publishing Co., 1977), p. 525.

25. C.D. Stein, "Objective Management Systems: Two to Five Years After Implementation," *Personnel Journal*, 54 (October 1975): 525.

26. Swanson et al., *Police Administration*, p. 514.

27. Ibid., p. 514.

28. Roberto Michels, *Political Parties*, trans. by Eden and Cedar Paul (New York: Dover, 1959).

29. Swanson et al., *Police Administration*, p. 120.

30. Thibault et al., *Proactive Police Management*, p. 212.

31. G. Douglas Gourley, *Patrol Administration* (Springfield, IL: Charles C. Thomas Publisher, 1974), p. 72.

32. Alfred I. Schwartz and Sumner N. Clarren, *The Cincinnati Team Policing Experiment: A Summary Report* (Washington, DC: Police Foundation, 1977), p. 2.

33. U.S. Department of Justice, National Evaluation Program, *Neighborhood Team Policing* (Washington, DC: U.S. Government Printing Office, 1977), pp. 10–13.

34. Thibault et al., *Proactive Police Management*, p. 217.

35. Schwartz and Clarren, *The Cincinnati Team Policing Experiment*.

36. Walker, *The Police in America*, p. 94.

37. George L. Kelling, "Police Field Services and Crime: The Presumed Effects of a Capacity," *Crime and Delinquency* 24 (April 1978): p. 179.

38. Lawrence W. Sherman, C. H. Milton, and T.V. Kelly, *Team Policing: Seven Case Studies* (Washington, DC: Police Foundation, 1973).

39. Charles E. Lindblom, "The Science of 'Muddling Through,' " *Public Administration Review* 19 (Spring 1959).

40. Ronald G. Lynch, *The Police Manager*, 2nd ed. (Boston: Allyn and Bacon, Inc., 1978), p. 70.

41. Douglas McGregor, *The Human Side of Enterprise* (New York: McGraw-Hill, 1960).

42. William G. Ouchi, *Theory Z* (New York: Avon Books, 1981).

43. Thibault et al., *Proactive Police Management*, p. 103.

44. Robert Tannenbaum and Warren H. Schmidt, "How to Chose a Leadership Pattern," in *Business Classics: Fifteen Key Concepts for Managerial Success* (Cambridge, MA: Harvard University Press, 1975), pp. 115–24.

45. Lynch, *The Police Manager*, p. 76.

46. Ibid., p. 78.

47. Everett C. Hughs, *Men and Their Work* (Glencoe, IL: Free Press, 1958).

48. Paul M. Whisenand and George E. Rush, *Supervising Police Personnel* (Englewood Cliffs, NJ: Prentice Hall, 1988), pp. 198–201.

49. Ibid., p. 201.

50. Richard Terrill, *World Criminal Justice Systems: A Survey* (Cincinnati, OH: Anderson Publishing Co., 1984), p. 253.

51. Walker, *The Police in America*, p. 285.

52. Swanson et al., *Police Administration*, p. 291.

53. Sanford Cohen, *Labor in the United States* 4th ed. (Columbus, OH: Charles E. Merrill Publishing Company, 1975), p. 179.

54. Swanson et al., *Police Administration*, p. 15.

55. William J. Bopp, "The Boston Police Strike of 1919," in William J. Bopp, ed., *Police Administration* (Boston, MA: Holbrook Press, Inc., 1975), pp. 135–44.

56. Ibid., p. 136.

57. Ibid., p. 143.

58. Walker, *The Police in America*, p. 289.

59. Swanson et al., *Police Administration*, p. 299–300.

60. Cohen, *Labor in the U.S.*, p. 191.

61. Erdwin H. Pfuhl, Jr., "Police Strikes and Conventional Crime," *Criminology* 21 (November 1983): 489–503.

Chapter 13. Critical Issues in American Policing

1. Edith Linn and Barbara Raffel Price, "The Evolving Role of Women in American Policing," in Abraham S. Blumberg and Elaine Niederhoffer, eds., *The Ambivalent Force*, 3rd edition (New York: Holt, Rinehart and Winston, 1985), p. 78.

2. Antony Simpson, "The Changing Role of Women in Policing," *Law Enforcement News*, Vol. 1, No. 3 (March 1976): 16.

3. Peter Horne, *Women in Law Enforcement* (Springfield, IL: Charles C. Thomas, Publisher, 1980).

4. Linn and Price, "The Evolving Role of Women in American Policing," p. 70.

5. Ibid.

6. Ibid.

7. Patricia W. Lunneborg, *Women Police Officers: Current Career Profile* (Springfield, IL: Charles C. Thomas, 1989).

8. Susan Ehrlich Martin, *Breaking and Entering: Policewomen on Patrol* (Berkeley: University of California Press, 1980).

9. Ibid., pp. 186–87.

10. Linn and Price, "The Evolving Role of Women in American Policing," pp. 69–70.

11. Peter B. Bloch and Deborah Anderson, *Police-women on Patrol: Final Report* (Washington, DC: Police Foundation, 1974).

12. Ibid.

13. Anthony V. Bouza, "Women in Policing," *FBI Law Enforcement Bulletin* (Washington, DC: U.S. Department of Justice, September 1975).

14. William Geller, *Crime File—Deadly Force* (Washington, DC: National Institute of Justice, n.d.).

15. Ibid., p. 3.

16. Ibid.

17. Paul Takagi, "A Garrison State in a 'Democratic' Society," *Crime and Social Justice* 1 (Spring–Summer, 1974): 27–33.

18. *Tennessee v. Garner*, 53LW 4410-18 (March 27, 1985).

19. Victoria L. Major, "Law Enforcement

Officers Killed, 1980–1989," *FBI Law Enforcement Bulletin* (Washington, DC: U.S. Government Printing Office, May 1991), pp. 2–5.

20. Geller, *Crime File—Deadly Force*, p. 2.

21. *Time* (April 8, 1985): 30.

22. James F. Fyfe, "Always Prepared: Police Off-Duty Guns," in Blumberg and Niederhoffer, eds., *The Ambivalent Force*, pp. 334–35.

23. Ibid., p. 336.

24. Ibid., p. 337.

25. Herman Goldstein, *Policing a Free Society* (Cambridge, MA: Ballinger Publishing Co., 1977), p. 201.

26. Patrick V. Murphy and T. Plate, *Commissioner* (New York: Simon and Schuster, 1977), p. 167.

27. Maurice Punch, *Conduct Unbecoming: The Social Construction of Police Deviance and Control* (London: Tavistock Publications, 1985), p. 28.

28. Samuel Walker, *The Police in America* (New York: McGraw-Hill, 1983), p. 230.

29. *Law Enforcement News*, John Jay College of Criminal Justice, New York, April 15, 1991.

30. From Randy L. LaGrange, "The Future of Police Consolidation," *Journal of Contemporary Criminal Justice* 3 (February, 1987): pp. 6–16.

31. President's Commission on Law Enforcement and Administration of Justice, *Task Force Report: The Police* (Washington, DC: U.S. Government Printing Office, 1967), p. 68.

32. Ibid., p. 308.

33. V.L. Marando, "The Politics of City-County Consolidation: Reform, Regionalism, Referenda and Requiem," *Western Political Quarterly* 32 (1975): 409–21.

34. E. Ostrom and R.B. Parks, "Suburban Police Departments: Too Many and Too Small," in Louis H. Masotti and Jeffrey K. Hadden, eds., *The Urbanization of the Suburbs* (Beverly Hills, CA: Sage Publication, 1973), pp. 367–402; R.B. Parks, "Police Patrol in Metropolitan Areas: Implications for Restructuring the Police," in E. Ostrom, ed., *The Delivery of Urban Services* (Beverly Hills, CA: Sage Publications, 1976), pp. 261–83; B.D. Rogers and C.M. Lipsey, "Metropolitan Reform: Citizen Evaluations of Performances in Nashville-Davidson County, Tennessee," *Publius* 4 (Fall, 1974): 19–34.

35. E. Ostrom, R.B. Parks, and G.P. Whitaker, *Patterns of Metropolitan Policing* (Cambridge, MA: Ballinger Publishing, 1978), p. 3.

36. R.D. Gustely, "The Allocational and Distributional Impacts of Governmental Consolidation: The Dade County Experience," *Urban Affairs Quarterly* 12 (1979): pp. 349–64.

37. J.E. Benton and D. Gamble, "City/County Consolidation and Economies of Scale: Evidence from a Time-Series Analysis in Jacksonville, Florida," *Social Science Quarterly* 65 (1984): 190–98.

38. U.S. Department of Justice, National Institute of Justice, Research in Action, *AIDS and the Law Enforcement Officer* (Washington, DC: U.S. Government Printing Office, November/December 1987), p. 5.

39. Ibid.

40. Walker, *The Police in America*, p. 243.

41. James Q. Wilson, *Varieties of Police Behavior* (New York: Atheneum, 1972), p. 30.

INDEX

PHOTO CREDITS